WOMEN ADMINISTRATORS IN HIGHER EDUCATION

HISTORICAL AND CONTEMPORARY PERSPECTIVES

Edited by

JANA NIDIFFER AND
CAROLYN TERRY BASHAW

State University of New York Press

Published by
State University of New York Press, Albany

Printed in the United States of America

For information, address State University of New York Press,
90 State Street, Suite 700, Albany, NY 12207

Production by Cathleen Collins
Marketing by Anne M. Valentine

Library of Congress Cataloging-in-Publication Data

Women administrators in higher education : historical and contemporary perspectives /
edited by Jana Nidiffer and Carolyn Terry Bashaw.
p. cm. — (SUNY series, frontiers in education)
Includes bibliographical references and index.
ISBN 0-7914-4817-7 (alk. paper) — ISBN 0-7914-4818-5 (pbk. : alk. paper)
1. Women college administrators—United States. I. Nidiffer, Jana, 1957– II. Bashaw,
Carolyn Terry. III. Series.

LB2341.W5719 2001
378'.0082—dc21 00-036522

10 9 8 7 6 5 4 3 2 1

To Jayne Thorson whose courage inspires me and
kindness sustains me, and
to Jim Terry who has always been there.

WOMEN ADMINISTRATORS IN HIGHER EDUCATION

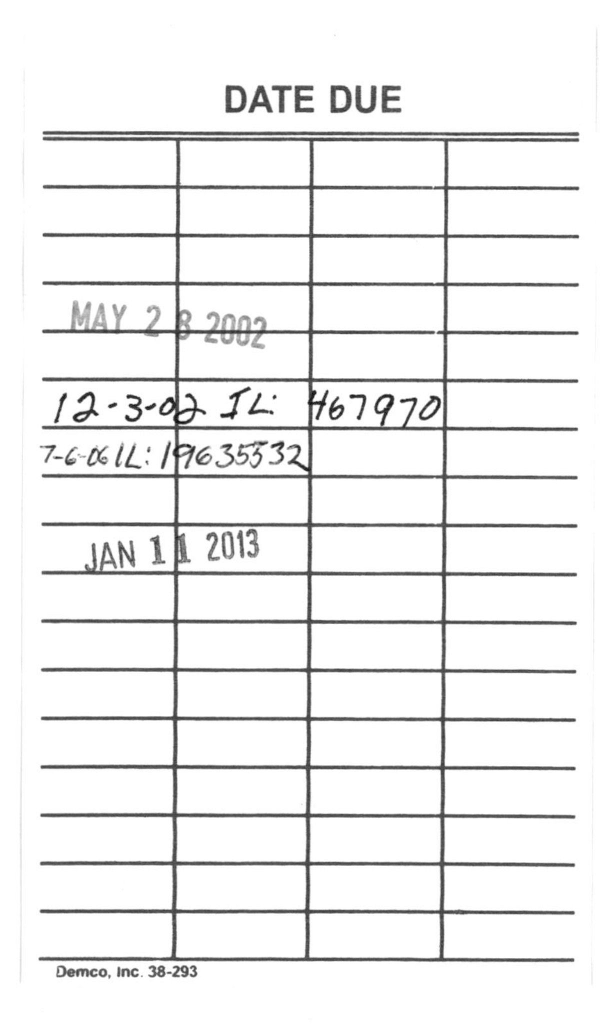

SUNY series

FRONTIERS IN EDUCATION

Philip G. Altbach, Editor

The Frontiers in Education Series draws upon a range of disciplines and approaches in the analysis of contemporary educational issues and concerns. Books in the series help to reinterpret established fields of scholarship in education by encouraging the latest synthesis and research. A special focus highlights educational policy issues from a multidisciplinary perspective. The series is published in cooperation with the School of Education, Boston College. A complete listing of books in the series can be found at the end of this volume.

Contents

Tables and Figures

Acknowledgments

From both of us:

We have been working on this project a long time and we wish to acknowledge the catalyst for our professional collaboration, Linda Eisenmann, who told both of us about each other's work. Linda is a generous colleague and warm friend.

Several people associated with SUNY Press were quite helpful at different stages of the manuscript. Many thanks to Philip Altbach, Priscilla Ross, Jenny Doling, and Cathleen Collins. Judith Contruci provided the invaluable technical service of turning individual chapters produced on multiple computers with myriad software programs into a unified text—a task that felt especially daunting to us.

We also wish to extend many heartfelt thanks to the contributors of this volume—Vivan Acosta, Cynthia Farr Brown, Linda Jean Carpenter, Candace Introcasso, Susan Jones, Susan Komives, Sharon McDade, Joan Paul, and Karen Doyle Walton. Their groundbreaking scholarship is indispensable and their patience during the process is greatly appreciated.

From Jana:

I appreciate the many friends, colleagues, and students who are continually supportive. I wish to express my deepest gratitude to Jayne Thorson whose humor and cracker-jack editing improves my work and enhances my life.

From Carolyn:

I would like to thank Carol Miller and Judith Shoen for their technical expertise, patience, and friendship while assisting in the preparation of this manuscript. I extend my sincere gratitude to John W. Langdon of the History Department at Le Moyne College for his encouragement of this project from its inception and his unwavering support for the story of women and higher education.

On a more personal level, I would like to thank Emily Gibson for her emotional and spiritual support, her humor, and her incisive sermons, which always point to what truly matters in this life. Finally, and always, I am grateful each and every day for the love and support of my husband, Louis Bashaw.

Introduction

Quiet Inspiration and Hard Work: The Impact of Women Administrators

JANA NIDIFFER AND CAROLYN TERRY BASHAW

In 1996, a student in the history of higher education course at the University of Massachusetts, Amherst, commented on what he gained as a contemporary professional by studying the contributions of his female predecessors. He captured the value of knowing our legacy:

> The advancement of women, black or white, in any field has been slow-coming, but we are seeing the direct results where deans, chancellors, even presidents of the universities are female. The women of today's education services owe a thanks to the women of the nineteenth century who tested the will of the educational institutions and ended up winning a very tough battle.[1]

Such comments make the hearts of history professors beat a bit faster. They also make us realize that within the professional literature, the work of historians and the work of scholars on current topics of higher education, only occasionally inform each other. Unfortunately, these two discrete literatures are seldom read by the same audiences. Yet, practicing administrators, historians, and higher education scholars share an interest in the study of female administrators from myriad perspectives. We therefore invited contributions from two scholarly traditions to form a single volume that will inform and inspire both audiences.

Scholarship on Women of the Past and the Present

Both the historical and contemporary scholarly traditions, at times, discuss women's inequality in higher education in terms that imply that women are the "other," exceptions to the norm, victims, or characters in "ain't it awful" stories. While it remains important to reveal the discrimination that still exists today and to portray women of past eras accurately, it is equally important to value their contributions and recognize that their accomplishments were, and are, many and varied.

In this spirit, we conceptualized this book. The contributing authors go beyond elucidating the problems. Instead, they reflect on women administrators as change agents—acting upon institutions of higher education rather than always being acted upon. The authors tell the stories of not only presidents, but a full array of women in administrative positions, all of whom exerted leadership on behalf of women students, faculty, or other administrators. The historians generate a new respect for the change agents of the past and unveil a rich context for the dilemmas facing contemporary administrators. The contemporary scholars build on this history and apply new theories and data to our understanding of women administrators today. The historians, in turn, use the theories of contemporary scholars to guide their reinterpretations and new visions of the past. Thus, a cycle emerges where scholarship from two different traditions becomes mutually reinforcing and results in an exponential growth in what we know about women as college and university administrators.

In the pages of this volume, many stereotypes are broken. Common cultural stereotypes of deans of women, nun presidents, and P.E. teachers as silly, vapid, bothersome, or ineffectual are proved false. Deans of women, women religious presidents, as well as their secular counterparts, and physical educators in fact made significant contributions that improved the material well being of women students in the first half of the twentieth century. What did these women accomplish?

- They produced spaces for women students on the coeducational campuses that disregarded them and forced institutions to provide adequate resources.
- They created colleges and provided opportunities for women faculty unavailable elsewhere.
- They looked after the physical well-being of women and demonstrated to the larger world that women were capable of physical activity, even athletics.
- They exerted power and leadership—again showing the larger world that women held such capabilities.
- They formed professional networks and organizations.
- They were activists on behalf of women students—their primary constituency—even in the post–World War II era of the 1950s, often considered a nadir decade for women's activism.

Of equal importance, within the pages of this volume new scholarly ground is broken. The writers on contemporary women administrators expand our knowledge with scholarship informed by a knowledge of the past, but venturing into new intellectual territory. What is learned about contemporary women administrators?

- The formidable battle waged by women athletic directors to provide parity for women and insist that the principles of Title IX are upheld.
- The first statistical portrait of women Chief Academic Officers is groundbreaking primary data that illustrates the influential role women play as senior administrators as well as the challenges and triumphs of the position.
- The leadership women Senior Student Affairs Officers exert to improve the campus climate, employing strategies often reminiscent of their fore-mothers, deans of women.
- A new way of considering, not just the equity involved in selecting more women as institutional presidents, but the strategic advantage of rethinking the skills and attributes required of the modern CEO, including characteristics emphasized in female socialization and therefore prevalent in women.

Quiet Inspiration and Hard Work

In the last fifteen years, the volume of historical scholarship on the experience of women in higher education has increased significantly. The stories, strategies, triumphs, and tribulations of women students, faculty members, and administrators are beginning to be told. Much of this work is inspiring, demonstrating the strength and passion of women who claimed the right to a life of the mind. These women were altruistic in a significant sense. They committed their professional energies to improving higher education for all women. They worked hard, paved the way for the women who followed, and quietly inspired the next generation of administrators to continue their battles and the next generation of students to aspire to their full potential.

For example, the founders, first presidents, and early administrators of women's colleges faced an undeniably daunting challenge. In an era when it was believed that educating women was unnecessary or even dangerous, they built institutions and helped define what it meant to be an educated woman. Along their way, the early presidents demonstrated that women could lead and manage—two skills that most of society presumed were restricted to men. The institutions they created provided women students incredible opportunities to learn and supplied women professionals the chance to teach or administer the college. These institutions continue to give women unparalleled possibilities.

Historians have also revealed that women's administrative networks were broader and deeper than one might imagine. The legacies of women physical educators and deans of women remain largely unfamiliar. The conflicts they faced, the compromises they engineered, and the concessions they won link their histories unquestionably and instructively to the fortunes of their successors.

Historical analysis of the careers of these pioneers makes us keenly conscious of the dissonance between superficial answers and deeper historical reality. A growing number of historians, eschewing conventional scholarly wisdom, have identified and evaluated rich collections of primary sources which provides a broader and deeper understanding of the role of women administrators in higher education. Their historical observations concerning these women reveal both the challenges they faced and the contributions they made to higher education for women and to the history of one of the defining institutions of modern life in the United States.

Our volume reminds contemporary women administrators in college sports that conflict on campus and within the profession is not merely a post-Title IX occurrence. Exploration of the history of women physical educators in higher education reveals that they encountered challenges from at least three sources: institutional administrators, women students, and colleagues within the profession. Despite questions concerning their academic credibility and personal attacks, pioneer administrators in women's physical education programs consistently pursued their goal of maintaining and enhancing the health and the athletic opportunities of college women.

Contemporary women student affairs officers can learn much about pragmatism and professionalism from their immediate predecessors, the deans of women. In a historical study of women and the professions, Penina Glazer and Miriam Slater found that a contingent of early professional women succeeded by eschewing direct competition with men through the formation of their own professions.[2] Our historical scholarship concerning deans of women confirms their findings. Deans of women were among the most dedicated and persistent of professional innovators. Working at the very margins of campus and professional life, they nevertheless oversaw the expansion of women students' access to the full range of campus life, the establishment of a national professional organization that exists to this day, and the creation of a legitimate body of scholarly literature concerning their profession.

Historical consideration of women administrators' predecessors compels us to reconsider and, hopefully, to replace easy answers with deeper, larger truths. Early women administrators were far less pliant than stereotypes suggest. Their stories offer instructive insight into contemporary administrative practice and decisively reflect on-going generational bonds among the practitioners and both their protégés and their students. Therefore, women administrators presently working in higher education do not operate in a historical vacuum. Historical precedent, both consciously and unconsciously, informs their professional environment and their professional decisions.

The legacy of these pioneers lives on in the work of today's professional women presidents, provosts, deans of students, and athletic directors who continue to work for equity and parity for women. As role models, the leadership of today's women undoubtedly serves as inspiration to untold numbers of other women on campus. As a new century begins, supporters of women's access to American higher education can take some comfort. Women compose slightly more than one-half of all undergraduates, earn one-third of the doctoral degrees, and constitute one-third of the faculty. Women no longer serve as presidents only of single-sex institutions; they now lead an increasing number of prestigious private and well-respected public colleges and universities.

Yet women continue to lack full access and equality of opportunity. We must rely on today's leaders—those in positions who have considerable formal authority and the capacity to enact the vision of the office-holder. Today's senior administrators have the opportunity to exercise leadership in higher education in ways only dreamed about by the early pioneers.

If this assertion is true, women can exert a notable impact on higher education. Yet with this possibility comes a potential dilemma. In the past, female administrators were unambiguously defined by their primary constituency—women. What are the implications for contemporary female administrators required to serve the entire community, not just "all the women of the university"? Do women have a particular obligation to create what poet Adrienne Rich referred to as a "women-centered university"?[3] These questions are being tackled by scholars within the frameworks of organizational and feminist analysis. This work is informative to historians of the so-called "nadir decades" of the twentieth century—the 1930s through the 1960s. During these years, women's place in the academy was in transition as the image of the domesticity prevailed in the popular mind, belying the undercurrent of feminist activity, especially by women working in higher education. Understanding how these women in the past successfully negotiated two seeming oppositional stances is made easier by the work of current scholars who study the analogous phenomenon of the 1990s.

So, with this volume we begin a fruitful scholarly exchange that benefits both professors and practitioners of higher education. Women administrators, past and present, work as change agents, but changing an institution as hidebound as higher education is no easy task. Organizational theorists posit that administrators wishing to be successful at change require a thoughtful understanding of institutional culture. Historians then utilize the theories of organizational scholars to demonstrate how the exclusion of women from the dominant culture of higher education made change an even greater challenge. But turnabout is fair play. Historical knowledge provides a deeper appreciation and understanding of the academic culture that assists both the organizational scholar and the contemporary administrator. Contemporary scholars extol the benefits of understanding institutional culture and savvy administrators know that operating without such an understanding is perilous. But institutional culture is brought into finest relief in times of conflict, and history elucidates those moments of antagonism—the times when previously unarticulated beliefs and assumptions are verbalized and forced into open debate, thus revealing the attitudes of those both for and against an idea. Women's entry into and subsequent participation in higher education was such a point of conflict. As a result, two scholarly traditions and bodies of knowledge emerged and now recognize their symbiosis.

Overview of Contents

Collectively, the chapters within this volume illuminate both the historical foundations of the dilemmas and the current realities, link the past with the present and contemplate the future.

Throughout the history of American higher education, there has been a direct correlation between the presence of female students and the number of women in the faculty or administration. Therefore, the history of women professionals within higher education begins in the 1830s with the founding of single-sex women's education and the first brave attempts at the dangerous experiment of coeducation. Jana Nidiffer's chapter, "Crumbs from the Boys Table," illustrates the tremendous controversy that surrounded the higher education of women during its first century. This chapter explores how proponents of women's education, especially the women professionals working within the colleges and universities, refuted each argument and overcame each obstacle. This chapter provides the foundation that places in context all the subsequent hard work and quiet inspiration of women administrators.

Three chapters explore the relationship of women to the power and responsibilities of the most senior position on campus—the president. The first is Cynthia Farr Brown's chapter, "Patterns of Leadership," in which she explores some of the earliest examples of women presidents at Wellesley, Bryn Mawr, and Trinity Colleges, and the College of New Rochelle. Looking closely at the experience of these four presidents, she reveals what they considered their leadership priority—mission. Each president built an institution that promoted rigorous academics as well as community and inspiration, and demonstrated the intellectual and professional potential of women. Their stories illustrate the importance of male mentors and allies for women stepping out of the traditional female sphere. This examination of leadership styles is a fascinating window not only on the specifics of the presidential role, but on the nature of gender roles, social norms, and the central issues within women's higher education as well.

The second chapter on the presidency builds on Brown's chapter and further examines an often overlooked contingent among leaders—the women religious who founded and built Roman Catholic institutions. Candace Introcaso in her chapter, "Determination in Leadership," examines the ways in which women religious presidents of women's colleges combined determination, humility, and faith to provide higher education for Roman Catholic women. Working within one of the primary patriarchal institutions in the world, sister presidents established a national network of colleges for women in the United States. Particularly intriguing are Introcaso's observations concerning the role of humility in both the success and frustration that these women encountered. She explores the ways in which this trait—so necessary in the religious life of community and so antithetical to traditional conceptions of institutional leadership in higher education—simultaneously enhanced and impeded their presidencies.

The position of provost is often dubbed the "internal president" because of the increasing off-campus demands of presidents. Sharon McDade and Karen Doyle Walton conducted a statistical study of the women Chief Academic Officers (CAO) at four-year colleges and universities in the United States. Like many other scholars in this volume, their chapter, "At the Top of the Faculty," breaks new ground. Scholars have yet to produce substantial research concerning CAOs of either gender. Thus, Walton and McDade's analysis of contemporary women holding this office represents a significant contribution to the study of women administrators in higher education. Based upon their research findings, they draw a concise portrait of women CAOs currently serving in colleges and universities. McDade and Walton reveal that despite the many challenges contemporary women CAOs encounter, they nevertheless remain enthusiastic about and dedicated to their work and encourage other women to enter the field.

The third chapter on the presidency deals with recent literature on leadership theory and its relationship to women. In "New Leadership for a New Century," Jana Nidiffer demonstrates how most of the skills traditionally associated with leadership such as power, control, or charisma may be less relevant to successful leadership in the future than they were in the past. Other characteristics, such as team-building, facilitating, and sense-making—those identified as the "emergent skills"—are more critical to leadership in the future. It is intriguing, but generally unacknowledged, that while both men and women are capable of possessing the emergent traits, such characteristics are typically associated with women. Nidiffer speculates that if female presidents do in fact have a "women's way of leading" that such skills may prove to be a *strategic* advantage for institutions that hire more women as senior executives. She then examines recent biographical sketches of women presidents and describes how their ideas about leadership embody the emergent skills.

The first female administrators who were not themselves founders of seminaries or colleges were mid-nineteenth-century matrons or disciplinarians hired to monitor the propriety of young women in the first coeducational colleges. At the turn of the twentieth century, coeducational universities began hiring a new type of administrator. They hired ambitious and talented women with strong academic backgrounds and a mission to improve the material and intellectual lives of women in the university. The new deans of women were not content with the limited role of matron and sought to expand the role and develop "deaning" as a recognized profession. These efforts were the foundation of modern student affairs administration. Jana Nidiffer's chapter, "Advocates on Campus," tells this story through the careers and strategies of four women who were instrumental in the process: Marion Talbot, University of Chicago; Mary Bidwell Breed, Indiana University; Ada Louise Comstock, University of Minnesota; and Lois Kimball Mathews, University of Wisconsin.

Since the inception of the office, deans of women encountered skepticism about if not hostility toward their work. Challenges to the profession intensified after World War II. In her consideration of deans of women during this period, Carolyn Bashaw challenges the traditional view of historians of women and of higher education concerning the activism of academic women during the Cold War era. In " 'Reassessment and Redefinition' The NAWDC and Higher Education for Women," Bashaw analyzes the *Journal of NAWDC,* 1956–1971, and finds that deans of women—despite attacks on their profession—responded with both feminism and foresight in their concern for the vitality of women's higher education in the United States. Deans of women concluded that to retain and to maintain the vitality of women's higher education, the profession must respond to changes in population, purpose, and paradigm.

During the earliest days of women's higher education, only two administrators attended to women students' needs—a dean of women and a health professional. Increasingly women students, as well as concerned educators, recognized the importance of physical education to their well-being. Joan Paul, in "Agents of Social Control: The Role of Physical Educators as Guardians of Women's Health, 1860–1960" explores the challenges faced by the earliest women physical educators in establishing collegiate programs in physical education. Critics on and off campus challenged their academic credentials and occasionally questioned their femininity. Institutional authorities were often reluctant to accord sufficient space to their programs. Despite such obstacles, Paul concludes that these women viewed their work in broad terms, determined to serve as supervisors of women's physical activities and general health, and, most importantly, as agents of social control.

After the mid-century, physical education for women expanded to include athletic programs, yet parity for women remains a distant dream. Linda Carpenter and Vivian Acosta in "Let Her Swim, Climb Mountain Peaks," conclude that by accepting Title IX, women leaders in collegiate athletics placed the interests of their women students first. As a result, they limited their own future professional prospects in many ways, both as administrators and as coaches. The subsequent merger of women's and men's athletic departments meant that many women physical educators either worked under the supervision of less-qualified men or lost their jobs entirely. Furthermore, with the improved salaries for coaches of women's intercollegiate sports, the number of successful male applicants for these jobs increased dramatically. Carpenter and Acosta discover that despite these circumstances, women coaches and administrators relied upon networking and other tactics to improve their circumstances.

Eventually, the administrative structure that included both a dean of women and a dean of men on campus came to an end, often in the name of "administrative efficiency." In their place, a dean of students was hired, frequently the former dean of men, resulting in a net loss of women in senior positions within student affairs. In "Contemporary Issues of Women as Chief Student Affairs Officers" Susan R. Jones and Susan R. Komives document the glass ceiling—how women have yet to achieve parity in senior positions despite their strong representation in the profession. Instead, they are clustered at the lower and middle levels. Despite an abundant presence in graduate preparation programs, women comprise a majority only in the more "nurturing" fields within student affairs. Jones and Komives also explore the quest of student affairs professionals to assert a more humanistic perspective amid the positivist values of the academy, an effort that resulted in student affairs being perceived as even more "feminized" and therefore further marginalized. The authors lament a shift in the research focus of scholarship from gender analysis to a more gender-neutral approach, a phenomenon that resulted in less scholarship on women. The chapter concludes with a discussion of several key issues within the profession and their impact on women.

Women in higher education and their partisans faced an unusual, internal challenge in the late 1950s and early 1960s as a contingent of women professionals and undergraduate women questioned the value both of women's professional organizations and of the dean of women. In " 'To Serve the Needs of Women,' " Carolyn Bashaw contends that in response, the AAUW and the NAWDC reaffirmed the unique scholarly and administrative contributions of women to the academic community. Cognizant of the connection between the power of money and the potential for professional careers, the AAUW reaffirmed its commitment to the growth of the Fellowship Program. Determined to counter attacks on the profession, the NAWDC emphasized the academic component of the dean of women's work and encouraged deans of women to redefine their relationship to faculty and students.

We began this project convinced of the value of both historical and contemporary approaches to uncovering the experiences of women administrators in higher education. At the completion of this work, we remain convinced, and indeed heartened, inspired, and encouraged by the range of scholars who share our views. We believe that these various studies—historical, quantitative, theoretical—inform each other and reflect the vitality this enterprise.

Notes

1. Many thanks to Dan Bureau for permission to quote his reading response paper from Jana Nidiffer's History of Higher Education course, University of Massachusetts, Fall term, 1996.

2. Penina M. Glazer and Miriam Slater, *Unequal Colleagues: The Entrance of Women into the Professions, 1890–1940* (New Brunswick: Rutgers University Press, 1987), 217–219.

3. Adrienne Rich, "Toward a Woman-Centered University," from *On Lies, Secrets, and Silence: Selected Prose, 1966–1978* (New York: W. W. Norton, 1979).

P A R T I

Historical Background

CHAPTER 1

Crumbs from the Boy's Table

The First Century of Coeducation

JANA NIDIFFER

In the very first novel written by a woman graduate of a coeducational university describing her experience, Olive San Louis Anderson (publishing under an anagram of her initials, SOLA) barely concealed her frustration and dismay.[1] Even her title, *An American Girl and Her Four Years in a Boy's College,* is revealing. Locating her story at the fictitious University of Ortonville, but in reality writing about the University of Michigan, Anderson told of her isolation and lack of integration into full university life. Although Michigan during the latter decades of the nineteenth century was regarded as one of the better universities in terms of providing opportunities for women, Anderson's story unmasks any pretense that women's admission to a university implied equal opportunity. "The girls are not expected to have much class spirit yet, but are supposed to sit meekly by and say 'Thank you' for the crumbs that fall from the boys table," she wrote. Yet at the same time, Anderson felt her "bosom swell with pride" to be attending such a great institution and knew she was given an opportunity that very few women before her had ever experienced.[2]

Such was the dilemma of coeducation. The climate for women was hostile and the social cost was enormous, but the opportunities were unparalleled. In the 1830s women first entered the handful of all-female academies that were newly opened. Located primarily in the East, the two most notable were Troy Female Seminary in upstate New York and Mount Holyoke Seminary (later College) in Massachusetts. In that same decade, Oberlin College of Ohio opened its doors to women embarking upon the experiment of educating young men and women together. By the 1930s, women's participation in higher education reached its zenith. Regrettably, the gains up to that point were soon eclipsed by the social and political conservatism of postwar America.

Not until the late 1970s did participation rates for women equal, and then surpass those of the 1930s.[3]

During the first century of women's higher education, from the 1830s to the 1930s, the myriad arguments against women's higher education in general and coeducation in particular were articulated and refuted—refuted at least in the minds of most women! By the 1930s, the preponderance of previously all-male institutions, except the most elite and the most militaristic, were opened to women. Yet, although women enrolled in record numbers, they did so amid the doubts, dire predictions, fears, and resentment foisted on them by a wary society. The religious, intellectual, biological, and social arguments against women's higher education reveal a great deal about the attitudes and beliefs of America's dominate white middle-class, as well as the growing importance of higher education in the social and economic welfare of the nation.

The Separate Spheres

The cornerstone of resistance to women's higher education was the very Judeo-Christian heritage on which the country was founded. Laws and social practices reflected the pan-Protestantism integral to early America. This belief system included a conviction that women were to be subservient, first to a father, then to a husband, and, at all times, to God. People believed in a divinely ordained world order. God meant things to be exactly as they were. It followed therefore that women were confined to the domestic sphere of life, and men participated in the political, economic, and social spheres of the communities.[4] Women were expected to conform to the "cult of true womanhood" that demanded piety, obedience, purity, and domesticity.[5]

Prior to the American Revolution, American colonial colleges chiefly prepared boys to enter the ministry, politics, or academic life. Some gentleman farmers of the South attended, usually the College of William and Mary, but few men needed much formal education.[6] The idea of a woman attending college seemed absurd, since she could never become a minister, politician, statesman, or farmer.

The ferment surrounding the American Revolution, specifically the Enlightenment-inspired, Jefferson-invigorated ideas about the inherent rationality of human beings led some women to question their lack of educational opportunity. As Barbara Miller Solomon illustrated, a few outspoken women such as Abigail Adams and Mercy Otis Warren agitated for more education for women and girls and radicals such as Mary Wollenstonecraft called for greater political participation and recognition.[7] A few academies formed to offer post-elementary preparation, but the revolutionary zeal that inspired the Founding Fathers to seek more freedom and opportunity for themselves did not extend to women.

Such attitudes are not surprising. Even Jean-Jacques Rousseau, one of Thomas Jefferson's intellectual inspirations, outlined his view of women's education quite clearly. In *Emile,* Rousseau's treatise on child development and pedagogy published in 1762, he stated, "A woman's education must therefore be planned in relation to man. To be pleasing in his sight, to win his respect and love, to train him in childhood, to tend him in manhood, to counsel and console, to make his life pleasant and happy, these are the duties of woman for all time, and this is what she should be taught while she is young."[8]

As the young country grew, increased mercantile opportunities created the beginnings of a significant middle class. A trend toward urbanization began, especially in the East. With fewer people working family farms where the work of women and children often meant the difference between starvation and survival, the gender spheres grew even more immutable. More men left the home to work and the economic contribution of "women's work" became less obvious. Demand for common schooling increased for both sons and daughters. Religious fervor spurred literacy rates as more citizens sought at least the ability to read the Bible, an essential trait of Protestantism. Even higher education began to change, too, albeit slowly at first. The young colleges that were springing up like weeds across the East and Midwest offered a few more pragmatic areas of study including courses in political economy, engineering, and English. Even the South, where the number of colleges was fewer, experienced a time of remarkable growth.

The growth in common schooling, combined with increased business opportunities for men, created a demand for teachers that women could fill. The revivalist spirit of the second Great Awakening simultaniously stimulated a need for missionaries. Beginning in the 1830s, a smattering of seminaries and colleges such as Troy and Mount Holyoke, Oberlin and Antioch, seized the chance to educate women for these two new roles.[9] A social contract was struck. Women could continue their educations and find intellectual and professional fulfillment in work that was genuinely needed. Yet these two roles only minimally expanded the edges of the female sphere—women remained obedient Christians and nurturers of children.

Male educators grudgingly accepted the idea of women's higher education in order to fulfill specific, pragmatic needs. However, most educators assumed that women did not have the intellectual capacity to study the same subjects as men. At Oberlin, for example, women enrolled in the "Ladies Course," a less demanding version of the literary course that men studied. The revered classical education designed to train the logical minds of men was thought beyond women. If they studied at all, it should be the domestic arts, "finishing" subjects such as sewing, drawing, or French, or disciplines of minimal rigor and importance such as science.[10] Throughout the country, however, women educators held different expectations for their students.[11] The early curriculum created by Emma Willard at Troy and Mary Lyon at Mount Holyoke was as demanding as many of the other antebellum colleges and more rigorous than some.

Higher education for women was one of the gains reformers sought in the so-called First Wave of feminism of the late 1830s and 1840s. Susan B. Anthony, Elizabeth Cady Stanton, and other women's rights advocates, included women's education in the *Declaration of Sentiments* at the first Women's Rights Convention in Seneca Falls, New York in 1848.[12] For the social and political progressives of the 1840s, however, the abolition of slavery emerged as the more important and more urgent societal problem. Women were essentially asked to place their agenda on hold. After the Civil War, many feminists were disappointed that women's suffrage was not included when the Fifteenth Amendment to the Constitution gave African American men the vote. Although suffrage remained a goal, most political energy on behalf of women from the late 1860s to the turn of the century was focused on winning the chance to go to college.

The passage of the Morrill Act in 1862 brought several changes to American higher education, but more important than any single change was the overall development of a significant public sector of higher education. Prior to 1860, the majority of institutions were private—at least in the contemporary understanding of the term. Although the distinction between public and private colleges was not as clearly delineated as might be believed, the two sectors increasingly assumed distinguishing characteristics. For women, the private sector of previously all-male colleges remained largely closed for decades, but equivalent women's colleges including the Seven Sisters Colleges (Mount Holyoke, Smith, Wellesley, Radcliffe, Barnard, Vassar, and Bryn Mawr) were begun in the 1870s. Some women's colleges were little more than finishing schools, but most quickly became serious, rigorous liberal arts colleges. Oberlin, Antioch, and a few others remained anomalies—private, coeducational colleges.

By-in-large, coeducation was a phenomenon of the public sector, at the smaller normal schools and the state universities. As more and more public institutions admitted women, the debate regarding coeducation grew.[13] This acrimonious and long-lasting debate has been compared to the debate surrounding abolition in terms of the intensity of emotions on both sides of the issue and the numbers of middle-class men and women involved.[14]

The Biological Bogy

By the middle of the nineteenth century, science—specifically biology—was used to justify the differences between the genders. British philosopher, Herbert Spencer, inspired much of this type of thinking. Spencer believed that the body was a closed biological system—the expenditure of energy in one part, necessarily deprived another part. Spencer's major contribution was his work in applying the conclusions of Charles Darwin to the full range of human activities. He believed that "specialization of function" was critical to both social and biological evolution. This included specialization between men and women—each of whom had their prescribed roles.[15] So, the separate spheres and a separate system of educating women were not only as God ordained, they were as Darwin predicted.

One of the first widely read attacks on coeducation emerged from the medical community. In 1873 a former member of the Harvard Medical School faculty, Dr. Edward H. Clarke, published his views on women's education in a small book entitled, *Sex in Education; or, a Fair Chance for the Girls.* Clarke based his views on the proposition that biology was destiny.[16] He argued that women's brains were less developed and could not tolerate the same level of mental stimulation (meaning higher education) as men's so they should not be taught in the same manner as men.[17] More importantly, however, Clarke linked intense brain activity with the potential malfunction of the reproductive "apparatus," especially if women were overtaxed during the "catamenial function" (menstruation).[18] He therefore concluded that a separate system of women's higher education was needed, and was vehemently opposed to coeducation, which he considered a "crime before God and humanity."[19]

Clarke's book had a tremendous impact and opponents of women's education used it extensively. Clarke's book was also extremely popular. On one hand, *Sex in Education* addressed two issues that fascinated the educated public—the "experiment" of women's higher education and the application of evolutionary biology to social issues. Furthermore, the book discussed these issues with "readable prose and decidedly non-Victorian candor about female physiology."[20] It was almost titillating.

Response on campuses and in college towns, women's clubs, medical schools, reading circles, and anywhere that people were debating women's education was overwhelming. Clarke's book was all the talk. Although the University of Michigan had been coeducational for three years by 1873, "everyone" was reading the book and on one occasion two hundred copies were sold in one day! At the University of Wisconsin, where antagonism toward coeducation was intense in the 1870s, the regents of the university used Clarke's findings to justify withdrawing support for women's education. "It is better that the future matrons of the state should be without university training than that it should be produced at the fearful expense of ruined health," commented a regent.[21]

Proponents of women's education were shocked and angered by Clarke's wrong-headed, but unfortunately persuasive theories. M. Carey Thomas, future president of Bryn Mawr College, recalled, "We did not know when we began whether women's health could stand the strain of education. We were haunted in those days by the clanging chains of the gloomy specter, Dr. Edward Clarke's *Sex in Education*."[22] Feminists denounced Clarke, argued that his conclusions were faulty, and pointed out that his theory was based on only seven case studies, one of whom was not even a college student. Of those subjects who were students, not even one woman attended a coeducational institution.[23] Proponents wrote several articles in the leading women's publication, *Women's Journal,* illustrating the good health and stamina of college women. Members of the Association of College Alumnae (ACA) conducted a survey and used empirical evidence to refute Clarke, stating that 78 percent of college women were in good health.[24]

In her study, Rosalind Rosenberg concluded, the "growing emphasis on the power of biology revealed anxiety over the increasing instability of sex roles."[25] While many opponents embraced the "ruined health" thesis of Dr. Clarke, others opposed women's education because it was "socially undesirable."[26] Throughout the 1870s and 1880s, the anxiety surrounding changing gender roles was often expressed as a fear of "masculating" or "un-sexing" women, making them unfit for marriage. Annie Nathan Meyer, founder of Barnard College, recalled with sadness her father's prediction when she announced her intention to seek higher education. "You will never be married," he said. "Men hate intelligent wives."[27]

Although critics were numerous, coeducation also had influential friends. Early women's rights advocates believed that coeducation was the only way to achieve equity for women so that they might emerge from their "separate sphere."[28] Activists such as Susan B. Anthony, Lucy Stone, and Julia Ward Howe argued that coeducation was "the only means of reaching the ideal of equal education."[29] Others such as Elizabeth Cady Stanton believed coeducation would improve relationships between the sexes. "If the sexes were educated together," she said, "we should have the healthy, moral, and intellectual stimulus of sex everquickening and refining all the faculties without the undue excitement of senses that results from novelty in the present system of isolation."[30] Most middle-class feminists believed in the need for education to improve conditions for women.

After the Civil War there were strong pockets of local support and women's clubs of the era who actively campaigned for coeducation. Comprised primarily of older women denied the opportunity of a college education, these clubs worked diligently on behalf of their daughters and younger sisters. They lobbied university administrations and state legislatures, and convinced husbands and brothers to support legislation that would open public colleges to women.[31]

Doors Open

Colleges and universities, however, were not "overwhelmed by egalitarian considerations" and on the whole did not admit women enthusiastically.[32] Only a few institutions were persuaded to adopt coeducation as a result of women's campaigns. Cornell University, located in the same region as Seneca Falls, admitted women in 1872 after a long campaign by both male and female women's rights advocates.[33] Most institutions opened to women for a variety of other, economically oriented reasons. The new Morrill Act–funded colleges and their sister state institutions notoriously experienced serious financial pressures in their early years from the 1860s through to the 1880s.[34] The responses of Michigan and Wisconsin to such economic considerations were typical.

It is simple to assert that when taxpaying parents in Michigan argued that the state was obligated to educate both sons and daughters, the regents of the University of Michigan voted to admit women in 1870. It was considerably cheaper than supporting a separate, female institution. But the story is much more involved.

Women had been agitating for admission for almost twenty years. After all, the 1837 charter of the university said it was "open to all persons of the state." Although the legal thinking of the era excluded women from the category of "persons," several citizens of Michigan did not. In 1853, the State Teachers Association sought higher education for the state's secondary school teachers, including women. In 1858, Sara Berger petitioned the Board of Regents on behalf of herself and twelve women for admission, but her request was tabled. When the petition was finally heard, President Henry Tappan—the man hailed as building Michigan into a great university based upon the idealized German model—declared his opposition:

> After [the admission of women] no advancement is possible. . . . The standard of education must now be accommodated to the wants of girls who finish their education at 16–20, very properly, in order to get married, at the very age when young men begin their education.[35]

The Regents did not relent until 1870 when James B. Angell (in general, a supporter of coeducation) was president. The pressure from taxpayers was too large to ignore and all efforts at a separate women's institution were deemed financially ruinous.

Substantial Civil War causalities caused a drop in male enrollment and colleges needed tuition revenue. The growing number of students in public elementary schools prompted states to seek a cheap supply of teachers. Women students paid tuition and women teachers were often paid only half of what men earned so they were cheap labor indeed. In Wisconsin, after considerable lobbying by the State Teachers Association (as was the case in Michigan), women were admitted to the university in 1863. However, Wisconsin limited its admission to the newly created normal department. Wisconsin was not unique; several institutions introduced coeducation reluctantly and gradually, allowing women only in certain departments or courses of study.

Thus coeducation came into being because it served a state need or pressure from taxpayers or other groups. State and university officials did not bother much about the intellectual or personal benefits which accrued to the women themselves.[36]

Yet, no matter the reason, young women took advantage of the opportunity presented in the midwestern universities. Barbara Miller Solomon identified the women who went to college between 1870 and 1890 as the "first generation."[37] These pioneers were serious, purposeful, and single-minded. They were stereotyped as mannish and often joyless, yet they were very much aware that they were the first of their gender to receive such opportunities and they labored under the tremendous expectations placed upon them.

The first woman to attend Indiana University, Sarah Parke Morrison, wrote of her experiences of 1867, "When the decision was announced [that she would attend the university] no one in the family encouraged it. This was more than they bargained for."[38] But she did attend and was so aware of the many stares she received that she wore a large hat her first few months on campus to avoid men's eyes. She was also aware that she was scrutinized and felt considerable pressure to perform well. She noted that a "woman must come up to the mark, must be careful to establish no precedent injurious to her interests. . . . To fail would be worse than not to try."[39] She felt she always overcompensated: "I think that perhaps I had had about of enough Latin, I had chosen to make a point of it, but I rather read more than really required 'to not lower the standard.' "[40]

First-generation women represented only 2.2 percent of their age cohort (18 to 21 year-old women), but they represented 35 percent of all college students. Slightly over 70 percent of all first-generation students were in coeducational institutions.[41] By example they proved that women could withstand the intellectual rigors of college and remain healthy. They performed well academically and several pursued careers in medicine, science, teaching, and social work. A number entered higher education—a few as professors, others as the first professional women administrators, deans of women, physicians, or health and physical education supervisors.[42]

The lot of the first generation was perhaps not as dour or bleak as the stereotype. Despite the taunts and stares and even the isolation, many college women experienced considerable personal satisfaction and meaningful personal freedom greater than that of the average woman of the nineteenth century. In fact, the relative autonomy and fulfillment that the college experience provided prompted a more poignant question, "After college, what?"

The fiction written by women college graduates is revealing. The tone of the standard "commencement chapter" is frequently bittersweet, because the authors know that life after college will be more limited and constrained. Often the central woman character laments being a misfit—feeling unfulfilled as a housewife, but not welcome in the work world.[43]

Yet despite uncertain futures and the hostility from men, women came to campuses in droves. As time passed, the women found that some men were increasingly receptive to the idea of female friends and classmates. Correspondingly, several women savored friendships and working relationships with men, which again was not a typical nineteenth-century female experience. Occasionally, friendship led to romance, and among college women who married, several married classmates.[44] Most women, however, viewed an intellectual and professional career as one life choice, and marriage and motherhood as another. Combining career and marriage was unthinkable for the first generation. As a result, college women did not marry and have children at the same rate as their non-college-educated peers.[45] Unfortunately, this situation prompted yet another round of attacks on coeducation.

Race Suicide and Other Concerns

In the mid-nineteenth century, critics of coeducation charged that educating women was an abomination before God. Within a few decades the argument became more personal. Opponents concluded that the strain of education hurt the individual woman. At first they feared her masculinization and then her "ruined health" as Dr. Clarke predicted. As the nineteenth century came to a close, however, coeducation was deemed to be causing grievous harm to the larger society. The academic success and low birth rates of college women shifted the arguments against coeducation to the slightly different, yet integrally related, notion of "race suicide."

Anxiety regarding acceptable sex roles combined with increasing xenophobia and anti-immigration sentiments. This wave of attacks upon women's education focused on the fact that college-educated women married later, if at all, and had fewer children than their less-educated contemporaries. Critics blamed a college education for the falling marriage and birth rates and the increasing divorce rates among white, native-born Americans.[46]

The critics were numerous and prominent. Charles Eliot of Harvard, psychologist G. Stanley Hall, and President Theodore Roosevelt warned Americans that the "best classes" were not reproducing themselves.[47] Throughout the Progressive Era, scholars and commentators published articles on the issue. In 1907, Paul J. Möebius, a German-born physician wrote, "If we wish a woman to fulfill her task of motherhood fully, she cannot possess a masculine brain. If the feminine abilities were developed to the same degree as those of the male, woman's maternal organs would suffer and we should have a repulsive and useless hybrid."[48]

In a 1915 *Journal of Heredity* article simply entitled, "Education and Race Suicide," the author argued that every college-educated woman should have at least three children "in order to prevent the race from actually declining in numbers."[49] The topic was even the subject of concern in college courses. A student in Harvard's "Principles of Sociology" in 1904 recorded in his notebook, "higher education has somewhat the same effect [on population] as celibacy. Those securing higher training multiply less rapidly than others. Whether this is due to education or not is undecided, but it seems to be. Now it seems certain that if the educated people multiply slower than non-educated, intellectual deterioration is sure."[50]

The critics enjoyed the advantage of statistics. Approximately one-half of the first-generation college women married, in contrast to a marriage rate of 90 percent for non-college educated women.[51] Women who went to college after 1890 had higher marriage and birth rates than the first generation, although they were still lower than the rest of the population. However, the percentage of women attending college was still so small that even if one-half or one-third of them did not marry, the vehemence of the attacks was out of proportion to any real population danger.

In addition to race suicide, a new criticism emerged during the Progressive Era accusing coeducation of feminizing male students and the institutions themselves. The fear of feminization was a preoccupation at the turn of the century and received considerable attention in the popular press, which encouraged American men to be more manly, athletic, and aggressive.[52] Increasing industrialization and urbanization were commonly believed to be rendering men too soft. But some critics considered higher education to be the real culprit. They charged that coeducation was responsible for the loss of manly verve. Ironically and largely unnoticed, such criticism implied that women wielded enormous power and depicted men in quite unfavorable terms. Such criticism was, in fact, a response to the growing prevalence of coeducation and especially to the academic success of women students.[53] The secretary of the Western Association of Collegiate Alumnae commented adroitly in 1905, "the very success of the movement, which amounts to a great revolution affecting one-half of the human race, has roused men to resist its progress."[54]

The "success" of coeducation was measured in two ways. The first was simply the sheer number of women in colleges and universities. By the late nineteenth century more institutions were coeducational than single-sex. Coeducation had become the dominant mode of educating students in the United States. By 1920, women were almost half of all higher education students and 80 percent of them were in coeducational institutions.[55]

The second benchmark was the intellectual success of women. At the University of Chicago between 1892 and 1902, women earned 46 percent of the baccalaureate degrees but 56.3 percent of the Phi Beta Kappa keys. Similar levels of accomplishment occurred elsewhere. Women's academic success prompted some universities to impose limits on the number of honors women were eligible to earn.[56]

Antagonism toward women students was manifest in the inequitable distribution of resources that universities bestowed on them. In general the Midwestern universities did not provide women with housing, medical care, or physical education facilities, despite the fact that such facilities existed for men by the 1870s.

Access to a gymnasium was quite important because of the concerns regarding the health and fitness of women students. Typically, universities initially barred women from the gyms and then gradually relented to pressure by granting limited access. When access was granted it was usually at times deemed less desirable by men, during the dinner hour for example. Some presidents, such as William Rainey Harper of Chicago, argued that women and men could not use the gymnasium at the same time for reasons of propriety. To Harper's declaration, Dean Marion Talbot wryly noted, "they [men and women] could swim together in the ocean and dance together on the ballroom floor even though, in the former case, the costumes of women were much scantier than those allowed in the gymnasium."[57]

Of greater concern was the paucity of scholarship money available to women. Universities awarded little, if any, of their available funds to female students. Of the class of 1903 at the University of Chicago, 88 men (12.6 percent of the total male undergraduates) and 85 women (14.2 percent of the female total) were admitted to Chicago's graduate school. Ten of the men received fellowships while only three of the women received financial assistance.[58] In response, local club women and YWCAs developed the practice of raising scholarship money for students.[59]

Male students made it difficult for women to enter their preserve. Photographs of lecture halls of the era reveal a pattern of strict segregation.[60] Women were explicitly ridiculed under the guise of humor as misogynistic cartoons and stories filled campus newspapers, literary magazines, and yearbooks. "Coeds," as they came to be called, were excluded from clubs, eating halls, music groups, honorary societies, and most activities associated with campus prestige.[61]

Sarah Parke Morrison, the first woman graduate of Indiana University, described her feelings when her recitation in class was followed by a hurtful comment from a classmate:

> Mr. Dunn, whom I had noticed as a rather superior young gentleman, astonished me by making some rather slighting remark. For the first time, I lost my temper, but higher power preserved me from losing my tongue. It probably was intended as a test. If I was mad internally, I could not permit my cause to suffer, even for myself. Professor Wylie was placid, apparently oblivious of the critic and me further for that time.[62]

Unfortunately, not only students exhibited their hostility. Faculty members sometimes ignored women in the classroom, refused to answer questions, or prohibited discussion. Faculty often addressed mixed classes as "gentlemen" and called women "Mr. __," ignoring their obvious gender. On some occasions, even official university policy ignored or excluded women.[63]

In response, college women established a separate student culture in much the same manner as adult women in the larger society.[64] They formed women's literary and debating clubs, wrote women's magazines and newspapers or special "women's pages" inside the dominant campus publications, and they formed sororities. Depicted in the diaries and letters of women students as well as in the fiction written by them and about them, these special, all-female worlds were cozy and valuable assets for coping with the daily indignities of campus life. Despite their obvious drawbacks, alumnae remembered the female worlds fondly.

Changes in Higher Education

In a predictable fashion, the criticism leveled at coeducation spoke volumes about the changing nature of the relationship between higher education and the economy. As the twentieth century dawned, established professions were organizing and nascent occupations were working hard to professionalize. Professionalization required the training and credentialing of aspirants. Higher education assumed the role of gatekeeper to the professions and, consequently, the middle class. As more graduate schools opened and entry to high-status jobs depended less on family name, the hierarchy of prestige among institutions began to codify. Men resented the places taken and honors won by women at the premier state universities.

Many changes occured within higher education as well. The fear of feminization of the institution was spurred by the modifications in the curriculum and the pattern of course selection demonstrated by both genders. Women students were the catalyst for several curricular changes, including two women-oriented additions to the curriculum in the first few years after the Morrill Act. Coeducation and the need for teachers prompted universities to create normal departments, and "domestic" studies, eventually known as home economics, was introduced. One of the earliest was at the University of Iowa which established its program in 1871. Several other state universities followed within a decade or two.[65]

The role of home economics in the history of women's education is equivocal. Many educators, both male and female, supported women gaining the practical training it offered. Others viewed it as a step backward into the kitchen. Different faculties focused on the various aspects of the discipline—scientific, social, economic, or domestic—but the steady growth of enrollments across universities demonstrated its popularity with students. It was also a viable option for women who, with their home economics degrees, found steady employment in industry and social service, especially before

World War I.[66] However, home economics departments became a ghetto of sorts for women academics unable to secure positions in other disciplines. Even women who had advanced degrees in other subject areas such as chemistry, for example, were relegated to home economics departments. By 1911, over 60 percent of all female professors at coeducational institutions were housed in one discipline—domestic science.

These two fields—teacher preparation and home economics—absorbed the majority of female enrollments in the nineteenth century. By 1900 there were 61,000 women in coeducational institutions; 43,000 were enrolled in education departments and 2,000 were studying home economics.[67] After 1900, women students and educators sought other types of courses related to women's interests. The growing numbers of women involved in the reformist movements of the Progressive Era created demand for courses on topics such as child psychology, marriage and family, social work, settlement work, poverty, and charity.[68]

Coeducation caused other modifications in the curriculum. Faculty and administrators noticed a disturbing trend in the liberal arts colleges of coeducational institutions. Men and women demonstrated different patterns in course selection for both their major areas of study and their electives. Men were deserting the humanities and languages. They gravitated instead toward the sciences and some of the new social science disciplines, especially economics and political economy. Women did the opposite; they chose the humanities and languages (the very disciplines they were thought incapable of understanding a few decades earlier!) and the new discipline of sociology.

Faculty members in the humanities complained vociferously that women were feminizing, and therefore devaluing, their disciplines by driving the men away.[69] Many educators, including presidents such as Benjamin Wheeler of Berkeley and early deans of women such as Marion Talbot, addressed the issue. Most concluded that men and women chose different courses based on vocational interests and employment possibilities, rather than inherent differences in aptitude or ability. Women entering teaching or social work still benefited from the humanities, languages, or sociology. Men, the majority of whom planned to enter business or the professions, found less use for humanities courses.[70] Despite this explanation for the phenomenon, it was argued that reversing the effects of feminization required more male students and separate courses of study for each gender.

Several universities contemplated restricting female enrollment, segregating men and women in all subjects, or eliminating coeducation altogether. Mrs. Jane Stanford, chief benefactor and mother of the institution's namesake, was very worried about feminization. She decreed that female enrollment could never exceed five hundred. Boston University initiated a "More Men Movement" and Wesleyan abandoned coeducation altogether. Even at the University of Chicago, where coeducation had been part of the university from its beginning, President William Rainey Harper held deep reservations about educating men and women together.

Harper worried that coeducation might remove sexual distinctions and he suggested segregated instruction in the junior college (freshman and sophomore years). His plan went into effect in 1902, but lasted only a few years. Chicago's dean of women, Marion Talbot, led the protest against segregation, but the plan was abandoned by the administration only when it proved too costly and cumbersome.[71] In 1908, President Charles Van Hise of Wisconsin uttered similar sentiments and created a storm of controversy so great that reinstated the position of dean of women to alleviate the criticism that he was antagonistic toward women.[72]

The question of whether women and men required separate or distinct educations was not new. As Rosalind Rosenberg noted, "[U]ntil the turn of the century women faculty and women's rights leaders opposed [segregation in the classroom]. As higher education came to appeal to a broader spectrum of young womanhood, however, courses fitted to women's domestic interests gained support."[73] In the early twentieth century, the issue became more cloudy. Differences in employment possibilities and future social roles caused both male and female educators to agree that some forms of separate education were desirable.[74] For those educators who wanted separate educations to overcome feminization, several trends within the university including departmentalization, specialization, and the expansion of professional schools made the task easier.[75]

The movement toward departmentalization as an organizational structure and specialization among faculty members began in the 1880s, but was a stronger force after 1900. Prior to that time, there had been more interdepartmental activity. As departmental and faculty interests narrowed, clear gender distinctions emerged. The separation of the theoretical (considered masculine) from the practical (feminine) was a common division. For example, psychology divided into experimental versus clinical fields. Theoretical sociology was made distinct from professional social work. Home economics became less interdepartmental and more feminized. Prior to 1900, home economics departments employed women faculty from a variety of usually science-oriented disciplines. Institutions without specific departments offered home economics courses under the rubric of other disciplines such as economics, political economy, chemistry, sociology, or public health. Eventually home economics became a discrete department with specific faculty training and concentrated increasingly on domestic issues.[76]

The professional schools of law, medicine, business, and divinity were dominated by male students and fostered a social ethos that women did not belong. Eliza Mosher's Quaker upbringing had instilled in her a sense that women were equal to men. She assumed her mother shared this belief so was shocked by her reaction to Mosher's plans to enter medical school: "I would sooner pay to have thee shut up in a lunatic asylum . . . than to have thee study medicine."[77] Fortunately, Mosher's mother relented and Mosher became one of Michigan's earliest woman graduates of the medical school in 1875. Discouraged or ignored by most of her professors and even called a "hen medic" by President James Angell, Mosher persisted and went on to a successful medical career. She later served as the first dean of women at the University of Michigan, ushering in health reforms and encouraging women to get more exercise, abandon their corsets, and wear sensible shoes.

Only social work graduate programs, newly formed in the Progressive Era, had significant female enrollments.[78] Therefore, more male-oriented professional schools were established in order to increase the number of men on campus. Universities established such schools at an accelerated rate. An economist at the University of Chicago summed up the thinking of the era in 1902:

> The congestion of numbers [of women students] is now largely due to the fact that the undergraduate courses are practically used by women as an advanced normal school to prepare for teaching. Just so soon as proper support and endowments are given to work which offers training for careers in engineering, railways, banking, trade and industry, law and medicine, etc. the disproportion of men will doubtless remedy itself.[79]

Conclusion

During the first century of women's higher education, the presence of women on a campus was a tangible sign of an institution's lack of wealth and prestige. As President Van Hise of Wisconsin noted, "The reasons which led to coeducation were then purely economic. The western states in these early days were too poor to support two high grade educational institutions."[80] The rather condescending attitudes of Eastern educators, especially Charles Eliot of Harvard, further fueled resentment toward women students. Eliot stated in 1894 that men and women aged fifteen to twenty years were not "best educated in intimate association" but noted that coeducation may "nevertheless be justifiable in a community which cannot afford anything better. . . . Coeducation has the advantage of economy. . . . Many of the colleges of the West were established for both men and women because the churches or the people could not afford two colleges in a single commonwealth."[81]

Consequently, the presence of women on campus was a painful reminder to the men at Wisconsin or Michigan that they were not at Harvard or Yale.[82] In response, a few institutions—Wisconsin, Stanford, Chicago, and Wesleyan, for example—on much stronger fiscal ground after 1900 than before, attempted to limit or eliminate coeducation. These attempts, however, were socially, politically, or financially costly and were not sustained.[83] In the generally expansive and pro-democracy mood of the Progressive Era, a retreat from access was unacceptable.

Women were largely ignored and resented until the early part of the twentieth century, but the daily life for women on campuses altered rather dramatically after World War I. The patterns of social life among male and female students changed as Victorian strictness regarding heterosexual relationships eased. When college men became interested in dating and marrying college women, the women no longer wanted a separate existence. As the strangeness of being a woman in college diminished, and women seemed content to be at college for the good times. As Helen Horowitz described in her history of student life, men gained prestige through multiple avenues—sports, extracurricular achievement, and even occasionally academics. Women gained prestige by being sought after by men with prestige. As Horowitz puts it, "women glowed in reflective light."

Numerically, women's participation in higher education hit a high-water mark in the 1930s, but the gains soon faded. Comparative rates of participation were not reached until the 1970s ushered in another wave of feminist activity that focused attention on women's intellectual and professional potential. This time the colleges responded with a few more tangible supports including women's studies departments and women's centers.

The resistance to women's higher education did not magically disappear once the university doors were open. Through the first century, legal barriers were easier to surmount than attitudinal ones. Resentment and prejudice lingered. Virginia Woolf described the underlying subtext against which women struggled as habits of mind that were "tough as roots, but intangible as sea-mist."[84]

Vestiges of these same attitudes are still prevalent, manifest in what Bernice Sandler and her colleagues described as the "Chilly Climate." In fact, the climate can be positively cold at the sites of the most recent struggles for coeducation at the Citadel and the Virginia Military Institute. Whether our institutions' climates are cold, chilly, tepid, or even warm, the conflict over women's education is our legacy. The drama of the first century forms the backdrop against which women currently participate in higher education. Our history shapes the struggles and the agendas of contemporary female administrators, requiring hard work but often providing quiet inspiration.

Notes

1. SOLA, *An American Girl and Her Four Years in a Boy's College* (New York: D. Appleton and Company, 1878).
2. Ibid., 49–50.
3. Patricia A. Graham, "Expansion and Exclusion: A History of Women in American Higher Education," *Signs: Journal of Women in Culture and Society* 3 (1978): 759–73.

4. See Rosalind Rosenberg, *Beyond Separate Spheres: Intellectual Roots of Modern Feminism* (New Haven: Yale University Press, 1982), for how social thought moved beyond the notion of the separate sphere, largely due to the work of early women social scientists.

5. Historian Barbara Welter coined the phrase "The Cult of True Womanhood" to describe the sphere of life for American women in the nineteenth century. A woman was measured by four cardinal virtues—piety, purity, submissiveness, and domesticity—which prepared her for her exclusive roles as daughter, wife, and mother. See Barbara Welter, *Dimity Convictions: The American Woman in the Nineteenth Century* (Athens: Ohio University Press, 1976), 21–41.

6. Frederick Rudolph. *American College and University: A History* (New York: Alfred A. Knopf, 1962).

7. See Barbara Miller Solomon, *In the Company of Educated Women* (New Haven: Yale University Press, 1985).

8. Jean-Jacques Rousseau. *Emile*, trans. Barbara Foxley (London: 1911), quoted in Charlotte Williams Conable, *Women at Cornell: The Myth of Equal Education* (Ithaca: Cornell University Press, 1977), 184.

9. There were fewer than six coeducational colleges before the Civil War. See Rudolph, *American College and University,* 311. Oberlin College was quite interesting because it also admitted African American students and provided a rare antebellum instance of integrated education.

10. Prior to the Civil War, the study of some sciences and engineering was considered less demanding and rigorous than the more formal classical curriculum. At Harvard and Yale, students who studied science—in scientific schools only tangential to the campus, not central—were awarded the lesser Bachelor of Science degree in lieu of the Bachelor of Arts. Also, the work of Kim Tolley illustrates that women in the early academies studied a considerable amount of science and that their curriculum was indeed collegiate level. See Kim Tolley, "Science for Ladies, Classics for Gentlemen: A Comparative Analysis of Scientific Subjects in the Curricula of Boy's and Girl's Secondary Schools in the United States, 1794–1850," *History of Education Quarterly* 36 (Summer 1996): 129–53.

11. See Christie Farnham, *Education of a Southern Belle* (New York: New York Univerity Press, 1994) for a description of the antebellum colleges for women in the South, for example.

12. Lynn D. Gordon, *Gender and Higher Education in the Progressive Era* (New Haven: Yale University Press, 1990), 101.

13. Sally Schwager pointed out that arguments for and against women's education and for and against coeducation were not always identical. At times they were even at cross purposes. For the most part, this chapter discusses the issue of whether to educate men and women *together,* rather than the more general question of whether to educate women at all. See Sally Schwager,

"Arguing for the Higher Education of Women: Early Experiences with Co-education" (Qualifying Paper, Harvard Graduate School of Education, 1978), 3. For one of the earliest historical treatments of the coeducation debate, see Thomas Woody, *A History of Women's Education in the United States,* 2 vols. (New York: Science Press, 1929; reprint, New York: Octagon Books, 1980), 2: 255–94.

14. Patricia A. Palmeri, "From Republican Motherhood to Race Suicide," in *Educating Men and Women Together: Coeducation in a Changing World,* ed. Carol Lasser (Urbana: University of Illinois Press, 1987), 54.

15. Rosenberg, *Beyond Separate Spheres,* primarily chapter 1.

16. Ibid., 6.

17. For fuller information on Clarke's views, the circumstances surrounding the book's publication, and the response it generated see Sue Zschoche, "Dr. Clarke Revisited: Science, True Womanhood, and Female Collegiate Education," *History of Education Quarterly* 29 (Winter 1989): 545–69.

18. Rosenberg, *Beyond Separate Spheres,* 1–27, especially, 5–9; Zschoche, "Dr. Clarke Revisited," 545–46.

19. Edward H. Clarke, *Sex in Education: Or, A Fair Chance for the Girls* (Boston: James R. Osgood and Co., 1873; reprint, New York: Arno Press, 1972), 48.

20. Ibid., 127.

21. Zschoche, "Dr. Clarke Revisited," 546–47.

22. Rosenberg, *Beyond Separate Spheres*, 12. Zschoche, "Dr. Clarke Revisited," 564, makes the point that the ACA's rebuttal illustrated that women had learned to use science to fight science. Yet that was, in itself, a conundrum because it demonstrated their acceptance of the ascendance of science in the debate surrounding women's education.

23. Ibid.

24. Feminists responded with a collection of essays. See Eliza Bisbee Duffey, *No Sex in Education: Or, A Fair Chance for Both Boys and Girls: Being a Review of Dr. E. H. Clarke's Sex in Education* (Philadelphia: J. M. Stoddart & Co., 1874).

25. Rosenberg, *Beyond Separate Spheres*, 19–20. The results of the survey were published in 1885.

26. See Lynn D. Gordon, "Co-Education on Two Campuses: Berkeley and Chicago, 1890–1912," in *Woman's Being, Woman's Place: Female Identity and Vocation in American History,* ed. Mary Kelley (Boston: Hall, 1979), 172; and Elizabeth Seymour Eschbach, *The Higher Education of Women in England and America, 1865–1920* (New York: Garland Publishing, 1993), 87.

27. Eschbach, *Higher Education in England and America*, 87.

28. Rosalind Rosenberg, "The Limits of Access: The History of Coeducation in America," in *Women and Higher Education in American History,*

eds. John Mack Faragher and Florence Howe (New York: W. W. Norton & Company, 1988), 107.

29. Eschbach, *Higher Education of Women in England and America,* 99.

30. Ibid., 100.

31. Gordon, *Gender and Higher Education,* 24.

32. Ibid., 21.

33. Rosenberg, "Limits of Access," 110. Boston University was another example. Rosenberg pointed out that the proximity of Ithaca to the women's rights agitation of upstate New York contributed to the success of the campaign.

34. The financial concerns of these new state colleges were enormous and have been documented by other historians. See Nevins, *State Universities and Democracy,* 26–29 and Rudolph, *American College and University,* 253–55. The constant need for more and regular appropriations was answered in 1890 when a second Morrill Act was passed. In this legislation, Congress stipulated that states would not receive their appropriations if they denied admission to the land-grant university on the basis of race. States could, however, establish a separate land-grant college for African Americans and seventeen states chose that route. The second Morrill Act, therefore, has the dubious legacy of perpetuating the separate but equal doctrine that would take over half a century to rend asunder.

35. Quoted in Dorothy Gies McGuigan, *A Dangerous Experiment: 100 Years of Women at the University of Michigan.* (Ann Arbor: Center for Continuing Education of Women, 1977), 18.

36. Gordon, *Gender and Higher Education,* 22–24; Rosenberg, "The Limits of Access," 110–11. See also Sally Schwager, "Educating Women in America," *Signs* 12 (Winter 1987): 362, who summarized the arguments of historian Jill K. Conway.

37. Barbara Miller Solomon identified the initial three generations of students: the first generation attended from 1870 to 1889; the second from 1890 to 1909; and the third from 1910 to 1930. She argued that there were important distinctions among the three generations, but especially between the first and second. See Solomon, *In the Company of Educated Women,* 95. Lynn D. Gordon, on the other hand, stated that there were only two generations, one from 1870 to 1890 and a second one from 1890 to 1920. She argued that there were fewer distinctions between the two groups than had been depicted by other historians. See Gordon, *Gender and Higher Education,* 30–33. In either case, the first generation was characterized similarly by both historians.

38. Sarah Parke Morrison, "Some Sidelights of Fifty Years Ago," *Indiana University Alumni Quarterly* 6 (October 1919): 532.

39. Ibid., 531.

40. Ibid., 533.

41. Gordon, "Co-Education on Two Campuses," 171. Much of the original statistical information on women's participation in higher education is provided in Newcomer, *A Century of Higher Education,* 46.

42. Gordon, *Gender and Higher Education,* 30–31.

43. Shirley Marchalonis, *College Girls: A Century in Fiction* (New Brunswick: Rutgers University Press, 1995), especially, 161–62 in chapter 8.

44. Rosenberg, "The Limits of Access," 115.

45. For a discussion on how college women perceived their after-college choices, see Solomon, *In the Company,* 116–40.

46. Lynn D. Gordon, "The Gibson Girl Goes to College: Popular Culture and Women's Higher Education in the Progressive Era, 1890–1920," *American Quarterly* 39 (Summer 1987): 215. Zschoche, "Dr. Clarke Revisited," 563, also noted how women's biology influenced the views of the medical and psychological communities until well into the twentieth century.

47. Gordon, "Gibson Girl," 215.

48. Paul J. Möebius, *Concerning the Physiological Intellectual Feebleness of Women,* quoted in Tama Starr, compiler, *The "Natural Inferiority" of Women: Outrageous Pronouncements by Misguided Males* (New York: Poseidon Press, 1991), 195.

49. Robert J. Sprague, "Education and Race Suicide," *Journal of Heredity* 6 (April 1915): 159. The author's reference to "the race" referred to native-born, Anglo-Saxon Americans. The undisguised racism and elitism of the argument was remarkable.

50. Albert Goodnow Waite (Harvard, class of 1905), Notebook for Economics 3, "Principles of Sociology" with Professor Carver. Harvard University Archives, Cambridge, Mass.

51. Gordon, *Gender and Higher Education,* 32.

52. Ibid., 43.

53. See especially Rosenberg, *Beyond Separate Spheres,* 44.

54. Palmeri, "From Republican Motherhood to Race Suicide," 57.

55. Newcomer, *Century of Higher Education,* 37, 46, and 49. The 1920s peak of almost 50 percent fell considerably during the next four decades. By the 1980s, however, women represented a majority of undergraduates.

56. At Berkeley, for example, Lillian Moller Gilbreth earned Phi Beta Kappa recognition in 1900 but also learned that no women were awarded the key. The university reasoned that men were in greater need of the honor when looking for a job. See Gordon, "Co-Education on Two Campuses," 187. Also, Rosenberg, "The Limits of Access," 113.

57. Marion Talbot, *More Than Lore: Reminiscences of Marion Talbot* (Chicago: University of Chicago Press, 1936), 177.

58. Ibid., 134–35.

59. Solomon, *In the Company,* 72–73; Gordon, "Gibson Girl," 214; Rosenberg, "The Limits of Access," 114.

60. Rosenberg, "The Limits of Access," 112; Gordon, *Gender and Higher Education,* 25.

61. Gordon, "Co-Education on Two Campuses," 173–75.

62. Morrison, "Some Sidelights of Fifty Years Ago," 534.

63. Rosenberg, "The Limits of Access," 113.

64. Horowitz, *Campus Life,* 68, 193–220. Most male historians spend very little time describing the life of women undergraduates. For example, neither Rudolph nor Veysey devote long discussions to undergraduate life for women. Both describe certain activities and behaviors as the "norm" when, in fact, they were norms for men only. Women historians such as Solomon (*In the Company*) and Gordon (*Gender and the Progressive Era*) redress the balance and illustrate the different cultures for women in coeducational universities. See also Freedman, "Separatism as Strategy," for a discussion of the creation of separate cultures for women during the Progressive Era.

65. Newcomer, *Century of Higher Education,* 90.

66. Solomon, *In the Company,* 85–87.

67. Ibid., 90–91.

68. Gordon, *Gender and Higher Education,* 35; Newcomer, *A Century of Higher Education*, 90; and Rosenberg, "The Limits of Access," 118–20.

69. Solomon, *In the Company,* 80–81; Gordon, "Co-Education on Two Campuses," 179.

70. See Gordon, "Co-Education on Two Campuses," 179, 187; Solomon, *In the Company,* 82; and Mary Bidwell Breed, "Women and the Academic Curriculum," *The Missouri Alumni Quarterly* (June 1907): 214–19.

71. Gordon, "Co-Education on Two Campuses," 186–88; and Rosenberg, "The Limits of Access," 115.

72. Curti and Carstensen, *The University of Wisconsin,* 2: 81–86. At that time there was a dean at Wisconsin but she was not a faculty member. Van Hise wanted to reinstate the office with faculty rank as it had been from 1898 to 1901 when the university had its first dean of women.

73. Rosenberg, "The Limits of Access," 118.

74. It is important to note the distinction that several women educators made between forming separate women's communities and encouraging separate curriculum opportunities. As Estelle Freedman pointed out, most feminists adopted separatism as a strategy in the years from 1870 to 1920. This was a factor behind the women's club movement and the founding of many women's colleges. Between 1870 and 1900, women educators on coeducational campuses desired a separate women's community for many of the same reasons, however, they did not want a separate curriculum for fear that it would be deemed inferior. After 1900 or so, some educators began to soften their views about the curriculum and believed that women were served by such women-oriented courses of study as domestic science.

See Estelle Freedman, "Separatism as Strategy: Female Institution Building and American Feminism, 1870–1930," *Feminist Studies* 5 (Fall 1979): 512–29.

75. Rosenberg, *Beyond Separate Spheres,* 48.

76. See Rosenberg, "The Limits of Access," 118, as well as Rosenberg, *Beyond Separate Spheres,* 48–50.

77. McGuigan, *A Dangerous Experiment*, 63.

78. Students were not typically prepared for teaching or nursing in graduate schools.

79. Rosenberg, *Beyond Separate Spheres,* 48–49.

80. Charles Van Hise, "Educational Tendencies in State Universities," *Educational Review* 24 (December 1907): 509–11. Also quoted in Woody, *A History of Women's Education* 2: 256.

81. Quoted in Woody, *A History of Women's Education* 2: 257. See also Rosenberg, *Beyond Separate Spheres,* 31.

82. Rosenberg, "The Limits of Access," 111.

83. Charles Van Hise of Wisconsin received massive criticism including the public anger of the wife of a prominent Regent for his suggestion of gender-segregated classrooms; William Rainey Harper and the faculty of Chicago discovered that operating separate facilities was too costly; Stanford imposed a quota on the number of women admitted that lasted for a few decades, but was eventually overturned; and the decision at Wesleyan to return to an all-male college was not sustained for long. For a recent history of Wesleyan, see David B. Potts, *Wesleyan University, 1831–1910: Collegiate Enterprise in New England* (New Haven: Yale University Press, 1992).

84. Quoted in *Dangerous Experiment,* p. 106.

PART II

Academic and Institutional Leadership

CHAPTER 2

Patterns of Leadership

The Impact of Female Authority in Four Women's Colleges, 1880–1910

CYNTHIA FARR BROWN

Women's movement into powerful positions, such as the presidential or chief executive officer role, forms a distinct moment in the development of many women's colleges in the late nineteenth century. Similarities in generation, life stages, even in personality, unify them to some degree, though class, culture, and religion mark important differences. To overcome the doubts of others about their ability, as women, to exercise power, they employed a variety of strategies, with long-term consequences for the character of their leadership.

All shared a vision concentrated on mission and ethos. They set critical precedents, putting practices in place and building institutional reputations. The success or failure of their colleges, they rightly believed, rested on their ability to map out a coherent mission. Thus few devoted much energy to issues such as endowment drives or alumnae cultivation. Instead they concentrated on developing faculty, attracting students, and garnering publicity.

These women leaders cultivated both female and male allies; indeed some of the strongest support for female leadership came from men. This type of alliance had existed in many seminaries, but not to the same extent. Not surprisingly, many of these women had strong relationships with fathers, uncles, or other male relatives, and built friendships or alliances with men before assuming power. This was no small achievement in the mid-nineteenth century, where women speaking in public, much less hiring faculty or presenting budgets, was still viewed with suspicion.

Each of these women had to come to terms with the seminary model and respond to it. The seminary emphasized rigorous academics, women's potential for paid employment, the formation of a close-knit society, and inspirational leadership, and these were aspects that female college leaders frequently carried over into the new institutions. Piety, hierarchical power structures, the sheltering of students from controversy or the world outside the college, and traditional gender roles, also part of seminary culture, were a more controversial legacy.

Case studies of the advent of female executive leadership at four women's colleges—Wellesley College (Massachusetts), Bryn Mawr College (Pennsylvania), Trinity College (Washington, DC), and the College of New Rochelle (New York)—allow the exploration of some of the ways in which women tried to navigate the promise and perils of female leadership. Striking similarities, as well as important differences, mark their experiences. Taken as a whole, the coming of female leadership provides an important window into gender roles, social norms, and the development of higher education for women in turn-of-the-century America.

Wellesley College

The advent of female leadership at Wellesley, the first college where a woman was both named and exercised power as chief executive officer, was fraught with symbolism—and with the potential of failure. Alice Freeman, Wellesley's second president and first true female leader, faced an even greater challenge: how to move from the personal, highly centralized control of college founder Henry Durant to a more egalitarian power structure.

Wellesley was founded in 1870 and opened in 1875 by ex-attorney turned lay preacher Henry Durant and his wife Pauline after the deaths of their children. They intended Wellesley to provide women with an education comparable to that given men at Harvard, dispensed within an evangelical Christian framework and based on the seminary ideal, which would shape young women's physical, moral, and emotional development. Henry Durant had declared, "Women can do the work, I will give them the chance." Yet he also believed that women's nature and proper social role were fundamentally different from men's, that women were the only force capable of countering social decay. He appointed an all-female faculty; yet he also personally controlled the college down to its landscaping. The friction between Durant's ideals, echoing those of the seminary, and those of the science- and research-based German universities then influencing American higher education, precipitated a crisis over female leadership.[1]

Durant initially appointed Ada Howard, a former seminary head, as president. Plagued by vague illnesses and championing an old-style pedagogy, Howard implemented Durant's policies, including the unpopular ones. The college's high academic standard necessitated opening a preparatory department. A requirement that all faculty be members of an "evangelical" faith proved increasingly unworkable, while many considered Durant's penchant for exhorting on behalf of personal salvation as almost fanatical.[2]

These divisions were reinforced by Durant's faculty appointments. Some were graduates of Mount Holyoke, the preeminent New England seminary, and loyal to Durant, Howard, and seminary-style piety and submission. Others rejected these values and criticized Howard, and the latter were the faculty who could and did win student loyalty. As Patricia Palmieri notes, these strong faculty women "used the community created for them to come together on their own behalf."[3]

Student rebellion and faculty criticism escalated; at the same time both Howard and Durant suffered from increasing invalidism, and Durant ceased governing in person. In 1877 Durant began to look for his successor. He found her in the person of Alice Freeman, a young graduate of the University of Michigan recommended to him by his friend, Michigan president James Angell.[4]

Then twenty-three, Alice Freeman had achieved a seminary and later college education while balancing family demands in helping to support her younger siblings. She had chosen the University of Michigan over Elmira and Vassar because she believed it had the better curriculum. One of only twelve women in her class, she formed lifelong attachments to these other Michigan women students. Among other accomplishments, Freeman helped achieve women's admission to the all-male YMCA, which reformed as the Student Christian Association. She also excelled academically. After graduation she worked at a Wisconsin girls' seminary and began graduate work in history at Michigan. She turned down Wellesley appointments in 1877 and 1878, continuing to assist her family. She accepted Henry Durant's third offer after the death of her beloved sister Stella.[5]

Alice Freeman's leadership was rooted in both nineteenth-century sensibilities of romanticism, piety and domesticity, and newer ideas such as faith in science and belief in women's intellectual abilities. She "reconciled the new and the old conceptions of women," giving her the power to win over both older, more conservative members of the college community and younger, liberal allies. Freeman accomplished this transformation in part by formulating a unique philosophy, which she termed "heart culture." She believed in working closely and sympathetically with people and being accessible to them.[6]

Durant associated her with himself in making decisions, training for her intended role, yet the two also clashed. In their major confrontation Durant demanded that she counsel a student on religious matters. Freeman responded she couldn't do so with a girl she barely knew. Durant ordered her to do so, because "now" was the day of salvation. Freeman told him he knew nothing about it as he had never been a girl, and Durant backed down, accepting her point of view.[7]

Freeman demanded Durant refocus the college's mission and governance before she would agree to take over. Negotiations were under way to accommodate her when he died in October 1881. A month later the trustees announced that Freeman was the acting president. By honoring Durant's last wishes they ensured that his utopia would be transformed. Freeman spent the rest of her life serving Wellesley, remaking it from a seminary-college hybrid into one of the leading women's colleges. She ensured that succeeding Wellesley leaders would share these goals because she had the power to guide the choosing of the next three presidents from the board of trustees, on which she served after her marriage and resignation from the presidency.[8]

Freeman redistributed power, entrusting much internal administration to the senior faculty, organizing twelve departments and consulting regularly with their heads, who made policy and did the hiring. Faculty formed the Academic Council, which legislated academic policy, with her blessing. The female faculty had finally come into its own after the long years of seminary-style submission. Under subsequent presidents, picked at Freeman's behest or with her blessing as a powerful member of the board of trustees, the faculty would be pruned of a number of older, more conservative, less credentialed women allied with the Durant-inspired "old guard."[9]

By the time of her 1887 resignation to marry George Herbert Palmer, Freeman had significantly altered the college's structure and the president's role. Wellesley no longer offered seminary-level work. Faculty had a larger sphere of personal autonomy and a clear role in college governance and policy-making. Adherence to evangelical Protestantism was no longer a prerequisite for faculty. Perhaps most importantly, students could admire not only the theory of female academics, activists, and leaders, but witness them in action, thanks to Alice Freeman Palmer's persistence in challenging the waning tenets of Victorian culture and suggesting ways that old and new woman could merge identities. The "girl president" had successfully liberalized curriculum, college life, and faculty expectations, while retaining important ties to Henry Durant's ideals of community, refuge, and women's achievement.[10]

Bryn Mawr College

The advent of women's leadership at Bryn Mawr, delayed ten years from its opening by trustee hesitations, depended on a happy coincidence: the woman best fitted by training and ability for the post was also a member of a family prominent in the Orthodox Quaker sect that founded the college. By exploiting this fact, M. Carey Thomas overcame initial opposition and assumed the presidency. Yet she achieved this victory only by dividing the very men who put her in charge, a circumstance that later led to a crisis over her leadership.

The idea of a women's college sponsored by Orthodox Friends sprang from several sources: the opening of coeducational Swarthmore College by the rival Hicksite sect in 1864; an 1872 speech at the Orthodox Friends–supported Haverford, which advocated higher education for women; and the 1876 founding of Johns Hopkins by an Orthodox Friend. The Haverford speech fell upon the receptive ears of Dr. James Taylor, a bachelor who intended to leave his fortune to philanthropy. He began discussing the idea of establishing a school for female Friends. A group of like-minded men, leaders in the Philadelphia, New Jersey, and Baltimore Orthodox Friends communities, many of them graduates and managers (trustees) of Haverford, convened an educational conference in Baltimore in 1877. Taylor continued his conversations and even consulted fellow planner James Thomas's daughter Martha Carey, then a junior at Cornell, who dissuaded him from founding the college as an annex to Johns Hopkins.[11]

Johns Hopkins's first trustees included four men instrumental in Bryn Mawr's story: Francis King; his cousin James Carey Thomas; John Work Garrett; and Charles Gwinn. The first two were prominent, liberal Friends. Garrett was the powerful president of the Baltimore and Ohio Railroad, and Gwinn a former attorney general of Maryland; both were members of Baltimore's Episcopal establishment. All four had daughters, mutual friends who could influence their fathers: Elizabeth King, Martha Carey Thomas, Mary Garrett, and Mary Mackall (Mamie) Gwinn. All in their early twenties when Hopkins opened, these young women formed a "Friday Evening Group," part consciousness-raising, part mutual support. All wanted to go to college; each would contribute to women's emancipation through education or political action. Their experiences helped convince their fathers that women needed educational opportunities.[12]

By 1880, at another Quaker-sponsored educational conference, women participated, including Carey Thomas's mother Mary Whitall Thomas. Bryn Mawr was organized the same year, following Dr. Taylor's death. Mary Thomas, well aware of her daughter's interests, urged her to apply for a position in the new college.[13]

Martha Carey Thomas was twenty-four in 1880 and struggling along a remarkable educational path. Eldest child of a prominent Quaker family, Thomas had developed a strong affinity for "the cause" of women's emancipation, probably following the lead of her much-admired aunt, charismatic author and preacher Hannah Whitall Smith. She also drew from the less radical example of her mother, who held positions in the Baltimore Yearly (Friends) Meeting, the Women's Christian Temperance Union, and the YWCA, as well as organizing religious revivals.[14]

Thomas's pursuit of education across the barriers of social expectation, finances, and family obligation would be a story often told and much embroidered by herself and others. After private Quaker primary school, she boarded at Quaker Howland Academy. With pleading she received permission to attend Cornell, graduating with honors. Back home, admission to Johns Hopkins's classics graduate seminars did not lead to a degree, and she withdrew. More persuasion resulted in permission to pursue the doctorate in Europe, first at Leipzig, then Berne, and finally Zurich. The enormity of her achievement—a PhD summa cum laude in 1882—was a reality that all of the legends could not outweigh.[15]

Thomas rebelled against evangelism, forming a romanticized, theistic philosophy through which she rejected most organized religion. She formed fast friendships within the Friday Evening group; two of these women, Mamie Gwinn, who accompanied her to Europe, and Mary Garrett, became the successive companions of her maturity.[16]

The young woman who returned in triumph from Leipzig was proud, outspoken, and direct; she imagined for herself an intellectual, Bohemian existence. Thomas valued loyalty, bearing, and good taste, though not herself always capable of these qualities, and cultivated a knowledge of the books and people she thought authoritative. She attempted to incorporate these views into her educational and moral universe as well as those of Bryn Mawr. Often bold, sometimes her impetuosity overrode common sense.[17]

She had written of her doctorate, "I hope it shows that I can be useful . . . and then I am glad for 'the cause's' sake." Her beliefs fueled a desire "to protest against the misery and oppression of a girl's life," especially barriers keeping them from education. She would apply for the presidency of Bryn Mawr, conceiving of the college as an educational center for women and as a place to further women's equality. Given their very different perspectives, it was inevitable that her ideas and those of the trustees would collide.[18]

Taylor left explicit instructions for the college's trustees that emphasized a religious mission and "a very high degree of refinement of heart, mind and manners." The college's initial catalogue, the First Circular (1883), included seminary staples such as "physical culture" and drawing. Bryn Mawr would "develop womanly character" and give "religiously guarded education" that would prepare female Friends for their role in the often isolated Quaker world. Taylor envisioned that graduates who worked would teach school. Little distinguished this plan from that of any other sectarian-sponsored seminary or college.[19]

Despite Wellesley's example, the trustees thought that a man should be in charge, and appointed their chair, James Rhoads, first president. They made no provision for female trustees and no statement that women would form an important faculty element. Yet in deference to social mores, the trustees decided to appoint a woman to enforce discipline. They chose M. Carey Thomas, mistakenly believing she would assist them in maintaining guarded education. Instead their choice opened the door to a vigorous and far-seeing woman who would alter the mission and course of Bryn Mawr.

Though disappointed, Thomas accepted the deanship in April 1884. "It will be a pleasure to say things which cry aloud to be said and are yet seldom said to students beginning the search after them," she observed.[20] The appointment ended a period of uncertainty which, like other periods before, had shown Thomas that there were few roads for highly educated women to travel.

She embarked on an inspiring tour of leading eastern women's colleges that spring, most admiring Wellesley:

> To sit, as I sat today, in chapel and look down upon a woman president read prayers to an audience of 500 women and 70 professors and teachers—all women, not a man's influence seen or felt; or to watch the girls in trousers swing on rings . . . ushers in a new day.[21]

Thomas persuaded the trustees to redraft the college plan, and her ideas dominate the Second Circular (1884). Among her successful proposals were required entrance examinations and appointing to the faculty only those holding or close to completing the PhD. She also championed the creation of a graduate school, persuading the trustees to offer fellowships in each graduate department organized, laying the foundations for a true women's university. Graduate work would bolster the college's image and attract quality faculty, as well as demonstrate confidence in women's abilities.[22]

Thomas did not initially challenge the curriculum's religious elements, or indicate her own drift from the Society of Friends. She would consciously mute her ideas, even later during her presidency, in order to maintain a pretense of piety. Finally, she successfully appealed to the trustees' desire for excellence in curriculum, faculty and students in making and enacting plans, because her own ideas were often highly successful. This appeal would carry her through many crises.[23]

Once the college opened in 1885, she and President Rhoads divided duties harmoniously. Rhoads handled general policy, finances, faculty appointments, and religious life. Thomas turned her position into a platform from which to reform the college. Besides her original duties of student supervision, advising, record-keeping, and interviewing potential faculty, she assumed wide power over educational policy. Thomas taught the two-year required sequences in English literature, thus putting her in long-lasting contact with all students. She also used her father to access the trustees, even attempting to participate in areas outside her defined duties, such as the curriculum.[24]

Increasingly, Thomas and the trustees clashed. One reason was her perceived liberalism. During one dispute the trustees attempted to get her to drop Shakespeare, Fletcher, and Beaumont from her courses. She compromised by agreeing to bowdlerize some passages. She would not, however, police student reading. One trustee later resigned because of her liberalism. And Thomas's own scarcely concealed contempt for several trustees did not ease her way; privately she referred to them as "that ponderous body," and "stupid Philadelphia Quakers." She no doubt communicated these opinions to them, however indirectly.[25]

The board in turn played a rigidly avuncular role toward her, advising her to mingle in Philadelphia society and watching to be sure she attended weekly Meeting. She recapitulated her family role as eldest child: head of the junior branch of the family, subject to trustee paternalism. Yet Thomas could also count on her connections to and the liberality of certain trustees to give her a solid bloc of five votes, meaning she need only persuade two other trustees to have a majority.[26]

The trustees realized that Thomas was reshaping the college far more than they had anticipated. She had once told her mother, "Thee must not think that because I am not a missionary in your sense that I have no missionary spirit." She turned the family mysticism into intellectual ardor, substituting academic ritual for religious worship. Thomas resolved the common conflict educated women of her generation experienced between leading their own lives and the "family claim" by melding the male-dominated intellectual and community-oriented female worlds, much as the Wellesley faculty had under Alice Freeman. Thomas was a minister of rationalism, working to shape student beliefs and supporting the scholarly aims of the faculty. Worse, from the perspective of the trustees, this redirection succeeded: enrollment grew, the graduate program, limited to 100 students, attracted four or five applicants for each fellowship position, and after the first year, the number of Friends applying dropped to a mere handful.[27] The two-year crisis over whether Thomas would become Bryn Mawr's second president revealed that despite her success and Wellesley's example, conservative ideas about women's place dominated among the trustees. Long lobbying, a lack of viable male candidates, her own ability, and eventually monetary inducement of her friend Mary Garrett finally led to her selection, but at the price of harmony between Thomas and the trustees.

In 1892 Rhoads recommended Thomas to succeed him. Four trustees firmly thought that putting the dean in charge would end Taylor's conception of the college, believing that given Taylor's directions, they had "an obligation to make the College more Friendly." Thomas's solid bloc of support included her father, uncle James Whitall, and Rhoads; cousin David Scull often disagreed with her ideas but supported her on her merits, and mediated with the conservative faction. The five remaining trustees were swing votes; three were needed to form the necessary majority.[28]

Thomas resolved to remain only if elected president and life trustee, as Rhoads had been. The conservatives were terrified, Thomas believed, of making her president. They tried to persuade her to serve as dean under another male president, citing a "duty to sacrifice myself" for the good of the college. She threatened to resign.[29]

During the subsequent negotiations, Thomas took over most of Rhoads's duties, further alarming the conservatives. When Rhoads finally resigned in February 1893, effective the following year, the conservatives forced the issue of guarded education. The trustees appointed a subcommittee to decide whether the college conformed with Joseph Taylor's intent. Several favored strengthening the college's religious elements, scaling down academic goals, perhaps even reorganizing as a seminary or without graduate work, all of which upset Thomas.[30]

Her allies counseled patience. This was not her way, and while she followed this advice publicly, her almost daily letters to Mary Garrett revealed her frustrations. She wrote she did not want to "waste more years of my life" under the collective thumb of the board, "building up this house of cards that 13 irresponsible men can in a moment destroy." Yet she fought on tenaciously because she still considered Bryn Mawr the best platform from which to advance women.[31]

Help arrived from an unexpected quarter. Mary Garrett took a direct interest in the college, donating sculptures, paying off property taxes, and offering to purchase an important classical library. On March 28, 1893, she offered $10,000 annually should Thomas become president. James Thomas, apprised of this offer, wrote a letter to the other trustees citing his daughter's successes and abilities, and concluding, "If she were a man you would appoint her without hesitation." The trustees continued to stall. They pursued their newest idea: having Rhoads remain with a (male) vice-president to assist him, a position for which they interviewed candidates.[32]

Meanwhile the subcommittee reported. Several measures resulted: Friends were to be preferred for faculty appointments, and students had to register their religious affiliations and places of Sabbath worship. The trustees declared that Taylor meant Bryn Mawr to have neither a lower nor a higher standard than Haverford. Many of these same issues would continue to complicate Thomas's relations to the trustees in the years to follow. Yet without other alternatives, and needing Garrett's contribution, the trustees negotiated, and Thomas yielded on some points. She stopped seeking a trustee's seat, and Rhoads agreed to stay another year. Under these terms she was elected president on November 17, 1893. One trustee, alienated beyond repair, resigned. Lingering acrimony may have foreclosed an inauguration; with uncharacteristic lack of fanfare, Carey Thomas became president of Bryn Mawr, the post she held for the next twenty-eight years.[33]

Her coming to power, while a victory for women's education, produced a mixed legacy for female leadership. She had resolved none of the issues that produced the crisis, and the rifts created remained for years. Her personality, ideas, and sense of oppression precluded a more favorable resolution. Unlike

Alice Freeman, she could not meld the old and the new woman; personal and gender conflict were virtually inseparable in her case. The locuses of power divided along a gender line created by conservative versus liberal conceptions of women's role. Nor did her temperament allow much compromise. Despite her attempts to combine the female world and the world of the intellect, Carey Thomas felt herself at the mercy of men's chauvinism. There were no woman to turn to for support, no network, no appeal to a new ideology. If not for her family connections and Mary Garrett's money, she might never have become president. A sense of precariousness, of continual vigilance against opposition both real and imagined, would inform her often turbulent presidency.[34]

Trinity College

The coming to power of women leaders at Trinity College engendered particular difficulties. There were two issues: whether Catholic women's colleges should emulate the curricula and culture of non-Catholic institutions such as Vassar, Wellesley, and Bryn Mawr; and the degree of control that a nominally cloistered religious order could and should exercise. Both issues persisted past the college's opening, and the latter produced a clash between the sisters and the laywomen who assisted them, ending the college's first administration. Trinity's leaders experienced conflict along the twin fault lines of women's intellect and women's power like that apparent in the transitions of Wellesley and Bryn Mawr to female leadership. Only the forms in which the conflict played out differed.

The Sisters of Notre Dame de Namur (usually abbreviated SND) was founded by Sr. Julie Billiart in 1804 to educate poor children, particularly girls. Notre Dame schools soon gained a reputation for excellence, enhanced by the founding of teacher-training colleges in Belgium and England. In 1840 the first American-based Sisters of Notre Dame settled in Cincinnati. New academies and convents opened rapidly in the 1880s and 1890s under the order's second American provincial, Trinity co-founder Sr. Julia (McGroarty).[35]

Sr. Julia had emigrated from Donegal, Ireland with her family to Cincinnati, becoming the first American sister of the Sisters of Notre Dame in 1845 at eighteen. She held a series of administrative posts in Roxbury, Massachusetts, Philadelphia, and in Cincinnati under the order's Provincial, Sr. Louise, training to succeed her. In December 1886, following Sr. Louise's death, Sr. Julia became eastern and midwestern provincial. During her fifteen-year tenure she founded fifteen convents and built the order's novitiate and the Chapel of the Summit cathedral. The number of pupils enrolled in Notre Dame schools quadrupled to over ninety thousand, and the number of sisters rose from 850 to over 1,300. Sr. Julia centralized provincial government and teaching, publishing a unified "Plan of Study" for all Notre Dame schools, and instituting common exams. She appointed a superior of schools to oversee curriculum and common exams and made teacher training a priority.[36]

Sr. Julia, who operated with great latitude under the order's Europe-based Superior General, retained a sense of independence and had a knack for creating community, in part by being accessible, in part by correcting through positive rather than negative examples. She chafed somewhat under social prescriptions; when mulling her response to the Vatican regarding criticism of Trinity, she confided to her secretary "that if she were a man she would put on her hat and go off to see the Pope."[37]

Despite her liberalism, when conversations about a college began, Sr. Julia admitted, "I had always said that I was opposed to Higher Education [for women]."[38] She was persuaded by her advisors and, most importantly, by the superior of Notre Dame's small Washington, D.C. convent, Sr. Mary Euphrasia (Taylor).

Born Ella Osmonia Taylor, she had grown up in Virginia's slave-owning, Episcopalian upper class. When the Civil War came, she and her sister were shuttled off to various schools: the Piedmont Institute, Charlottesville, Columbia Female College, a seminary in South Carolina, and finally the Patapsco Female Institute in Maryland. Ella Taylor admired Patapsco's charismatic president, Almira Phelps, one of the great seminary leaders, and no doubt this experience influenced her ideas about women's education. Four years after graduating from Patapsco, in 1871, she journeyed north and converted to Catholicism, though what precipitated this decision is not clear. Ella entered the Notre Dame convent in Philadelphia, perhaps choosing a teaching order due to Almira Phelps's influence. She taught in a Boston convent until becoming superior of the Notre Dame school and convent in Washington in 1893. Sr. Mary Euphrasia maintained a strong sense of self, sometimes interpreted as stubbornness. In old age she would publish, in a Notre Dame magazine, articles about her childhood written under her birth rather than her religious name. Such assertion sometimes led to questions about her adherence to her vows.[39]

In the late 1890s Sr. Mary Euphrasia wanted to open an academy in Washington, but also broached the idea of a college at a Shrove Tuesday dinner in 1897, celebrated in Philadelphia with Sr. Julia and her two closest advisors, Srs. Mary Borgia and Georgianna. Sr. Julia agreed to the idea of a large academy, recalling, "The undertaking [of a college] did not appeal to me; I saw no possibility of our reaching out to so great a work. . . . But here was a question involving the whole Institute [order]." She authorized Sr. Mary Euphrasia to bring the college idea before James Cardinal Gibbons, meanwhile writing to Notre Dame's Superior General.[40]

The dynamic of dinner previewed the dynamic of the next three years: Sr. Julia's caution, Sr. Mary Euphrasia's advocacy, and the proactive stance of Srs. Georgianna and Mary Borgia. Yet the unformed ideas of Sr. Mary Euphrasia did not of themselves result in Trinity College. They needed a "catalyst": the advice and guidance of Rev. Dr. Philip Garrigan, then the young vice-rector of the Catholic University of America. An able administrator with an active interest in education, he revealed that two other orders had already petitioned to open a female annex to the university, which the trustees approved but which the Apostolic Delegate had vetoed, and that school had turned away twenty women, all of whom had entered Protestant colleges where they might lose their faith. He broached the subject of a true college as "the need of the times, the especial need of the place. It is what the present system of boarding schools is tending towards."[41]

Garrigan advised Sr. Mary Euphrasia to consult Vassar and Wellesley catalogues and urging her to do for Catholic women "what Vassar and Wellesley and Bryn Mawr are doing for American [Protestant] women."[42] Sr. Mary Euphrasia became the order's agent in this activity. She found the site, met with local prelates, and solicited support from lay men and women. Sr. Julia supervised by mail, sending Srs. Georgianna and Mary Borgia to Washington several times. She secured permission from the order and later from Rome and drafted the first prospectus and curriculum, as well as the college's "moral plan." She also chose the college's name, assigned the new faculty, and sent two future deans abroad for a year of study and observation at Notre Dame schools. Finally she named the first trustees, all women religious, in the summer of 1897.[43]

The two co-founders balanced one another. Sr. Mary Euphrasia was enthusiastic, almost impatient about opening the college. She understood the importance of seeking "every assistance that the influence of those high in station can afford us!" She also understood the importance of doing so personally, which while it took her beyond the cloister, greatly aided the college.[44]

Sr. Julia did not plan to go public until after June 15, 1897. By then much of the groundwork would be laid and initial allies won over, including the liberal "American cardinal," Cardinal Gibbons. He supported the plan from the first, and in June 1897, sent his official letter of commendation.[45] But before Sr. Julia could release a public announcement, a news leak began the chain of events that nearly ended Trinity. The publicity heightened Rome's scrutiny. In August a handful of conservative clerics sent their version of the story to Rome, including the lie that Trinity would be coeducational. They tied Trinity to the "Americanism" movement that had begun to concern the Pope. Added to the brew were the cultural and power rivalries of Irish- and German-American Catholics, played out in quarrels over Cahenslyism and Catholic University's mission.[46]

Sr. Mary Euphrasia urged moving forward, but Sr. Julia advised, "wait, study, and above all pray." Cardinal Gibbons reiterated his support, but an aide to the Apostolic Delegate questioned the Superior General's approval. Sr. Mary Euphrasia had to cope with reporters, perhaps the first time a woman religious responded to national media inquiries; she even gave a press conference.[47]

Spurred by favorable publicity, Sr. Julia visited Washington during the fall, helping cement earlier plans. Word of Rome's non-interference came in mid-November, but problems within the order continued. During a summer visit to Belgium, Sr. Julia asked the Superior General to "Forbid the work." She replied ambivalently: "But I cannot, I might be going against the will of God." Sr. Julia would be pained by the Superior General's doubts to the end.[48]

Efforts to raise an endowment continued. Sr. Mary Euphrasia organized a Ladies Auxiliary Board of "prominent" women with affiliates across the country. Yet overall progress slowed for lack of funding. The first regular trustees' meeting, held in October, elected Sr. Mary Euphrasia secretary-treasurer and, by virtue of being treasurer of the Auxiliary Board, liaison between the two. The Auxiliary Board grew impatient, informing an "astonished" Sr. Mary Euphrasia in November that they would dissolve unless building began; Sr. Julia reiterated her decision to complete an endowment before beginning. Then all agreed to rally around a Washington lecture by famed orator Bishop John Lancaster Spalding of Peoria.[49]

Spalding spoke on "Women and Education" on January 16, 1899. The highly successful lecture rallied opinions and purses to Trinity's cause. He backed women's higher education and a Catholic role in it, implicitly giving the American hierarchy's support to Trinity. Members of rival orders attended along with Cardinal Gibbons and the Apostolic Delegate, further unifying support. Reprinted in pamphlet form, "Women and Education" successfully furthered Trinity's mission. Bishop Spalding provided an even greater service, however: to the sisters he declared, " 'Mother Julia should begin [to build] at once.' " Sr. Julia finally decided the moment had come. Ground was broken June 21, and first faculty was called to the order's Massachusetts novitiate for summer instruction by professors from Harvard and the Massachusetts Institute of Technology. The college opened in November 1900.[50]

Despite early success, leadership issues plagued Trinity. Sr. Julia ran the college without making either herself or Sr. Mary Euphrasia president. Because her reasons have not been recorded, why Sr. Mary Euphrasia did not receive this position is a matter of speculation. It may be that the younger woman's enthusiasm, lack of exposure to higher education, and willingness to overstep her vows in going to the public, persuaded Sr. Julia to look elsewhere for leadership.[51]

Sr. Julia entrusted the presidency to an outsider, Sr. Lidwine of the Sacred Heart. Though personally popular, Sr. Lidwine's tenure lasted only fifteen months, twelve of them in Sr. Julia's shadow. The provincial resided at the college for much of that time and made most of the decisions. This is clear from faculty minutes, in which Sr. Julia dominated and Sr. Lidwine seldom spoke. The list of the president's duties reinforces this impression: they included mostly ceremonial roles such as opening the college and appearing "in Parlor, in Papers" as its head. She had no power to make policy or engage Catholic University faculty to teach. Her responsibility for the "Principles and Roles of College life" probably meant she was the disciplinarian of students.[52]

After Sr. Julia's unexpected death in November 1901, Sr. Lidwine faced a crisis. The conflict began over financial mismanagement, but soon gravitated to the role of the laywomen. The dispute pitted the Ladies' Auxiliary Board against the trustees. One board faction, later described by Rev. Garrigan as "very high-toned ladies . . . who wanted to control the Board . . . [and who] wanted to make this a high aristocratic school," desired a leadership role. Another was content to stick to raising money. This division was exacerbated when Sr. Lidwine voted with the board's president, displeasing an influential member. In protest, thirteen women resigned in January, 1902. Sr. Lidwine then urged the trustees to dissolve the Auxiliary Board.[53]

At the next trustee meeting the dean, Sr. Josephine Ignatius, disagreed with Sr. Lidwine openly about whether she could forbid the board from meeting. She warned "that the College would be blamed" for any problems. The trustees' pro tem chair, Rev. Garrigan, suggested that the Auxiliary Board be suspended, not dissolved. This solved the immediate problem. But even before this meeting, it must have been clear that relations between Sr. Lidwine and other community members had deteriorated beyond repair. She resigned, and the next day Sr. Georgianna arrived to take her place. Given the timing of Sr. Georgianna's arrival, the decision to replace Sr. Lidwine must have been made several weeks before.[54]

Sr. Mary Euphrasia's case was convoluted. The college project had sapped her energy, her relationship with Sr. Julia, and perhaps her ability to focus on religious life. There were questions about finances, and she may have favored a strong Auxiliary Board role. She went to the Namur motherhouse in September 1901, whether at her own or the order's request is unclear, returning early in 1902 with a new assignment to Cincinnati. She had spent only one night under Trinity's "red roof," and would never return there. It is hard to imagine that she was not disappointed.[55]

With her departure the founders' era ended. The partnership of Srs. Julia and Mary Euphrasia, and of others, had produced not only a pioneering enterprise—the first Catholic-sponsored women's college founded as a college—but proved strong enough to weather a storm of political and ideological criticism that might have submersed less steadfast leaders. Not only the physical shape, but the academic emphasis of Trinity College extended from the expectations and vision of its founders. And as at Wellesley, the reach of these women, particularly of Sr. Julia, extended beyond their tenure into subsequent leadership generations.

Yet problems remained. As in the case of M. Carey Thomas, familial disagreements were patched up without addressing underlying problems. The role of Catholic University, especially of individual advisors like Rev. Garrigan, remained strong but undefined, and the relation of the college to the SND order was uncertain. The future cooperation of lay and religious women was in jeopardy. Women were in charge and on the faculty, but the scope of their power was unclear. Resolving these problems would occupy several subsequent leaders.

College of New Rochelle

The founding of the College of New Rochelle (originally St. Angela's College), more than that of any other institution profiled here, reflected the guiding hand of one woman: Mother Irene Gill, founder and first executive officer. She personally solicited funds, appointed trustees, and organized the college's curriculum, faculty, and regulations. Yet New Rochelle's founding also contains a deeper story of cooperative leadership. The college rose from previous foundations, following ideals held by the Ursuline sisters who created it. A single community of the order nourished the college but also built an unparalleled tradition of cooperation with secular faculty and advisers. Finally, New Rochelle's leaders encouraged a vocational emphasis in curriculum, making the complex mixture of religious belief, educational ideals, and pragmatism still more intricate.

While the various Ursuline orders shared a common foundation by St. Angela Merici in the sixteenth century, they were not organized under a single hierarchy until 1900. All Ursuline communities were cloistered and used co-adjuctor sisters for domestic work. This freed the sisters for the order's mission: children's education and later female academies. A parallel, though less-developed, mission was that of teacher training began as early as 1534, when St. Angela founded a women's teacher training school.[56]

The focus of early Ursuline academies was twofold: the teaching of Christian doctrine, and "formative training" in language, history, and household arts. The order hoped the sisters' "spirit . . . is communicated to the pupils, and this . . . naturally and constantly penetrates the whole." This philosophy resembled Alice Freeman's "heart culture." The Ursulines were the first to adopt Jesuit education for women, and later this tie connected New Rochelle to Jesuit-sponsored Fordham University.[57]

In 1855 a group of Bavarian-born Ursulines went from the order's first American convent in St. Louis to establish a day and boarding school at East Morrisania, the Bronx, New York. The community attracted numerous Irish American postulants and opened a pioneering parochial school and academy in St. Jerome's parish. In 1873 the Rev. James Boyce, pastor of St. Theresa's

Church on Henry Street, then in the midst of the city's large Irish American enclave, made a similar request. The Henry Street sisters were mostly Irish. In 1881 the new parish priest, Rev. Michael C. O'Farrell, urged community autonomy. There may have been some social friction over this issue: stories survive of how the East Morrisania community allowed members to drink beer, while St. Theresa sisters banned all alcoholic drinks, reflecting Irish-American cultural proscriptions.[58]

In 1881 five nuns, five novices, and two lay sisters formed the Ursuline Community of St. Theresa. The community included Sister Irene Gill, then twenty-five; her educational mentor Mother de Pazzi Brady; and Mother Seraphine Leonard, later a New Rochelle administrator. The community's identity as the "Irish" Ursulines would last well into the next century. In 1884 the community opened a private academy, where Sr. Irene worked as assistant to the director.[59]

Mother Irene was born Lucy Gill in Galway, Ireland. In 1868 she journeyed with her mother, brother, and sister to New York, leaving her other siblings behind. Lucy Gill attended St. Catherine's Academy on West Broadway, conducted by the Sisters of Mercy, the order one of her sisters had entered in Ireland, and another sister, the one who immigrated with Lucy, entered in New York. Both family and academy moved uptown, where Lucy Gill met the Ursulines. She entered the East Morrisania convent, making her final vows in 1879. Sister Irene first taught at the Henry Street school. Here her leadership and the order's growth quickly became intertwined, and with them the germination of New Rochelle.[60]

Though described as "gentle" and deeply religious, Mother Irene was also capable of righteous anger and mindful of earthly ways in which to accomplish her goals. Masterful in decision-making, with an "excellent" memory and magnetic personality, Mother Irene focused on all kinds of projects. She could be "most exacting" in everything from neatness of dress to classroom disciplinary techniques. While holding numerous high offices, she frequently performed menial work and self-mortification. Yet this personal humility was joined to pride in the accomplishments of the order and the college, as if she could feel about these institutions what as a nun she was constrained from feeling personally.[61]

The career of Mother Irene was inextricably linked to that of her blood sister, Mother Augustine, who entered St. Theresa's in 1885. Ten years younger than her sister, Irene entered the convent at nineteen. Like her sister she taught at the St. Theresa's school and academy; she also taught for a time at the order's seminary in Middletown, New York. Prior to the opening of the college she worked at the Park Avenue academy. She and her elder sister would divide most of the leadership duties at New Rochelle for many years.[62]

The pedagogic genesis of New Rochelle lay in St. Theresa's next project. With the escalating demand for parochial school teachers, the sisters available could not meet the need. Also, teaching was a desirable occupation open to Irish American women. Finally, the board exams required for a city teaching license necessitated preparation. Thus teacher training was in great demand. To answer this need, the mother superior of St. Theresa's, Mother de Pazzi, following St. Angela's example, organized the first Catholic normal school in the city for both public and parochial school teachers in 1883. By welcoming any women religious, the school raised preparation standards and training in all Catholic schools, at a time when most women, let alone cloistered nuns, lacked teaching certification. Laywomen attended at least as early as 1886. Graduates were very successful both in passing the exams and in becoming department heads and principals.[63]

By this time Mother Irene directed the academy, which became known as "Mother Irene's school." She became superior at St. Theresa's in 1893, the same year the academy received its Board of Regents charter, the first Catholic high school so recognized in New York. By the early 1890s the Henry Street community was largely Jewish; the Irish had moved uptown. Academy enrollment declined, though that of the board classes continued to rise. In 1896 the sisters leased a house on 94th Street while Mother Irene explored sites in New Rochelle for their permanent move.[64]

The local priest, Father O'Farrell, was a friend of New Rochelle parish priest Father Thomas McLaughlin, who wanted Ursulines to teach in his parochial school. Mother Irene agreed. Father McLaughlin steered her to "Leland Castle," a burned-out former luxury inn that she bought and opened as a primary school, vindicating the idea that Catholics outside the city would support an academy.[65]

Meanwhile, following the passage of a mandatory teacher training law, the board classes became examination review classes. In 1900 the Ursulines moved most of their operations to the Park Street academy, which had begun offering college-level courses in the mid-1890s. Demand for these courses grew among both sisters and lay teachers, which "deeply impressed" Mother Irene with the necessity for a Catholic women's college.[66]

By now over twenty years had passed since the formation of the St. Theresa community. The manifest success of their enterprises no doubt sparked the idea of founding a college. Mother Irene probably made that decision herself, as she chose the twenty-fifth anniversary of her profession, July 4, 1904, to announce the plan. This celebration, one of the few personal occasions most women religious observed, underlines the personal nature of New Rochelle's founding, and its close connection to her ideas.[67]

Despite the lack of a Catholic women's college in New York, Archbishop John Farley was reluctant to approve this "wild idea." Some clerics referred to it as "Irene's folly." Only by "persistent pleading" did she obtain the required permission. She could not bring the college into being alone, however. Her hesitancy and unfamiliarity with procedures are evident in the surviving correspondence: the application for the Regents' charter, erased over and over, which needed to be recopied; the necessity of resubmitting some motions to the trustees to ensure that all was in order.[68]

She relied upon a network of male advisers, the nucleus of a group she would consult in the years ahead. It included her old friend Father O'Farrell, Father McLoughlin, state Board of Education member William H. Buckley, and Dr. Augustus Downing, city and state educational administrator. Buckley and Mother Irene met through her blood sister, Sr. Philomena of the Sisters of Mercy in Albany. Mother Irene consulted with him about a charter until it was given in June 1904. Buckley accepted a position as trustee soon after.[69]

Dr. Augustus Downing was first director of the New York teacher training school and a state regent. He had assisted St. Theresa's academy in obtaining its charter in 1893. Later he became first assistant state commissioner of education, and referred to himself as " 'the godfather of the college.' " Mother Irene also had less formal relationships with influential men such as John J. Wynes Jr., editor of the diocesan paper *The Messenger,* who confirmed the archbishop's support for the project.[70]

The college opened in September 1904, under the name St. Angela's College, in honor of the Ursuline's founder. Because it grew out of both a community and an educational tradition, leadership continued seamlessly from one to the other. While a priest was named president, it was well understood that he was a figurehead. Mother Irene was chief executive and hand-picked the trustees until the 1920s, and her advisers had urged her to make the board a rubber stamp.[71]

Yet she was not the public persona of the college; as early as 1908, an alumna recalled, "we rarely laid eyes on her, except in the chapel." The role of liaison with students and faculty belonged to Mother Augustine. She was more approachable, in charge of discipline and student activities. Later accounts name her the first Dean, though she never held that formal title. She was the go-between from students to her sister, lauded for her charm and "quick appreciation," receiving credit for the college's early "congeniality." She also served as superior of the community (1909–15), and thereafter the sisters alternated in this role into the 1930s, further underscoring their partnership of governing both community and college.[72]

To help run the college, Mother Irene even turned outside the Catholic community. The most noteworthy example was her hiring of Louise Tucker, first professor of pedagogy. Tucker had received her M.A. from Columbia and taught in the city's public schools. After reading an article about the new college she sought out Mother Irene and offered her services. Tucker would represent the college to the public schools and the Brooklyn Training School for Teachers, meetings the cloistered nuns could not attend.[73]

Though Mother Irene dominated New Rochelle, her handling of daily affairs apparently ended in 1909, when her term as Provincial of the Ursulines'

Eastern Province began. This post required extensive travel and attention. While she maintained a role at the college, she handed over its day-to-day administration. She was still the final arbiter of major decisions, including the renaming of the college in 1910, giving the school a "more universal aspect" and emphasizing the primacy of its educational mission.[74]

The creation of the College of New Rochelle, building on a previous mission and refocusing the educational aims of one community of the order, was inspired by Mother Irene. Though a distant figure to students, her vision and her decisions clearly set the path of the college's early years. The cooperation between the lay and religious worlds, the reliance on a group of well-placed advisors, decisions such as renaming the college that focused attention on the academic rather than the religious aspects of the school, and the desire to establish and maintain high academic standards, all sprang from Mother Irene, putting her in the company of the other strong, pioneering leaders profiled here.

While little controversy marked the coming to power of women at New Rochelle, there were elements of tension. The role and level of activity of the trustees, for example, would receive frequent examination but no resolution in later years. The use of secular faculty, especially secular women, would spark other conflicts. Finally the high level of personalization of leadership as exemplified by Mothers Irene and Augustine would lead to problems as well as triumphs. The nature of women's power was as thorny, though in less dramatic ways, at New Rochelle as it had been at Wellesley, Bryn Mawr, and Trinity.

Lessons in Power

What themes emerge from these varied stories of coming to power? Some critical precursors for first-generation leaders were the backing and continued support of one or more well-placed male mentors; administrative ability or experience, preferably both; and an appeal to more than one of the various constituencies of the institution. While these qualities may also have been necessary for their male counterparts, the very fact of women leaders was problematic at each college. The reinforcement of female power with the strength of male support, whether in the form of a cardinal or a paper board of trustees for the Catholic schools, or family connections or proximity to the all-powerful founder at the secular ones, was a necessity. One wonders how much additional mentoring or backing a Daniel Coit Gilman or James Angell felt he needed once in office; one imagines it cannot have been of this magnitude.

The ambivalence about handing over true executive power to women exploded into strenuous opposition at Bryn Mawr, while the combination of the founder's wishes and a strong female base kept the level of conflict at

Wellesley fairly subdued. Still, there emerged by the 1890s no sense that women could unquestionably assume power; and the meaning of power, the ability to make change, was still largely untested even at Wellesley, where Alice Freeman Palmer had only begun her sweeping slate of reforms. Yet Freeman Palmer, with her capacity to cooperate, build consensus, and empower constituents had a less-contentious presidency. In chapter 5, Jana Nidiffer further explores the relationship of gender-based characteristics and successful leadership.

The appointment of women leaders at Trinity and New Rochelle was never in question. Yet female leaders at both felt compelled to keep the trappings of male supremacy. Succession brought authority, but the unstated premise of that authority was obedience to the male-controlled Church as well as to the discipline of the order. Thus the archbishop of Baltimore continued to stir the Trinity pot, and faculty from Catholic University continued to lead meetings, advise on curriculum, and maintain a paternal guardianship over the school. The male trustees of New Rochelle, not to mention its succession of priest-presidents, continued to occupy the public gaze as that college's "leaders," however fictive their power over day-to-day operations. Candace Introcaso, in chapter 3, discusses both historical and contemporary women presidents in the context of both lay and religious life, including their connection to concepts of women's roles and to the church hierarchy.

Of all those who came to power in this study, the only one who sought her position was M. Carey Thomas, and even she was eventually torn about the wisdom of continuing against trustee opposition. In the other cases there is either no evidence about attitudes, or evidence that the nominated leader tried to refuse or felt ambivalent about her succession. Duty, persuasion and obligation guided them, not personal ambition or compelling vision. From a late-twentieth-century vantage point, it is likely that many of these women lacked confidence and rode into office on past performance. Questions about their ability, their role, their relation to the men and women who supported them, provided the starting point to many a presidency.

Finally, each of these pioneering leaders confronted the task of aligning social, personal, and intellectual expectations for their young institutions. At Wellesley and Bryn Mawr this meant confronting seminary and cultural ideas about the place of women and the centrality of religion, and pitted the young leaders against the college's founder or his representatives. At Trinity conflicts about the authority of Rome over the American church engulfed the college for a time, while there was no doubt that a particularly American conception of women's education would be the model for this first independently founded Catholic women's college. And at New Rochelle, where again permission to proceed was given with some reluctance, the founder maneuvered to maintain the autonomy necessary to achieve her goals, hidden behind the face of male authority. The pioneer generation of leaders achieved much but left a number of central issues unresolved or partially resolved, in part because of the convolutions of expectation and ideals. The shape of women's leadership had assumed several forms by 1910, but the outcomes of women coming to power were yet to emerge.

Notes

1. See Jean Glasscock, ed., *Wellesley College 1875–1975: A Century of Women* (Wellesley, MA: Wellesley College, 1975); Florence Converse, *The Story of Wellesley* (Boston: Little, Brown and Co., 1915); and Patricia A. Palmieri, "In Adamless Eden: A Social Portrait of the Academic Community at Wellesley College 1875–1920," Ed.D. diss., Harvard University, 1981. Quotation from Ada Howard, "Reminiscences of Henry Fowle Durant," 1DD1, Ada Howard Papers, Wellesley College Archives (hereinafter WCA).

2. Howard, a Mount Holyoke graduate, had served as lady principal at Knox College and later headed her own secondary school. On her role and the early years of Wellesley, see the Wellesley College Calendar, 1876–77 and 1877–78; Frances Robinson Johnson to her mother, Jan. 8, 1876 and Feb. 4, 1877, 6C, Class of 1879, Box 1, WCA; *Wellesley Magazine* (1895–96): 167–68; Alice Payne Hackett, *Wellesley: Part of the American Story* (New York: E. P. Dutton, 1949), 69; and Converse, *The Story of Wellesley,* 37. On the preparatory department, see Converse, *Wellesley,* 26. On religion, see Glasscock, ed., *Wellesley College 1875–1975,* 17–18, and Converse, *Wellesley* 23, 27.

3. Student estimations of faculty are in Estelle M. Hurll, "Professor Lord and Old Wellesley," *Wellesley Alumnae Quarterly* 5 (Oct. 1920): 1; Patricia A. Palmieri, " 'In Adamless Eden,' " 63.

4. Criticisms of Howard may be found in: Diary entry, Louise Manning Hodgkins, Oct. 9, 1881, Hodgkins Unprocessed Papers, WCA; Alice Payne Hackett, *Wellesley,* 48; Florence Converse, *Wellesley,* 38; Helen Merrill, "The History of the Dept. of Mathematics," 3L, Math Department Folder, WCA. See also: Frances Robinson Johnson to her mother, June 4, June 11, June [11?], June 18, and Thursday [n.d.; June], 1876, 6C, Class of 1879, Box 1, WCA; and Mary Knowles Ferry to "My Dear Frank" and "My Dear Parents," June 11, 1876, WCA.

5. See George Herbert Palmer, *Alice Freeman Palmer* (Boston: Houghton Mifflin, 1908), esp. 25; Alice Freeman Palmer, "Why I Am an Optimist," clipping, April 5, 1902, 1DD2, Alice Freeman Palmer: General, WCA. James Angell as quoted in Dorothy Gies McGuigan, *A Dangerous Experiment: 100 Years of Women at the University of Michigan* (Ann Arbor, MI: Center for Continuing Education of Women, 1970), 71–72. Her own recollections appear in "Three Types of Women's Colleges," in George H. and

Alice Freeman Palmer, *The Teacher: Essays and Addresses on Education* (Boston: Houghton Mifflin, 1908). On the Student Christian Association, see Kate Upson Clark, "Alice Freeman Palmer," *Ladies Home Journal* [n.d.; 1902?]. See also Alice Payne Hackett, *Wellesley,* 57; and Glasscock, et al., "The Founders and Early Presidents," in *Wellesley College 1875–1975,* ed. Jean Glasscock. Palmer received an honorary doctorate from Michigan in 1882.

6. Caroline Hazard, "Personal Recollections of Alice Freeman Palmer," in *From College Gates* (Boston: Houghton Mifflin, 1925), 208. On heart culture, see George Herbert Palmer, *Alice Freeman Palmer,* 75–76; see also: ALS (collection of letters by community members), Leila S. McKee to Miss Perkins, Feb. 5, 1903, WCA. Student perceptions may be seen in Carrie Park Harrington to her family [n.d.; Nov.? 1881] 6C, 1883 Class Records, Carrie Park Harrington Papers, WCA.

7. Katharine Lee Bates, "The Purposeful Women Who Have Reared the College from Struggling Babyhood to Glorious Womanhood and the Men Who Have Aided Them," *Boston Evening Transcript,* May 16, 1925; on her role, Alice Payne Hackett, *Wellesley,* p. 68; on Freeman and Durant's conflict see Lyman Abbott, "Snapshots of My Contemporaries," *The Outlook* 128 (Aug. 24, 1912), 645.

8. Jean Glasscock, ed., *Wellesley,* 24; George Herbert Palmer, *Alice Freeman Palmer,* 154. Katharine Lee Bates, "An Intimate Study of a Rare Woman," *The Congregationalist and Christian World,* May 16, 1908. Patricia A. Palmieri, " 'In Adamless Eden,' " describes the ensuing years and Palmer's role. The one flaw in this structure, Freeman believed, was Mrs. Durant's tenure as treasurer. She insisted on having real power, in tandem with the president, which Freeman labeled "the cause of all the difficulty which now exists." Alice Freeman to George Herbert Palmer, April 24, 1887, in *An Academic Courtship: Letters of Alice Freeman Palmer and George Herbert Palmer,* ed. George Herbert Palmer (Cambridge, MA: Harvard University Press, 1940), p. 160. Mrs. Durant seldom challenged Alice Freeman Palmer and the more liberal trustees outright; I believe her adherence to traditional female deference ensured this.

9. Marion Pelton Guild, "Historical Sketch of Wellesley College," in *History of Higher Education in Massachusetts,* ed. George Bush (Washington, D.C.: Government Printing Office, 1981), 432; Legislation of Wellesley College, Sept. 1908 [Article III: Academic Council], WCA. Patricia A. Palmieri, *In Adamless Eden* (New Haven: Yale University Press, 1995, part I, ch. 3) describes the program to dismiss certain faculty, and makes clear that Palmer was its chief architect.

10. Louise McCoy North referred to Alice Freeman Palmer as the "girl president" in an untitled autograph manuscript, n.p., WCA.

11. The lives and work of these men have yet to be explored. For James Whitall Thomas's role in helping found Johns Hopkins, see Helen

Lefkowitz Horowitz, *The Power and Passion of M. Carey Thomas* (New York: Alfred H. Knopf, 1994), 47–48. See William C. Dunlap, *Quaker Education in Baltimore and Virginia Yearly Meetings* (Philadelphia: University of Pennsylvania, 1936); *Proceedings of a Conference on Education in the Society of Friends* (Baltimore: William K. Boyle and Sons, 1878). Carey Thomas's Cornell career is described in Helen Lefkowitz Horowitz, *The Power and Passion of M. Carey Thomas,* ch. 3. See also Cornelia Meigs, *What Makes a College? A History of Bryn Mawr* (New York: Mcmillan, 1956), 16.

12. Horowitz, *The Power and Passion of M. Carey Thomas,* 75–76, 78; the further careers of its members are discussed passim. A brief description of the Friday Evening Group and its members also appears in Marjorie Housepian Dobkins, ed., *The Making of a Feminist: Early Journals and Letters of M. Carey Thomas* (Kent, OH: Kent State University Press, 1979).

13. *Proceedings of a Conference on Education in the Society of Friends at Haverford College* (Philadelphia: J. H. Culbertson Co., 1880). Mary Whitall Thomas to M. Carey Thomas, Jan. 30, 1880, reel 61, frame 709, in *The Papers of M. Carey Thomas in the Bryn Mawr College Archives,* ed. Lucy Fisher West. (printed reel guide and index and microfilm, 207 reels, Woodbridge, CT: Research Publications International, 1982; hereinafter Thomas Papers).

14. Horowitz, *The Power and Passion of M. Carey Thomas,* is the best assessment of Thomas and her career. On her family, see Helen Thomas Flexner, *A Quaker Childhood* (New Haven: Yale University Press, 1940); Barbara Strachey Halperin, *Remarkable Relations: The Story of the Pearsall Smith Women* (New York: Universe Books, 1980); Robert Allerton Parker, *The Transatlantic Smiths* (New York: Random House, 1959).

15. This career is summarized through her own letters in Marjorie Housepian Dobkin, ed., *The Making of a Feminist;* and in Horowitz, *The Power and Passion of M. Carey Thomas.*

16. For some interpretations of gender roles and female relationships at this time, including the historical construction of lesbian identity, see Lillian Faderman, *Odd Girls and Twilight Lovers: A History of Lesbian Life in Twentieth-Century America* (New York: Columbia University Press, 1991); Carroll Smith-Rosenberg, "The New Woman as Androgyne: Social Disorder and Gender Crisis, 1870–1936," in Rosenberg, *Disorderly Conduct: Visions of Gender in Victorian America* (New York: Alfred A. Knopf, 1985), 245–96. Thomas's shifting attitudes toward religion are traced in some detail in Horowitz, *The Power and Passion of M. Carey Thomas.*

17. Horowitz, *The Power and Passion of M. Carey Thomas.* See also Edith Finch, *Carey Thomas of Bryn Mawr* (New York: Harper & Brothers, 1947), 173, 185, 230, 233; Cornelia Meigs, *What Makes a College?* 70–71.

18. M. Carey Thomas to Mary Whitall Thomas, Nov. 30, 1882, reel 32, frame 212. Thomas Papers; Meigs, *What Makes a College?* 35–37.

19. Taylor's wishes are contained in his 1877 will, quoted in Meigs, *What Makes a College?* 28–29; see also Horowitz, *The Power and Passion of M. Carey Thomas,* 162–63. On the general quality and composition of women's education at this time, see Barbara Miller Solomon, *In the Company of Educated Women* (New Haven: Yale University Press, 1987). Circular No. 1, Bryn Mawr College (Bryn Mawr, 1883). Bryn Mawr College Archives (hereinafter BMCA). On religiously guarded education see Margaret Bacon, *The Quiet Rebels: The Story of the Quakers in America* (Philadelphia: Lippincott, 1970), 154 ff. Meigs maintains the trustees were flexible about the concept of guarded education, but it is clear that the controversy over Thomas becoming president was a referendum on this issue. See Meigs, *What Makes a College?* 29 ff.

20. M. Carey Thomas to Mary E. Garrett, May 3, 1884, reel 15, frame 437. Thomas Papers.

21. See M. Carey Thomas, Report to the President and Trustees, Bryn Mawr College, June 7, 1884. See also her "Note Book" of the 1884 trip she made to other women's colleges: Bryn Mawr, Organization of Bryn Mawr, 1884, Note Book 1, reel 166, beginning with frame 554. Thomas Papers. Quotation from M. Carey Thomas to Mary E. Garrett, May 3, 1884, reel 15, frame 437. Thomas Papers.

22. Horowitz, *The Power and Passion of M. Carey Thomas,* esp. ch. 10. The contrast in the original and Thomas-inspired plans is evident in comparing Circular No. 1 and Circular No. 2, Bryn Mawr College (Bryn Mawr, 1884).

23. Horowitz, *The Power and Passion of M. Carey Thomas.* The conscious muting of ideas and behaviors may also be seen in Cynthia Farr Brown, " 'Putting a *Woman* in Sole Power': The Presidential Succession at Bryn Mawr College, 1892–1894," *History of Higher Education Annual* (1988), 84–90.

24. Horowitz, *The Power and Passion of M. Carey Thomas,* esp. chapters 11 and 12; Finch, *Carey Thomas,* 154, 161–62, 166, 170–72.

25. Brown, " 'Putting a *Woman* in Sole Power.' "

26. Horowitz, *The Power and Passion of M. Carey Thomas,* esp. ch. 12; Finch, *Carey Thomas,* 167–69, 170; Meigs, *What Makes a College?* 23–26.

27. M. Carey Thomas to Mary Whitall Thomas, Oct. 1883, reel 32, frame 397, Thomas Papers. Direct religious imagery appears in her letter to Mary Garrett, May 28, 1884, reel 15, frame 442, Thomas Papers. The idea of teacher as minister is clear from her style and her tendency to bring highly secular, feminist ideas into her chapel talks; many of the notes for these talks appear in her papers.

28. The four opposed were brothers Philip and John Garrett (no relation to Mary Garrett), Francis Cope, and Edward Bettle. This list has been reconstructed from correspondence both before and after the event. See M. Carey Thomas to Mary Garrett, March 8, 1891, reel 16, frame 396, Thomas Papers; James Rhoads quoted in Finch, *Carey Thomas,* 210–11. The evaluation of the swing voters depends on a reading of trustee minutes through 1916; analysis of the Thomas correspondence; and information in Meigs, *What Makes a College?* pp. 23 ff. The trustees operated by majority vote rather than Quaker consensus.

29. M. Carey Thomas to Mary E. Garrett, March 23, 1893, reel 17, frame 413, Thomas Papers.

30. The votes appear in Trustees' Minutes for March 1893, BMCA. See also Horowitz, *The Power and Passion of M. Carey Thomas,* esp. ch. 13.

31. M. Carey Thomas to Mary E. Garrett, March 9, 1893, reel 17, frame 366, Thomas Papers.

32. Garrett's donations appear in the Trustees' Minutes of March, 1893. BMCA; and in Horowitz, *The Power and Passion of M. Carey Thomas,* 257–59. See James Thomas, circular letter, April 13, 1893, recorded in Trustees' Minutes of April 14, 1893, BMCA; the vice president scheme appears in Trustees' Minutes, April 4 and July 7, 1893, BMCA.

33. M. Carey Thomas to Mary E. Garrett, March 10, reel 17, frame 372; and March 22, 1893, reel 17, frame 408, Thomas Papers. The resolutions appear in the Trustees' Minutes for July 1893, BMCA. See Brown, " 'Putting a *Woman* in Sole Power'," esp. 87 ff.; on the arrangements, Cornelia Meigs, *What Makes a College?* 68–69.

34. Horowitz, *The Power and Passion of M. Carey Thomas.*

35. There is no modern history of this order. See Sr. Mary Patricia [Butler], *A Sketch of the History of Notre Dame* (Washington, D.C.: Trinity College, 1925), and her *American Foundations of the Sisters of Notre Dame de Namur* (Philadelphia: Dolphin Press, 1928). See also Sr. Helen Louise [Nugent], *Sister Louise* (New York: Benziger Brothers, 1931). They are called "de Namur" to distinguish them from the School Sisters of Notre Dame, another teaching order.

36. Sr. Helen Louise [Nugent], *Sr. Julia, Sister of Notre Dame de Namur* (New York: Benzinger Brothers, 1928): on her early life, pp. 1–18; on her career, pp. 25, 30–41; see also Sr. Mary Patricia [Butler], *A Sketch;* Sr. Helen Louise [Nugent], *Sr. Julia,* 140 ff. and 254–65; Sr. Mary Patricia [Butler], *American Foundations,* esp. pp. 38–39.

37. Quotations from Sr. Agnes Loretto to Sr. Mary Borgia, Sept. 20, 1897, Box: Sr. Julia McGroarty, Folder: Opening of Trinity College, Trinity College Archives (hereinafter TCA).

38. Sr. Julia, Letter to "My Dear Sisters," Feb. 2, 1901, p. 5. Drawer 2. Folder: MS History, TCA.

39. Sr. Angela Elizabeth Keenan, *Three Against the Wind: The Founding of Trinity College,* Washington, D.C. (Westminster, MD: Christian Classics, 1973), 38–47. There is a tradition that she was actually baptized before leaving North Carolina by Rev. James Gibbons, later Cardinal Gibbons, a strong supporter of Trinity; but there is no way to substantiate this. Keenan, *Three Against the Wind,* 60, 48–58. On her character, Sr. Agnes Loretto to Sr. Mary Borgia, Sept. 25, 1897, Box: Sr. Julia McGroarty, Folder: Opening of Trinity College, TCA; and Sr. Mary Patrick [Butler], *American Foundations,* 552. Ella Osmonia Taylor, "In the Midst of Things 1861–71," TS, Drawer 2, TCA.

40. "Mrs. Talty's Account of the Purchase of Land and Other Memorabilia," in Sr. Columba Mullaly, *Trinity College: The First Eighty Years 1897–1977* (Baltimore: Christian Classics, Inc., 1987) [Appendix I], 541; Sr. Mary Euphrasia Taylor, "Foundation of Trinity College," 1–3. Three notebooks, TCA (hereinafter "Foundation").

41. Mary Hayes, SND, "The Founding Years of Trinity College, Washington, D.C.: A Case Study in Christian Feminism," paper delivered at the Conference on the History of Women Religious, June 27, 1989; Sr. Mary Euphrasia Taylor, "Foundation," 22–23.

42. Rev. Philip Garrigan to Sr. Mary Euphrasia, March 16, 1897, TCA. See also Sr. Mary Euphrasia Taylor, "Foundation," 27.

43. See generally Sr. Mary Euphrasia Taylor, "Foundation"; and Sr. Columba Mullaly, *Trinity College,* ch. 2. The "moral plan" probably referred to the statement of purpose and discipline. On the trustees, see Sr. Mary Euphrasia Taylor, "Foundation," 185.

44. Sr. Mary Euphrasia to Sr. Julia, May 25, 1897, as quoted in Sr. Columba Mullaly, *Trinity College,* 29.

45. On the publicity plan, Sr. Columba Mullaly, *Trinity College,* pp. 6–8; on the cardinal's role see [Sr. Mary Euphrasia Taylor, "Foundation," 35, 42–43, 44–45; the cardinal's letter is reprinted in Sr. Columba Mullaly, *Trinity College,* xiii.

46. Sr. Columba Mullaly, *Trinity College,* 30–31 recounts the episode. See also Thomas T. McAvoy, *The Great Crisis in American Catholic History 1895–1900* (Chicago: Henry Regnery Co., 1957); John Tracy Ellis, *The Formative Years of Catholic University* (Washington, D.C.: Catholic University Press, 1946); and Peter Hogan, S.J., *The Catholic University of America: The Rectorship of Thomas J. Conaty* (Washington, D.C.: Catholic University of America, 1949).

47. Sr. Julia to Sr Mary Euphrasia, Aug. 25, 1897. Quoted in Sr. Julia, Letter to "My Dear Sisters," 10; see Sr. Columba Mullaly, *Trinity College,* 35–40.

48. See Sr. Mary Euphrasia Taylor, "Foundation," following 250; Sr. Julia to Sr. Mary Euphrasia, Feb. 9, 1898; Sr. Columba Mullaly, *Trinity College,* 36, 42. Quotation from Sr. Helen Louise [Nugent], *Sr. Julia,* 281.

49. The early genesis of the board is described in Sr. Columba Mullaly, *Trinity College,* 46–48; Sr. Mary Euphrasia to Sr. Julia, March 14, 1898, Drawer 2, Folder: 1898, TCA. See also Dean's Notebook, Oct. 10, 1900, 1, TCA; and Sr. Columba Mullaly, *Trinity College,* 501.

50. Sr. Columba Mullaly, *Trinity College,* 53–55, quoting from Sr. Mary Euphrasia Taylor, "Foundation"; Bishop Spalding quoted in Sr. Julia, Letter to "My Dear Sisters," 27; Thomas J. Conaty to Sr. Mary Euphrasia, Jan. 18, 1899. TCA. On the final controversy, Sr. Julia, Letter to "My Dear Sisters," 30; the building and other aspects of opening the college are well covered in Sr. Columba Mullaly, *Trinity College.*

51. Sr. Mary Euphrasia was not sent to study at one of the training colleges in Europe, nor was she mentioned as president in the list of the corporate members that Sr. Julia prepared. Thus the decision was probably made well in advance of the opening of the college.

52. See "Record of Teachers Meetings at Trinity College" [1900–1911], esp. meeting of April 21, 1901, 23, TCA. On the activities of Sr. Julia, see esp. "Record of Teachers Meetings at Trinity College" [1900–1911]. TCA. List of president's responsibilities from dean's notebook, 2 [n.d., 1900], TCA.

53. See Sr. Columba Mullaly, *Trinity College,* ch. II; on the crisis, see Board of Trustees of Trinity College Minutes, 48–49, TCA; Philip Garrigan, TS: Speech, Dec. 17, 1914, 4–5, Drawer 2. Folder: Dr. Garrigan, TCA.

54. Board of Trustees of Trinity College Minutes, 49. As it happened, Sr. Josephine Ignatius was wrong about the resignations but right about public opinion.

55. In cmphasizing the break in 1902 I am revising the interpretive chronology offered by Sr. Columba Mullaly, who sees one continuous period from 1899 to 1908. Sr. Mary Euphrasia ended her career teaching at the order's San Jose, California school. She retired to Dayton, Ohio about 1916 and died there on April 14, 1918.

56. There is no modern history of the Ursulines. See *Rules and Constitutions of the Roman Order of the Order of St. Ursula* (Exeter, UK: Catholic Records Press, 1937), 78; Marguerite Aron, *The Ursulines,* trans. Mother Angela Griffin, O.S.U. (New York: Declan McMullen Co., 1947).

57. Marguerite Aron, *The Ursulines,* 102–3; philosophy from Roman Order of Ursulines, *Reglements* (1705 edition), ch. IV, V, as quoted in Sr. Mary Jane Cuddy, O.S.U., "History of the College of New Rochelle," 42. Unfinished M.A. thesis, c. 1941, Box: Organization/Development/History: Early Years, 1904–30 (hereinafter referred to as "History"), College of New Rochelle Archives (hereinafter CNRA). On the Fordham connection, Rev. Joseph N. Moody, sermon, Oct. 24, 1936, Box: Foundation/Development/Administration, Folder 3, CNRA.

58. Sr. Mary Jane Cuddy, "History," 10; personal interview with Sr. Mary Russo O.S.U., March 6, 1990, New Rochelle, New York.

59. Mother Thomas Aquinas, "History of the College of New Rochelle 1904–1974," Box: Organization/Development/History, Folder: History of CNR, 1904–1974; personal interview with Sr. Mary Russo, March 6, 1990.

60. Sr. Gertrude Farmer, "Biography of Mother Irene Gill," 1968, 1, Box: Mother Irene Gill, CNRA; "Reverend Mother Irene Gill," obituary, Dec. 24, 1935, Box: Mother Irene Gill, CNRA.

61. Sr. Gertrude Farmer, "Biography," 10, 12; "Reverend Mother Irene Gill," 2.

62. Sr. Thomas Aquinas, "Mother Augustine Gill, First Dean of C.N.R.," *Alumnae News* 15.1 (Winter 1938): 1.

63. Sr. Mary Jane Cuddy, "History," 10, 12. St. Francis Xavier, an academy in Brooklyn, offered such classes, but in the days before the bridge was built city residents could make little use of them; Martha Counihan O.S.U., "Mother Irene Gill: Still in Our Hearts," *The Tatler,* 15 (Oct. 14, 1977); Sr. Mary Russo O.S.U., "A History of the Eastern Province of the US of the Roman Union of the Order of St. Ursula, 1535–1989," TS (1989), 35. CNRA. See also Sr. Mary Jane Cuddy, "History," 11.

64. Mother Xavier Fitzgerald O.S.U., "Memoirs," quoted in Sr. Mary Jane Cuddy, "History," 10–11; Mother Gertrude Farmer, "Biography," 4; Mother Thomas Aquinas, "History"; Sr. Mary Russo, "A History of the Eastern Province," 36.

65. Sr. Gertrude Farmer, "Biography," 7; Sr. Mary Jane Cuddy, "History," 15–16. The price was $35,000, and to pay it Mother Irene traded the Locust Ave. property and received a mortgage from the Iselin family. Legend has it that Adrian Iselin, by then a trustee of the college, tore up the mortgage on the occasion of Mother Irene's thirtieth anniversary of profession. On the first year of the school, Sr. Mary Jane Cuddy, "History," 17. Chartered by the state regents on March 22, 1898, the school's five original trustees included Mother Irene and Father O'Farrell. Charter of the Ursuline Academy of New Rochelle, Box: Organization/Development/History: Material for the Early Years, CNRA.

66. Sr. Mary Jane Cuddy, "History," 12–13, 17; Sr. Mary Russo, "A History of the Eastern Province," 38; Mother Gertrude Farmer, "Biography," 6. Little information about these courses survives, which probably were not accredited but may have been a bridge between high school and college-level work.

67. Sr. Mary Jane Cuddy, "History," 18.

68. Sr. Gertrude Farmer, "Biography," 8; Sr. Mary Jane Cuddy, "History," 19. See William H. Buckley to Mother Irene Gill, May 26, 1904, June 18, 1904, and June 22, 1904, Box 2, Folder 6, CNRA.

69. William H. Buckley to Mother Irene Gill, May 26, 1904, Box 2, Folder 6; Mother Thomas Aquinas, "History"; Thomas P. Keough to Mother Irene Gill, Sept. 11, 1905, Box 2, Folder 5, CNRA; William H. Buckley to

Mother Irene Gill, Oct. 14, 1905, and Mother Irene Gill to the Board of Regents, Oct. 30, 1905; copy of Minutes of the Board of Trustees Meeting, held Nov. 25, 1905 and dated Dec. 4, 1905, Box 2, Folder 5, CNRA.

70. Augustus S. Downing to Mother Augustine Gill, Feb. 20, 1911, Box 2, Folder 4, CNRA; Sr. Mary Jane Cuddy, "History," 13–14; John J. Wynes Jr. to Mother Irene Gill, June 30, 1904, Box 2, Folder 6, CNRA.

71. She could even determine the chair of the board. See, e.g., Edward J. McGuire to Mother Irene Gill, Feb. 1, 1918 and April 15, 1918, Box: Trustees, Folder: Correspondence, 1904–20. See also Edward J. McGuire to Mother Augustine Gill, Jan. 17, 1924, Box: Board of Trustees, Folder: Correspondence, 1921–43, CNRA.

72. Agnes Keating Muldoon '08, "Pioneer Days at CNR," Founder's Day Talk, 1951, 2; Mother Thomas Aquinas, "Mother Augustine Gill." On the college atmosphere, Mary Hennessey Birmingham '08, "Reminiscences," 1–2, 1952, CNRA.

73. Louise Tucker to Mother Irene Gill, Jan. 26, 1906, Box: Foundation/Development/ Administration, Folder: Correspondence, State Education Dept., 1905–7, CNRA.

74. Sr. Mary Russo, "A History of the Eastern Province," 68–69. Louise de Montivzin, "Mother Irene Tells about the Founding," *New Rochelle Tatler,* 514 (March 24, 1926): 1, CNRA.

CHAPTER 3

Determination in Leadership

Pioneering Roman Catholic Women Presidents

CANDACE INTROCASO

The story of women's access to higher education in the United States is woefully incomplete without examining the contribution of the Catholic women religious, or sisters, who were pioneers in the leadership of women's colleges. Indeed, for at least the first six decades of the twentieth century, the preponderance of women college presidents were women religious heading Catholic institutions. Their presence in a male-dominated arena paved the way for future generations of women presidents.

This is a complex story. Buried within the archives of religious orders and the histories of individual colleges, is the tale of courageous women who labored tirelessly on behalf of women's education, as did their colleagues in chapter 2. Their story is not so much about individuals who as college presidents did things that garnered significant public attention. Rather, it is the story of women in leadership positions who quietly, with little fanfare, built a cohort of colleges that historically made a significant impact on the enterprise of higher education in the United States, particularly higher education for women.

The late Sister Magdalen Coughlin, former president and chancellor of Mount Saint Mary's College in Los Angeles, called her predecessors in Catholic higher education women whose "vision and faith, pluck and shrewdness joined with superior minds and hard work" to accomplish what no other group of women have in the history of the Catholic Church—in the history of the world. In essence, Coughlin stated, women religious established colleges that have left "a tremendously wide and deep wake of accomplishments in individual human lives, in American higher education and in the Church."[1] Furthermore, they did so not only with limited resources but also with an unlimited supply of determination and courage.

An overriding theme pervading the story of sister presidents, whether one examines them as individuals or as a group, historically or in the present day, is that they relied on sheer determination and will to change women's lives through education. Oftentimes confronted by financial constraints or facing opposition from Church officials, these women possessed an uncanny ability to read the signs of the times. They have historically led these institutions to respond to changes in higher education, adapting the curriculum to meet the needs of their students, and developing extension programs and evening and weekend schedules to address the needs of returning women and part-time adult students.

One cannot tell the story of sister presidents apart from the religious congregations, or orders, that founded and sponsored these colleges. In reality, these sister presidents were part of a much larger contingent of Catholic sisters who established schools to meet the emerging need to educate an immigrant Church in the United States. In many cases, religious zeal motivated these sisters, many of whom were immigrants themselves, to overcome numerous obstacles and to respond to the educational needs of the Church.

Initially, all the presidents of these Catholic women's colleges were sisters, oftentimes, holding dual leadership positions, college president and congregational head. With little or no formal preparation to head a college, these early presidents were successful in large part because they had the backing and support of their religious order. Couple this with the firm conviction that what they were doing was the will of God, and one can begin to understand that this endeavor was deeply rooted in faith.

Contemporary sister presidents have been educated in some of the most prestigious institutions of higher education in this country and are well prepared to assume a college presidency. However, decreases in the number of women religious over the past thirty years have reduced the pool of sisters available to preside over the colleges founded by religious orders. Currently, in the 117 Catholic colleges and universities in the United States that share a common heritage of foundation by a religious order, fewer than half have sister presidents. Issues of leadership, legacy, and institutional Catholic identity are common topics of debate among Catholic educators today.

Before exploring the present state of leadership in Catholic colleges founded by women religious, it is important to examine the contributions of sister presidents to the education of women in the historical context in which these Catholic women's colleges were established. In Catholic higher education, the motivations and purposes of higher learning for women in the nineteenth century begins in the academies for young women. These are the institutions from which many sister presidents emerged to assume leadership in women's higher education.

A Heritage with Purpose

Coughlin observes that from the beginning, Catholic sisters in the United States were associated with education. They come from a heritage with purpose, beginning with the French Ursuline sisters who established the first Catholic women's academy in New Orleans in 1727.[2] To explain when and why Catholic education for women began, one must acknowledge the fact that historically these schools were established to serve an immigrant Church.

Edward Power asserts that the population of Catholics in colonial America was so small that it would have been impossible to support a college prior to the late 1700s. In 1770, there were only twenty-two thousand Catholics living in the colonies. That number increased very slowly until the first significant wave of immigration in the early decades of the nineteenth century saw the population increase to 1,616,000 by mid-century.[3]

Barbara Solomon observes that the establishment of academies, seminaries, and so-called colleges in the late eighteenth and early nineteen centuries laid the foundation for women's higher education.[4] Among the precedents for the education of women in the United States were the female seminaries such as those founded by Emma Willard at Troy, New York, in 1821 and by Catherine Beecher at Hartford, Connecticut, in 1828. Mount Holyoke College also had its beginnings as a seminary established by Mary Lyon in South Hadley, Massachusetts, in 1836. These female seminaries became prototypes for women's institutions in other regions of the country.

In 1837, Oberlin College, in Ohio, admitted women with full collegiate status, inaugurating coeducational higher education. However, single-sex higher education for women made its appearance in the nineteenth century with the founding of a number of institutions including Vassar in 1865, Smith and Wellesley both in 1875, and Bryn Mawr in 1885. Frederick Rudolph reports that these colleges adopted a curriculum from the classical course of study developed at such places as Yale, Amherst, and Williams.[5]

Higher education for Catholic women in the nineteenth century is noteworthy only for its absence. There were a number of convent schools and academies. Like the seminaries established by women in the Northeast, Catholic academies founded by sisters also emerged by 1850. The Sisters of Providence, in 1841, established Saint Mary-of-the-Woods on the frontier of what was later western Indiana. In 1847, the Sisters of Charity of New York founded an academy for women located on an upper Fifth Avenue tract of land that is now part of Central Park. Nevertheless, it was not until the close of the century that the first Catholic women's college, the College of Notre Dame of Maryland, founded in 1896, upgraded itself from academy to collegiate status.

There are a number of reasons for this neglect of Catholic women's higher education. Catholics and Protestants alike shared cultural attitudes toward women's intellectual abilities as indicated in chapter 1. The Catholic hierarchy, along with many others, believed that women were by nature incapable of serious higher learning. Because of women's natural inferiority, many believed that they neither needed nor could profit from higher learning. Many people posed the question, "Would a college education make a better wife and mother?" To a Catholic priest-professor, who thought that "the best diploma for a woman was always a large family and a happy husband, the answer to this question was an unequivocal 'no.' "[6]

Administrators in Catholic men's colleges, as did their counterparts in public institutions described earlier, offered more specific reasons for excluding women. Power observes that if women were admitted to Catholic men's colleges, provision would have to be made for living accommodations, and women living on campus in the company of male students "would destroy good order, discipline, intellectual concentration, and morality."[7] Thus, higher education for Catholic women in the United States took a different path than did the men's colleges, and Catholic sisters forged the way.

While male Catholic education in the United States began with the establishment of colleges that were, in reality, a combination of elementary and secondary schools, education for Catholic women has its origins in the academies established to educate young girls. According to Power, 115 Catholic girls' schools were founded between 1829 and 1852.[8] Women's religious congregations or orders directed all but three of these. Such schools provided the scholastic foundation for Catholic women's colleges that appeared around the turn of the century.

The curriculum of these schools followed the course of the day for girls' education. Until the late 1870s, the curricula was predominantly practical, with an emphasis on purely elementary studies and the arts. There were some deviations from this practice worthy of notice. Making concessions to domestic training and the arts, many of these academies introduced courses in Latin, logic, or ethics. There is also some indication of a variety of teaching methods which recognized individual differences. The introduction of Latin into the curriculum marked a movement toward more liberal learning and laid a foundation for the establishment of women's colleges.

The Emergence of Catholic Women's Colleges

The meeting of the Catholic hierarchy in the United States which was responsible for the founding of the Catholic University of America in 1889, was inadvertently the same driving force behind education for Catholic women. The Third Plenary Council of Baltimore, a meeting of America's bishops, laid the foundation for the collegiate education of women. The council legislated a complete system of parochial schools to meet the needs of the growing Catholic population in the United States. While there appears to be little or no regard for the quality of school instruction or for the need for qualified teachers to implement the bishops' mandate, the establishment of parochial schools demanded the education of women to staff these institutions.

Throughout the nineteenth century, the pedagogical preparation for sisters who taught in Catholic schools was primarily a matter of apprenticeship and practical experience. The academies operated by religious communities also functioned as informal teacher-training schools. Philip Gleason notes that these mechanisms were clearly inadequate. A number of factors, including the expansion of high schools, the setting of educational standards by new accrediting bodies, and the apparent intention on the part of states to exercise closer supervision over education at all levels, necessitated the preparation of a substantial number of teachers for Catholic schools.[9]

Given the central role of women religious in the emerging Catholic enterprise of parochial education, the establishment of means to provide sisters with professional training produced a number of innovations. At Catholic University, which announced in 1895 that it would admit lay persons, Gleason reports that the university annually rejected as many as twenty women applicants.[10] The administrators of the university maintained the traditional view that the sexes should be educated separately. This position forced Catholic women, including religious sisters, to attend secular institutions that many believed threatened their religious faith. Thus, when the Sisters of Notre Dame de Namur, whom Cynthia F. Brown analyzes in chapter 2, discussed with university officials their plans to open an academy for girls in the vicinity of Catholic University's campus in Washington, D.C., authorities urged them instead to establish a college. Though some conservatives raised objections to having a women's college located so close to the university, the Sisters persisted in their efforts and, in 1900, Trinity College opened its doors as the first Catholic women's college that did not emerge from an academy.

Gleason reports that the fourteen colleges for women that were included in the 1918 Catholic Education Association's (CEA) first list of accredited colleges, comprise a fairly representative sample of the approximately seventy institutions that came into existence in the first three decades of the twentieth century. Of these fourteen, only one, Trinity College, did not have its foundation as a Catholic girls' academy. The remaining colleges illustrate the most common pattern for the development of Catholic women's colleges, that is, the addition of collegiate studies to an existing academy.[11] Table 3.1 provides a list of the colleges that appeared on the CEA's accreditation list in 1918.

TABLE 3.1
Catholic Colleges for Women, Catholic Education Association's 1918 List of Accredited Colleges

College	*Location*	*Founded*	*Founding Order*
College of Notre Dame of Maryland	Maryland	1896	School Sisters of Notre Dame
St. Elizabeth's	New Jersey	1900	Sisters of Charity of New Jersey
Trinity	Washington, D.C.	1900	Sisters of Notre Dame de Namur
Rosary	Illinois	1901	Dominican Sisters of Sinsinawa
St. Mary's	Indiana	1903	Holy Cross Sisters
College of New Rochelle	New York	1904	Ursuline Sisters
College of St. Catherine	Minnesota	1905	Sisters of St. Joseph of Carondelet
Georgian Court	New Jersey	1908	Sisters of Mercy
D'Youville	New York	1908	Grey Nuns
Saint Mary-of-the-Woods	Indiana	1909	Sisters of Providence
College of St. Teresa	Minnesota	1910	Sisters of St. Francis
St. Xavier	Illinois	1915	Sisters of Mercy
Clarke	Iowa	1915	Sisters of Charity of the Blessed Virgin Mary
Marygrove	Michigan	1918	Sisters, Servants of the Immaculate Heart of Mary

Gleason further reports that between 1926 and 1949, the number of Catholic women's colleges approved for membership in the National Catholic Education Association (NCEA) increased from 25, with approximately 5,600 students, to 97, with about 32,000 students. These colleges varied in quality, but the better ones were truly exceptional places. For example, the College of St. Catherine in St. Paul had the first Phi Beta Kappa chapter of any Catholic institution and Trinity College in Washington, D.C. produced more Ph.D. candidates in the humanities and social sciences between 1936 and 1950 than any other college of its size in the country.[12]

Early Presidential Leadership

In her recent book on sponsorship, *Independence and a New Partnership in Catholic Higher Education,* Ursuline Sister Alice Gallin, historian and former executive director of the Association of Catholic Colleges and Universities, identifies a common early pattern of presidential leadership in Catholic colleges that congregations of women religious founded. Oftentimes, Gallin explains, the college president was also the head of the congregation, that is, the same woman held both leadership positions. In many cases, another sister held the position of college dean and functioned from that position as the actual chief administrator of the college.[13]

Such was the case in the history of the oldest Catholic women's college, the College of Notre Dame of Maryland. Founded in 1896 by the School Sisters of Notre Dame (S.S.N.D.), Sister Mary David Cameron reports the order chose as its founding president the head of the sisters' eastern province in Baltimore. Mother M. Theophila Bauer held the title of president until her death in 1904. At her side was the college's first dean, Sister Mary Meletia Foley, who served in that capacity from 1895 until her death in 1917.[14]

An early history of the college provides a picture of this first sister president. A native of Bavaria, Mother Theophila, came to the United States in 1848, in one of the first waves of sisters sent from the community's motherhouse in Munich, Germany, to educate the growing population of German immigrants. She was a recognized leader among the School Sisters of Notre Dame in United States and a likely choice to guide the new endeavor in higher education.

In 1877, after being named superior of the eastern province of the order in Baltimore, Mother Theophila took up residence at Notre Dame of Maryland and established the sisters' community while supervising the elementary and secondary schools that the sisters operated on campus. A tiny, dignified nun, her initial responsibilities included paying the debt for the campus land and supervising the construction of the college's buildings.

The college dean's primary responsibility was curriculum development. Sister M. Meletia Foley, a native of Wisconsin, became dean when the first class entered College of Notre Dame of Maryland. She had initially served as directress of the academy, formally called the Notre Dame of Maryland Collegiate Institute. Responding to the growing need to provide women with higher studies, she took a curriculum already advanced beyond typical secondary studies and developed it into a full baccalaureate degree program.[15]

The College of Mount Saint Vincent in Riverdale, New York, provides another example of an early model for presidential leadership, albeit a departure from the pattern established at many of the colleges women religious established, including those examined in chapter 2. Founded by the Sisters of Charity of New York, the College of Mount Saint Vincent has its roots in the Academy of Mount Saint Vincent, established in 1847. Late in the century, the academy began to offer post-secondary courses to students to provide the equivalent of one year of college work at the time of graduation.

In 1910, the sisters established the first women's college within New York City limits. The academy charter was officially amended and in the following year, the Regents of the State University of New York granted permission to confer baccalaureate degrees. However, unlike the College of Notre Dame of Maryland, where the head of the School Sisters of Notre

Dame became the first college president, the first president of the College of Mount Saint Vincent was New York Archbishop John Farley.

Church law governs religious life, and congregations of religious sisters may be either pontifical, which means they are under the authority of the pope, or diocesan, which places them under the direct authority of the local bishop. This further means that the appropriate Church authority approves the constitutions, or proper law governing the order. The Sisters of Charity of New York, a diocesan order, is thus under the authority of the head of the archdiocese of New York.

For most of the history of the College of Mount Saint Vincent, the head of the Archdiocese of New York served as the president of the college. While a Sister of Charity functioned as dean of the college and attended to the daily administrative duties a president usually performed, it was not until 1956, under the leadership of Cardinal Francis Spellman, that a Sister of Charity became president of the college. Sister Catharine Marie O'Brien, who had served as dean of the college since 1937, became the first Sister of Charity president.[16]

These two examples of early presidential leadership in Catholic women's colleges are not unique. This pattern was quite common and reflects the customary practice for these institutions in the first half of the twentieth century. However, following the Second World War, increases in enrollment and a movement within Catholic higher education to move Catholic institutions into the mainstream of American higher education produced further developments. In particular, the need to address educational issues pertinent to sisters and other women provided the means for sister presidents to become more visible and vocal.

One example comes from St. Mary's College in South Bend, Indiana. In the early 1940s, Catholic women's colleges were eager to improve their programs of religious education. However, the sisters and other women who constituted the majority of their faculties, could not prepare themselves by doing advanced work in theology since seminaries taught that subject and prohibited women from attending. To address this problem, the president of St. Mary's College in South Bend, Indiana, Sister Madeleva Wolff, began St. Mary's School of Theology in the summer of 1943. Gleason reports that in its first decade of operation, over nine hundred sisters and many lay women enrolled in the program, twenty-five of whom earned the doctorate and eighty-two the master's degree.[17] Sister Madeleva Wolff was a pioneer in her efforts to provide women access to theological education.

By the middle of the twentieth century, the Catholic women's colleges had closer connections with the teaching profession than did other Catholic institutions of higher education, and given the preponderance of women teachers, it is fair to say that many graduates of these colleges went into education. There is no question, according to Gleason, that the women religious who operated these colleges were closer to the teaching profession than were other Catholic educators, and as a result were attuned to the developments in education, particularly in emerging certification requirements.[18]

The shift toward coeducation in Catholic colleges and universities had a significant impact on the women's colleges. Although only about one in five Catholic schools was coeducational, Gleason reports that many presidents of women's colleges remained skeptical of the trend.[19] They were particularly disturbed by men's schools that became coeducational without consulting the women's colleges in the area. In some cases, the men's colleges competed unfairly by offering women students lower tuition and other incentives. Although economic necessity doubtless played a role, women religious involved in Catholic higher education were deeply troubled by this injustice, which may have contributed to their new spirit of assertiveness manifested in the 1950s.

That assertiveness, coupled with a desire for more professional development on the part of Catholic women religious, is apparent in the Sister Formation Movement that emerged in the 1950s and that had as one of its main objectives the determination to improve the training of teaching sisters. One of the effects of this movement was the increase in the number of Catholic women's colleges, which had already been multiplying throughout the twentieth century.

The need to provide women religious with professional studies was connected to the formation, or religious training, of sisters. The leaders of many religious congregations favored an integrated program where academic and spiritual elements were properly combined. They took the position that this could only be provided when the young sisters were kept separate from lay students. As a result, the Sisters Formation Movement produced educational institutions known variously as juniorates, motherhouse colleges, or Sister-Formation colleges.

Most of these colleges for sisters could not meet the basic criteria for accreditation. By 1960, there were ninety-three such institutions with enrollments of fewer than fifty-five students; over half had been founded since 1950; and only three were accredited. Fearing the consequences of these actions, the executive committee of the college and university department of the National Catholic Education Association formally expressed its concern at "the undue multiplication of new, small, unaccredited Catholic colleges."[20] However, the determination to provide higher education to religious sisters and other women continued to motivate religious congregations to found new colleges despite the opposition of the NCEA.

This was the case at La Roche College, a small, Catholic college in western Pennsylvania. Founded in 1963 by the Congregation of Divine Providence, it was not until 1984 at the funeral mass for the founder of the college, Mother Mary Kenneth Kearns, that the homilist, the Most Reverend John B. McDowell, Auxiliary Bishop, D.D., Ph.D., told the following story.[21]

Bishop McDowell relates that in the early 1960s, the NCEA had commissioned a study, endorsed by the National Conference of Catholic bishops, to look into the establishment of new Catholic colleges. The study showed there were too many small colleges, and because they were small many questioned both the education and Catholic value. The mortality rate for such colleges was high, and so the bishops decided to do everything possible to prevent their establishment.

The Bishop of Pittsburgh, John J. Wright, told McDowell to establish rigid rules to prevent such colleges from being established in his diocese. McDowell established a blue ribbon committee to govern the establishment of new colleges in Pittsburgh. The committee instituted strict regulations, including five rules that he believed were virtually impossible to meet. McDowell related in his homily that "I liked to characterize the rules as conditions drawn up by the Harvard board of directors which would govern the establishment of Yale."

Without meeting these rigid requirements, no Catholic college could gain approval by the diocese for foundation. Many religious orders in Pittsburgh that wanted to establish colleges declined when they read the requirements. Mother Mary Kenneth made an appointment to see Bishop McDowell, who at the time was responsible for all Catholic education in the diocese. Mother Mary Kenneth told the bishop of her desire to begin a new college in the North Hills of Pittsburgh with a mission to educate sisters. The bishop tried to dissuade her, but she was determined. He finally gave her the strict requirements the blue ribbon panel established, assuming that was the last he would hear about the matter. He related in his homily, "She never said a word."

To his utter dismay, Mother Mary Kenneth returned several months later having fulfilled all the requirements, including the five rules. She announced to him, "We're ready to go!" Bishop McDowell had no choice but to allow her to proceed with plans to found La Roche College. Within weeks, the Commonwealth issued the charter, and, to add insult to injury, according to McDowell, she asked him and Bishop Wright to serve on the first board of directors. While Mother Mary Kenneth Kearns was never president of La Roche College, it was her leadership in the religious order and her determination that propelled this college into existence at a time when the Church leadership was opposed to such actions.

The Transformation of Catholic Higher Education

The 1960s can best be described as a decade of tremendous upheaval in the Catholic Church. The Second Vatican Council, 1962–65, an assembly of the world's bishops to address issues of renewal, modernization, and ecumenism, resulted in significant changes in the Catholic Church and in its institutions. For Catholic colleges and universities, 1966 marked a period in which there was a "sudden and dramatic trend toward 'secularization' of Catholic higher education," which changed the relationship between Catholic educational institutions and the religious orders that founded them and owned them.[22] In the late 1960s, many schools transferred formal ownership of their colleges to a lay board of trustees. Some comment is necessary here to underscore further the importance of this change in governance structure and of its impact on the position of president.

In the mid-to-late 1960s, the American Catholic institutions of higher education began drastically to change their individual institutional governance formations. Prior to that time nearly all Catholic colleges and universities were either dependent subsystems of the sponsoring religious order or were independent corporations that mandated that members of the sponsoring religious order serve as board members. There were several motivations behind this change in governance structure.[23]

First, the themes of pragmatic change and cultural adaptation that characterized the Second Vatican Council certainly had an effect on the Catholic Church in general and on these institutions in particular. The documents that emerged from Vatican II clearly emphasized a new role for the laity in the Church and it can be surmised, within Catholic institutions as well. Second, this atmosphere of post–Vatican Council openness "combined with economic, political and social forces in the United States to create a climate in which the inclusion of laypersons on governing boards seemed philosophically, morally, and pragmatically desirable."[24]

Thus, in the late 1960s and the 1970s, many Catholic colleges and universities changed their governance structures to conform to the American normative standard. They accomplished this by formally separating the college or university from the founding order and by including laypeople as voting members on these new independent boards of trustees. These changes also moved Catholic colleges to a better legal position to receive federal and state support and helped to remove from the religious orders the heavy financial burden of supporting these colleges and universities.

This initiative to separate religious orders from the colleges they founded was not totally without modification. Many orders retained some control over the institutions they founded by instituting a two-tiered governance system. In these cases, the top tier is composed solely of the leadership of the founding religious order and is the highest authority at the college. The second tier, the board of directors of the college, often has significant representation from the founders as well. In other cases, many orders were able to reserve certain powers, for instance, addressing such areas as changes in the mission, dissolution of the corporation, transfer of property, and selection of the president.

Changes in the governance structure and in the composition of boards of trustees were precursors to what was to follow in terms of changes in presidential leadership of Catholic colleges. A number of studies of the American college presidency conducted in the past two decades explains the changing profile of women presidents overall and sister presidents particularly.

In the late 1970s, the Committee on College Sponsorship of the Association of Catholic Colleges and Universities (ACCU), commissioned a study on the Catholic college presidency. The author of the study, Louis Gatto, at the time president of Marian College, states that "Initially, the study was intended to survey only the lay presidents of Catholic institutions of higher education in an effort to learn more about them."[25] However, as the committee formulated the questions and refined the survey instrument, its members decided that the study would be more significant if it were expanded to include all 211 presidents of the ACCU membership. The survey garnered a 69 percent response rate.

It is not surprising that over ten years after changing the governance structure of Catholic institutions, there was growing interest in learning about their presidents. Of the 146 respondents, there were eighty males and sixty-six females. The study revealed that the vast majority of Catholic college presidents were still members of religious orders. In fact, 78 percent of the respondents were priests, brothers, or sisters. Of the thirty-two lay presidents who answered the survey, only two were women. In other words, as late as the early 1980s, 97 percent of the women presidents of Catholic colleges were sisters.

The study revealed some mildly intriguing facts about the sisters who were presidents of Catholic colleges in the early 1980s. The median age for the sister presidents was 54.5 years of age, in comparison to the priest and brother presidents at 52, and the lay president median age of 49. These sister presidents had an average presidential tenure of about five and one-half years in comparison to six years for the male religious and only three and one-half years for all the lay presidents. Of the two women presidents who were not sisters, one was married and had one child.

In a broader study of college presidents conducted by the American Council on Education (ACE) Center for Leadership Development, Madeleine Green reveals some other facts about the changing face of the American college presidency. Of the 2,105 presidents who responded to the survey in 1986, only 200 were women and of these, thirty percent, or sixty, were members of religious orders.[26] While it is safe to say that in the broader arena of American higher education, sister presidents were no longer the predominant women presidents, what was happening in the institutions which they initially founded? What do scholars know about sister presidents today? Do they continue to represent the majority of presidents in the colleges founded by women's religious orders? Again, it is necessary to look more broadly at the picture of these institutions to adequately get a picture of the women who lead them.

The Sister Presidents Today

It might be safe to say that even today there are few sister presidents with name recognition beyond the vicinity of their own campus. However, there are some sister presidents who have made significant contributions to American higher education. For example, Franciscan Sister Joel Read, president of Alverno College, a Catholic women's college in Milwaukee, has presided over that college's rise to national prominence in the area of competency-based assessment.

Perhaps the only sister president to head a non-denominational college is Holy Names Sister Kathleen Ross, the founding president of Heritage College. Situated on the reservation lands of the Yakama Indian Nation in central Washington, Heritage College was founded in 1982 to serve a place-bound population of Native Americans and Hispanics who had no other opportunities to pursue higher studies. Ross was recently awarded a prestigious MacArthur Fellowship for her efforts on behalf of multicultural higher education.

There are many other sister presidents who have had distinguished careers as Catholic college presidents. However, in the late 1970s, leaders of the colleges founded by women religious began to see the advantages of collaborating as a group of institutions with a common heritage. The collective power and resources of these colleges could accomplish what few could do alone. The time was right to explore this collaborative advantage.

Today the colleges and universities the congregations of women religious founded are commonly known in Catholic higher education circles as the Neylan colleges. Neylan is the surname of two biological sisters, Edith and Genevieve Neylan, who bequeathed a sum of money to support the work of sisters in higher education. The story of the Neylan colleges begins in 1978, when nine presidents and six other sisters, representing eleven of these colleges, met in an informal group to seek ways to enhance the educational leadership of their colleges. The participants in this initial conference, representing some of the oldest Catholic women's colleges, were among the leaders in women's Catholic higher education. The minutes of this meeting indicate that at the time there were some ninety-six sister presidents in the United States, and the nine attending presidents concluded that it was time to discuss the future of these institutions.

The group raised a number of concerns. Who speaks for Catholic higher education, especially the small liberal arts college with a particular mission to women? What is the relationship of these colleges to the founding religious congregations? How can the presidents speak to the special concerns of women's colleges, including identity, role, values, or as coeducational colleges with a special concern for the roles of women? Why do these colleges lack visibility in the wider world, and what is the image of sister presidents?

Underneath all these issues was a basic concern for survival. Will the colleges sisters founded live into the twenty-first century?[27]

The participants of this first meeting stated for the minutes that "The central question then became, how shall we move into the twenty-first century among such currents, keeping our institutions in a growth posture? Inevitably, it was thought, some will not meet the challenges of these currents, but nonetheless, the leadership among Catholic higher education ought to explore together ways of doing so, laying out options, strategies, etc., to build the future. For, like it or not, we have come to the end of an era, and though we have a strong and proud tradition in our past, our responsibility is to the future." This visionary group of women made a goal statement at this time proclaiming, "As a group of administrators in Catholic college settings, we propose to position ourselves in such a way as to be able to contribute to shaping, the changing role of women, the emerging forms of ministry in the church, the changing forms of higher education and in so doing to gain national visibility for Catholic higher education with a particular mission for women."[28]

The most significant outcome of this meeting was the establishment of a support system to assist the presidents with the task of planning for the future of these colleges. That organization became known initially as the Neylan Conference, and later, by its present title, the Neylan Commission. Perhaps what is most important about the establishment of the Neylan Commission in the late 1970s, is the realization by the sister presidents that it was time to act collectively, to come together as a group of institutions to accomplish what alone no college could.

In the 1980s, the Neylan Commission sponsored four national conferences that brought together sisters and others, primarily women, who were engaged in the work of higher education. The participants for the most part were all affiliated with colleges sponsored by women's orders. These conferences addressed the role of women religious in higher education and explored areas for collaboration among these institutions. Among the early initiatives was an Outreach to Minorities project at ten Neylan colleges that focused on ways to increase minority recruitment and retention.

The Neylan colleges and universities currently number 117. Using the Carnegie classification system, there are forty-seven masters and fifty-one baccalaureate granting institutions, and nineteen colleges awarding associate degrees. Twenty-eight of these institutions are women's colleges. Nonetheless, with a total enrollment of 209,154 students, 76 percent of students attending these colleges are women. An examination of a recent government report on graduates indicates that women graduates of these colleges have a strong commitment to service professions as evidenced by the fact that in 1995 the three top degrees awarded were in the Health Professions and Related Sciences, Education, and Business.

While sisters constitute the majority of top-level leadership in Catholic colleges founded by orders, the number of other women presidents and men presidents of Catholic colleges has increased significantly over the past two decades. Today 70 percent of the presidents of Neylan colleges and universities are women. There are eighty-two women and thirty-five men presidents at these colleges. Of the women presidents, fifty-seven are sisters.

Not surprisingly, there remains much concern over the transition from a majority of sister presidents to other presidents and this is actually addressed more broadly in terms of discussions over how the legacy of the founding religious congregations will be maintained in the future as the number of sisters serving in these institutions decreases. This is what is at the crux of the transition from sister presidents to lay presidents, the importance of continuing the commitment to educating women and other underserved populations in the future.

In recent research on what is the nature of Catholic identity at American Catholic colleges founded by women's congregations, Candace Introcaso found that where Catholic identity is strongest, the president plays a key role in transmitting the legacy of the founders. Presidential leadership is critically important to maintaining a Catholic identity, and the president is vital to the clarification and articulation of an institution's Catholic identity. Included in this study were presidents who are members of founding religious congregations as well as other women presidents. The findings indicate there is very little difference between sister presidents and other presidents in terms of the Catholic identity of the college. The difference lies in *intentionality,* that is, lay presidents make the articulation of the Catholic identity more deliberate. What may formerly have been taken for granted when the visible head of the college was a sister must now be voiced.[29]

Can lay presidents say and do things that a sister president cannot? People interviewed at colleges with lay presidents answered affirmatively. The members of religious congregations interviewed in this study often expressed humility as a reason for not publicly recalling the contributions of the founders. The value placed upon humility is historically part of the life of sisters, who often do not adequately articulate their achievements. So, even in their own colleges, they were reluctant to emphasize their own contributions. Lay presidents bring a certain credibility to the process of recalling the importance of the founding congregation to the college or university, a process that may be unavailable to a sister president since such an action might appear to be self-serving.

The full story of sister presidents is still waiting to be told. Retrieving the countless individual stories of courage and determination, including those recounted in chapter 2, from the archives of religious congregations and their colleges will take a concerted effort on the part of historians and archivists. It may take a revisionist's approach to capture the true contributions of scores of women who were pioneers in providing higher education for so many women. It may take a process of transformation, that is, going back to reclaim what has been lost, whether in the name of humility, or in a time period when the contributions of all women, not just sister presidents, did not receive adequate recognition. Truly, the legacy of the first women presidents is alive at the colleges and universities that continue to hold a commitment to educating women and in the women presidents who continue that commitment.

Notes

1. Magdalen Coughlin, "A Heritage with Purpose: Women Religious in Higher Education," in *A Call to New Leadership: Women Religious in the Ministry of Higher Education Conference Report* (Baltimore, Md.: College of Notre Dame of Maryland Public Relations Office, 1983), 1.
2. Ibid.
3. Edward J. Power, *Catholic Higher Education in America: A History* (New York: Appleton-Century-Crofts, 1972), 25–26.
4. Barbara Miller Solomon, *In the Company of Educated Women: A History of Women and Higher Education in America* (New Haven: Yale University Press, 1985), 14.
5. Frederick Rudolph, *The American College and University: A History* (New York: A. Knopf, 1962), 310–11.
6. Power, *Catholic Higher Education*, 273.
7. Ibid.
8. Ibid.
9. Philip Gleason, *Contending with Modernity* (New York: Oxford University Press, 1995), 87.
10. Ibid., 10.
11. Ibid., 89.
12. Ibid., 227.
13. Alice Gallin, *Independence and a New Partnership in Catholic Higher Education* (Notre Dame, Ind.: University of Notre Dame Press, 1996), 5.
14. Mary David Cameron, *The College of Notre Dame of Maryland 1895–1945* (New York: Declan X McMullen Company, Inc., 1947), 112–13. See also *The Heritage We Claim,* College of Notre Dame of Maryland, Centennial Anniversary Publication, 1996, 13.
15. Ibid., 117.
16. Public Relations Department, College of Mount Saint Vincent, 1994. See also Richard P. McBrien, ed., *The HarperCollins Encyclopedia of Catholicism* (San Francisco: HarperCollins Publishers, 1995), 1098.
17. Gleason, *Contending with Modernity*, 258–59.

18. Ibid., 227.

19. Ibid.

20. Ibid., 234.

21. For full text, see Most Rev. John B. McDowell, sermon, June 11, 1984, Congregation of Divine Providence Archives, Allison Park, Pennsylvania.

22. Andrew M. Greeley, *From Backwater to Mainstream: A Profile of Catholic Higher Education* (New York: McGraw-Hill, 1969), 17.

23. Martin J. Stamm, "Report in the Governance of American Catholic Higher Education Institutions in 1992," in *Current Issues in Catholic Higher Education: Catholic Education: New Partnerships in the Service of the Church* (Washington, D.C.: Association of Catholic Colleges and Universities), 10.

24. Ibid.

25. Louis Gatto, "The Catholic College Presidency: A Study," in *Current Issues in Catholic Higher Education: Purposes in Leadership* (Washington, D.C.: Association of Catholic Colleges and Universities), 24.

26. Madeline F. Green, *The American College President: A Contemporary Profile* (Washington, D.C.: American Council on Education, 1988), 8.

27. Minutes of the First Neylan Conference. St. Mary-of-the-Woods College, June 1978.

28. Ibid.

29. Candace Introcaso, "The Strength of Institutional Culture: Reframing Catholic Identity," Ph.D. diss., Claremont Graduate School, 1996, 391.

CHAPTER 4

At the Top of the Faculty

Women as Chief Academic Officers

KAREN DOYLE WALTON AND SHARON A. McDADE

The faculty is the heart and soul of any academic institution. At the top of the faculty is the chief academic officer (CAO)—bearing the title of provost, vice president for academic affairs, or dean, among others. The CAO provides leadership for all academic operations—the core business of higher education.[1] Her responsibilities include the academic curriculum, faculty, students, and budget. No administrator other than the president, as illustrated in chapters 2, 3, and 5, has such an institutionally broad range of responsibilities, has oversight of such a large segment of the institution's finances, or affects so many of the institution's employees or customers. Hence the CAO is usually the second in command after the president of the college or university. The chief academic position is the stepping stone to the presidency for one-quarter of the presidents,[2] making it the most fertile preparation for that highest office.

Despite the irrefutable importance of the CAO, scholars of higher education administration have written little about that position in general, and even less about women who serve as CAOs. Although previous studies address the relationships between the two top positions from the perspective of the presidency (and usually in retrospect), few scholars examine the historical or contemporary careers of CAOs. Extant CAO surveys include insufficient women to support valid gender comparisons. One study that related leadership behaviors of men and women CAOs found no significant differences; and when they were perceived to exist, they tended to have more to do with the gender of the evaluator than the gender of the CAOs.[3]

The project described below is important because it is the first study to profile women CAOs of United States colleges and universities and to document their career paths. In the last twenty-five years, there have been five major, comprehensive studies of the presidency[4] in addition to numerous other publications. However, besides a few doctoral dissertations, small-scale studies, and hortatory articles, Kathryn M. Moore's 1983 study of career paths of provosts, deans, and presidents provides the only serious national data on CAOs.

Women are underrepresented in senior positions within higher education. Furthermore, there are too few scholarly studies of their contributions to higher education.[5] Women comprise the majority of higher-education students, but women faculty fare poorly compared to men with respect to rank, tenure, and salary. In 1992, only 36% of the 717,334 full- and part-time faculty were women, including 50% of lecturers, 47% of instructors, 43% of assistant professors, and 41% of associate professors, but only 18% of full professors. In 1991, 75% of full-time male faculty were tenured, compared to only 58% of full-time female faculty.[6] Women professors are concentrated in traditional women's areas such as nursing (98%) and education (56%), in contrast to engineering (6%) and the natural sciences (23%).[7]

In 1996, women earned less than their male counterparts in each academic rank: $32,090 versus $35,720 for lecturers, $30,340 versus $31,550 for instructors, $38,630 versus $41,250 for assistant professors, $46,030 versus $49,390 for associate professors, and $58,990 versus $66,740 for full professors.[8] Men outnumbered women in senior positions in administration at all types of institutions, coming closest to parity only in external affairs (48% women) and student services (47% women).[9] In 1995, 453 women held college and university presidencies (16% of all institutions), including 277 who headed 14.9% of the 1,855 four-year colleges and universities.[10] Although these figures are low in absolute terms, they are high in relative terms, since the percentage of female presidents of colleges and universities is higher than the percentage of female CEOs of most other significant social institutions in the world.[11]

Of the 453 women presidents in 1993,[12] 26% were chief academic officers immediately preceding their presidencies (33% at public four-year institutions). Thus, to fully understand the dynamics of women moving into presidencies, it is necessary to study women in the CAO position, because the ascent of women into top leadership positions does not happen by accident, as other chapters in this volume confirm.[13] This study addresses three questions: (1) Who are the women in CAO positions in four-year colleges and universities? (2) What are their career paths and aspirations? and (3) What factors influence their pursuit of these aspirations? Women in CAO positions remain anomalies; most women who rise to the position are the first of their gender in that role at their institutions, making female CAOs boundary breakers within the internal organization of colleges and universities.

The CAO Position in the Literature

There is very little documentation, historical or otherwise, on the academic vice presidency. Perhaps this is because the CAO position is a relatively recent innovation in higher education. In fact, the first was not appointed for more than two hundred years after the founding of Harvard College, when Ephraim Gurney became its dean in 1870.[14] Previously, the president, with the assistance of faculty, performed the necessary academic administrative tasks.[15] Most CAO literature consists of personal essays. Little is empirically based, and all is dated.

In 1984, Louise Allen provided a descriptive profile of the typical CAO. Allen's essay,[16] although not empirically based, drew on her years as a CAO and presented her observations on the job. According to Allen, a typical CAO was a Caucasian male in his late 40s or early 50s, articulate, well-read, and "usually rather good-looking."[17] He held an academic-discipline doctorate, although sometimes in higher-education administration, and continued to do limited instruction, advisement, and research. He rose to the CAO position through a career path of professor, department chair, and dean. While he still occasionally attended his academic discipline's conventions and perhaps even presented a paper, for the most part his job made it increasingly difficult to continue his research, and his focus was shifting to administration.

The typical CAO was a member of several administrator organizations, a frequent consultant for an accrediting agency, and a member of the boards of educational entities. As CAO in the early 1980s, he earned between $30,000 and $60,000, depending on the size of the institution. He spent the majority of his career at the same type of institution; and if he became a president, it was at the same type of college or university. According to Allen, the 5 percent of all CAOs at that time who were female were mostly at women's colleges or members of Catholic religious orders and were similar to male CAOs in terms of personal demographics and career paths,[18] an assertion other studies support.[19]

Literature on the CAO position reinforces its reputation as "the toughest job in any college or university."[20] The CAO is in a delicate but pivotal position with respect to faculty, students, and administration. In one way or the other, the CAO controls or influences curriculum, instruction, and educational values.[21]

Since the CAO is typically the second in command after the president, the alliance must be close and work well for the health and growth of the institution.[22] A common model for this alliance has the president addressing an institution's outside audiences. The CAO, however, serves the inside constituencies, primarily the faculty and students.

Perhaps because of these outside/inside roles, the previous literature rarely linked the CAO with fund raising, the major outside responsibility of a president. However, it is of note that a campus figure who asserts such significant power and responsibility regarding the institution's mission has been absent from the fund raising responsibility that has gained significant magnitude over the past fifteen years. While the CAO position may have been the springboard position to a presidency in previous decades when academic expertise was the *sine qua non* for leadership success, now presidential search committees highly value fund-raising experience. Felicetti challenged CAOs to become more involved in fund raising and commented that CAOs who fail to do so will have difficulty in making the transition to a presidency.[23]

The criteria for selection as a CAO generally includes a doctoral degree, some faculty experience, presumably including teaching and scholarship; knowledge of curriculum development and evaluation; the ability to work well with all types of people; the capacity to provide leadership; and the ability to solve problems.[24] While CAOs in several studies admitted that experience as a researcher and teacher were not necessary preparation for the role, there is agreement across studies that degrees and scholarly pedigrees earn CAOs respect from their faculty constituency. In those studies, CAOs felt the most important preparation was experience in other administrative positions, where they learned the business of higher education, budgeting, political skills, understanding, and patience.[25] CAOs also cited linkage in networks and participation in professional development programs as key learning opportunities, providing skills not fully developed as they ascended the ranks.[26]

Methodology and Data Sources

In order to provide a baseline of data about women chief academic officers, a fifty-three-item survey was developed and pilot tested in the winter of 1991. The instrument included questions derived with permission from two sources: the 1985 survey of women college and university presidents conducted by the ACE Office of Women in Higher Education[27] and Kathryn Moore's 1983 survey entitled "Leaders in Transition."[28] Questions solicited biographical and employment information as well as data about job characteristics and career aspirations.

The survey included the 1,378 four-year colleges and universities in the United States in the Carnegie classification categories of Research I and II, Doctoral I and II, Master's comprehensive I and II, and Baccalaureate liberal arts I and II, excluding professional and specialized institutions. Phone calls were made to the offices of any CAOs for whom gender could not be determined solely through names.[29] This process yielded 208 female CAOs representing 15.1 percent of the qualifying institutions.

Each female CAO received a packet including a cover letter on stationary from the Pennsylvania American Council on Education's National Identification

Program for the Advancement of Women in Higher Education Administration (PACE/NIP). Over four months during the spring of 1991, two mailings of the survey packet and two follow-up postcards yielded 179 completed surveys for an 86 percent response rate. Analysis included descriptive statistics such as frequencies and tests of statistical significance (chi-square, t-tests, and ANOVA) using SPSS. Percentages for missing data (no response) are not reported.

Women in CAO Positions in Four-Year Colleges and Universities

Institutional Characteristics

The largest single group of women CAOs (49.7%) were at Baccalaureate I and II liberal arts colleges, while 35.8% were at Master's I and II comprehensive institutions, and 12.8% at Research I and II, Doctorate I and II, universities. ANOVA showed significant differences between institution groups with female CAOs based on Carnegie Classification and size, using average enrollment figures of 1,141 at liberal arts institutions, 4,961 at comprehensive institutions, and 10,186 at doctorate-granting institutions. Few women have broken into the ranks of CAO positions at large doctoral institutions. Twenty-three, or 12.8%, were at women's colleges. Two-thirds of the women CAOs were at independent institutions, including 63.7% of those at liberal arts institutions, 28.2% at comprehensive institutions, and 6.5% at doctoral/research institutions.

Personal Characteristics

The average age of the women CAOs was 52.7 years. Approximately one-eighth (12.8%) of the respondents indicated that they were members of minority groups, including African-American 6.7%, Hispanic/Latina 2.8%, and Native American .6%. Most of the women (92%) were born in the United States. Catholics comprised 38.0% of the women; 30.2% Protestant, 10.1% Jewish, 11.7% other religions, and 10.1% with no religious preference. One-fifth (20.7%) were members of Catholic religious orders, representing 54.4% of the total Catholic women CAOs. Almost half of the women (45.8%) were married, a third (30.7%) had never been married, 16.8% were separated or divorced, 3.4% widowed, and 1.7% had a committed partner. Among married CAOs, 72.0% were in first marriages. Half of the women (49.7%) had children.

First-born children (55.9%) were overrepresented; 13.4% were second of two children, 18.4% were middle of three or more children, and 10.1% were youngest children. Someone other than parents reared only five respondents.

While the women CAOs were in high school, more than half (52.0%) of their mothers worked outside the home, most of them working full-time. Half of the parents had at least some college education, including 43.5% of mothers and 47.4% of fathers. A quarter of the fathers (22.3%) had graduate or professional degrees, as did 9.5% of the mothers. Most fathers had white collar (34.6%) or professional jobs (31.3%); of the mothers who worked outside the home, 20.1% were in white-collar jobs and 10.6% in education.

Educational Background

Women's college alumnae represented 36.9% of the respondents, with Wellesley College graduating four, the largest group. Major baccalaureate fields listed in decreasing frequency were English, history, education, sociology, French, chemistry, nursing, mathematics, biology, and economics, with English majors being more than twice as numerous as any other. Most (96.1%) had doctoral degrees (84.4% PhD, 10.1% Ed.D.) with the remaining having professional degrees. In descending order, doctorate fields were humanities/fine arts, social sciences, education, and the sciences. Columbia University granted doctorates to eight of these women, the largest alma mater group. They financed their doctoral degrees through teaching assistantships (44.1%), fellowships (35.8%), research assistantships (25.1%), work on grants (15.6%), other appointments (8.4%), administration (4.5%), and residence hall supervision (2.8%). Ten (5.6%) had received honorary degrees.

Professional Background

Since CAOs serve as leaders of their institutions' faculties, there is an expectation of faculty experience and publications. Half (49.2%) were tenured, but some institutions' statutes preclude administrators from academic rank and tenure. However, women CAOs at doctorate-granting universities were more often tenured than those at other types of institutions. The women CAOs held all academic ranks: 68.2% were full professors, 14.0% were associate professors, 1.1% assistant professors, 1.1% at the instructor rank, and the rest were ineligible for academic rank because of their institutions' policies concerning administrative positions. While most of the women had published, 6.7% had never done so. Most (83.6%) had written at least one article or monograph; 43.0% had co-authored an article or monograph. A quarter of the women had authored or co-authored at least one book (25.2% and 24.0%), 22.8% had edited an article or monograph, and 17.9% had edited a book.

On average, women CAOs had spent 21.7 years in higher education. More than half (58.1%) had participated in at least one of the major professional development programs. ACE/National Identification Program (NIP) has been an important professional-development connection for women CAOs;

39.7% participated in the ACE/NIP networks, and 22.3% in an ACE/NIP National Forum. As for the major national professional-development programs, 15.6% of the CAOs had participated in Harvard's Institute for Educational Management, 12.3% in the HERS/Bryn Mawr Program, and 8.4% had been ACE Fellows. Of those who participated, the following percentages of the respondents viewed the activity as being directly related to their advancement: 15.5% for ACE/NIP, 22.5% for ACE Forum, 33.0% for IEM, 50.0% for HERS/Bryn Mawr, and 80.0% for the ACE Fellowship Program.

Women in the CAO Position

For 80.4% of the women, these were their first CAO positions; however, 10.1% were holding their second CAO jobs, 7.8% their third, and 1.1% were in fourth CAO positions. At the time of the survey, 64% had been CAO for five years or fewer, 19.0% six to ten years, and 10.2% eleven to nineteen years. Only 5.0% of the respondents stated that the CAO job had always been a goal; another 49.2% noted that it had become a goal as they ascended the administrative ladder.

However, 21.8% answered that the job had been thrust upon them, but they grew to like it; or it was suggested to them as their duty (4.5%). More than half (54.2%) indicated that they were "intentional" as opposed to "unintentional" administrators.[30] Reasons (high or very high) for moving to a CAO position included: (1) the challenge of the duties and responsibilities (86.6%), (2) attraction to the mission of the institution (77.7%), (3) competence of colleagues (65.9%), (4) congeniality of colleagues (65.9%), (5) readiness for a change (64.8%), (6) geographic location of the institution (50.3%), (7) salary (40.8%), (8) increased status and responsibility (40.8%), (9) potential for advancement (36.9%), (10) institution's physical facilities (19.0%), (11) retirement plan benefits (15.6%), (12) spouse employment opportunities (10%), and (13) family education opportunities (8.4%).

Approximately one-quarter of the women CAOs made salaries over $90,000 in 1990–91. The salary range distribution included 3.4% making less than $40,000; 11.2% making $40,000 to $49,999; 19.0% making $50,000 to $59,999; 12.3% making $60,000 to $69,999; 14.0% making $70,000 to $79,999; and 12.3% making $80,000 to $89,999. The lower salaries were for positions at liberal arts and comprehensive colleges. The lowest salaries for women CAOs at doctorate-granting salaries were in the $60,000-plus range, with 70.0% of these CAOs earning over $90,000. The fact that larger numbers of women CAOs are members of religious orders accounts for the lower salaries for comprehensive and liberal arts institutions. Traditionally, salaries for members of religious orders are low, in keeping with the service orientation of their religious vows. Chapters 2 and 3 underscore the essentially altruistic nature of these women.

Obtaining the CAO Position

Women pursued CAO positions by increasing their activities on several fronts. Almost half (42.5%) began reading advertisements for CAO jobs in *The Chronicle of Higher Education*. Many took active steps to increase their professional visibility (39.7%), sought professional-development activities to enhance their strengths (39.7%), told well-placed male (32.4%) and female (29.1%) colleagues of their career interests, developed new contacts (26.3%), and asked people for nominations (25.1%). Other strategies for obtaining the CAO position included seeking professional-development opportunities to address deficiencies (25.1%), talking with members of the ACE/NIP staff (16.8%), becoming acquainted with CAOs (10.6%), and seeking major speaking opportunities (8.4%). Only 2.8% contacted or were contacted by executive search firms. Nominations were statistically more important for women who became CAOs at doctoral institutions (ratio of 3 to 1) and less important at comprehensive and liberal arts institutions (ratio of 1 to 2).

The most common first recruitment contact was through a nomination (40.8%). Other sorts of initial contacts included encouragement by the institution (31.3%), direct application without nomination (25.7%), and contact by a search committee chair (15.6%) or committee members (7.8%). Almost half (44.1%) of the women CAOs were internal candidates for their positions, with 20.7% receiving direct appointments to their positions, and 17.9% initially served as acting CAOs.

CAOs had varying opinions of the characteristics that were of greatest importance to the search committee, the president, and themselves regarding their appointments. The women maintained that search committees emphasized educational philosophy and vision (56.4%), personal style and presence (54.7%), and administrative experience (48.6%), followed by scholarship (29.6%). The CAOs contended that presidents placed greatest emphasis on philosophy and vision (72.6%), personal style and presence (64.2%), administrative experience (63.7%), and political acuity (31.3%). Scholarship ranked seventh in perceived presidents' priorities at 22.8%. The women themselves ranked philosophy and vision first (81.6%), personal style and presence second (70.4%), administrative experience third (66.5%), and political acuity fourth (45.8%). In retrospect, women CAOs wished they had tended to more of the practical issues of their terms of employment during their initial negotiations. They wished they had paid more attention to sabbatical leaves (28.5%), other leaves of absences (21.2%), involuntary-separation policy (21.2%), entertainment budget (20.7%), and performance evaluation (20.1%).

Current Orientation to the Job

In general, the women CAOs were satisfied with their performance: 66.5% strongly agreed that they were doing a good job; another 32.4% agreed. Only

7.2% concluded that they were not working well with their president, 2.3% were not working well with the other senior officers, and only one CAO noted she was not working well with her faculty. Satisfaction ratings for the job were high: 52.5% were highly satisfied, 36.9% were satisfied, and 8.9% were somewhat satisfied. After years in the position, CAOs wished that they had more experience and training in financial management (44.7%), conflict resolution (38.0%), negotiation skills (35.8%), and federal and state policy issues (31.3%).

Women CAOs at doctorate-granting institutions expressed a different orientation to their needs. Those women felt they had sufficient experience in financial management (74.2%) and conflict-resolution (83.9%). Women CAOs at liberal arts institutions (45.5%) felt more of a need for conflict resolution training than did CAOs at doctoral institutions (19.4%), suggesting that since liberal arts institutions are smaller, those CAOs spent more time adjudicating personnel disputes and felt less prepared for this part of their jobs. Women CAOs at liberal arts institutions also wished they had more experience in administrative ranks before ascending to the CAO position (26.1%), compared to those at doctorate-granting institutions (3.2%). It may be that the number of administrative career rungs are fewer at liberal arts institutions because of their smaller size than at doctoral institutions where, because of larger size, there are more and a greater variety of line and staff administrative positions in which aspiring CAOs can gain experience.

Why stay in the CAO job? Reasons "high" or "very high" were similar to those that attracted the women to the jobs in the first place. Substantial numbers of women remained in the job because of the duties and responsibilities of the position (89.3%), mission and philosophy of the institution (83.8%), congeniality (71.5%) and competence (70.9%) of colleagues, geographic location (52.5%), increased status and prestige (45.3%), and salary (43.0%).

Career Aspirations of Women CAOs

Almost half the women CAOs had not participated in any searches in the past five years (46.9%). Others, however, were greatly in demand: 34.2% had been in multiple searches (11.7% in two searches, 16.8% in three to five, 5.7% in six to twenty). Of those involved in searches, 31.8% had been offered other CAO positions but refused or declined the offers, while 26.8% withdrew from CAO searches before they received offers.

When considering career options within the next three to five years, 63.1% aspired to a presidency, while only 22.3% thought a presidency was a likely next move. When contemplating their futures, these women CAOs expressed a variety of preferences. The largest percentage preferred remaining in their current CAO positions (36.9%), while others contemplated moving to a presidency at another institution (24.0%), becoming CAO at another institution (14.0%), returning to the faculty (11.2%), becoming president at the current institution (10.1%), retiring (5.6%), or leaving higher education (2.8%).

Statistically significant differences in career aspirations appeared across institutional groups. Women CAOs at doctorate-granting institutions thought that remaining in their current positions was the most viable option (77.4%), compared with women CAOs at liberal arts institutions (59.1%) and women CAOs at comprehensive institutions (83.3%). In contrast, more women CAOs at comprehensive institutions thought it most likely that they would go on to presidencies at other institutions (9.7%) compared to those women at doctoral or liberal arts institutions (27.8% each). However, more women CAOs at doctoral institutions thought their most likely next career move would be back to the faculty (67.7%), compared with 44.3% at liberal arts institutions and 35.0% at comprehensive institutions. This may suggest that women CAOs at comprehensive institutions perceive these colleges to be more welcoming to women in leadership than are liberal arts or doctoral institutions. The issue of women's leadership styles and the contemporary presidency is explored further in chapter 5.

Reasons for changing positions included personal and institutional factors. For 73.2% of the women, the lure was a new challenge, 49.7% sought a higher salary, 25.1% had family considerations, and 19.0% were bored with their current jobs. Institutional factors included desire for a stronger funding base (53.6%), an institution with greater prestige (43.0%), different problems (40.8%), a larger institution (30.7%), a better geographic location (27.9%), an institution with fewer problems (24.6%), and an institution with more feminist values (17.9%). Boredom was a more important factor for women CAOs at liberal arts institutions (67.6%) compared to comprehensive (26.5%) and doctorate-granting (5.9%) institutions. CAOs may surmise that they quickly master the intricacies and problems of smaller liberal arts institutions, while the larger doctoral and comprehensive institutions present more rapidly-changing challenges.

Profile of a Typical Female Chief Academic Officer

The survey data provide the following profile: a typical female CAO is fifty-three years old, of Caucasian-European descent, born in the United States, and the first child of a mother who worked outside the home. Her parents had high school diplomas and possibly some college education. She is married and is equally likely to have or not have children. She obtained a Ph.D. in humanities and financed that degree through work as a teaching assistant, has spent twenty-two years in her higher education career, and has had an average scholarly career. She has participated in at least one of the major higher education professional development programs, most typically the ACE/NIP network or forum. This is her first CAO position, and she has served for fewer than five years. The CAO position became a goal after she had spent some years in administrative positions, but it had not always been her objective.

She was attracted to the CAO position because of the duties and responsibilities of the job itself and her belief in the educational mission of the institution. The congeniality and competence of the people at the institution are important to her. The job probably came to her without overt and explicit effort, although she probably increased her visibility within the higher-education community in key ways as the possibility of a move to the position became more feasible. For the most part, she contends that she negotiated well for her CAO job, although she wished she had given more thought to the issues of time off for intellectual renewal and departure from the job. She maintains strongly that she is doing a good job and is working well with her president, other senior staff, and faculty. She is satisfied in her job. While she may have wished for more experience in specific areas before entering this position, overall she feels prepared.

The typical female CAO stays in her job for the same reasons that attracted her to it in the first place—the duties and responsibilities of the job and the mission of the institution in which she serves. While she probably has not been sought in other searches and thinks she will remain in her current position for the next three to five years, she is eyeing presidencies and contemplating other options. She is considering a job change because she wants new challenges and a higher salary.

Although the women tried to increase their visibility within the higher education community, and especially among women's groups such as ACE/NIP, relatively few had participated in the more prestigious professional development programs that provide visibility and comparisons with larger numbers of men. Very few women made contacts with search firms at a time when more institutions were enlisting such assistance to enlarge the pool of candidates, especially with women and people of color.

Advice to Aspiring Women Chief Academic Officers

The respondents were generous and candid in giving advice to aspiring women CAOs. With respect to preparation for the job, they prescribed the traditional career path of faculty member, chair, and dean, establishing firm grounding in one's discipline through teaching, scholarship, and publication. Their advice was to gain administrative experience in related areas, such as budgeting and personnel management. Furthermore, they maintained that potential CAOs must seek help from others through a mentor who can be trusted and admired. Aspiring women CAOs should also attend professional meetings and develop networks with other academic administrators and acknowledge that "politics" need not be a dirty word.

Responding CAOs freely offered personal advice: Make certain you can deal with conflict and prosper under adversity, not taking personally the complaints and criticisms of faculty, students, and staff who just need to vent their frustrations. Develop a tough skin, do not panic, and learn to juggle, finding ways to handle stress so as not to compromise one's own physical or mental health.

CAOs concluded that the position requires a strong constitution, love of the work, abundant endurance, total involvement, and a good sense of humor. They contend that a fair and consistent managerial style is essential for survival in the position. Furthermore, they advise women who wish to succeed as CAOs to concentrate on doing the job well without trying to be an "old boy," or worrying about being a woman doing the job. Finally, the successful CAO must be a good listener and observer of behavior.

Conclusion

This study is only a beginning, but it suggests strategic directions for future research and presents hypotheses for testing by other investigators. Longitudinal tracking of women CAOs may be an important bellwether for the status of women in higher education administration. Indeed, this study, along with the consideration of contemporary presidential leadership in chapter 5, represent pathbreaking contributions to the larger issue of women as leaders in higher education. Perhaps it is appropriate to end this report of a survey that represents the opinions of 86 percent of the women chief academic officers in the country with the advice of two of them: "Help other women" and "Go for it! It's rewarding and fulfilling."

Notes

1. David G. Brown, ed., *Leadership Roles of Chief Academic Officers*, New Directions for Higher Education Series, no. 47 (San Francisco: Jossey-Bass, 1984).

2. Marlene Ross, Madeleine F. Green, and Cathy Henderson, *The American College President: A 1993 Edition* (Washington, D.C.: American Council on Education Center for Leadership Development, 1993).

3. Catherine Kirby, "A Comparative Study of the Perception of Leadership Behaviors of Men and Women Chief Academic Officers of Small, Independent Colleges," Ph.D. diss., Miami University, 1987, abstract in *Dissertation Abstracts International* 48-05A (1987): 1126.

4. These studies include Michael D. Cohen and James G. March, *Leadership and Ambiguity: The American College President* (New York: McGraw-Hill, 1974); Commission on Strengthening Presidential Leadership, *Presidents Make a Difference: Strengthening Leadership in Colleges and Universities* (Washington, D.C.: Association of Governing Boards of Universities and Colleges, 1984); Clark Kerr and Marian L. Gade, *The Many Lives of Academic Presidents: Time, Place and Character* (Washington, D.C.: Association of Governing Boards of Universities and Colleges, 1986); Kathryn M. Moore, *The Top Line: A Report on Presidents', Provosts', and Deans' Careers* (University Park: The Pennsylvania State University, 1983); and Judith G. Touchton, Donna Shavlik, and Lynne Davis, *Women in Presidencies: A Descriptive Study of Women College and University Presidents* (Washington, D.C.: Office of Women in Higher Education—American Council on Education, 1993).

5. Mariam K. Chamberlain, ed., *Women in Academe: Progress and Prospects* (New York: Russell Sage Foundation, 1988) and Adrian A. Tinsley, Cynthia Secor, and Sheila Kaplan, eds., *Women in Higher Education Administration*, New Directions for Higher Education Series, no. 45 (San Francisco: Jossey-Bass, 1984).

6. Cecilia Ottinger and Robin Sikula, "Women in Higher Education: Where Do We Stand?" *Research Briefs* 4.2 (1993).

7. Linda Knopp, "Women in Higher Education Today: A Mid-1990s Profile," *Research Briefs* 6.5 (1995).

8. American Association of University Professors, "Not So Bad: The Economic Status of the Profession 1995–1996," *Academe* 82 (March-April 1996): 14–22.

9. College and University Personnel Association, *Administrative Compensation Survey* (Washington, D.C., 1995).

10. Judith G. Touchton and D. Ingram, *Women Presidents in US Colleges and Universities: A 1995 Higher Education Update* (Washington, D.C.: Office of Women in Higher Education—American Council on Education, 1995).

11. Judith A. Sturnick, Jane E. Milley, and Catherine A. Tisinger, eds., *Women at the Helm: Pathfinding Presidents at State Colleges and Universities* (Washington, D.C.: American Association of State Colleges and Universities, 1993), p. 5. See also Touchton and Ingram, p. 2, and Touchton, Shavlik, and Davis, 2.

12. Touchton, Shavlik, and Davis, 1.

13. Richard J. Ernst, "Women in Higher Education Leadership Positions—It Doesn't Happen by Accident," *Journal of the College and University Personnel Association* 33 (Summer 1982): 19–22.

14. John S. Brubacher and Willis Rudy, *Higher Education in Transition, A History of American Colleges and Universities:* 3rd rev. ed. (New York: Harper & Row, 1976).

15. Francis E. Rourke and Glen E. Brooks, *The Managerial Revolution in Higher Education* (Baltimore, Md.: Johns Hopkins University Press, 1966).

16. Louise H. Allen, "On Being Vice President for Academic Affairs," *Journal of the National Association of Women, Deans, and Counselors* 47 (Summer 1984): 8–15.

17. Ibid., 9.

18. Ibid., 10.

19. William K. Jackson, "The Professional Preparation of Chief Academic Officers of Private, Four-Year, Liberal Arts Colleges Accredited by the Southern Association of Colleges and Schools," Ed.D. diss., University of South Carolina, 1981, abstract in *Dissertation Abstracts International* 42-05A (1981): 1989. See also Beverly T. Watkins, "Typical Chief Academic Officer: He's 50, Earns $61,000, Has Been on the Job 5 Years, and Wants to Be a President," *The Chronicle of Higher Education* 31 (November 27, 1985): 21.

20. See Allen, "On Being Vice President," 8–15. See also Sandra. L. Barker, "The Influence of Academic Deans on Colleagues and Superiors," in the *American Educational Research Association Division Journal* (San Francisco: ERIC Document Reproduction Service No. ED 251 055, October 23–30, 1984); James Martin, James E. Samels, and Associates. *First Among Equals: The Role of the Chief Academic Officer.* Baltimore, MD: The Johns Hopkins University Press, 1997, vii; and Bill Ritter, "A Pair of Aces: How The Partnership of a President and Vice President Helps Advance a University," *Currents* 10 (January 1984): 20–22.

21. These sources include Harold Enarson, "The Academic Vice President or Dean," in *Administrators in Higher Education: Their Functions and Coordination*, ed. Gerald P. Burns (New York: Harper and Brothers, 1962); Arthur J. Dibden, ed., *The Academic Deanship in American Colleges and Universities* (Carbondale: Southern Illinois University Press, 1968); C. E. Floyd and C. N. Batsche, "The Leadership Role of the Academic Vice President," in *Multicultural Education: Strategies for Implementation in Colleges and Universities*, ed. J. Q. Adams and Janice R. Welsch (Macomb: Western Illinois University, 1992), 2: 99–106; F. A. McGinnis, "The Dean and His Duties," *Journal of Higher Education* 4 (April 1933): 191–96; Van Cleve Morris, *Deaning: Middle Management in Academe* (Champaign: University of Illinois Press, 1981); Jancye J. Napora, "A Case Study of the Academic Planning Process," in the *Annual Forum of the Association for Institutional Research* (Denver, Colo.: ERIC Document Reproduction Service No. ED 220 030, May 16–19, 1982); George J. Petrello, "An Analysis of Formal Long-Range and Strategic Planning as a Guide for Effective Leadership," paper presented at the Annual Meeting of the Society of Educators and Scholars, Louisville, Ky., October 10–11, 1986; Robert S. Shea, "The Role of the Provost in American Colleges and Universities," Ed.D. diss., Columbia University, 1967, abstract in *Dissertation Abstracts International* 28-09A (1967): 3440.

22. Barbara Ettorre, "Who Is This Person? Focus on the Number Two," *Management Review* 82 (February 1993): 10–15. See also Janet J. Lathrop, "Sharing Leadership: The Nature of Relationships between Presidents and Chief Academic Officers in Colleges and Universities," Ed.D. diss., Columbia University Teachers College, 1990, abstract in *Dissertation Abstracts International* 51-07A (1990): 2283, and Ritter, "A Pair of Aces," 20–22.

23. Daniel A. Felicetti, "The Role of the Academic Vice President in Fundraising," in *Research Report No. 143* (Ann Arbor: University of Michigan, ERIC Document Reproduction Service No. ED 318 381, 1989).

24. John N. Mangieri and John W. Arnn Jr., "Responsibilities and Qualifications of the Chief Academic Officer: Past, Present, and Future," *Journal for Higher Education Management* 7 (Summer/Fall 1991): 11–18.

25. Literature confirming this includes Dana M. Aaron, "The Perceptions of Incumbent Chief Academic Officers Regarding the Importance of Selected Factors in the Prediction of Success of Applicants for that Position," Ph.D. diss., Bowling Green State University, 1978, abstract in *Dissertation Abstracts International* 39-07A (1978): 3936; Robert L. Abel, "Administrator Background and Influence: A Study of the Effect of Background upon Perceived Influence of Chief Academic Officers and Chief Fiscal Officers in Sixty-two Major Public Research Universities," Ph.D. diss., the University of Iowa, 1979, abstract in *Dissertation Abstracts International* 41-01A (1979): 0117; and Marilyn Jane Amey, "Academic Vice Presidents in Action: An Analysis of Four Areas of Leadership Competency" Ph.D. diss., The Pennsylvania State University, 1989, abstract in *Dissertation Abstracts International* 50-07A (1989): 1956. See also Barker, "Influence of Academic Deans," 5; Elwood B. Ehrle and John B. Bennett, *Managing the Academic Enterprise: Case Studies for Deans and Provosts* (Washington, D.C.: American Council on Education/Macmillan, 1987); Marjorie D. Lewis, "Academic Leadership and Community College Chief Instructional Officers at Selected Single-College Districts (Chief Instructional Officers)," Ph.D. diss., Claremont Graduate School, 1992, abstract in *Dissertation Abstracts International* 53-08A (1992): 2626; Charles W. McKee, "A Study of Institutional Decision-Making by the Chief Academic Officers and the Chief Business Officers in Southern Colleges and Universities" (Ed.D. diss., The University of Tennessee, 1992), abstract in *Dissertation Abstracts International* 53-07A (1992): 2265; and Emmanuel O. Uzoigwe, "Management Styles and Demographic Characteristics of Chief Academic Officers," Ph.D. diss., The University of Toledo, 1994, abstract in *Dissertation Abstracts International* 55-03A (1994): 0440.

26. Madeleine F. Green and Sharon A. McDade, *Investing in Higher Education: A Handbook of Leadership Development* (Washington, D.C.: American Council on Education/Orryx, 1991).

27. See Touchton, Shavlik, and Davis, 55.

28. Kathryn M. Moore, "The Top Line: A Report on Presidents', Provosts', and Deans' Careers," *Leaders in Transition: A National Study of Higher Education Administrators* (University Park: The Pennsylvania State University Press, 1983), 1–6.

29. Higher Education Publications, *1991 Higher Education Directory* (Falls Church, Va.: Higher Education Publications, 1991).

30. Sharon A. McDade, "Intentions of Becoming an Administrator: Implications for Leadership Learning and Practice," *Journal of Continuing Higher Education* (in press).

CHAPTER 5

New Leadership for a New Century

Women's Contribution to Leadership in Higher Education

JANA NIDIFFER

> There are about as many female college presidents in this country as there are whooping cranes in the world. The rate of increase in the latter is probably higher.
>
> —Ellen E. Chaffee, ASHE Presidential Address

During the past two decades American higher education has come under considerable scrutiny. Ours is not the first era in which citizens are highly critical of higher education nor will it be the last, but faultfinding is now a conspicuous component of national discourse. The list of criticisms is familiar: high costs; underworked and overpaid professors; inattention to undergraduate education; political correctness run amok; esoteric or useless research; poor teaching; poor student performance; inflated administrative salaries; lethargy in responding to advancing technologies; neglect of national labor and economic needs; the failure of shared governance; and the travesty of tenure.

The 1983 publication of "A Nation at Risk," was followed shortly thereafter by Allan Bloom's influential *Closing of the American Mind.* Bookstore shelves were stocked with titles that reflected the national mood, including: *Killing the Spirit; Illiberal Education; The Moral Collapse of the University; Tenured Radicals; Profscam;* and recently, *Generation X Goes to College,* and *Bright College Years.*[2]

Books are not the only source of discouraging words for higher education; newspapers and magazines regularly publish articles detailing current problems. Of greater concern, however, are the actions of state legislatures and boards of trustees who have increased what might be described as either "micro-managing intrusion" or "appropriate oversight" depending on one's point of view. This recent spate of antagonism has prompted many scholars, institutional presidents, political leaders, and other interested parties to ask how such problems developed and what might be done about them. Inevitably, such inquiries lead to the question of leadership.

Leadership in higher education is a much-studied phenomenon. Cynthia Farr Brown and Candace Introcaso provide examples of historical scholarship on presidents and examine what lessons may be learned from studying the past. Other scholars focus more closely on the present. Over thirty years ago, the interest in leadership accelerated when critics blamed campus unrest partially on ineffective presidents. Scholars have drawn on multiple sources to form myriad theories about leadership within higher education. They used studies of leadership within corporations and the military as a foundation, then expanded the literature with their own empirical studies of institutional presidents. These studies were then interwoven with the organizational scholarship on higher education. A rich and complicated literature resulted; one that attempted to illuminate this most complex human phenomenon, including a few studies that concluded that leadership does not matter at all![2]

This chapter summarizes pivotal theories of leadership in higher education, including the nature of metaphors used to describe the college presidency. First, noting that most scholarship on leadership was constructed using male norms, the traditional theories of leadership are reexamined through a gendered lens in terms of their implications for women presidents. Second, alternatives to the traditional theories, or the "emergent" literature, are discussed in terms of their implications for women. The analysis of these two bodies of literature leads to the conclusion that the multiple competencies identified as essential to successful leadership are associated with women by virtue of sex-role socialization. As a result, I suggest a broadened view of characteristics of good leadership and, within this expanded definition, propose a competitive advantage for women presidents. To test whether women, in fact, manifest the competencies that socialization theory predicts, recent biographical sketches of women presidents are analyzed to discern leadership styles.

Good Leaders Are Both Made and Born—Male (?)

American culture, and therefore American higher education, is awash in images of what a leader should look like, act like, and be like. These images and beliefs are powerful yardsticks by which candidates for presidencies at colleges and universities are measured. Invariably, these ideals and models are male. As Luba Chliwniak succinctly noted, "organizational arrangements carry the supposed natural differences into the workplace and in doing so, men are expected to hold dominate positions while women provide deference and support."[3] In a 1992 article discussing the need for new leadership in community colleges and the dearth of women chosen for such positions, Marilyn Amey and Susan Twombly argued, that presidential search committees select certain candidates and eliminate others based on strongly held cultural beliefs about leadership and leaders.[4]

Leadership attributes such as aggression, vision, strength, determination, and courage are consistent with, and usually positively associated with, the masculine traits that result from the ways boys are commonly socialized within American society. Even the physical characteristics of leaders such as height and appearance are frequently male, and also typically white and middle class. As a result, Amey and Twombly concluded, women candidates often fail to *look like* leaders in the minds of search committees and are thought to lack what is *really* needed to be president. Therefore, both male and female members of search committees select men to be presidents more often than women.[5]

These strongly held cultural beliefs about leaders and leadership are frequently expressed in the metaphors used to depict leaders. Joseph Crowley conducted a fascinating historical study of the metaphors describing the office of the presidency as well as individual college presidents, both real and fictional. He confirmed Amey and Twombly's hypothosis that cultural ideas about leadership are overwhelmingly masculine.[6] Metaphors used to portray the presidency include: boss, hero, titan, daring pioneer, superman, viceroy, gladiator, visionary, broker, orator, pilot, papal figure, quarterback, helmsman, mediator, preacher, and father. Crowley's study revealed that these images apply to both the antebellum "old-time college presidents," as well as to a cadre of men who served later in the nineteenth century and were often hailed by traditional historians as the greatest university presidents in our history—Charles Eliot (Harvard), David Starr Jordan (Stanford), Charles Van Hise (Wisconsin), James Angell (Michigan), William Rainey Harper (Chicago), Daniel Coit Gilman (Johns Hopkins), and Andrew White (Cornell).[7]

In a patriarchal society, leadership and power are the roles, responsibilities, and privileges assigned to men. Because men fill these roles, our cultural images, attitudes, and beliefs associate men with leadership. Skills and attributes valued in men become the qualities prized in leaders. As a result, members of society begin to accept with little question or hesitation that leadership simply must be associated with time-honored masculine traits. Professor of psychology. M. Elizabeth Tidball succinctly noted, "virtually all work roles that men occupy are defined in masculine terms to such an extent that the attributes associated with the job description are indistinguishable from the attributes associated with masculinity."[8]

In ways both subtle and profoundly complex, members of society cultivate desirable traits in boys with the hope that such virtues will manifest themselves in grown men. Therefore, as a society, we confidently assume that men are more likely to possess these traits than women. Male monopoly on these qualities is either the result of nature (biology and genetics) or nurture (sex-role socialization), or an important, mutually reinforcing combination of the two where socialization plays a key role.[9] The power of sex-role socialization is documented by scholars in several disciplines. After reviewing numerous studies on socialization, Cynthia Fuchs Epstein concluded that "overwhelming evidence created by the past decade of research on gender supports the theory that gender differentiation—as distinct, of course, from sexual differentiation—is best explained as a social construction rooted in hierarchy, not in biology."[10] For women seeking leadership positions this presents a dilemma. How can they cope in "this paradigm, where sex role and occupational role share a common identity, where being and doing coalesce?"[11]

Unlike candidates whose leadership acumen is obvious to a search committee (e.g., "*he* looks the part"), individuals who, by virtue of their gender, race, class, or some other variable, appear unlikely to posses leadership traits, must overtly demonstrate their competence and "prove themselves" to be good leaders. The "born" leader may have advantages in establishing *his* presidency, but there are several significant drawbacks to choosing a president based on cultural ideas of leadership.

One obvious limitation is the human cost. The leadership potential of countless individuals perceived as lacking the requisite skills is never brought to fruition. To provide women the opportunity to lead institutions, the American Council on Education (ACE) established the Office of Women in Higher Education (OWHE) in 1972 to document the dearth of women in senior positions and advocate for equal opportunity for women candidates. In 1977, OWHE established the National Identification Program (NIP) to recognize promising women administrators and assist them in preparing for presidencies.[12]

OWHE raised arguments beyond the equity issue. OWHE's leaders stressed that women had equitable representation in electoral politics and the consumer economy and should, therefore, have a leading voice in education.[13] As early as 1984, women's advocates argued that women and people of color should be leaders on campuses and role models to young women and students of color.[14] The equity, fair representation, and role-model arguments emphasized either the benefits to the individual woman chosen as president or the members of the community she served, but did not stress the potential benefits to the institution.

Limiting who is perceived, and therefore subsequently chosen, as a leader stifles the individuals whose aspirations are dashed. It also deprives higher education of their talent and insight and the hope that new leaders might find new solutions to persistent problems.[15] In fact, outsider status might abet women's capacity to seek innovative approaches.[16] "If we are to successfully restructure higher education to be more responsive to our dynamic, global society," argued Anita Harrow, "women must join the higher education leadership ranks at a faster rate. . . . It is time for new voices, new perspectives, new strategies, new ways of working with people; all qualified individuals capable of making significant contributions to the advancement of higher education must have the opportunity to serve."[17]

The second shortcoming of choosing presidents based on outmoded cultural beliefs is the conceivable mismatch of skills and needs. Cultural beliefs about leaders dictate not only their appearance, but the characteristics and skills they possess. Hopefully, the skills attributed to the leader are, in fact, the precise skills needed to lead the institution. Yet what if this correlation is not as strong as believed? What if the collection of skills necessary to lead colleges and universities successfully in the present environment or the future is different from the collection of skills previously needed? What if the masculine skills so valued by society represent only a subset of leadership skills and the skills socialized in women represent the remainder?[18] Institutions may experience a ruinous disconnect between what they look for in a leader and what is actually required of a president. As Amey and Twombly noted in their analysis of the gendered images in the community college literature:

> Ideas about leadership are shaped and constrained by beliefs and images about the kind of leadership called for and the characteristics required in those who assume leadership positions. The language in which these images are communicated serves both symbolic and political purposes—defining legitimate leadership regardless of contextual demands for leadership. Obviously, the consequences of images that no longer fit can hamper the effectiveness of an institution.[19]

Organizational and Leadership Theory in Higher Education

The actual job requirements of college presidents interests both organizational and leadership theorists. These two literatures overlap and inter-relate in significant ways and have moved in similar intellectual directions over the past several years. Understanding the general direction of this scholarship and its recent insights is critical to understanding women and leadership.

In their book *Making Sense of Administrative Leadership: The "L" Word in Higher Education,* Estela Bensimon, Anna Neumann, and Robert Birnbaum, cogently summarized and discussed the strengths and weaknesses of recent ideas in organizational and leadership theory.[20] First, they noted that trait theories dominated the early scholarship, but hold less sway today. Derived from eighteenth- and nineteenth-century philosophers and historians subscribing to a "Great Man" notion of history, trait theory asserts that effective leaders possess certain character traits that ineffective leaders do not, such as boldness, vigor, confidence, courage, strength, and even specific physical traits.[21] Although not discussed explicitly, most of the desirable traits listed are associated with men or masculinity. In the final analysis, the authors concluded that "no traits have proven to be essential for successful leaders and trait theories are no longer a major focus of organizational research."[22]

Second, they discussed theories of power and influence. Theorists in this school examine how leaders influence followers or the reciprocal relationship between leaders and followers. Social power theories predict that leaders can influence because of their office (official), their personality (informal), or a combination (formal). Five different types of power were considered: legitimate (office held), reward (power to bestow awards), coercive (capacity to punish), expert (perceived expertise), and referent (when followers identify with and care for the leader).[23] In studies relating types of power to follower performance and satisfaction, the authors found that coercive power was negatively correlated, legitimate power was essentially neutral, studies of reward power were inconclusive, while expert and referent power were generally positively correlated with satisfaction and productivity.[24]

Social influence theories emphasize the exchange between leader and follower. Leaders have power, but it is constrained by follower expectations. The authors cited studies in which leaders actually increased their power by empowering others. Success in this paradigm requires leaders to either fulfill follower expectations or change them. Transactional leaders meet follower expectations by following a relationship where both parties exchange things of value. On the other hand, transformational leaders seek to *change* follower expectations.

According to James McGregor Burns transformational leadership occurs when "one or more persons engage with others in such a way that leader and follower raise one another to higher levels of motivation and morality. Their purposes, which might have started out as separate but related, as in the case of transactional leadership, become fused."[25] Transformational leaders are often concerned with "end values such as liberty, justice, and equality."[26] As such, transformational leadership is viewed as a more ethical form of leadership.[27] Transformational leadership has more recently become associated with the capacity to change an organizational culture. In this sense, the capacity to change followers is still prevalent, but the high premium placed on change in the direction of greater morality is diminished.

Behavioral theories of leadership focus on what leaders actually "do" rather than their traits or sources of power. One set of theories places behavior on a continuum from authoritarian to democratic; productivity increases as the leader's style moves toward the democratic end of the continuum. Another group of studies analyzes whether leaders are concerned with tasks or relationships. Here, the most productive leaders are those who can do both, in appropriate circumstances. However, the literature is contradictory regarding the precise combination of task and relationship orientation that is most effective.[28] More than likely, the absence of a definitive prescription reflects the increasing belief that successful leadership is contingent upon context.

Contingency theories predict that good leadership is situationally specific. These theories are similar to behavior theories, but focus on forces external to the organization rather than the internal orientation of the leader. Some contingency theories examine forces that either substitute for or counteract leadership. When leaders are too constrained by rules to effect change, have little control of rewards, or when subordinates look primarily to other professional peers for "approval, recognition, or standards of performance" leadership is neutralized.[29] Employee unions, intrusive boards of trustees, and tenure are often cited as leadership-neutralizing elements within higher education.

The aforementioned theories all assume a certain rationality and linearity of organizations. The cultural and symbolic theories represent a paradigmatic shift because they "assume that organizational structures and processes are invented, not discovered."[30] Participants share evolving meanings, values, and beliefs that constitute the organization's culture.[31] Leadership, in these theories, stresses the "management of meaning."[32] Leaders may influence culture, but culture cannot be "managed" in the traditional sense of the word. In fact, culture can significantly constrain leaders.

The cultural and symbolic theories of leadership are intriguing because several organizational theorists within higher education emphasize the importance of culture.[33] When institutions are viewed as cultural systems, effective leaders give symbolic meaning to events that others may see as perplexing, senseless, or chaotic. Changing the culture is difficult, thus true transformational leadership may be rare. However, through attention to social integration and symbolic events, leaders may sustain and strengthen the existing culture. Such leaders are interpretive, rather than linear, and are concerned with how people see, feel, and understand their lives.

As contingency theory predicts, the nature of appropriate or effective leadership is best understood within the context of the organization.[34] Universities and colleges are described as various institutional types: Bureaucracy, Colleguim, Political System, or Organized Anarchy.[35] In a comprehensive study of organizational literature, Lee Bolman and Terrence Deal asserted that organizations can be viewed through four "frames" or lenses which generally correspond to the above institutional types: Bureaucratic, Human Resource, Political, and Symbolic.[36] These frames are windows through which leaders view the organization and they foretell the leader's most likely response in a given situation.

Other studies of higher education corroborate the basic institutional typography, but Bolman and Deal also considered the fact that organizations are rarely discrete types.[37] In fact, a college or university could easily manifest elements of all the various types within one institution. Successful leaders must therefore be sufficiently "cognitively complex" and able to view their organization through multiple frames, depending on the situation.[38] This is especially relevant in the current climate in which higher education is viewed as increasingly enigmatic and leadership as "a set of myths reinforcing organizational constructions of meaning."[39]

Cognitive theories of leadership are based on the above notion. A cognitive leader pays selective attention to events and takes credit for successes, attributing them to internal causes (e.g., ability and effort), and shifts blame for failures to external causes such as bad luck or task complexity. The success of cognitive theories may be due to the perceptions of followers as much as what leaders actually "do."[40]

Bensimon, Neumann, and Birnbaum's discussion of leadership theories is comprehensive but not exhaustive, and is now over a decade old. The 1990s, however, was a fertile decade for leadership scholarship. Some of the more recent entreaties long for a return to strong, traditional, or even militaristic styles of leadership.[41] Other contemporary voices in the debate encourage a more explicit adoption of the corporate model of leadership and management. While some of these works are grounded scholarship, others are merely exhortations. But there is another recent strain of leadership research which deserves closer analysis. Referred to as the emergent literature, these studies of leadership have a decidedly different cast.

On the whole, emergent leadership theory is based on the belief that society is changing. Old-style leadership is anachronistic in today's complex, global, information-rich, interconnected culture in which higher education's leaders deal with multiple constituencies.[42] Emergent leadership is more collectivist in nature, assuming a "relational context" in which leaders share power, information, and decision-making with other group members.[43] Emergent leaders are participatory, flexible, ethical, authentic, connective, and team-oriented.[44] The skills of empowerment, communication, collaboration, and even healing are emphasized.[45]

Theoretical Implications for Women Presidents

Past studies of leadership used male norms and women leaders were assumed to have adopted these norms.[46] Brown's work in chapter 2 is a delightful exception because she analyzes how women presidents interpreted and exercised power. However, in the main, male-based assumptions undergird most leadership theory. Therefore, it is important to reconsider the leadership literature in light of the impact these theories may have on women as potential presidents. Before embarking on such a re-analysis, it is necessary to state a few key assumptions.

In my analyses, I use the terms "masculine" and "feminine" to describe a collection of behaviors, traits, and attitudes that are traditionally and culturally associated with men and women. Scholar Virginia Valian refers to such cultural labels as gender schema—the "implicit, or nonconcious hypotheses about sex differences."[47] Gender schema assume men and women are different based on a combination of nature and nurture and as a result, each gender manifests different behaviors in various aspects of life. Gender schema are reinforced by sex-role socialization which dictates the appropriate behaviors associated with masculinity and feminity. Individual men and women who violate such cultural norms, may suffer social, emotional, or psychological consequences. As a result, gender schema are quite powerful, despite the cultural and political changes brought by the feminist movement and analogous efforts to redefine masculinity.

Valian convincingly argues that gender schema pervade our culture, yet aspects of using the gender schema are troubling. First, many educated people want to believe such schema do not dictate their judgments and actions, especially when the task is as important as selecting a president. Second, the schema are by their very nature essentialist. While "masculine" and "feminine" capture a concept, the words rely on stereotypes and are hopelessly inadequate when describing an individual man or woman. Despite these caveats, gender schema are a valuable analytic tool when examining the implications of leadership theory on women.

What Would a Gendered Re-analysis Reveal?

Trait theory, largely based on a collection of masculine characteristics, is generally dismissed by contemporary leadership theorists. Since studies failed to demonstrate any *single* set of traits that predicts effective leadership in all circumstances, the old, time-honored list of attributes that dominates cultural images of leadership has little worth. The collection of skills and attributes that make effective leaders is more encompassing and, according to contingency theory, varies according to circumstances. Fundamentally, an institution and its president must form a compatible match.[48] While this sounds simple, it is not the case in many presidential searches.[49] Search committees may not realize or may remain reluctant to admit that several forces on campus effectively neutralize traditional leadership and that networking, bridge-building, communication, and "meaning management" are the skills required rather the more romantic or heroic notions of conventional leadership.

Studies relating types of power to worker productivity and satisfaction are also quite revealing when analyzed through a gender lens. In higher education men hold the preponderance of senior positions and therefore have access to more legitimate power (office held), more resources (reward power), and the capacity to hire and fire (coercive power). Respectively, these forms of power are neutrally, unclearly, and negatively associated with productivity and satisfaction. The most stereotypically masculine power base, coercive power, is also the most negative. Within higher education, it is not surprising that expert and referent power are more effective in managing an institution of highly educated, autonomous professionals.

Power is a fascinating subject within feminist analysis. Despite derisive comments or jokes, the majority of feminist organizational analysis does not call for utopian organizations functioning in the absence of power, although serious feminist critiques of the more abusive forms of legitimate and coercive power are prevalent. However, research indicates that men and women use power differently.[50] Men often perceive power within a scarcity model, or a zero-sum game. Women, in contrast, are more likely to believe that leaders actually increase their power by empowering others.[51] In this mindset, power is "generative, not distributive."[52] Social power theory defines leadership as the capacity to influence the activities of others. Here, charisma, distance, mastery, and mystery can play vital roles. But this approach is criticized by, among others, Nannerl Koehane, the former president of Wellesley College and currently president of Duke University. Koehane asserts that a president dedicated to mystery and separateness cannot become a skillful team-builder, a skill she sees as critical for effective leadership.[53]

Transactional and transformational leadership theories also have ramifications for women presidents. Bernard Bass argues that effective leaders must utilize both strategies.[54] Transactional leaders generally conform to the culture and thereby earn willingness on the part of followers to accept change. This builds trust and followers become favorably disposed to change *in* the directions inspired by the transformational leader. Interestingly, that the gender-role characteristics most employed by transformational leaders are the "feminine" traits,[55] such as speaking in the "care voice" (as defined by Carol Gilligan), sharing—rather than hoarding—information, and the willingness to be reflective about one's own practice.

The implications for women presidents from the behavioral theories of leadership are rather straightforward. Democratic styles are correlated with higher productivity than autocratic styles and successful leaders strive for a balance between task and relationship orientation. The autocratic "taskmaster" is *not* an efficient or effective leader. Participatory leadership is the style most preferred by faculty members and seen as most compatible with academic culture. Women leaders, in general, are more participatory and democratic, and rarely focus exclusively on task.[56]

The ramifications for women from the cultural and symbolic theories of leadership are more speculative. The ideas associated with the symbolic frame in Bolman and Deal's analysis are not necessarily female nor are they consistent with the strong, heroic, masculine-inspired images of leaders. Symbolic theories incorporate the importance of rituals, stories, myths, theater, humor, and cultural interpretation.[57] Obviously, neither men nor women have an automatic monopoly on the employment of such skills.

Discerning the implications for women presidents in the more traditional schools of thought on leadership requires carefully drawn inferences and some intellectual speculation. It is much easier to see the gender implications in the emergent literature. Emergent leaders are collaborative, empowering, connective, communicative, authentic, and team-oriented. As Linda Kuk noted, "the skills required for these approaches overlap the skills and attributes associated with female socialization and 'voice' [as defined and described by Carol Gilligan]."[58] Chliwniak confirmed Kuk's observation, demonstrating that women were more likely to exhibit emergent traits, even to the extent of the language they used in daily conversation.[59]

In an article on connective leadership, Jean Lipman-Blumen cogently discussed the rationale behind the emergent approach to leadership. Connective leadership combines elements of both transactional and transformational leadership, an approach regarded as highly effective. Lipman-Blumen described three achieving styles: direct, instrumental, and relational. Of these, only the direct style has been privileged. A direct style stresses individualism, but in the current climate, institutions need leaders who can connect to multiple constituencies. Women's socialization presupposes them to be connective leaders, she argued. Therefore, women should not deny how they are socialized and adopt behaviors of men. In adopting male behaviors women relinquish the competitive advantage they have as connective leaders.[60]

In summary, numerous scholars, both male and female, seriously question whether the skills traditionally associated with leadership in higher education remain effective today or will be viable in the future. Leaders within higher education are likely to find that military-inspired, top-down, or heroic leadership is counter-productive.[61] A gendered interpretation of the primary theories of leadership, combined with the emergent studies, prescribes an alternative collection of proficiencies and expertise for leaders. As Chliwniak summarized:

> When cross-referencing postmodern, nonhierachical leadership theories and models with gender-related research and scholarship, it becomes evident that the gender-related characteristics, described as innate to most women, encompass the very characteristics leadership theorists claim to be the most effective.[62]

Model of Women Leaders' Comparative Advantage

Why then are men more frequently chosen to be leaders? Men are considered "natural" leaders because social expectations of male behavior and masculine attributes coincide with the skills and characteristics historically deemed important in leaders, such as strength, courage, power, and so on. In this traditional view of leadership, proficiencies typically associated with feminine attributes are virtually absent. Figure 5.1 depicts this "feminine-deficit" model of leadership. In this model, men have an obvious advantage. They "naturally" possess the critical leadership competencies because of their socialization. Women, on the other hand, do not. To acquire the requisite skills, women must violate cultural expectations of gender roles and choose to "act like a man" in order to secure a presidency. The result is a painful "double bind"—women are incompetent if too feminine or abnormal if too masculine.

The opposite situation, a "masculine-deficit" model, is also represented in figure 5.1. In this model, attributes primarily associated with female socialization are primarily deemed desirable. Here the emergent skills dominate and the preponderance of traditional competencies are rejected. Women are socialized to possess the needed proficiencies, while men must work to acquire them. This model rests on the assumption that women's ways of leadership represent a discrete alternative to the male "beau ideal." However, this model is as limiting as the former. Rather than broadening and embellishing the definitions of leadership, it is but a second, restrictive alternative.[63]

A more desirable model, therefore, recognizes a fuller array of leadership competencies. Thus, the accepted definition of successful leadership can draw upon the best elements of the traditional and emergent scholarship. In this model, the skills demanded of a leader include a blend of stereotypically male and stereotypically female attributes—perhaps an integrated set of abilities.[64] The precise mixture of competencies depends, of course, on the individual and the context of the institution; there is no single, ideal type of leader.

The theoretical literature on leadership supports the contention that within such an integrated mixture, the typically female traits are more advantageous than typically male traits. Thus, choosing a man for a leadership role has no automatic advantage. In fact, because male skills have been historically privileged in the larger society, women may actually be more adept at exhibiting male traits than men are at assuming female attributes.[65] The ability to broaden their range of behaviors and perspectives by incorporating traits of the dominant gender may provide women with a competitive advantage for leading institutions.

There are several advantages to choosing leaders based on an integrated collection of characteristics. One benefit is the psychological health of the president. As Marvalene Hughes asserted, "balanced sex role development

Mixture of Gender-Related Leadership Competencies	F | M "Feminine-Deficit" Model	F | M "Integrated" Model	F | M "Masculine-Deficit" Model
Consequences for:	Socialized Competencies (S)		Acquired Competencies (A)
Women	S | A	S | A	S | A
Men	S | A	S | A	S | A

* Socialized (S) attributes or competencies are those that one comes by "naturally" while Acquired (A) proficiencies must be learned and might represent acting across gender expectations. Thus, the larger the (S) component of the leadership model, the more advantageous that model is for one gender or the other.

Figure 5.1 Hypothetical Model of Women Leaders' Comparative Advantage

suggests that the healthy, competent adult in contemporary society—regardless of sex—is that individual capable of expressing a broad range of traits and characteristics in situationally-appropriate circumstances."[66]

A second important benefit is that women will be perceived as capable of academic leadership.[67] As Bryn Mawr president Mary Patterson McPherson stated, "we all know that there is nothing in the job description that women cannot do just as well as men."[68] Yet the benefits of more women assuming presidencies extends beyond equity considerations or the importance of role models. The greater potential is that women may connect "the characteristic strengths of their gender to the power of their office."[69] Women can bring a different type of leadership to higher education, enabling institutions to respond more effectively to the challenges of the new millennium. Chliwniak predicted that, the impact could be far reaching, affecting models and modes "in classrooms, boardrooms and scholarship."[70] No doubt, such change will be resisted. As Elizabeth Minnich described, it is not easy to start listening to voices you are unaccustomed to hearing, but society must move away from "the false universialization that has taken a very few privileged men from a particular tradition to be . . . the norm, the ideal for all."[71]

Real Women Presidents

Gender-based theories of leadership are compelling, but do they go beyond theory and predict actual behaviors? Do women actually exhibit the emergent, female-associated, leadership skills while working as presidents?

Alice Eagly and several colleagues completed four meta-analyses on various aspects of this question.[72] In their analysis of leadership style and gender, Eagly and Blair Johnson considered studies conducted in three ways: leaders acting within organizational settings; laboratory settings; and self-assessment inventories of individuals not currently in leadership positions.[73] Eagly and Johnson constructed two continua representing different dimensions of leadership on which each endpoint exemplified typical sex-role expectations. The first continuum gauged the interpersonal (female) versus task (male) orientation of leaders; the second measured style, ranging from democratic (female) to autocratic (male).

Their results are interesting and significant. In all three types of studies, women were in fact more democratic than men. However, women were only more interpersonally oriented only in laboratory settings or self-assessments. In actual organizational settings, there was little gender difference in the task-orientation of male and female presidents. The authors hypothesized that the gender differences were evident in the preponderance of the other studies because of biology, socialization, and sex-role spillover. The overwhelming power of the male-dominated culture of most organizations, and of leadership positions in particular, causes women in actual jobs to modify their sex-typical behavior (relationship-orientation) to more closely align with organizational norms.

Scholars of socialization and the impact on women's professional lives have described the sex-role incongruity that women experience when assuming managerial roles.[74] Women are evaluated by both superiors and subordinates on their femininity as well as their competence as leaders. To reiterate the double bind, if they act in a way that is too feminine, they risk losing their authority; too masculine and they are also judged harshly.[75] Not surprisingly, women espouse the value of the emergent skills, but are reluctant to utilize them extensively. Consequently, women leaders are not always viewed by their constituents as acting on their stated ideals. This dynamic was demonstrated by Margaret Jablonski in a recent study.[76] She interviewed seven women presidents who described their leadership style as empowering, collaborative, and communicative. She then questioned faculty members to determine whether their perceptions of the leader corroborated the president's self-assessment. Predictably, some faculty members on each campus, especially women faculty, did not always corroborate the president's perception. Whether the discrepancies found resulted from by an inaccurate self-assessment on the part of the president or overly critical faculty members was unclear. Nevertheless,

Jablonski raised interesting issues that could be studied more extensively with different approaches.

In one such approach, future scholars might identify specific actions and behaviors that correspond to the emergent and more female-identified leadership attributes. Presidential behavior could then be observed, recorded, coded, categorized, and assessed to determine whether the espoused leadership values are in fact acted upon. Such results would not depend upon the perceptions of followers, which may be biased in any number of directions.

A second approach would consider the relationship between the scholarly literature about college presidents and the perceptions of practitioners—sitting presidents. Women presidents would be asked to read a selected portion of the above-mentioned literature and reflect upon whether it adequately describes the skills needed for a president and whether women are more inclined to manifest the needed skills. In other words, does this literature "ring true" to sitting women presidents? Scholars of higher education are sometimes criticized for not making their work of more immediate use or relevance to practitioners; perhaps "field testing" theoretical literature in this manner would be useful.

A third approach is the examination of biographical or autobiographical literature on women presidents in which they were not answering direct questions about their leadership style per se. Within the language of the personal stories, women tell about their backgrounds, subsequent rise to the presidency, and views of the office. In so doing, their convictions regarding leadership style are revealed in ways that are conceivably more authentic than when asked directly by an interviewer to comment upon leadership style. There remains, of course, the concern of social desirability bias in which subjects respond in public (or in essays that will be published) in a manner they believe to be publicly acceptable or approved. Such a bias is difficult to eliminate in any qualitative research. However, when subjects are asked to respond to several issues, in which the ones of most interest to the researcher are embedded, the likelihood of an authentic response is increased.[77]

Using this approach, I analyzed the espoused leadership styles of ten female college presidents. In the last two decades, a few biographies, autobiographies, or collections of "mini-autobiographies" on women presidents have been published.[78] One the most recent publications in this genre is *Against the Tide: Career Paths of Women Leaders in American and British Higher Education,* edited by Karen Doyle Walton, co-author of the previous chapter on women chief academic officers.[79] *Against the Tide* is a collection of twenty "profiles" or "mini-autobiographies" of American and British presidents.[80] For purposes of this chapter and to avoid any possible confusion or bias resulting from differences in language use between American- and British-style English, only the ten profiles of American presidents were analyzed. Each profile was ten to fifteen pages long, and although Walton provided very little demographic information, most presidents offered a few clues about their ages. It is reasonable to assume that most of the presidents were in their fifties or sixties. Of course, all are highly educated. Five of the presidents hold Ph.D.s in the humanities (history, philosophy, linguistics, and two in English); three are scientists (geography, zoology, and chemistry). One woman is an anthropologist and another holds a doctorate in special education. No other demographic data are given in sufficient detail to provide comparisons.

Walton asked each woman to write about her personal journey to her current position. She provided minimal guidelines as to style, and asked the women to address some or all of a long list of subjects, including:

> personal background, educational background, career paths, helps (such as mentors) and hindrances encountered, recruitment for her present position, scholarly activities, public activities, acquiring and developing her leadership style and skills, personal strengths, conflict management, stress, job satisfaction, and encouraging other women to pursue careers in higher education.[81]

Walton intended to use the profiles to reveal similarities and differences between the career paths of British and American leaders. As the list intimates, Walton was most curious about the collection of experiences that led to the presidency. She did not analyze leadership styles in a theoretical sense, but noted that she was interested in whether an autobiography might reveal whether leadership attributes are innate or acquired and how an autobiography might reveal such insights. My goal, however, was only to discern their espoused philosophy of leadership.

The ten American presidents profiled in Walton's book and their positions at the time of their interviews were: Paula Pimlott Brownlee, former president of Hollins College (Virginia); Carol Cartwright, president of Kent State University (Ohio); Martha Church, president of Hood College (Maryland); Mary Maples Dunn, president of Smith College (Massachusetts); Vera King Farris, president of Richard Stockman College (New Jersey); Carol Harter, president of University of Nevada–Las Vegas; Bette Landman, president of Beaver College (Pennsylvania); Mary Patterson McPherson, president of Bryn Mawr College (Pennsylvania); Diana Natalicio, president of University of Texas at El Paso; and Judith Sturnick, former president of Keene State College (New Hampshire) and the University of Maine at Farmington.

Within the ten profiles, references to leadership skills and styles were identified. Because this was not the primary focus of each essay, often such references were brief. Three presidents hardly mentioned the topic. Mary Maples Dunn did not comment on her leadership style, but noted the importance of women in senior positions. While in graduate school as a working mother, a woman dean convinced Dunn that completing school and having children were both possible. Dunn commented that such advice seemed unlikely to come from a male provost.[82] Like Dunn, Paula Pimlott Brownlee assumed that a professional woman could not have a family as well, but she had a mentor who successfully juggled both and proved very inspirational. Her only comment on leadership was, "I believe that [my] domestic experience also helped me develop some of the skills that later would prove essential for an academic administrator," but she did not elaborate.[83]

Similarly, Diana Natalicio did not address her specific leadership style. She mentioned that she thinks it is disingenuous for presidents to discuss how much they disdain administrative work and yet choose administration as a career. She acknowledged that she did not attain her position without help from others, "I first understood that wanting to do something and being good at it, though important, were not sufficient conditions for success. I understood that others had to do their part to create opportunities." Although she said that her gender had not caused any particular obstacles, this quote is revealingly inconsistent with that assertion:

> I sometimes am asked whether being a woman president presents special challenges to me. In general, my response is that it doesn't seem to make all that much difference. . . . It is obvious that women still represent a small minority of university presidents and that there continue to be those faculty, students, and alumni who are not totally comfortable with the idea of a woman executive. My strategy in dealing with this attitude is to ignore it. During the seven years that I have been president, I believe that I have changed more attitudes by doing my job well than by worrying about or debating those attitudes.[84]

Higher education scholar Luba Chliwniak categorized many leadership attributes as falling on the "male" (traditional) or "female" (emergent) ends of various spectra.[85] Of the remaining seven profiles, five presidents acknowledged that their styles included examples of both masculine and feminine traits. In essence, they presented the integrated mixture that I suggest produces successful leaders.

Martha Church was guided by her philosophy of "women helping women and my deep commitment to the educational needs of women of varying ages and backgrounds."[86] She continued, "as a woman, I have been alert to spot and correct inequities and to suggest not doing something because of the message involved, for example, meeting only in states that have ratified the Equal Rights Amendment."[87] Church believed she could accomplish her goals if she kept fifteen tenets of leadership in mind. Of these tenets, several reflected the female end of the various continua of leadership styles including: belief in people as colleagues not to be manipulated; preference for discussion and sharing information instead of confrontation; belief in delegation with no "end runs" permitted; commitment to fair and scrupulously honest interactions on every level; willingness to hear criticism and take action on it where appropriate; and desire not to use a position only to gain another one. For Church, there was little room for the mystery and mastery noted in traditionally masculine leadership scholarship. None of her other tenets reflected the masculine extremes of the style continua. Most of Church's tenets were simply not found in the gendered leadership literature. For example, her remaining tenets included knowing when it was time to leave or taking time off for renewal.[88]

Vera King Farris's presidency was marred by racist incidents against her and copious amounts of harsh criticism. She philosophically placed such concerns behind her and strove as president to educate the community about racial equity. She maintained, "if the constituents leave a college carrying the same prejudices with which they entered, one wonders, ultimately what college is all about. . . . I am hopeful that the academy also can produce the solution to the human problems and provide a model of cooperation, of people living and learning in peace and harmony."[89] Farris' style displayed a good balance between task orientation and relationship:

> For me, the most appealing attribute of higher education administration is the opportunity to get a task accomplished, especially because in our field the goal often is the acquisition or dissemination of knowledge that will continue to improve the lot of humans. . . . The battery of skills and talents necessary to achieve process and policy development include leadership, persuasion, listening, communicating, and team building.[90]

She added, "understanding what it means to be a faculty member and how to work with and motivate faculty is an important asset for a college president."[91]

The title of Carol Harter's essay reveals her integrated approach to leadership, "Tough Mind, Kind Heart." As a student, she was discouraged from a possible chemistry major because "girls didn't do chemistry and math." Consequently, she now takes mentoring very seriously. "I also tried to mentor and promote other women and minorities who heretofore had not had opportunities in the 'hard' management arenas that finance and administration traditionally represent on our campuses," she stated.[92] Like Church, Harter listed ten specific traits that are important to leadership. Harter's list also included principles not discussed in the emergent literature such as enjoying one's self and staying physically fit. In a more traditional vein, she listed doing extraordinarily well, becoming politically sensitive while retaining integrity, and establishing a leadership presence. Her more emergent items included sublimating the ego, indulging a people-orientation, having a future orientation, and embodying and encouraging teamwork.[93]

Bette Landman learned to adopt an integrated leadership style by observing a male president who was gentle and caring to a fault. She described her leadership style succinctly, "[a] president does not lose by being perceived as an individual who can make hard decisions and still be caring. In the final analysis, being respected may be more important than being beloved."[94] Her leadership was filled with being "honest and fair" and she had but two central tenets—to trust her instincts and to be a good listener. She concluded, "I'm still trying to learn how and when to delegate and how to fully empower others."[95]

Mary Patterson McPherson took a different approach to writing her profile and quoted extensively from two speeches given on earlier occasions. In a 1992 keynote address at a Bryn Mawr conference on Women and Leadership, McPherson discussed the distinctiveness of feminine rhetoric which is analogous to feminine leadership style. She quoted scholar Karlyn Campbell, " 'structurally, feminine rhetoric is inductive, even circuitous, moving from example to example, and is usually grounded in personal experience. . . . The tone tends to be personal and somewhat tentative, rather than objective and authoritative.' "[96]

McPherson discussed explicitly the relationship of gender and leadership:

> each of you will need to decide by your own experience how much and what kind of a factor gender is in leadership and how much power inheres in qualities that are gradually becoming loosened from identification with only one gender. Gender is both a destiny and a decision—it is something we are born into, fated to, with the whole weight of its past and present social pressures. It also is something we each must define, develop, and deploy in a quite individual way, so it does not inhibit but rather enhances the talents, intelligence, and gifts that we bring.[97]

McPherson summarized her leadership style, "the fundamental qualification for education leadership, in my view, is a habit of interest in others and a penchant for involvement in complex situations."[98]

The final two of the ten profiles discussed only attributes described in the emergent literature. Carol Cartwright studied chemical engineering and recalls, "the chilly reception I received in 1958 as a student in a primarily male field taught me some important lessons about what happens to a student when there is a less-than-supportive atmosphere."[99] She possessed an overriding commitment to make life better for the students on her campus. "Students invest more than money and time in a college education. They trust us with their dreams."[100] In terms of leadership, Cartwright stated, "future solutions must take new approaches to solving problems and must incorporate new styles of leadership."[101] She viewed her leadership skills as the ability to take in discussion, live with ambiguity, and build consensus. "The key to being an effective leader and communicator is being comfortable with who you are — being confident in yourself and your style."[102] She also believed in sharing information, "Most people appreciate the facts and can deal with the realities of decision making. They want to be 'in the know.' "[103] She added:

> I agree with Harland Cleveland, who said that in today's horizontal society, the traditional modes of leadership—recommendations up, orders down—simply will no longer work. . . . In my role as president, I think about leadership tasks and leadership trust. The leadership task for change is to make it clear that people have permission to discuss and debate the issues and make recommendations. The leadership trust is that people believe that something will happen when they make proposals and have solutions to problems.[104]

Judith Sturnick expressed her belief in the power of sharing information and mentoring:

> Authentic power springs from the opportunities to mentor others, . . . to find ways to promote individuals internally on the campus, to inspire students (especially women) to dream more dramatic dreams, to help create a collegiate community, . . . to leave human and intellectual legacies, and to have loved—and been loved—by many people in the process . . . During these years of leadership, I also have learned that mentoring is especially important for women to offer to other women. We need male mentors, too; but women understand the language and realities of other women in a unique way. It may even be that female mentors help us work our way through the long struggles we have with our mothers.[105]

She also reflected, "[t]here are times in one's life when a person has to be willing to put his or her job on the line in order to preserve one's principles. Therefore, one of the greatest gifts we can give each other as women leaders and potential leaders is to tell each other the truth of our individual lives, instead of our gilded, self-serving myths."[106]

Cumulatively through these ten profiles, the women espoused a leadership philosophies that sometimes contained traditional elements, but also emphasized emergent traits. The majority possessed an integrated mixture. Interestingly they espoused these beliefs in an essay where their primary task was to describe their journeys to a presidency. These types of revelations may be more authentic than those gathered when the primary task is to espouse leadership philosophy. This analysis compliments the growing body of literature demonstrating that women bring important and potentially unique insights and skills to leadership positions. Future research must assess whether their espoused leadership theories are operationalized.[107]

Potential Lost

If women are not actually leading in the emergent ways that they espouse (and which leadership theory suggests is effective) why is the idealism embraced by women not coming to full fruition? A cynical view would emphasize that the emergent skills are impractical, idealist, or unrealistic and that espousing such utopian rhetoric is good public relations, but bad management. Yet, scholars imply that the emergent skills are advantageous and perhaps even vital for higher education. What aspects of colleges and universities impede the implementation of such promising styles of leadership?

Several theorists, including feminist organizational scholars, identify various structural barriers to women utilizing the emergent skills more fully. The more systemic analyses discuss the overwhelmingly patriarchal nature of higher education as an organization, root and branch.[108] Even the language used to describe organizations' structures and goals and the jobs people perform within them, is patriarchal in origin and meaning. Estela Bensimon, in a feminist reinterpretation of Bolman and Deal's frames, found that the language used to label the frames and the concepts therein are gendered—male.[109] Eagly and Johnson offered a slightly more benign, and I believe less likely, structural interpretation.[110] They proposed that gender differences inside organizations are minimized because there are published guidelines for behavior. They further argued that organizations socialize *all* members. Moreover, both men and women are chosen for positions by the same criteria (ostensibly) and therefore must conform to it.

In addition to structural barriers, organizational culture can thwart women presidents with overt criticism, harassment, or more subtle forms of discomfort. Research reveals that women are taken less seriously in the most stereotypically male aspects of the job such as fiscal affairs or management of the physical plant.[111] Eagly, Makhijani, and Klonsky's meta-analysis on the evaluation of leaders illustrates that women are more frequently criticized than men, and the criticism is even harsher if women adopt a masculine style of leadership. Again, women presidents risk the notorious double bind.

Not only are women criticized, but aspects of the academy that are associated with women or femininity are marginalized. Thus, inferior status is assigned to women's studies and women's scholarship. The marginalization is also apparent in the relative prestige of quantitative versus qualitative research methodology, the comparative prominence of "soft" and "hard" disciplines, and the low importance assigned to "women's work"—nurturing (including many aspects of student affairs), secretarial, clerical, or support functions.[112]

The infamous "Chilly Climate" in higher education is well documented.[113] Women endure countless tangible inequities, such as fewer resources, fewer opportunities, and sexual harassment. Innumerable, but often less perceptible, "micro-inequalities" accumulate. Women are acutely sensitive to symbols of exclusion, hostility, and neglect. The compounding effect of fewer opportunities for administrative promotion perpetuates the "pipeline problem"—resulting in too few women in positions that are stepping stones to presidencies.[114] The pipeline problem will be addressed only when the barriers to women's full participation are eliminated. These barriers are delineated and well documented and need not be repeated here.[115] However, barriers are not artifacts of the past, but remain firmly in place today, as the dearth of women presidents attests. Although the percentage of all college presidencies held by women has grown in the last decade—reaching 16.5 percent in the late 1990s, compared to 9.5 percent ten years earlier—it remains closer to demographic parody than demographic parity.[116]

Potential Found

Women exercising authority in higher education is not a new phenomenon nor is it limited to the office of the president. The chapters in this volume collectively show that women have exerted a force in higher education for well over a century. Brown and Introcaso examine presidential leadership, and Carolyn Bashaw and I demonstrate how deans of women exercised executive ability and used what power they had to provide "genuine access" for women. Susan Komives and Susan Jones illustrate how contemporary Senior Student Affairs Officers, extolling the virtues of the emergent attributes, exhibit considerable leadership on campus. Joan Paul, Linda Carpenter, and Vivian Acosta reveal the leadership displayed by physical educators and athletic directors, while Sharon McDade and Karen Doyle Walton demonstrate that the position of chief academic officer may, in fact, be the most influential on campus. Today, women in many varied positions are valuable leaders. They continue the tradition begun by Marion Talbot in 1881 when she created what became the AAUW—they form networks of women, gaining professional insights and encouragement from each other.

Women presidents are among those who meet to share strategies, insights, solutions, and dreams. The first meeting of women presidents was held in December of 1990 and was sponsored by OWHE of ACE. At that meeting Margaret McKenna, president of Leslie College in Cambridge, Massachusetts, voiced this sentiment, "[a] quality of leadership . . . often attributed to women is compassion. Female presidents are more likely than their male counterparts to be more concerned with how policy and practice affect people than how they affect the bottom line. . . . The question for us is, How do we use the values that society often assigns to women, like compassion and people-centeredness, as a way to make changes [and to] bring about reform?"[117]

In 1993, OWHE sponsored a subsequent meeting, the Women Presidents' Summit. The participants issued "A Blueprint for Leadership: How Women College and University Presidents Can Shape the Future." The Blueprint contained an outline of public policy issues to which the women presidents pledged to lend their voices and energies. They argued that women hold a unique perspective and vision that rarely informs pressing social issues such as global peace, the environment, and the economy. The "Blueprint" emphasized the distinctiveness of a woman president's point of view.

The most recent meeting of women presidents was held in November 1997 and participants echoed a similar theme. The multiple agencies sponsoring the event reflected the growing interest in the leadership potential of women presidents. A quote from Constance H. Buchman on the cover of the conference program eloquently expressed the tone of the meeting: "Women are poised to shape American values publicly on a scale to which they have never before had access. Much is riding on whether and how they choose to lead."

Notes

1. National Commission on Excellence in Education. "A Nation at Risk: The Imperative for Educational Reform: A Report to the Nation and the Secretary of Education, United States Department of Education" (Washington, D.C.: The Commission, 1983); Allan D. Bloom, *Closing of the American Mind: How Higher Education Has Failed Democracy and Impoverished the Souls of Today's Students* (New York: Simon & Schuster, 1987); Page Smith *Killing the Spirit: Higher Education in America* (New York: Viking, 1990); Dinesh D'Souza, *Illiberal Education: The Politics of Race and Sex on Campus* (New York: Free Press, 1991); Bruce Wilshire, *The Moral Collapse of the University: Professionalism, Purity, and Alienation* (Albany: State University of New York Press, 1990); Roger Kimball, *Tenured Radicals: How Politics Has Corrupted Our Higher Education* (New York: Harper & Row, 1990); Charles J. Sykes, *ProfScam: Professors and the Demise of Higher Education* (New York: St. Martin's Press, 1988); Peter Sacks, *Generation X Goes to College: An Eye-Opening Account of Teaching in Postmodern America* (Chicago: Open Court, 1996); and Anne Matthews, *Bright College Years: Inside the American Campus Today* (New York: Simon & Schuster, 1997).

2. See Robert Birnbaum, "Presidential Succession and Institutional Functioning in Higher Education," *The Journal of Higher Education* 60.2, (March/April 1989) as an example. In the article, Birnbaum argues that if presidents made a difference to the institution then substantial changes would be noted when administrations change. This was not the case.

3. Luba Chliwniak, *Higher Education Leadership: Analyzing the Gender Gap,* ASHE-ERIC Higher Education Report, volume 25, number 4, 1997 (Washington, D.C.: ASHE, 1997).

4. Marilyn J. Amey and Susan B. Twombly, "Re-Visioning Leadership in Community Colleges," *The Review of Higher Education,* 15.2 (Winter 1992).

5. It should not be assumed that women are any more monolithic regarding their attitudes about leadership than men. Women are equally susceptible to cultural images of leaders and therefore believe that men make better presidents. Women's orientation toward leadership is changing, but not

at the same rate for all. Offerman posited a spectrum across traditional sex role expectations. See G. Ellis and J. Wheeler, *Women Managers: Success on Our Own Terms: Career Strategies for New Zealand Women* (Auckland: Penguin Books, 1991); and Lynn R. Offerman and Cheryl Beil, "Achievement Styles of Women Leaders and Their Peers: Toward an Understanding of Women and Leadership," *Psychology of Women Quarterly* 16 (1992): 37–56.

6. Joseph N. Crowley, *No Equal in the World: An Interpretation of the Academic Presidency* (Reno: University of Nevada Press, 1994).

7. A preeminent example of a scholar who describes the "old time college president" is Frederick Rudolph, *The American College and University: A History* (New York: A. Knopf, 1962). In addition to Rudolph, scholars who describe a cadre of men as the great presidents of higher education history include: Edwin E. Slosson, *Great American Universities* (New York: Macmillan, 1910); and Laurence R. Veysey, *The Emergence of the American University* (Chicago: University of Chicago Press, 1965).

8. From M. Elizabeth Tidball's inauguration speech for Russell Sage College in 1976, quoted in Helen S. Astin and Carole Leland, *Women of Influence, Women of Vision: A Cross-Generational Study of Leaders and Social Change* (San Francisco: Jossey-Bass, 1991), 22.

9. Florence Denmark, "Women, Leadership, and Empowerment," *Psychology of Women Quarterly* 17 (1993): 343–56.

10. From Cynthia Fuchs Epstein, *Deceptive Distinctions: Sex, Gender, and the Social Order* (New Haven: Yale University Press, 1988), quoted in Susan B. Twombly, "What We Know about Women in Community Colleges: An Examination of the Literature Using Feminist Phase Theory," *Journal of Higher Education* 64 (1993): 189.

11. Tidball quoted in Astin and Leland, *Women of Influence, Women of Vision.*

12. Donna Shavlick and Judy Touchton. "Toward a New Era in Leadership: The National Identification Program," in *Women in Higher Education Administration,* New Directions in Higher Education, no. 45, ed. Adrian Tinsley, Cynthia Secor, and Sheila Kaplan (San Francisco: Jossey-Bass, 1984).

13. Anita J. Harrow, "Power and Politics: The Leadership Challenge," in *Cracking the Wall: Women in Higher Education Administration,* ed. Patricia Turner Mitchell (Washington, D.C.: College and University Personnel Association, 1993).

14. Judith Eaton, "Tapping Neglected Leadership Sources," in *Emerging Roles for Community College Leaders,* New Directions for Community Colleges, no. 45, ed. Richard L. Alfred, Paul A. Elsner, R. Jan LeCroy, and Nancy Armes (San Francisco: Jossey-Bass, 1984).

15. Linda Kuk, "New Approaches to Management," in *Different Voices: Gender and Perspectives in Student Affairs Administration,* ed. Jane Fried

(Washington, D.C.: National Association of Student Personnel Administrators, 1994).

16. Ibid.

17. Harrow in *Cracking the Wall,* ed. Mitchell, 142 and 145.

18. There is, of course, a large dilemma posed by discussing individuals according to stereotypes. The larger point is that if men are chosen based on beliefs that they posses stereotypic traits, then such logic could apply to women as well. Especially if stereotypically female traits are demonstrated to be positively associated with effective leadership.

19. Amey and Twombly, "Re-Visioning Leadership in Community Colleges." See also Susan B. Twombly, "Gendered Images of Community College Leadership: What Messages They Send," in *Gender and Power in the Community College,* ed. Barbara K. Townsend (San Francisco: Jossey-Bass, 1995).

20. Estela M. Bensimon, Anna Neumann, and Robert Birnbaum, *Making Sense of Administrative Leadership: The "L" Word in Higher Education,* ASHE-ERIC Higher Education Report 1, 1989 (Washington, D.C.: School of Education and Human Development, The George Washington University, 1989).

21. In addition to Bensimon, Neumann, and Birnbaum's *Making Sense of Administrative Leadership*, I will cite other references were explanations of leadership theory may be useful. See also Denmark, "Women, Leadership, and Empowerment."

22. Bensimon, Neumann, and Birnbaum, *Making Sense of Administrative Leadership*, 8.

23. John R. P. French and Bertram H. Raven, "The Bases of Social Power," in *Studies in Social Power,* ed. Dorwin Cartwright (Ann Arbor, Mich.: Institute for Social Research, 1959).

24. Bensimon, Neumann, and Birnbaum. *Making Sense of Administrative Leadership*, 9.

25. James McGregor Burns, *Leadership* (New York: Harper & Row, 1978) 20.

26. Bensimon, Neumann, and Birnbaum, *Making Sense of Administrative Leadership*, 10.

27. John R. Wilcox and Susan B. Ebbs, *The Leadership Compass: Values and Ethics in Higher Education,* ASHE-ERIC Higher Education Report No. 1, 1992 (Washington, D.C.: ASHE).

28. Bensimon, Neumann, and Birnbaum, *Making Sense of Administrative Leadership*, 13.

29. Ibid., 19.

30. Ibid., 20–21.

31. Marvin W. Peterson and Melinda G. Spencer, "Understanding Organizational Culture and Climate," in *Assessing Academic Climates and*

Cultures, New Directions for Institutional Research, no. 68, ed. William G. Tierney (San Francisco: Jossey-Bass, 1991).

32. Bensimon, Newmann, and Birnbaum, *Making Sense of Administrative Leadership*, 22.

33. See, for example, Andrew T. Masland, "Organizational Culture in the Study of Higher Education," *Review of Higher Education* 8.2 (1985): 157–68, or William G. Tierney, "Organizational Culture in Higher Education: Defining the Essentials," *Journal of Higher Education* 59.1 (1988): 2–21, as examples of articles on culture in higher education.

34. See Bensimon, Newmann, and Birnbaum, *Making Sense of Administrative Leadership* for their discussion of this integration.

35. Gary L. Riley and J. Victor Baldridge, *Governing Academic Organizations* (Berkeley, Calif.: McCutchan Publishing Corporation, 1977) and Michael D. Cohen and James G. March, *Leadership and Ambiguity: The American College President* (Boston: Harvard Business School Press, 1974).

36. Lee G. Bolman and Terrence Deal, *Reframing Organizations: Artistry, Choice and Leadership* (San Francisco: Jossey-Bass, 1991).

37. See, especially, Robert Birnbaum, *How Colleges Work: The Cybernetics of Academic Organization and Leadership* (San Francisco: Jossey-Bass, 1988).

38. The Meaning of Good Presidential Leadership: A Frame Analysis," *The Review of Higher Education* 12.2 (Winter 1989): 107–23.

39. Bensimon, Newmann, and Birnbaum, *Making Sense of Administrative Leadership*, 23. Not all agree with this research perspective. For example, Fincher questions the value of new research, feels there is little to support the cultural vision of higher education. See Cameron Fincher, "Theory and Research in Administrative Leadership," in *Higher Education: Handbook of Theory and Research,* Vol. XI (New York: Agathon Press, 1996).

40. Bensimon, Newmann, and Birnbaum, *Making Sense of Administrative Leadership*, 23–24.

41. See Cameron Fincher, "Theory and Research in Administrative Leadership"; also Cameron Fincher, "Principles and Examples of Leadership," *Research in Higher Education* 36.6, 1995, 705–9; James L. Fisher, *Power of the Presidency* (New York: Macmillan Publishing, Co., 1984); and the Commission on the Academic Presidency, "Renewing the Academic Presidency: Stronger Leader for Tougher Times" (Washington, D.C.: Association of Governing Boards, 1996).

42. See Jane Fried, "In Groups, Out Groups, Paradigms, and Perceptions," in Jane Fried, ed., *Different Voices* and Thomas Stauffer, "A University Model for the 1990s," in *An Agenda for a New Decade,* ed. Larry W. Jones and Franz A. Nowotny (San Francisco: Jossey-Bass, 1990).

43. Florence Guido-DiBrito, Patricia A. Noteboom, Laura Nathan, and Joseph Fenty, "Traditional and New Paradigm Leadership: The Gender Link," *Initiatives* 58.1 (1996): 91.

44. Even within the business culture, such a movement is obvious. Note the popularity in the last several years of Total Quality Management and Participative Management. See popular management gurus such as Tom Peters in P. Aburdene and J. Naisbitt, *Megatrends for Women* (New York: Villard Books, 1992). A call for teamwork is the focus of Estela M. Bensimon and Anna Neumann, *Redesigning Collegiate Leadership: Teams and Teamwork in Higher Education* (Baltimore: The Johns Hopkins University Press, 1993). Other perspectives for leadership are: ethical—Wilcox and Ebbs, *The Leadership Compass*; empowering—Susan R. Komives, "New Approaches to Leadership," in Jane Fried, ed., *Different Voices*; authentic—R. W. Terry, *Authentic Leadership: Courage in Action* (San Francisco: Jossey-Bass, 1993); connective—Jean Lipman-Blumen. "Connective Leadership: Female Leadership Styles in the 21st-Century Workplace," *Sociological Perspectives* 35 (1992): 183-203.

45. Judith Sturnick in Larry C. Spears, ed., *Insights on Leadership: Service, Stewardship, Spiritual, and Servant-Leadership*; Denmark, "Women, Leadership, and Empowerment," 351–52; Margaret Jablonski, "The Leadership Challenge for Women College Presidents," *Initiatives* 57.4 (1996): 1–10. She suggests that the emergent skills are empowerment, shared decision-making, communication, collaboration.

46. Chliwniak, *Higher Education Leadership;* C. Desjardin "Gender Issues in Community College Leadership," *AAWCJC Journal,* 1989, p. 5–10; C. Johnson, "Gender and Formal Authority," *Social Psychology Quarterly* 56.3. (1993): 193–210; and C. Northcutt, *Successful Career Women: Their Professional and Personal Characteristics* (New York: Greenwood Press, 1990).

47. Virginia Valian, *Why So Slow: The Advancement of Women.* Cambridge, MA: MIT Press, 1998, 2.

48. Bensimon, Newmann, and Birnbaum, *Making Sense of Administrative Leadership*, 16.

49. Judith Block McLaughlin and David Riesman, *Choosing a College President: Opportunities and Constraints* (Princeton: Carnegie Foundation for the Advancement of Teaching, 1990).

50. Chliwniak, *Higher Education Leadership,* 49.

51. Ibid.

52. Susan Komives, "New Approaches to Leadership," in *Different Voices,* ed. Jane Fried, 48.

53. Bensimon, Newmann, and Birnbaum, *Making Sense of Administrative Leadership*, 38.

54. Bernard Bass, "From Transactional to Transformational Leadership: Learning to Share the Vision," *Organizational Dynamics* 18 (1990).

55. Michael Z. Hackman, Alison H. Furness, Marylyn J. Hills, and Tracy J. Patterson, "Perceptions of Gender-Role Characteristics and Transformational and Transactional Leadership Behaviors," *Perceptual and Motor Skills* 75 (1992).

56. Chliwniak, *Higher Education Leadership,* 46, 51, and 61.

57. Bolman and Deal, *Reframing Organizations.* See especially chapters 12, 13, and 14.

58. Linda Kuk, "New Approaches to Management," in *Different Voices,* ed. Fried, 64. See also Carol Gilligan, *In a Different Voice: Psychological Theory and Women's Development* (Cambridge: Harvard University Press, 1982).

59. Chliwniak, *Higher Education Leadership,* 49.

60. Lipman-Blumen, "Connective Leadership."

61. Discussions of the organizational nature of higher education using theses sorts of metaphors include: Bensimon, Neumann, and Birnbaum, *Making Sense of Administrative Leadership*; Birnbaum, *How Colleges Work*; Bolman and Deal, *Reframing Organizations*; and especially Cohen and March, *Leadership and Ambiguity.*

62. Chliwniak, *Higher Education Leadership,* 69.

63. I wish to thank Adrianna Kezar for her thoughtful comments on an early version of this work. In her dissertation, Kezar made a strong case for rejecting two discrete models of leadership (one male and one female) in favor of broadening our overall understanding of leadership theory. See Adrianna J. Kezar, "Reconstructing Exclusive Images: An Examination of Higher Education Leadership Models," unpublished doctoral dissertation, University of Michigan, Ann Arbor, 1996.

64. Carol. C. Harter, "Women, Leadership, and the Academy: Anecdotes and Observations," in Mitchell, ed., *Cracking the Wall.* See also Alice G. Sargent and Ronald J. Stupak, "Managing in the 90s: The Androgynous Manager," *Training and Development Journal* 43 (December 1989): 29–32, on adopting the best of both sexes.

65. Marvalene S. Hughes, "Feminization and Student Affairs," reprinted in Audrey L. Rentz, ed., *Student Affairs: A Professon's Heritage* (Lanham, Md.: University Press of America, 1994). See also Sandra L. Bem, "The Measurement of Psychological Androgyny," *Journal of Consulting and Clinical Psychology* 42 (1974).

66. Hughes, "Feminization and Student Affairs."

67. Guido-DiBrito et al., "Traditional and New Paradigm Leadership."

68. Walton, *Against the Tide,* 164.

69. Deborah M. DiCroce, "Women and the Community College Presidency: Challenges and Possibilities," from Barbara K. Townsend, ed., *Gender and Power in the Community College* (San Francisco: Jossey-Bass, 1995).

70. Chliwniak, *Higher Education Leadership,* 79.

71. Elizabeth K. Minnich, *Transforming Knowledge* (Philadelphia: Temple University Press, 1990), 2.

72. The four meta-analyses are: Alice H. Eagly and Blair T. Johnson, "Gender and Leadership Style: A Meta-analysis," *Psychological Bulletin* 108 (1990): 233–56; Alice H. Eagly and Steven J. Karau, "Gender and the Emergence of Leaders: A Meta-analysis," *Journal of Personality and Social Psychology* 60 (1991): 685–710; Alice H. Eagly, Mona G. Makjijani, and Bruce G. Klonsky, "Gender and the Evaluation of Leaders: A Meta-analysis," *Psychological Bulletin* 111 (1992): 3–22; Alice H. Eagly, Steven J. Karau, and Mona G. Makhijani. "Gender and the Effectiveness of Leaders: A Meta-analysis," *Psychological Bulletin,* 117 (1975): 125–45.

73. Eagly and Johnson, "Gender and Leadership Style."

74. Rosabeth Moss Kanter, *Men and Women of the Corporation* (New York: Basic Books, 1977) and Edward Lafontaine and Bonnie Jean McKenzie, "Being Out on the Inside in Higher Education Administration: Women's Responses to Role and Status Incongruity." *Journal of the National Association of Women Deans, Administrators, and Counselors* 48.2 (Winter 1985): 19–25.

75. Eagly, Makjijani, and Klonsky, "Gender and the Evaluation of Leaders."

76. Jablonski, "The Leadership Challenge for Women College Presidents."

77. Jerome Kirk and Marc L Miller, *Reliability and Validity in Qualitative Research* (Newbury Park, Calif.: Sage Publications, 1986).

78. Other examples of biographies, autobiographies, memoirs, or "war stories" of women presidents include: Judith Sturnick, Jane E. Milley, and Catherine A. Tisinger, eds., *Women at the Helm: Pathfinding Presidents at State Colleges and Universities* (Washington, D.C.: American Association of State Colleges and Universities, 1991); Johnnetta B. Cole, *Conversations: Straight Talk with America's Sister President* (New York: Anchor Books, 1993); Helen Astin and Carole Leland, *Women of Influence, Women of Vision: A Cross-Generational Study of Leaders and Social Change* (San Francisco: Jossey-Bass, 1991).

79. Karen Doyle Walton, ed. *Against the Tide: Career Paths of Women Leaders in American and British Higher Education.* (Bloomington, Ind.: Phi Delta Kappa Educational Foundation, 1996).

80. Walton uses the word "president" for the sake of convenience although several of the British senior administrators actually had other titles. However, all the Americans had the title of president.

81. Walton, *Against the Tide,* 7–8.

82. Ibid., 95–105.

83. Ibid., 37.

84. Ibid., 178, 186–89.

85. Chliwniak, *Higher Education Leadership,* 47–48.

86. Walton, *Against the Tide,* 70.
87. Ibid., 78.
88. Ibid., 72–73.
89. Ibid., 118.
90. Ibid., 110–11.
91. Ibid.
92. Ibid., 130.
93. Ibid., 131–32.
94. Ibid., 141.
95. Ibid., 145.
96. Ibid., 157.
97. Ibid., 158.
98. Ibid., 164.
99. Ibid., 57.
100. Ibid., 58.
101. Ibid., 57.
102. Ibid., 62.
103. Ibid.
104. Ibid., 63–66.
105. Ibid., 249–53
106. Ibid., 254–56.
107. Christopher Argyris and Donald Schön describe the differences between espoused theory and theory-in-use in *Theory in Practice: Increasing Professional Effectiveness* (San Francisco: Jossey-Bass, 1974).
108. See Joan Acker, "Hierarchies, Jobs, and Bodies: A Theory of Gendered Organizations," *Gender and Society* 4.2 (June 1990); and Marta B. Calas and Linda Smircich, "Re-Writing Gender into Organizational Theorizing: Directions from Feminist Perspectives," from Michael Reed and Michael Hughes, eds., *Rethinking Organizations: New Directions in Organizational Theory and Analysis* (Newbury Park, Calif.: Sage Publications, 1992).
109. Estela Bensimon, "The Meaning of Presidential Leadership: Alternatives to Charismatic Leadership," in *Women at the Helm* (1991), eds. Sturnick, Milley, and Tisinger.
110. Eagly and Johnson, "Gender and Leadership Style." Also, Kanter in *Men and Women of the Corporation* largely takes this view.
111. George Vaughn, "Black Community College Presidents," *Community College Review* 17.2 (1989): 21–26.
112. Arthur G. Jago, and Victor H. Vroom, "Sex Differences in the Incidence and Evaluation of Participative Leader Behavior," *Journal of Applied Psychology* 67 (1982).
113. Bernice R. Sandler, Lisa A. Silverberg, and Roberta Hall, *The Chilly Classroom Climate: A Guide to Improve the Education of Women* (Washington, D.C.: National Association for Women in Education, 1996).

114. Linda K. Johnsrud and Ronald H. Heck, "Administrative Promotion within a University," *The Journal of Higher Education* 65 (1994): 23–44. See Valian's discussion of microinequalities in *Why So Slow?*

115. There are numerous examples, but a particularly interesting one is Mary T. Flynn, "Questioning the System: A Feminist Perspective," in *Cracking the Wall,* ed. Mitchell.

116. Joyce Mercer, "Most College Presidents Are White Males, but Women and Minorities Post Gains," *Chronicle of Higher Education,* April 1, 1998. This story discusses the American Council on Education's "The American College President: A 1998 Edition," which is based on 1995 data. For a more in-depth profile of women presidents specifically, see Judith Touchton, Donna Shavlik, and Lynne Davis, *Women in Presidencies: A Descriptive Study of Women College and University Presidencies* (Washington, D.C.: ACE, OWHE, 1993).

117. Debra E. Blum, "Female Presidents Compare Notes, Urge Renewed Push for Reforms," *Chronicle of Higher Education,* December 19, 1990, p. A13.

PART III

Changing Lives: Women as Managers, Mentors, Guardians, and Healers

CHAPTER 6

Advocates on Campus

Deans of Women Create a New Profession

JANA NIDIFFER

Any woman who graduated from a coeducational college or university between the turn of the century and the early-1960s, probably had a dean of women on her campus. Until the 1950s, deans were virtually ubiquitous. For women who attended college after the 1920s and 1930s, the dean was probably perceived as exclusively responsible for the conduct for women students; she was less likely to be regarded as an advocate for women students in the face of the now well documented "Chilly Climate" inherent in coeducational institutions. In fact, most students, especially the well-behaved, probably had little if anything to do with the dean of women. Among the myriad changes that swept campuses in the 1960s was the continued decline in the numbers of deans of women. By the end of that decade, the out-of-classroom life of male and female students alike was typically served by a collection of student affairs professionals. By the 1970s, the position had all but disappeared.

In the popular imagination deans of women are often stereotyped as either matronly, curmudgeonly chaperones or an innocuous mother figures.[1] In fact, on more than a few occasions, women who remember their deans have commented that any depiction of deans of women as advocates is a bit startling. Yet neither the characterization of curmudgeon nor that of house mother is wholly accurate. During the Progressive Era, the position of dean of women was instead one "in which intelligent, well-qualified, well-educated women could exercise administrative skills and professional leadership and exert a unifying influence on behalf of women."[2] The early deans of women of the Progressive Era accomplished two major goals. These well-qualified, well-educated deans improved the material lot of women students, especially at midwestern state universities. In addition, and perhaps most importantly, the deans—at least a small cadre of leaders between the years of 1892 and

1916—forged a new professional identity for themselves as the first senior women administrators on coeducational university campuses. Their effort to create a profession for women reveals typical difficulties professional women faced in the early twentieth century.

The position of dean of women also played an intriguing historical role by being the first systemic, administrative response in higher education to cope with a new, and essentially unwelcome, population. There was one brief period when the College of William and Mary hired a "Master of the Indian School," to look after the few Native American students, but by 1721, the Indian School had faded away and it was not emulated at other colonial colleges.[3] The position of dean of women, on the other hand, was replicated widely. After World War II with the appointment of special officers to attend to the needs of returning veterans, hiring an administrator for a new or marginalized population on campus became a very common practice in higher education. But deans of women were the first!

Early History of Deans of Women

The position of dean of women was born in the antebellum liberal arts colleges of the midwest; it came of age in midwestern universities in the early twentieth century. Oberlin College opened its doors to women in 1833, an era in which propriety required the close supervision of unmarried young women in proximity to young men. The president and faculty quickly recognized such "problems which demanded the presence and supervision of an older woman."[4] The first woman to serve in this position at Oberlin was Mrs. Marianne Parker Dascom with the title of "Lady Principal of the Female Department."[5] The 1835 description of the Female Department in the college catalog indicated both Oberlin's desire to appease trepidation regarding coeducation and the scope of Mrs. Dascom's duties:

> Young ladies of good minds, unblemished morals, and respectable attainments are received into this department and placed under the supervision of a judicious lady, whose duty it is to correct their habits and mould the female character. They attend recitations with young gentlemen in all the departments. Their rooms are entirely separate from those of the other sex, and no calls or visits in the respective apartments are at all permitted.[6]

Antioch College in Yellow Springs, Ohio was also coeducational from its opening in 1854. President Horace Mann acknowledged that "[t]he advantages of joint education are very great. The dangers are terrible." Mann insisted on a boarding house for the young women. He stated, "I should deprecate exceedingly turning them out in the streets for meals."[7] This type of boarding house required a female supervisor, so a matron was hired.

When members of the Board of Regents of the University of Michigan were contemplating coeducation for their institution in 1858, they solicited opinions from educational experts of the day including Mann and Charles Grandison Finney, president of Oberlin. Finney replied that the results at Oberlin were "satisfactory and admirable" and offered the Board the following advice for ensuring success: "You will need a *wise and pious matron* with such lady assistants as to keep up supervision." (emphasis added).[8] Despite the positive outcome Finney reported, Michigan remained single-sex for another twelve years even though the charter of the institution said it was "open to all persons." It was a combination of political pressure from taxpayers and the pragmatic necessity of training women teachers that finally forced the university to open its doors to women in 1870.

The experiences of Oberlin and Antioch illustrated two important themes in the earliest history of deans of women. First, the "Lady Principal" was hired as a direct response to prevailing concerns regarding coeducation. Second, her duties were limited to supervision of living arrangements and the moral guardianship of the women students. As chapter 1 details, coeducation became more prevalent after the Civil War and so did the number of residential colleges employing lady principals, matrons, or preceptresses who supervised the women's housing. Swarthmore College was typical and engaged a "judicious matron" in 1872. By 1880, this practice was more common than not in the coeducational, liberal arts colleges of the Midwest.[9]

The pattern of hiring deans of women at midwestern *universities* was different, however, and it did not begin until the 1890s. The primary reason why many universities failed to employ a "wise and pious matron" from the outset was because the young state universities generally did not provide on-campus housing for women or men due to the persistent lack of resources. The women students were expected to lodge with family members or in local rooming houses. Without a specific dormitory, house, or female college to supervise, university presidents felt little imperative to hire a female administrator. For example, Indiana University (IU) experimented briefly with the position when Sarah Parke Morrison, Indiana University's first female graduate (1869), was hired to be a social advisor to women students in 1873. Morrison resigned her position after only two years and it remained unfilled for the next quarter of a century.[10]

In the late 1880s and early 1890s circumstances changed, leading to the appointment of women administrators. At a few universities, women students, their parents, and sometimes community members as well, agitated for the university to offer some living arrangements for the women students. Without supervised housing, middle-class parents and families who lived long distances from the campuses expressed reluctance to send daughters to college.[11] If boarding houses, residence halls, or sorority houses were created, an administrator was needed. The typical practice of using the boarding houses in town had grown unsatisfactory.

There were other catalysts, however, beyond the need to monitor a dormitory. As the 1890s progressed, faculty members on several campuses, with or without special residence halls for women, grew increasingly concerned about the extra-curricular activities of students. At the same time, faculty reluctance to handle such matters was intensifying. The growing demand for research productivity placed new pressures on faculty and created an unwillingness on their part to spend vast amounts of time on administrative details or student supervision. Nor would a president interested in research results want a faculty so engaged.[12]

It was interesting that the administrative response to excesses in student behavior, which included class "rushes" and violence in athletics, was a dean of *women* when it was generally acknowledged that it was male students who exhibited the most troubling behavior. Such reactions suggest that presidents were responding equally to a resurgence of anti-coeducation sentiment at the turn of the century and to the consequent uneasiness felt on many campuses.[13]

Chapter 1 delineates the specific causes for the battle over coeducation which was long and acrimonious. It became a rallying cry for feminists who had forgone their battle for suffrage to join the abolitionist movement before the Civil War. Coeducation was also the cause taken up by some education reformers who wanted teachers, by then a largely female occupation, to have a full college education. The high degree of negative feelings toward women on campuses created an environment that ranged from inhospitable to openly hostile. Therefore, administrators at coeducational universities in the 1890s were obligated to worry about the "woman problem." One response was hiring a dean of women. A pioneer in this regard was William Rainey Harper of the University of Chicago. Harper's dream was to make Chicago a western Yale and the generosity of John D. Rockefeller gave him the resources to lure prestigious eastern academics to the shores of Lake Michigan.[14]

Harper was determined to fashion a great university quickly by hiring proven administrators and established scholars. Harper was not an enthusiast for coeducation, but the charter of the university demanded it. In keeping with his desire to hire the most talented faculty that he could and the social expectation that college women needed supervision, Harper offered Alice Freeman Palmer, the former president of Wellesley College, the position of professor of history and dean of women for the university.

Palmer was reluctant to turn down an opportunity to become a female professor in a coeducational institution, for there were precious few such offers in 1892. She agreed, however, upon two conditions. Because her Harvard professor husband, George Herbert Palmer, was unwilling to leave Cambridge, Alice Palmer said she would only work in Chicago for twelve weeks a year. She also demanded that Marion Talbot, also a professor at Wellesley, be appointed as her deputy. Because of Palmer's schedule, Talbot was, in effect, the dean of women at Chicago, but became so officially upon Palmer's retirement in 1895.[15]

Becoming More Than "A Wise and Pious Matron"

With Talbot's appointment in 1892, the position of dean of women began to change. By 1916, the year in which the National Association of Deans of Women (NADW) was founded, a small cadre of women, mostly from midwestern institutions, had transformed the position into a profession. This chapter examines the careers of four such women and the strategies they employed to meet their twin goals of being advocates for women students and creating a profession for themselves. Each of the four women made a specific contribution to the evolution of the profession and exemplified a specific strategy for helping women. In addition, each woman was, at times, representative of other deans serving in the same era. The four women are: Marion Talbot, University of Chicago, 1892–1925; Mary Bidwell Breed, Indiana University, 1901–6; Ada Comstock, University of Minnesota, 1906–12; and Lois Mathews (later Rosenberry), University of Wisconsin, 1911–18. The process they went through to establish a profession is similar to that of myriad professions established in the early twentieth century. There were four steps that were especially salient to the deans' quest for professional recognition: laying an intellectual foundation; initiating collective activity; becoming an expert; and creating a professional literature and association.

Laying the Intellectual Foundation

Marion Talbot was a bright and ambitious young woman raised in comfortable circumstances whose family was part of the Boston intelligentsia. Julia Ward Howe and Louisa May Alcott were in her social milieu. Her father, Israel Tisdale Talbot, was passionate about health reform and the first dean of Boston University's medical school. In 1881, along with her mother, Emily Talbot, Marion founded the Association of Collegiate Alumnae (ACA), the forerunner of the American Association of University Women.[16] The ACA had a twofold purpose of "offering encouragement to young women wanting to go to college and expanding the opportunities for women graduates."[17]

The ACA made several important contributions to women's higher education over the years including the establishment of fellowships for graduate study that helped several women earn doctorates. During her years as dean of women at Chicago, Marion served as ACA president (1895 to 1897) and remained connected to the organization until her death. Urged by Marion in 1912, the ACA changed its criteria for accrediting institutions and demanded, among other things, that the college or university have a dean of women. In 1921, the ACA became the American Association of University Women. Later, in 1931, Talbot co-authored a history of its founding and accomplishments with another important dean of women, Lois Mathews Rosenberry.[18]

Talbot's concern for the postcollege fate of educated women was transformed at Chicago where she became devoted to making sure that the women students enjoyed the full advantages of the university while on campus. She understood the anti-coeducation sentiment that prevailed and she, like Breed, Comstock, and Mathews, wanted to change the university and make it a more hospitable environment for women. She began by creating the Women's Union in 1901, but employed many other strategies as well.

From the beginning, although Talbot was officially charged with looking after the undergraduate women, she actually considered all the women of the university community as her constituency. As dean, she was responsible for the provision and superintendence of adequate housing and the social supervision of students. In the residence halls where students of all ages mixed, she advocated a "house plan" that meant that the students were largely self-governed although each dorm had a woman with an academic appointment as the head resident. The freedom from supervision that this afforded was a tribute to Talbot's liberal attitudes toward and confidence in women students. A former student and faculty colleague of Talbot's recalled that she had a "warmheartedness, a quick understanding and sympathy, and a sincere and uncompromising evaluation of the rights and wrongs of a case. Her desire was always that women should go forth from the University with ability to think for themselves, to develop their powers to the utmost and to lead useful and gracious lives."[19]

Chicago was also the home of an important women's community off campus at the turn of the century. Women were active in several fields, but the most notable was the large women-dominated reformist community in Chicago led by Jane Addams and her associates at Hull House, founded in 1899. Addams was so frequent a speaker on campus and Hull House so often the host to many of the university's prominent sociologists, that she was virtually an adjunct faculty member.[20] She also sponsored meetings of women fellows (graduate students with fellowships) and other examples of formal and informal gatherings of students and faculty. Talbot used all the resources available to create a sense of community and simultaneously provided women with the intellectual opportunities available at a university such as Chicago.[21]

Talbot regularly surveyed "the women of the university" from her vantage point as dean and presented her findings in her annual reports to the president.[22] She emphasized the accomplishments of female professors, undergraduates, and graduate students to illustrate that "the presence of women did not mean the lowering of any standards."[23] She also wrote of difficulties and losses for women at Chicago. She rarely missed the opportunity to remind Harper that the women needed additional university funds and support. In her 1905–6 report to the president, she rather caustically pointed out that "the work in Physical Culture continues to gain in effectiveness in spite of the fact that the increase in the number of students is not accompanied by the corresponding increase in instructional force or equipment."[24] Her use of graphs, charts, and statistics sometimes allowed "the status of Chicago's women [to] speak for themselves."[25] On one occasion, she illustrated that the number of women faculty members was actually declining as time passed rather than increasing despite gains in the number of women earning the Ph.D. She noted that there were fifty-two women of academic rank in 1902–3 but only forty-five in 1903–4, a loss of 14 percent. As Ellen Fitzpatric noted, "Whatever her technique, Talbot's insistent refrain ensured that nothing would silence the voice of what William Rainey Harper called 'the woman side of the university.' "[26]

Talbot also articulated a purpose for women's education that she believed would both lay the intellectual foundations for the work of deans and minimize resistance to coeducation. She subscribed to several strains of late-nineteenth-century thought regarding intelligence and sex-role definition that were challenging conventional assumptions about the place of women in education and society. In terms of her efforts to professionalize deans, two of her beliefs were particularly relevant.[27]

First, she believed in a modernist notion about the inherent rationality of all human beings, which implied that women were as capable of intellectual thought as men. As she stated unequivocally in her book *The Education of Women,* "women have proved their ability to enter every realm of knowledge. They must have the right to do it. . . . Unhampered by traditions of sex, women will naturally and without comment seek the intellectual goal which they think good and fit."[28] Yet Talbot never completely relinquished all the vestiges of Victorian notions of propriety and separate spheres, other than intellectual, so the second component of her belief was that women were unique from men and required an environment that was special or distinct. Her beliefs in the benefits of a separate women's community placed Talbot firmly within the tradition of late-nineteenth-century feminists who adopted what Estelle Freedman referred to as "separatism as a strategy."[29] The women "preferred to retain membership in a separate female sphere, one which they did not believe to be inferior to men's sphere and one in which women could be free to create their own forms of personal, social, and political relationships."[30]

Creating essentially a separate-but-equal social life for women, as historian Joyce Antler has noted, often reinforced the sexual status quo by making the separate spheres seem immutable, and, perhaps, this actually limited the choices for women. Yet the creation of a discrete "social structure . . . was a positive response to the pervasive sexism on campus."[31] If any of the four deans engaged the merits of this debate, they left no written record. It was clear from their actions, however, that they followed the separatism strategy common to women prior to World War I and created a distinct women's community on campus.

Talbot fought a pitched battle at the University of Chicago to maintain coeducational classrooms, however. Anti-coeducation sentiment was strong at the turn of the century and in 1900, the university administration proposed the segregation of instruction for men and women in the Junior College (freshman and sophomore years). She galvanized the opposition because separate classrooms threatened her lifelong crusade to establish the intellectual equality of the sexes. The faculty voted to approve Harper's plan in the summer of 1902, but it never became fully operational, apparently dying of atrophy.

Talbot was attacked by those opponents of coeducation who argued that if women needed a separate social environment, they should be in separate classrooms as well. But Talbot firmly stated that mixed classrooms were the only way to insure equivalent educational opportunities and that the needed "special" environment was for the out-of-classroom lives of women. Thus Talbot acted as an intellectual bridge between the older view that feminine uniqueness implied intellectual limitations—"true womanhood"—and the belief that women were as rational as men, but still distinct—"new womanhood."[32] By asserting that women were academically capable in any field and the need for unique circumstances applied only to the social realm, she secured for women a safe place within the university, maintained propriety, and yet kept all avenues of mental exploration open. Her view laid the foundation for the professional work of deans.

Initiating Collective Activity

Talbot took the next step in professionalization and communicated her beliefs with other deans of women. She published widely in various education journals, especially the *Journal of the ACA,* but most importantly she initiated the first collective activity of deans by organizing the first professional conference. She decided to invite several women from other midwestern colleges and universities for a two-day conference in November of 1903.

Eighteen women, including the young chemistry professor and dean of women at nearby Indiana University—Mary Bidwell Breed—arrived in Chicago in the autumn of 1903.[33] All the deans represented institutions in the midwest (except the dean of the college of Barnard) so it was not surprising that the meeting's official title was the Conference of Deans of Women of the Middle West. Ten of the women were from private institutions while eight represented state universities. Twelve of the women held faculty appointments in addition to their work as deans.

Not surprisingly, the first substantive issue addressed was housing—the most pressing student need that deans faced. But they discussed a few other topics as well including the helpfulness of the League of Women and the YWCA, "Ways of Influencing Young Women," the effectiveness of "at homes"[34] with the dean, and self-government versus direct government.[35] The deans then voted to meet two years hence and passed a series of resolutions summing up the collective opinion of the group. Mary Bidwell Breed was then elected president of the 1905 meeting.

Some time in the two years intervening between the first and second meeting, a decision was made to limit the membership of the group to deans of women in state universities, except for founder Marion Talbot who represented a private institution. No record exists of who made the decision or why,[36] but when the deans met in Chicago in December of 1905, the gathering was convened as the *first* meeting of "The Conference of Deans and Advisors of Women in State Universities." With the exception of Lucy Sprague from the University of California, all participants were from midwestern institutions. The early leadership of the new profession was securely in the hands of women working in the midwestern, public sector.[37]

One interesting development at the 1905 meeting, however, was that the deans went beyond deliberations of the basic needs of students. The first resolution passed was on ways of making a community of women on campus which they believed was "absolutely necessary."[38] Deans of women were probably unique on their campuses in understanding the complexity involved in achieving what I term "genuine access." Typically, male administrators believed that admission to the institution was all that women needed. Deans, however, recognized that while the immediate concerns of housing, adequate meals, rest, and good health were necessary, the higher needs of women such as intellectual parity, career aspirations, leadership opportunities, and a sense of community must also be addressed. In this vein, the deans also discussed levels of scholarship and the place of domestic science in the curriculum, and were in almost unanimous agreement that the classroom should not be segregated by gender.[39]

The biennial conferences not only aided the individual women in the course of their daily jobs by recommending standards of practice, but they were also a mechanism for communication among one another. Most importantly, however, they helped shape an identity for the new profession. A conference illustrated that the number of practitioners was growing, that they had an articulated purpose and a field of expertise, and it placed deans of women within the tradition of all other university administrators of the era who were also forming professional organizations and developing professional identities.

Resistance to their presence and their work was a significant obstacle faced by deans on the state university campuses. Although Breed held a Ph.D. from Bryn Mawr and a record of scholarly accomplishment that included study in a prestigious German university laboratory, her problem of acceptance was illustrative. When she took up residence in Bloomington in the fall of 1901, she met with resentment from both students and faculty. President Swain, who recruited her, believed deans were desirable. He was impressed with both her eastern "sense of decorum" and her manner, which was "strict enough to enforce her code of gentlewomanly behavior."[40] The fact that he wanted a woman who combined scholarly accomplishment with gentlewomanly grace was again consistent with the prevailing notions of qualifications for the position. But several male faculty members expressed resistance to the idea of a dean of women—not because of her potential effect on students—but because they objected to having a woman with any administrative authority at any level on campus. By the time of Breed's appointment, only three other women had ever been *employed* by the university; the female contributors to the university had been professor's wives and town women.[41]

Breed also met resistance from students who believed a dean was an affront to their integrity or feared possible limitations on their newly found freedom.[42] Gertrude Martin, who later became a dean herself, recalled her undergraduate days at the University of Michigan when they learned of Marion Talbot at nearby University of Chicago. "We resented that Chicago dean of women as an unwarrantable criticism of the conduct of college women in general. We were very certain we needed no disciplining."[43]

Evidence left by students including letters and diaries suggests that deans on many campuses were successful in reversing resentment and converting it to a respect that sometimes verged on reverence.[44] Even allowing for the purplishness of late-nineteenth-century prose, the high level of regard seemed genuine.[45] Breed, for example, received a gift from students—a photograph of the statue of Hermes by the Greek sculptor, Praxiteles—for which she publicly thanked students in the newspaper.[46] The senior class of 1905 dedicated the *Arbutus* (yearbook) to her. This represented a significant departure from custom. Prior to that time, the yearbook had only been dedicated to sitting or former presidents or occasionally anonymous groups of university supporters such as the alumni or "the people of the state." Only twice before had the yearbook been dedicated to a faculty member and never had the male-run *Arbutus* paid tribute to a woman.[47]

Such high regard should not obscure the fact that deans and female students were not always of one mind. There were components of a generation gap and elements of a disciplinarian/disciplined relationship. There were also class tensions at times between the largely private-school educated deans and state university students. The deans—Talbot, Breed, Comstock, and Mathews—each came from upper-middle-class backgrounds, most had powerful fathers, and all had been, before becoming a dean, associated with an elite private institution. One of Comstock's close friends and colleagues, Lucy Sprague of Berkeley, who also came from a privileged background, was more vocal on this issue than other deans. At times, she expressed her uncomfortableness with the rough-hewn nature of the state university women students.[48]

Students and deans shared many political objectives, especially in reform-oriented areas, but many women students were pro-suffrage and thought the deans maddeningly silent on this issue. Students agitated for more freedom in male-female socialization which also caused a split between the two generations of women. Deans thought students were too frivolous; students thought deans were old-fashioned, perhaps sexually unfulfilled or even "deviant."[49] But overall, female students had very few adult female role models on coeducational campuses between 1900 and 1920 and even fewer advocates.

Breed's strategy to win over opponents was rather straightforward to a modern reader, but it was new at the time—she expanded her role beyond discipline, involved students in policies and program decisions, and advocated for women in ways that made tangible differences in their lives. She did not believe in elaborate "machinery" to regulate people.[50] Her approach was that of self-government, which had been the standard at eastern women's colleges for years. She asked students for their cooperation in her policies and responded in kind by fighting for little amenities and larger benefits. For example, once a student building was finally completed in the last months of her deanship, she argued for cooking facilities for the women's wing and coffee service in the women's parlor.[51]

The larger benefits came in the form of social opportunities. Breed knew that students required more from college than a place to live, however important that might be, and Bloomington had little to offer. Breed found some time to offer embellishments in the form of social gatherings and intellectual stimulation. As the university's historian put it, Dean Breed was "taxed to the limit of imagination and energy to break the drab monotony of college girls' lives."[52] She occasionally offered a lecture series on various subjects. She spoke on etiquette and the challenges of entering a professional field not already identified as acceptable for women (science, for example). She gave several popular travelogue lectures about her trip through France the previous summer of 1904.[53]

She hosted meetings for the Women's League, gave candy and chafing dish parties, provided opportunities for students and faculty to mix, and attended numerous receptions. On one occasion, she directed a play.[54] Breed, however, set her sights on providing Indiana's students and alumnae with a more tangible benefit—membership in the Association of Collegiate Alumni (ACA).

The ACA provided opportunities for leadership and support. Recognition, a form of accreditation, often brought material benefits (for example, scholarships and graduate school admission). Breed, a former president of the Pittsburgh Chapter, was convinced of the long-term benefits to women students and set out to make Indiana a member institution. It was often Breed's lot to fall prey to the slowly grinding wheels of change. She clearly set the membership process in motion, but failed to see her vision come to fruition during her tenure.

Becoming an Expert

The next phase of professionalization called for the development of expertise: deans became experts in women's education in coeducational settings. This phase, roughly from 1905–12, was marked by a growing professional maturity among the deans. Deans regularly published in educational journals, made connections to other professional women in education (especially the ACA), and became more "scientific," using techniques and language associated with scientific research. In 1911, Dean Gertrude Martin of Cornell conducted and distributed the first statistical research project on the work of deans. This intellectual activity, said Lucy Ward Stebbins (Berkeley's second dean of women), saved the profession from the "bog of discipline and decorum."[55]

Ada Comstock began her administrative career as dean of women at the University of Minnesota in 1906. She is perhaps best known as the long-term president of Radcliffe College, from 1922 to 1943, who eventually secured full membership (at least in theory) for undergraduate women at Harvard. However, she was also instrumental in helping deans of women develop their field of expertise. When Comstock arrived in 1906, she was immediately able to employ the strategies suggested by her colleagues for coping with the most basic deaning issues such as housing, so she was free to devote energy to other matters. She collected data on students and illustrated a systematic, more "scientific" approach to the job. In journal articles and speeches, she helped articulate the specific expertise deans needed, building upon the ideas of women's nature Talbot previously expressed. She then used her expertise as the basis for the campus programs she initiated.

Comstock's initiatives were dedicated to addressing the higher needs of women such as a sense of community, leadership roles, employment, and intellectual opportunities. As far as students were concerned, this was the strategy with the most tangible results. One of Comstock's first acts was to fight the use of the word "coed" in the Minneapolis and campus publications and the ridicule that women faced in the guise of humor. Although she was only partially successful, fighting public mockery became a cause embraced by several of her peers.

Creating a sense of community for the young women was Comstock's highest priority. The Alice Shevlin Hall, which provided women students with a physical place on campus to rest, study, eat, and associate with one another to ease the loneliness and feelings of isolation, was central to her mission.[56] In fact, she described Shevlin Hall as her most effective "tool."[57] Comstock recognized that universities were organizations created and run by men "and however kindly the individual members of the faculty may show themselves . . . the close discipleship which the young men may enjoy . . . [is] not so easily attainable to the young women."[58] In several respects, Shevlin Hall was not unlike contemporary women's centers found on many campuses today.

The mechanism Comstock used to develop leadership skills and responsibility in students was the Student Self-Government Association, which was voted in by students in December of 1906 for the purpose of aiding in the care and conduct of Alice Shevlin Hall. Such associations originated in the women's colleges and Comstock herself had participated in self-government while attending Smith College. Comstock believed that student-developed and student-enforced policies achieved more positive outcomes (especially in terms of greater compliance) than those dictated by administrators. In the meantime, the process taught students about leadership, consensus, law and order, and good citizenship.[59]

A student's need to finance her education, find suitable employment, and develop career aspirations was as important to Comstock as building a dormitory. She wanted to "fit" women for a greater variety of gainful occupations. In 1909, it was estimated that the average student needed between $350 and $450 to attend the university.[60] Comstock conducted research and found that 15 percent of women students were at least partially self-supporting (compared with 64 percent of the men). On average, the women earned $191 while their male classmates earned $306 per year on the job. The women worked in very female-oriented occupations including housekeeping, child care, office clerking, tutoring, and other secretarial work. Comstock believed that low salaries obligated women to work longer hours and she observed that the women often suffered from overwork and exhaustion. She also discovered that despite the hardship, the self-supporting women did as well academically as their nonworking counterparts.[61]

Comstock took it upon herself to oversee the employment of women, making sure that it was safe and fairly paid. She once said that "this aspect of the work of my office is of very great interest to me. It brings me in contact with many girls whom I am especially glad to know."[62] She used Shevlin Hall as a clearing house for job listings, but often the choices were limited. To increase employment opportunities, Comstock spent the Christmas vacation of 1911–12 walking up and down the streets of the Twin Cities trying to convince department stores of the sagacity of hiring women. She found that they "were particularly impregnable to the suggestion."[63]

Creating a Professional Literature and Professional Association

Successfully initiating programs such as those created by Comstock and insuring that women had full intellectual participation in the campus became the raison d'être of the young profession of dean of women. Some deans, however, believed that their work on behalf of students and their own sense of self-esteem would be enhanced and legitimated if the overall status of the position was elevated. Lois Mathews, at the University of Wisconsin from 1911 to 1918, was of such a mind. She believed that deans of women should also be members of the faculty and have more of the attributes normally associated with a profession—including a professional literature and formal training for aspirants.

Mathews was a protégée of Frederick Jackson Turner and the first woman to pass Harvard's Ph.D. examination in history—although her degree was from the Radcliffe graduate school, a bureaucratic anomaly created to award doctorates to women because Harvard would not. She was an assistant professor of history at Vassar and an associate professor at Wellesley College before moving to Wisconsin.

In her long and occasionally heated negotiations with Charles Van Hise, president of the university, she held out for the title of dean (rather than advisor as he suggested) and the rank of associate professor. She argued that an associate professorship carried more weight with students and faculty and contributed to the dignity of her office. She also noted that she might only spend a few years in administration and might choose to resume a full-time academic career, in which case she would need the rank of associate professor to secure her own future. When explaining why she did not relent, she said, "if I were to undertake so great and serious a task as the deanship of women in the University of Wisconsin, it seemed to me it would be my first duty to make it in stature what it is in opportunity; and at the same time to try to make it an example to other universities in that regard."[64]

Mathews's scholarly potential and productivity prior to entering Wisconsin was considerable—she published articles and wrote a very important book in 1909, *The Expansion of New England,* which had its last printing in 1962; her career as an historian was quite disappointing after she was made dean. Although she continued to teach, she did not contribute much after 1912 to the field of history. Unfortunately, Mathews's experience was very typical. All four women in this study were trained as faculty members and all four found their scholarly progress impeded by the exigencies of administrative positions.

Mathews was very dedicated to her new profession and brought to it the same intellectual vigor that she had applied earlier to history. While dean, she had numerous public-speaking engagements, published several articles, and spoke frequently at ACA and the biennial deans' conferences. She invited aspiring deans to visit her on the Madison campus to learn about the job. She organized a statewide conference for all women deans in Wisconsin, including those from small colleges and normal schools. In the summer of 1915 she taught a course in "College Administration for Women," which was the first of its kind taught in a public university and was offered concurrently with the first courses taught on the subject at Teachers College.[65]

Once appointed, Mathews set about making positive and tangible contributions to the women on campus, her work always guided by her convictions about women's education. One of her first outreach efforts to the young women coupled her skill as an historian with her desire to make female students feel that they were an integral component of the university's intellectual community. She published an article in the campuswide *Wisconsin Magazine* on the history and purpose of women's education.[66]

Women's education, she argued, needed to prepare women intellectually and in so doing, equip them to be useful—in the home or workplace. But deans of women were also concerned with civility and propriety and as Mathews added, women's education must also cultivate the right tastes.[67]

Mathews articulated some of her views in her dean's reports, thus formally sharing them with Van Hise and the Board of Regents. She wrote in 1912 that women's education was not merely a "duplication of men's education" and challenged the university to use its resources for the full development of women's possibilities.[68] She recorded her goals more fully in her dean's report of 1914. She stated that there were three principles that guided her work: (1) to do all she could to develop the potential of women's education; (2) to secure for women the highest possible individual development; and (3) to develop in women the highest social responsibility.[69]

In terms of activities for women, much of Mathews's work involved honing programs that already existed on campus or importing initiatives from elsewhere. For example, her first initiative was to revitalized the dormant self-government association. Establishing the annual vocational conferences—the first at a public university—was her second major initiative.[70] The conferences began in the spring of 1912 to offer women alternatives to teaching careers. As she said, "college women have for at least half a century . . . gone almost without exception into teaching. . . . [T]he enormous expansion of business has left teaching to the feminine part of the community because of the greater rewards offered men through professional life and mercantile enterprises."[71] Her philosophy behind establishing the conference was outlined in her annual report to President Van Hise:

> The teaching profession for women is so "overstocked" that salaries are kept down to a mere living wage, save in rare instances where teaching is combined with administration. The opportunities for women in business, welfare work, in play-ground work, in charities and correction associations, and in all lines opened up by household economics and its allied subjects are almost numberless and as yet there are not enough trained women to fill them.[72]

The conferences were large undertakings involving two or three days of speakers, presentations, and social events.[73] Mathews brought in women professionals from a variety of fields.[74] President Van Hise agreed to open the first conference and, although he praised Mathews's efforts, he was a bit cautious and stressed that teaching was indeed a worthwhile profession and should not be totally abandoned by women.[75] Perhaps because of her own experience of being widowed at a young age and therefore dependent on her professional skills for a livelihood, helping women find appropriate and remunerative careers was a cherished goal for Mathews. She successfully petitioned the university to hire a permanent vocational counselor for the women students. The conferences were so popular that men students soon agitated for the right to hold one of their own. While it is not clear if a men's conference came to pass, the vocational conferences for women lasted over thirty-five years.[76] The conferences did not include teaching until 1917 when there were widespread teacher shortages and, not surprisingly, the 1918 conference focused on war-related work for women.[77]

Her most lasting contribution, however, was her 1915 book, *The Dean of Women,* the first book ever written on the profession that eventually became known as student affairs. A second book on the subject did not appear until 1926.[78] Mathews held a particular vision for the profession. She wanted to be more than a wise and pious matron. She believed deans should be scholars, experts on women's education, and general advocates for women who expanded the social, vocational, and intellectual opportunities available to them. This book represented the collective wisdom of Mathews and her like-minded peers on issues ranging from teaching to supervision in the dormitories to how to organize an office. With all the pieces in place by 1916, the position had the vestiges of a profession.

The Next Generation

The new profession of dean of women opened up the possibility of administrative careers on coeducational campuses. Because of the direct relationship between the number of women students at an institution and the presence of women in the faculty or administration, women's colleges traditionally offered a few opportunities, but prospects at coeducational universities were scarce, especially before 1920.[79] Coeducational institutions, therefore, held tremendous promise for women who sought professional careers in universities, but who lived in the Midwest or other regions of the country where single-sex education was less common. Therefore, deans acted as the "entering wedge" in coeducational institutions.[80] As the first and often the only female administrators who either held a broad range of responsibilities or the sufficient rank needed in the institution to initiate policy proposals, "they had the most consistent effect in bringing more women into the professional community."[81] They also succeeded in making the position of dean *de rigueur.* Although women's needs were hardly an institutional priority, the vast majority of all types of coeducational institutions had a dean after 1920.

One cautionary note on the effect of the position of dean on professional women is in order, however. Like other women in nascent professions, the pioneering deans struggled and strategized to secure professional status, overcome resistance, secure acceptance, and gain recognition. Yet attaining the position was somewhat of a two-edged sword, perhaps analogous to the experience of academic women who sought appointments within home economics departments. Like home economics, being a dean provided women with opportunities for professional work, but it also contributed to the ghettoizing of women into administrative roles that became essentially student affairs positions and, consequently, undervalued by the academy. In addition, many of the early deans (those hired in the first years of this century) were women with credentials that should have earned them faculty posts. These highly trained "teaching deans" combined teaching and administration and held faculty rank, but their administrative duties inhibited scholarly advancement. One can only speculate on how many women reluctantly settled for a combined administrative/academic post because they were not offered a purely academic job.

It was this trend toward an exclusively administrative post, away from teaching and in the direction of student affairs, that defined the working lives of most deans of women who came after the pioneering cohort. Talbot, Breed, Comstock, and Mathews worked in large universities and simultaneously held faculty positions. However, deans of women were also hired in other types of institutions such as smaller colleges and normal schools. Deans in these environments (and in some universities) began to question the need for dual faculty appointments—they chose instead to emphasize the counseling, guidance, and regulatory nature of their work. A few women with this point of view were studying for a master's degree at Teachers College in the summer of 1916 when they formed the National Association for Deans of Women (NADW)—which eventually became the professional organization for all deans. However, the NADW, whose founding Carolyn Bashaw examines in chapter 7 placed very little emphasis on the importance of faculty rank to the position of dean.

Lois Mathews's vision of deans as scholars lost out to the newer vision of the profession that was shared by the newly created office of dean of men.[82] As student affairs practitioners, they suffered a lack of prestige within the academy. Therefore, in terms of the administrative influence of deans of women, the era examined, 1892 to 1916, represented a high point. Later decades saw it further reduced in stature when former deans of women, who had once reported directly to the president, subsequently became assistants who reported to male deans of students.[83] It is intriguing to speculate on whether the strategy that Mathews proposed—holding dual faculty/administrative appointments—might have helped the profession of dean of women maintain or even increase its prestige on campus. As a result of separating themselves from the faculty, deans were isolated from any important power base within the academy.

Is there a place in a modern coeducational university for a dean of women? If the original vision of the pioneering deans of women is being carried into the next century, perhaps the women leaders on campuses most responsible are not deans of students, but rather the heads of women's studies programs or women's centers. For many of these professionals, who often hold faculty positions, their missions are to secure parity in academic opportunity and build a women's community—a raison d'être not unlike that of Talbot, Breed, Comstock, Lois Mathews.

Notes

1. Katherine S. M. Phillips, "The Work of a Dean of Women," master's thesis, Teachers College, Columbia University, n.d. [probably 1919], 3.

2. Paula A. Treichler, "Alma Mater's Sorority: Women and the University of Illinois, 1890–1925," in *For Alma Mater: Theory and Practice in Feminist Scholarship,* ed. Paula A. Treichler, Cheris Kramarae, and Beth Stafford, 5–61 (Urbana: University of Illinois Press, 1985), 24.

3. J. E. Morpurgo, *Their Majesties' Royall Colledge: William and Mary in the Seventeenth and Eighteenth Centuries* (Williamsburg, Va.: The Endowment Association of the College of William and Mary, 1976), 67–69.

4. Lulu Holmes, *A History of the Position of Dean of Women in a Selected Group of Co-educational Colleges and Universities in the United States* (New York: Teachers College, Columbia University, Bureau of Publications, 1939), 109.

5. M. Kehr, "The Pioneer Days of the Dean of Women," *The Journal of the National Education Association* 27 (January 1938): 6–7, 6.

6. Oberlin College, *Second Annual Report, 1835,* 24.

7. Holmes, *History of the Position of Dean of Women,* 6–7.

8. Ibid., 7.

9. Earl J. McGrath, "The Evolution of Administrative Offices in Institutions of Higher Education in the United States from 1860 to 1933," Ph.D. diss., University of Chicago, 1936.

10. Katherine Rothenberger, "An Historical Study of the Position of Dean of Women at Indiana University," master's thesis, Indiana University, 1942.

11. Lynn D. Gordon, *Gender and Higher Education in the Progressive Era* (New Haven: Yale University Press, 1990).

12. Laurence R. Veysey, *The Emergence of the American University* (Chicago: University of Chicago Press, 1965).

13. Roslind Rosenberg, "The Limits of Access: The History of Coeducation in America." In *Women and Higher Education in American History,* ed. John Mack Faragher and Florence Howe, 107–29 (New York: W. W. Norton, 1988).

14. Gordon, *Gender and Higher Education.*

15. Ellen Fitzpatrick, "For the 'Women of the University': Marion Talbot, 1858–1948," in *Lone Voyagers: Academic Women in Coeducational Universities, 1870–1937,* ed. Geraldine Joncich Clifford, 85–124 (New York: The Feminist Press, 1989).

16. Ibid.

17. Rosenberg, *Beyond Separate Spheres,* 19.

18. See Marion Talbot and Lois K. M. Rosenberry, *The History of the American Association of University Women* (Boston: Houghton, Mifflin, 1931) for a complete history of the organization.

19. Ibid., 346–47.

20. Rosenberg, *Beyond Separate Spheres,* 33.

21. Gordon, *Gender and Higher Education,* 89–92.

22. Fitzpatrick, "For the 'Women of the University,' " 91.

23. Marion Talbot quoted from her reports to the president in Fitzpatrick, "For the 'Women of the University,' " 92.

24. Ibid.

25. Ibid.

26. Ibid. Her use of letters, charts, and other documentation was more thoroughly explored in Virginia Kemp Fish, " 'More than Lore': Marion Talbot and Her Role in the Founding Years of the University of Chicago," *International Journal of Women's Studies* 8 (May–June 1985): 237–41.

27. Roslind Rosenberg, *Beyond Separate Spheres: The Intellectual Roots of Modern Feminism* (New Haven: Yale University Press, 1982).

28. Marion Talbot, *The Education of Women* (Chicago: University of Chicago Press, 1910), 22.

29. Estelle Freedman, "Separatism as Strategy: Female Institution Building and American Feminism, 1870–1930," *Feminist Studies* 5 (Fall 1979): 512–29.

30. Ibid., 514

31. Joyce Antler, *Lucy Sprague Mitchell: The Making of a Modern Woman* (New Haven: Yale University Press, 1987), 98–99.

32. Freedman, "Separatism as Strategy"; Rosenberg, *Beyond Separate Spheres.*

33. Mary R. Potter, "Report of Committee on History of the National Association of Deans of Women," *National Association of Deans of Women Yearbook, 1927,* 212–27.

34. "At homes" were small gatherings in the dean's office or home. The conversation, accompanied by tea and refreshments, was guided by the dean for the purpose of discussing policies or problems.

35. Minutes of the Conference, 1903, p. 9.

36. Potter, "Report of Committee on History of the NADW," 217.

37. Mary Bidwell Breed, Correspondence, Dean of Women, 1901–1906, Indiana University Archives, Bloomington, Ind.

38. Potter, "Report of Committee on History of the NADW," 217.

39. Minutes of the Conference of Deans and Advisors of Women in State Universities, December 19–20, 1905.

40. Thomas Clark, *Indiana University: Midwestern Pioneer,* 2 vols. (Bloomington: Indiana University Press, 1970, 1973), 1: 320.

41. Rothenberger, "Position of a Dean of Women"; Clark, *Indiana University.*

42. Rosenberg, "Limits of Access," 118.

43. Martin, "Position of Dean of Women," 66.

44. Ruth Haddock, "A Study of Five Deans of Women," (Ph.D. diss., Syracuse University, 1952), Ruth Haddock Dissertation. Schlesinger Library, Radcliffe College, Cambridge, MA; Antler, *Lucy Sprague Mitchell*; Fitzpatick, "Marion Talbot"; Linda Eisenmann, " 'Freedom to be Womanly': The Separate Culture of the Women's College" in *The Search for Equity: Women at Brown University, 1891–1991,* ed. Polly Welts Kaufman, 54–85 in (Hanover: Brown University Press, 1991); H. Stephens (née Reed), University of Wisconsin, class of 1917, interview with author, July 20, 1992, Madison, Wisc.

45. In much of the historical work on deans, examples are given of the strategies the women used and the high praise they received from students. See, for example, Fitzpatrick, "For the 'Women of the University,' " 87–124 and Talbot's own account of her work, *More Than Lore: Reminiscences of Marion Talbot* (Chicago: University of Chicago Press, 1936). Letters from students lauding Talbot are found in Ruth Haddock, "A Study of Five Deans of Women." Lois Mathews was remembered very fondly by Mrs. Helen Stephens (née Reed), class of 1917, in an interview with the author, July 20, 1992. Other examples of praise include "Personal and Educational Contributions to UW of Mrs. Rosenberry Lauded," *Capitol Times,* April 22, 1942, 12. Linda Eisenmann noted the same phenomenon in her study of Anne Crosby Emery, the first dean of women at the University of Wisconsin and later of Pembroke College. See " 'Freedom to be Womanly': The Separate Culture of the Women's College," in *The Search for Equity: Women at Brown University, 1891–1991,* ed. Polly Welts Kaufman (Providence: Brown University Press, 1991), 55. See also Antler, *Lucy Sprague Mitchell,* 107, for the feelings of women at Berkeley toward Sprague.

46. "Words of Thanks," *Daily Student,* May 26, 1905, 2: 2.

47. Jo Ann Fley, "Student Personnel Pioneers: Those Who Developed Our Profession, Part I," *National Association of Student Personnel Administrators Journal,* 17 (Summer, 1979): 33.

48. Antler, *Lucy Sprague Mitchell.*

49. Gordon, *Gender and Higher Education;* Mathews, *Dean of Women.*

50. Mary Bidwell Breed (MBB), "The Control of Student Life," *Publications of the Association of Collegiate Alumnae* Series III, 18 (December

1908): 70–73. See also MBB, "Dean's Report," June 14, 1906, Indiana University Archives (IUA).

51. MBB to William Lowe Bryan, January 31, 1906, Breed Correspondence, IUA.

52. Clark, *Indiana University,* 2: 26.

53. See various articles in the *Daily Student:* April 14, 17, and 24, 1905; September 30 and October 5, 7, and 14, 1905.

54. See various articles in the *Daily Student:* September 29, October 3 and 5, and November 14, 1903; June 6 and September 24, 1904; and April 12, 1906.

55. Antler, *Lucy Sprague Mitchell,* 111–12.

56. Ada Comstock, "Report of the Dean of Women," in The President's Report, 1911–1912, *Bulletin of the University of Minnesota* 6 (January 1913): 157.

57. E. B. Johnson, ed., *Forty Years of the University of Minnesota* (Minneapolis: The General Alumni Association, 1910), 194.

58. Ada Comstock, "The Fourth R for Women," *Century Magazine* 117 (February 1929): 413.

59. Ada Comstock, "What Student Government Means," *Minnesota Alumni Weekly* (May 10, 1909): 4.

60. Johnson, *Forty Years of the University of Minnesota,* 195.

61. Ada Comstock, "Self Supporting Students," *Minnesota Alumni Weekly* (February 7, 1910): 11.

62. Ada Comstock, "The Office of Dean of Women," *Minnesota Alumni Weekly* (March 16, 1908): 4.

63. Ruth Y. Blanshard, "A Louise Comstock: Some of her memories of her life up to 1943, collected for reading to the Saturday Morning Club, March 16, 1974," 11.

64. Charles Van Hise, correspondence, to Lois K. Mathews, Dean of Women, 1911–1918. April 17, 1911, University of Wisconsin Archives, Madison, Wisc.

65. *The Daily Cardinal,* May 1, 1915, 4 and November 1, 1916, 6.

66. Lois Mathews, "A Half-Century of Higher Education for Women," *The Wisconsin Magazine* 9 (December 1911): 5–9. This was a very early example of women's educational history, written before (and therefore without the benefit of) the landmark study by Thomas Woody completed in 1929.

67. See Mathews, *Dean of Women,* 160–61 and several other references on the cultivation of higher tastes and civility.

68. Mathews, "Report of the Dean of Women," 1912, 200–210.

69. Mathews, "Report of the Dean of Women," 1914, 208–16.

70. For example, Marion Talbot had introduced vocational conferences at the University of Chicago in 1910. Margaret Dollar cites 1909 as the beginning of the vocational guidance movement when the ACA created their

Committee on Vocational Opportunities Other Than Teaching. It was further spurred when the Women's Educational and Industrial Union in Boston began concentrating on college women in 1910. By 1913, there were occupational bureaus in Boston, Chicago, New York, and Philadelphia. See Margaret C. Dollar, "The Beginnings of Vocational Guidance for College Women: The Women's Educational and Industrial Union, the Association of Collegiate Alumnae, and Women's Colleges," Ed.D. diss., Harvard Graduate School of Education, 1992.

71. Mathews, *Dean of Women,* 109.

72. Mathews, "Report of the Dean of Women," 1912, 207.

73. The archives of the University of Wisconsin have the programs for almost all of the early vocational conferences. The vocational conferences received a great deal of campus publicity that described the list of events. See *The Daily Cardinal,* April 1, 10, 11, 12, 13, 1912, all on page 1; October 15 and December 7, 1912, 4; May 2, 1913, 4; and December 2, 1914, 4.

74. The fields represented included journalism, medicine, social service, library work, and private secretary work. Mathews was especially interested in directing women into social service, which she defined as "Christianity applied to everyday living." See *The Daily Cardinal,* November 5, 1915, 4.

75. Emily Chervenik, "Thirty-Five Years of Careers Conferences," *Journal of the National Association of Deans of Women* 11 (March 1948): 145 and *The Daily Cardinal,* December 4, 1912, 4. Mathews's initiatives at Wisconsin were so well received that in 1918 she was invited to be a keynote speaker at vocational conferences the University of South Dakota. See *The Daily Cardinal,* May 1, 1918, 4.

76. Chervenik, "Thirty-Five Years of Careers Conferences," 145–48.

77. "War-Vocational Conference," program for the 1918 vocational conference, UWA.

78. Merrill and Bragdon, *Vocation of Dean.*

79. Geraldine J. Clifford, ed., *Lone Voyagers: Academic Women in Coeducational Institutions, 1870–1937* (New York: The Feminist Press, 1989).

80. Margaret W. Rossiter, *Women Scientists in America: Struggles and Strategies to 1940* (Baltimore: Johns Hopkins University Press, 1982), 2.

81. Clifford, *Lone Voyagers,* 13.

82. Barbara Catton, "Our Association in Review." *Journal of the National Association of Deans of Women,* 10 (1956): 3–9.

83. E. Greenleaf, "How Others See Us: ACPA Presidential Address," *Journal of College Student Personnel* 9 (July 1968): 225–31.

CHAPTER 7

"Reassessment and Redefinition"

The NAWDC and Higher Education for Women

CAROLYN TERRY BASHAW

The National Association of Women Deans and Counselors commemorated its fifty-fifth anniversary in 1971. This anniversary occurred during time of great change and turmoil in higher education in the United States. Students, faculty, and administrators alike grappled with a wide range of issues—those particular to campus life and those of national and international importance. The individual rights of students, the pervasive racism in the United States, and the escalating war in Vietnam numbered among the major foci of public discourse on campus.

Academic women—students, faculty, and the administrators discussed in this volume—numbered among the most insistent, yet hopeful, participants in that public discourse. Transformed by their involvement in the growing civil rights and antiwar movements and in the resurgent women's movement, they sought to extend the boundaries of discussion. Any consideration of individual rights, they contended, must include not only issues of race, of individual conscience in the face of law, but also of the central fact of gender.

Indeed, these women had genuine reason to be hopeful. The number and variety of women students had increased steadily. Prestigious single-sex men's institutions now opened their doors to women. Paradoxically, as Barbara Miller Solomon observed, by the 1970s, women's options for higher education eventually outnumbered those of men.[1]

In demanding that women's place in the academy be included in this contentious reexamination of higher education in the United States, these women continued a debate almost as old as the nation itself. How should a democracy educate its women? For over a century, contemporaries and historians alike raised myriad questions concerning the effects of higher education on women and of women on higher education.

None of these women remains more problematic for historians of higher education than does the dean of women, charged with the care of women students in coeducational institutions and founder of the modern student personnel profession. Born partly from institutional expediency—the need to supervise those few women students in the earliest coeducational colleges in the 1830s, as Jana Nidiffer explains in chapter 6—the office expanded dramatically to include, by the 1950s, virtually every coeducational institution in the United States. Conceived partly in response to revolutionary social change brought about by the admission of women to formerly all-male campuses, the office also disappeared in response to the revolutionary social change of the 1970s—the end of *in loco parentis* and the demand of women students for greater personal autonomy. Despite the very delineated institutional life span of the profession, mid 1830s–late 1970s, and the abundance of personal and institutional records, historians have barely begun to discern the effect of the dean of women on higher education in the United States. Examination of the profession in the post–World War II era, particularly, 1956–73, offers an instructive perspective from which to determine its contributions.

A pervasive aura of pride, concern, and hope suffused the celebration of the fifty-fifth anniversary of the NAWDC in 1971. A variety of speakers discussed the history of and prospects for the profession. Of particular significance in appreciating how deans of women perceived their profession and in interpreting its contribution to the history of women in the post–World War II era are the comments of Dorothy Truex, Director of Research and Program Development for the University Community, at the University of Oklahoma.

In her remarks, Truex offered congratulations, advocated candor, and issued a challenge. First, she identified an enduring connection between the profession of dean of women and the history of feminism in the United States. She contended that the National Association of Deans of Women, organized in 1916, reflected "the legacy of feminism" in the lives of its founders.[2]

Such a proud heritage she continued, could not belie two disquieting demographic circumstances that the profession faced in the early 1970s. Despite the dramatic increase in the number of women attending college in the 1960s, the status of the women grew "more ambiguous." Furthermore, membership in the NAWDC had decreased by 13.5 percent.[3]

Feminism and foresight, Truex concluded, sustained deans of women in meeting and mastering adversity throughout the history of the profession. As an example, she cited the organization's name change in 1956, from National Association of Deans of Women (NADW) to National Association of Women Deans and Counselors (NAWDC). The organization retained this name until 1973, when it became the National Association of Women Deans, Administrators, and Counselors (NAWDAC). In 1991, NAWDAC, again reflecting changes in the student personnel profession, became the National Association for Women in Education (NAWE).

For Truex, such a change suggested the nuanced nature of the profession. Although this change in part reflected a pragmatic response to decreases in the number of women holding the title dean of women, it also reflected the enduring feminist commitment of the profession to the advancement of women's educational opportunities through its acceptance of a wider spectrum of personnel workers. Truex reminded members that this willingness to embrace "reassessment and redefinition . . . at a time when feminism was at an all time low [indicates] that the deans are not easily discouraged."[4]

How valid are Truex's remarks? How might one document them? Did deans of women draw on feminism and foresight in their contribution to the higher education of women in the United States in the post–World War II era?

Explicit support for Truex's claims appears in the organization's scholarly journal. Founded in 1938, this publication, edited at Teachers College, Columbia University, not only reflected the growing maturity and ability of the profession, but also the innovative nature of scholars in the field. An examination of the *Journal of NAWDC*, 1956–73, confirms both the feminism and foresight of the NAWDC in its concern for the vitality of women's education.

Historians have until fairly recently embraced a static conventional wisdom in their assessment of the activities of women in the United States, 1945–60, and of the contribution of the deans of women. According to this interpretation, women in the immediate postwar era unquestioningly assumed primarily domestic roles. On college and university campuses, deans of women, complicit in this vision, monitored skirt lengths and sexual lapses until these women graduated and fulfilled their cultural destiny—marriage and motherhood.

Only recently have scholars begun to challenge this vision, utilizing historical evidence long hidden in plain sight. Two groups of historians have recast the historiographical landscape in which the NAWDC functioned, 1956–73. Historians of women and of women in higher education provide a provocative revisioning of both a period and one organization.

Joanne Meyerowitz contends that women of the 1950s in the United States remain an historically lost generation. Women's activism in the Progressive Era, Great Depression, and 1960s forms a coherent and compelling narrative, interrupted only by the headlong rush to the suburbs, the sink, and the scout troop in the 1950s. In their assessment of women in the immediate postwar years, Meyerowitz concludes that historians adopted the "conservatism and constraints approach."[5] The pervasive political conservatism, born in response to the Cold War, circumscribed not only public but also private behavior, particularly gender expectations.

Advocates of such a constrained historical perspective, Meyerowitz maintains, commit several errors in fact and in judgment. First, to subsume all women under the suburban domestic ideals ignores "women's agency"[6] even in times of cultural conservatism. Second, such a perspective ignores the variety of circumstances defining women in the United States—race, class, ethnicity, sexual orientation.

Historical revisioning of women in the 1950s undoubtedly "complicates our stories of the past."[7] Meyerowitz suggests that women in the 1950s represented not only a social and cultural conglomerate but also engaged in myriad activities, including paid labor, volunteerism, social activism, cultural rebellion, and traditional domesticity. Dismissing the traditional nostalgic and restrictive historical interpretation, Meyerowitz concludes that the era remains, rather, "a time of notable social change and actual complexity."[8]

Deans of women, invariably the highest-ranking women on coeducational campuses, contributed to the discussion of a wider social and cultural reality for women students and for professional colleagues. Central to this changing reality was the remarkable and sustained growth in the number of married women returning to the workforce by the mid 1950s. Susan Hartmann discovered that in response to this change in the labor force, a contingent of activist women founded commissions or agencies to enhance cultural acceptance of this new segment of the work force.

Especially active in this endeavor was the NADW, which in 1951, provided the American Council on Education with adequate funds to establish the Commission on the Education of Women (CEW).[9] Hartmann claims that the CEW, through its conferences, research, and publication "foreshadowed elements of the feminist movement that would emerge a decade later."[10] Such activism supports her contention that the immediate postwar years, 1945–1960, mark not an aberration in the activities of women in the United States, but rather "a transition period" preparing the foundation for the modern women's movement.[11]

Historians of higher education, in several recent studies of the dean of women, not only support Meyerowitz's and Hartmann's specific interpretation of the activities of women in the postwar United States but also situate the dean of women squarely in the ranks of other activist women professionals. To do so, they have utilized abundant primary collections heretofore relatively untouched, including personal correspondence, institutional records, and the rich NAWDAC archives. These scholars persuasively undercut the stereotypical assessment of the dean of women and reinterpret the quality and quantity of her contributions to the active public discourse concerning women played out both on campus and in the larger culture. In this growing field within the history of higher education, scholars evaluate the dean of women through the lenses of professionalization, race, and region.

Paula A. Treichler maintains that "for perhaps fifty years, it was an office in which intelligent, well-qualified women could exercise administrative skill and professional leadership and exert a unifying influence on behalf of women."[12] Geraldine J. Clifford insists that "the position of the dean of women had the most consistent effect in bringing more women into the professional community at coeducational colleges and universities."[13] Robert Arthur Schwartz credits deans of women with establishing the student personnel profession in the United States.[14] Jana Nidiffer explores the motivations, concerns, and professional rigor of the founders of the NADW.[15] Kathryn Tuttle assesses the effect of the student and women's movements of the 1960s and 1970s on the profession.[16] Patricia Bell-Scott acknowledges the significance of the dean of women in defining women's experience in African American coeducational institutions.[17] I evaluate the role deans of women played on coeducational campuses in the South in the first half of this century.[18]

Binding such studies into a coherent historiographical interpretation is the ability of these scholars to discern the unmistakable difference between bureaucratic bean-counting and genuine cultural leadership. Despite the demise of the office itself, they contend that these women—pioneers in coeducational institutions—left their mark upon generations of women and upon discourse concerning women's place on campus. Across chronological, racial, and regional boundaries, activist members of this profession worked tirelessly on behalf of women's present and future advancement.

To appreciate Truex's claims of feminism and foresight in the NAWDC, one must review briefly the founding and development of that organization. In his study of professionalism, Burton Bledstein asserts that between 1880 and 1920, middle-class men created the modern professions, a form of meritocracy based upon specialized training and single-minded dedication, as a way of realizing a "vertical vision," which emphasized personal achievement.[19] Central to this process, he asserts, was the establishment of professional associations, which defined qualifications and provided scholarly and social outlets for their members. Robert W. Wiebe identifies these newly emerging professionals as "self-conscious pioneers," exchanging "village values" for "bureaucratic values" of regularity, system, and continuity.[20]

Although men initially dominated the professional ranks, an increasing number of women as well aspired to such status. By 1890, a second generation of women, comprising over one-third of the total student population, enrolled in colleges and universities across the country.[21] In this same decade, a fearless cadre of women earned over 7 percent of the doctorates that institutions in the United States conferred.[22] Such education set them apart as pioneers among women. Equally anxious to fulfill their own "vertical vision," many pursued professional careers.

Joyce Antler maintains that professionalization requires "a gradual transformation of self, a transformation supported by new associations and new rewards."[23] Such a transformation, she concludes, which was in direct conflict with traditional gender roles, remained particularly difficult for women.

Everything that characterized them as professionals—training, single-minded dedication, and ego—challenged the time-honored claims of home and family.[24]

Aspiring women professionals chose between two options: either to enter a traditional field with its various obstacles, or to build new, female-dominated professions. Whichever path they followed, Nancy Cott suggests that women professionals confronted similar problems: the battle for "professional credibility" and the need "to outperform men in their rigor and standards."[25] Such formidable obstacles, however, did not deter dedicated women. Penina M. Glazer and Miriam Slater identify four strategies—superperformance, separatism, subordination, and innovation—by which women achieved productive professional careers. Of special interest are the innovators, women who created professional employment opportunities by appropriating "areas ignored by the established professions."[26]

Deans of women were just such innovators. In 1900, despite the dramatic increase in the number of women attending coeducational institutions and the corresponding increase in the number of deans of women, the position possessed none of the fundamental components of a genuine profession—formalized graduate training programs, a coherent body of research literature, and a professional association. Nevertheless, the women attracted to the position, like their middle-class, male counterparts, increasingly embraced the concept of a meritocracy based upon professional expertise. As chapter 6 explains, between 1900 and 1916, a core of dedicated deans of women began the difficult task of transforming a nonstandardized job into a legitimate profession.

The establishment of the National Association of Deans of Women grew out of over a decade of organizational activity at coeducational institutions in the Midwest and at Teachers College, Columbia University. Central to this activity was Marion Talbot, dean of women at the University of Chicago, 1892–1925. Determined that deans of women achieve their own "vertical vision," Talbot and other enterprising women established the framework of a modern profession—professional societies and graduate training programs.

In December 1903, Talbot and Martha Foote Crowe, dean of women at Northwestern University, hosted a meeting of eighteen deans of women. Two years later, the Conference of Deans and Advisors in State Universities was established with the support of Dean Talbot. This association drew its membership primarily from public institutions in the Midwest. The organization met biennially until 1922, when it became a division of the National Association of Deans of Women. In addition to this organization, beginning in 1911, a group of deans of women began meeting informally at the annual convention of the Association of Collegiate Alumnae.[27]

Equally as important as professional associations was the existence of reputable graduate training programs for deans of women. Although many deans attended Teachers College, Columbia University, before 1916, the institution offered no course work specifically designed for that purpose. In the summer of 1915, Kathryn Sisson McLean, dean of women at State Teachers College, Chadron, Nebraska, initiated an informal discussion group of graduate women at Teachers College. As a result of their lobbying efforts, coupled with faculty support, Teachers College offered its first graduate courses designed exclusively for deans of women in the summer session of 1916.[28] From that inauspicious beginning, the Teachers College Program, which eventually employed influential scholars such as Sarah Sturtevant and Ruth Strang, became the most prestigious training center in the country.

Like other professionals McLean and her colleagues realized that neither professional training, while essential, nor informal professional organizations such as the Conference of Deans of Women, while valuable, could foster national connections among deans of women. To achieve this end, the profession needed an official professional society that served deans of women across the country. In the summer of 1916, McLean made that dream a reality.

Learning that the National Education Association (NEA) would be holding its annual meeting in New York City, she asked that the Teachers College graduate students be allowed to hold an organizational meeting for deans of women. NEA officials agreed, and the women reserved the Horace Mann Auditorium for their sessions. Reflecting upon their plans, nearly fifty years later, McLean maintained that "we knew how deeply we cared about our program, but we didn't know how many would join us in our belief."[29]

Her worries were groundless, for, on Thursday, July 6, 1916, nearly two hundred persons attended the meeting. Rather than sponsor a bare-bones organizational conference, McLean, determined to attract support, invited some of the most prominent members of the profession, including Gertrude S. Martin, Advisor of Women at Cornell University, and Virginia Gildersleeve, dean of Barnard College, to address the audience.[30]

McLean's strategy succeeded. During the speeches, "unmistakable enthusiasm and interest grew," she recalled, "and when the meeting was over there was a great feeling of confidence and hope in the future of our association."[31] Meeting in executive session following the formal addresses, the deans organized the National Association of Deans of Women (NADW) and elected Kathryn McLean president.[32]

Throughout its history, the organization struggled, against financial and cultural challenges, to support the work of deans of women. Ten years after its founding, the NADW established a permanent headquarters office in Washington, D.C., and hired an executive secretary. Cognizant of the inability of many members to attend its annual conventions and of the need to disseminate the latest research in the field, the organization published, between 1922 and 1937, the *Yearbook*.[33]

The NADW met and mastered some of its greatest challenges during the Great Depression. Membership fell precipitously. Despite the decrease in dues, many members could not remain affiliated with the NADW, relying instead on state associations, or maintaining no formal professional ties.[34] Despite bleak circumstances, however, the organization survived and in 1938, in a great gesture of faith in the profession, discontinued the *Yearbook* and commenced publication of the *Journal of the NADW*. Edited by Ruth Strang of Teachers College, the *Journal*, for six decades, has published the latest research in the student personnel field.[35]

In the post–World War II era, the organization experienced continual restructuring. Several name changes occurred, to National Association of Women Deans and Counselors (NAWDC), 1956–73, to the National Association of Women Deans, Administrators, and Counselors (NAWDAC), 1973–91, and to its current name, the National Association of Women in Education (NAWE), in 1991. Conscious of both its past and its future, the NAWDAC maintains an historical archive at Bowling Green State University and continues to publish a scholarly journal, *Initiatives*. Although great changes occurred in the student personnel profession, which Jones and Komives analyze in chapter 10, and deans of women saw the demise of their office, there remain, over eight decades after the founding of the NADW, women administrators and student personnel workers dedicated to the profession and to the larger interests of women in the academy.

Although women students flocked to campus in greater numbers than ever before in the postwar years, Barbara Miller Solomon observes that their actual percentage within the undergraduate population decreased, at least until the late 1950s.[36] Three larger political and strategic factors, she contends, influenced the fortunes of women's higher education in those years. Between 1945 and 1956, she maintains that academic women suffered because of "the male influx into academia." Not only did they usurp women's space on the campus, they also superimposed on campus—because of their sheer numbers—"new patterns of college domesticity."[37] Because of the high rates of marriage among the GIs returning to campus, marriage and domesticity—more than ever in the history of higher education in the United States—became a campus social norm, imparting a potent cultural message to the primarily single, women students.[38]

Ironically, the intensification of the Cold War, suffused with male brinkmanship, altered, at least marginally, cultural expectations for college women. Solomon concludes that Russian initiatives in space, particularly the launching of Sputnik, awakened the United States to the need for developing its entire range of intellectual resources, regardless of gender. Congressional ratification of the National Defense Act in 1958 intensified the search and opportunities for talented women.[39] Thus, within the complex context of traditional domesticity and international geopolitical conflict, deans of women sought to maintain the vitality of women's higher education and of their own profession.

The appearance of numerous articles discussing the quality of higher education for women in the *Journal of NAWDC*, 1956–73, surprises no one. After all, expanding higher education of women created the office of deans of women in the first place. What does merit scholarly revisioning, however, is the quality of those articles, which so dramatically reflect the feminism and foresight of members of the profession. Possessed of a wider cultural vision, these women conducted research and wrote articles concerned not with discipline, but rather with discovery.

Consistent with their unique spirit of feminism, these scholars advised their colleagues that only through discovery of the cultural expectations affecting women could they begin to change the present and, perhaps, to secure the future. Only by refocusing attention away from the bureaucratic aspects of their work could they use their position on campus to discover, appreciate, and support women and their power to achieve. Amazingly, such articles, written nearly thirty years ago, reflect the perspicacity of these women in discerning and discussing questions concerning the higher education of women that contemporary culture has yet to resolve. Repeatedly, they reminded their colleagues that to retain and maintain the vitality of women's higher education, deans of women must recognize and respond to changes in population, purpose, and paradigm.

Throughout the entire life span of the profession, deans of women experienced almost continual change in the student population of women whom they served. For example, Barbara Miller Solomon suggests that for the first generation of women students who attended college between 1860 and 1880, the decision to pursue higher education was "unusual and complicated," and one that marked them as "social rebels."[40] Members of this single-minded company, Joyce Antler maintains, were "committed to obtaining a college degree above all other interests, including marriage and the creation of a family."[41]

Portentous change commenced, however, between 1870 and 1910, when the number of women attending coeducational institutions grew over twenty-three fold, from approximately 4,600 to 106,500.[42] This dramatic growth brought not only more women to coeducational campuses but also a greater variety of women. In her classic study of the dean of women, Lois Kimball Mathews, dean of women at the University of Wisconsin and a recognized authority in the profession, observed a decided change in the nature of the collegiate woman around 1890. No longer did the "sober-minded young women" dominate college campus. Instead, large numbers of women, with greater financial resources and fewer scholarly ambitions, matriculated, in search of " 'the college life.' "[43] By 1890, Solomon maintains that the first generation of self-conscious "pioneers" gave way to the " 'new woman' " of the emerging century.[44]

Deans of women encountered yet a more varied student population. Around 1920, aspiring middle-class parents, Helen Horowitz claims, had increasingly come to recognize the economic and social value of a college education for their daughters and sons.[45] With the ensuing proliferation of institutions of higher education, parents found that a college education was well within the reach of even those who were of modest financial means. With this increase came a fundamental change in the motivations of many women who sought college degrees. Alongside the serious women students who eschewed marriage and family in favor of academic achievements and productive careers were many who valued a college education "as a way station to a proper marriage."[46]

By the mid-1950s, deans of women confronted not only economic and motivational variations, but also much greater racial and chronological diversity among women students. Within the unprecedented numbers of women who flocked to coeducational campuses in this period were both new and traditional students. These women did not need discipline so much as they needed knowledge, support, advice, empathy, and role models. Research findings that appeared in the *Journal of NAWDC* during these years reminded deans of women that women's higher education remains vital only as it recognizes and responds to a more complex student population.

Public and private colleges and universities across the United States faced one of the greatest moral challenges to their lofty rationales for the transcendent value of higher education when increasing numbers of black students throughout the 1950s and 1960s demanded their right to partake of this tradition. Must institutions admit them? Should institutions admit them? If institutions admit them, what obligations beyond access to the classroom did this bring?

Gloria Josephs, assistant dean of students at Cornell University, observed that the increasing influx of African American students actually reflected a new kind of new student. Despite initial disquiet on both sides and in the larger culture, she observed that such change compelled perceptive administrators, indeed the entire university community, to reexamine the conflict between lingering tradition and burgeoning diversity within the academy. Out of that process could emerge constructive revision of both student evaluation and university governance.

Although African American students had attended virtually the whole range of white institutions of higher education since the antebellum period, they represented both an extremely circumscribed and homogenized segment of the African American population and a distinct minority on campus. Products primarily of the " 'black bourgeoisie,' " these persons, Josephs claimed, often had more in common with their white classmates than with the majority of their own race.[47]

Thus, in the mid-1950s, while the African American bourgeoisie remained, in many respects, new students on campus, there appeared an influx of new African American students. Josephs encouraged deans of women and other administrators and faculty to recognize this different sort of student, requiring a different sort of institutional response. Cognizant that many colleges and universities actively recruited these students for many of the right reasons, she nevertheless concluded that institutional responsibility for these persons did not end with the approval of an application for admission.[48]

Josephs maintained that the dean of women assumed a significant role in this process, both in discerning the identity and concerns of these students and in securing meaningful institutional response. For many of the new, African American students, often the products of urban ghettos, the university campus represented "foreign soil" indeed. She reminded deans that they must look beyond flattening categories such as race and perceive these young women as "sensitive intelligent, complex" persons, "pioneers"[49] in the fullest sense of the word.

According to Josephs, their presence on campus compelled a reexamination of classroom and boardroom procedures. As a consequence of the varied backgrounds of these students, faculty and administrators must face honestly their own "cultural bias," which could no longer be "swept under the rug."[50] In evaluating students, they must acknowledge their environment, and in governing students, they must attend to their concerns through face to face discussions. Only then could there be "a truly democratic campus."[51]

These observations, offered nearly three decades ago, now seem almost stereotypically and idealistically politically correct. Joseph's challenge to her colleagues, that "there is no turning back,"[52] rings sadly hollow. However, in the heady cultural landscape of the feminist and the student movements, such comments seem phenomenally forward-looking, especially as advice to deans of women, from within their own profession.

By the late 1950s, yet another group of women sought higher education. Older women, married or divorced—the linchpin of the nontraditional student population—matriculated in unprecedented numbers. Deans of women responded dramatically to this population. Numerous articles in the *Journal of NAWDC*, 1956–73, acknowledge its significance and advocate its acceptance.

Cognizant of the intellectual and strategic challenges that the Cold War presented to the United States, Annie Lee, a researcher at Indiana State University, reminded her audience that women represented "one of society's greatest untapped resources."[53] Expediency, if nothing else, necessitated the education of women, whether married or single, young or old. Realistically, however, Lee conceded that such broad-based acceptance of women's need for higher education necessitated a "reconstruction of attitudes in our society."[54] In pursuance of this goal, Lee and her colleagues disseminated research in which they examined the motivations, needs, and skills of nontraditional women college students.

Why did married women return to college? In addressing this and other pertinent questions, deans of women challenged the cultural conventional wisdom concerning married women and higher education. Barbara Doty, a psychologist, reiterated for her audience those stifling cultural proscriptions. Most older women who came to campus only for "frivolous, time-filling reasons,"[55] proved a poor short- and long-term risk. Not only was their academic performance inferior to other women students, but also they remained highly unlikely to use such skills through continuous, full-time employment in the workforce.

Cultural misconceptions concerning the educational motives of mature women students persisted because little research existed on this segment of the student population. In her study of married women students, Doty identified motivations for their returning to college. Some women simply wanted to learn, to enhance their knowledge. Others, unknowingly supporting Betty Friedan's finding in *The Feminine Mystique*, expressed frustration with club work and other time-filling suburban, domestic activities. Finally, some women sought education for financial reasons. They needed well-paying, productive employment either to provide for their children or for their own future.[56]

What do older women students need when they return to campus? Cora Myers, a nontraditional student, reminded deans of women that bureaucratic acceptance of mature women constituted merely a first step. Colleges and universities, she maintained, must implement policies that "enable us to return and to do well"[57]—the "genuine access" that Nidiffer identifies in chapter 6.

Mature women, Myers contends, despite their age and domestic responsibilities, bring a fresh breadth of experience to campus. To remain there, however, to maximize their experience and skills, mature women require specific, sensible institutional assistance of both a bureaucratic and personal nature.[58] Assured of such assistance, mature women can, indeed, be "a *valuable addition* to the university"[59] and to the Cold War culture.

Annie Lee, in her study of married women college students, identified a number of these concerns. First, institutions of higher education must recognize the realities of married women's lives and make genuine effort to address these through policies such as flexible scheduling and accessible child-care facilities. Furthermore, Lee contends that administrators must acknowledge and attack "faculty resentment and prejudice"[60] toward mature women students, which often manifested itself through the persistent problem of poor, if not inaccurate, advisement. Sufficient institutional recognition of and reaction against such sentiments, one of many "subtle factors"[61] frustrating mature women's educational advancement, remained essential to mature women's genuine acceptance and achievement on campus.

What skills do mature women students bring to campus and to the larger culture? Irma Halfter, director of testing at DePaul University, conducted research effectively demolishing the cornerstone of conventional wisdom concerning mature women students—"their inability to learn in later life."[62] Based upon comparative studies of the academic habits and achievements of traditional and mature women students at a sample of universities in Chicago, she found that, despite "long absence from formal study,"[63] mature women surpassed their young colleagues in classroom performance, not only in all subjects but also within each subject.

Mature women college students challenged cultural conventional wisdom not only in their academic performance but also in their vocational goals. Unwilling to return exclusively either to the kitchen, the volunteer network, or the country club, many of these women sought full-time employment. The majority of the mature women whom Barbara Doty studied intended to become teachers. While some naturally worked to enhance their children's lives and educations, others—whether married, divorced, or single—sought employment to secure their own long-term future.[64]

In the past three decades, nontraditional women students have changed the face of higher education in the United States. Mature women attend community colleges, public and private universities, and graduate programs of every sort. Increasing numbers and academic success, however, have not eradicated persistent problems and traditional expectations. Nevertheless, throughout the postwar decades, deans of women, through the *Journal*, consistently celebrated the value, articulated the needs, and acknowledged the potential contributions of these students.

If deans of women seemed rather idealistic in some of their statements concerning the vitality of women's higher education, then unmistakable realism marked their assessment of the challenges which the largest segment of women, the traditional population of eighteen- to twenty-two-year-old women, faced both on the campus and in the larger culture. Their articles concerning this group of students lend strong support to Joanna Meyerowitz's revisionist assessment of the complex nature of women's concerns and attitudes in the 1950s and early 1960s.

Women on the college campus reflected all shades of opinion concerning their rightful place in the world. On the one hand, deans of women encountered new, highly motivated women among the African American, and mature, women students. However, in their assessment of the traditional population, articles in the *Journal* reflect the same complexity of perspective as Meyerowitz contends existed in the larger culture. In other words, few of the traditional stereotypes persisted in all women. One did not see, for example, only ladylike, repressed spinster deans of women confronting a sea of would-be brides and mothers. Instead, college women pursued a variety of goals, marriage and family among them. Most deans of women operating from a distinctly feminist perspective, produced a variety of research exploring the reality that college women face, the risk factors they must overcome, and the response that perceptive deans of women should offer.

What sort of reality did traditional college women face? Writing in 1968, at the height of the student and women's movements on campus, K. Patricia

Cross suggested to deans of women that from the perspective of the causal observer, higher education approached "the final stages of removing the last vestiges of distinction between education for men and . . . for women."[65] Such integration had, indeed, been at the very heart of the coeducational venture, particularly in the eyes of many women. However, Cross, a perceptive commentator, reminded her audience of the paradox that lay at the heart of truth. The reality for college women was that, despite decades of institutional reform and campus activism, these students, in fact, reflected a complex of motivations and goals. Thus, at the very apex of the Free Speech, antiwar, civil rights, and women's movements on campus, Cross identified a persistent " 'feminine mystique' to which college women subscribe."[66]

Ruth Tokey, in a study of undergraduate women at Michigan State University, confirms Cross's observations. She isolated essentially two types of women students: the intellectually and the socially oriented. Intellectually oriented women valued independence and achievement. They sought privacy and articulated long term goals. While many hoped to marry, they preferred to do so after securing their career.[67]

Tokey discovered that socially oriented women, pursued short-term goals, the primary of which being marriage. Steeped in "the feminine tradition,"[68] these students exhibited deference and embraced conformity. Reflecting the concern of others in her profession, Tokey acknowledged the reality that while both groups included bright young women, all of these bright young women require perceptive counseling to choose wisely among a complex of options.

What risk factors must college women overcome? Research articles in the *Journal* reflect the concern of deans of women that the majority of their students still accepted the collegiate "feminine mystique" to which Cross alludes. Thus, five years after the appearance of Betty Friedan's pathbreaking work, *The Feminine Mystique*, and at the very moment when coeducation apparently reflected gender equality on campus, a number of scholars conclude that traditional expectations for women retain their potency. Anxious that their colleagues appreciate the risk factor that college women face, they present an articulate, incisive, and disturbingly persistent, description of traditional femininity.

Jean MacFarlane, a psychologist at the University of California at Berkeley, in a study of cultural factors affecting adolescent girls, concludes that during times of national emergency, such as the Cold War, the United States could ill afford the "civic or economic unproductivity"[69] of its women. The country, the family, the women themselves suffer as consequence. However, to reverse this trend, she maintains that deans of women, who spend four crucial years with those young persons, must have no illusions concerning the strength and seductiveness of traditional gender expectations.

Femininity, Esther Westervelt, a scholar of women's education from SUNY Stony Brook, contends is a culturally defined concept, which varies over time.

"Created by human beings [and] abolished by human beings,"[70] one must not confuse constructs such as femininity with natural law. Nevertheless, neither can one underestimate the investment which other aspects of society, including some on campus, have in its survival. For example, Jean MacFarlane reinforces the role of advertising in defining concepts of femininity. "Glamour advertisements brainwash" young women, communicating the obvious message that intelligence represents a "handicap to 'dates' " and brands a woman "unfeminine."[71]

Westervelt contends that "innumerable social sources . . . even our comic strips"[72] inculcate traditional feminine characteristics such as "passivity, dependence, emotionality."[73] Numerous women of all ages, she observes, embrace this concept of femininity, even when it "serves them poorly and ill fits the circumstances of their lives."[74] Of particular concern are the innumerable, competent young women who, even before they enter college, lose any concept of themselves as "unique, resourceful, and autonomous" persons.

Westervelt castigates not only the larger culture but also the campus for perpetuating this restrictive definition of womanhood. Traditional women students, like their African American and mature counterparts, more often than not derive restrictive, wrong-headed advice from faculty and other counseling personnel. Oblivious to campus realities such as "women's liberation, radical [feminism], and women's studies," Westervelt discovered that numerous faculty and other advisors encourage women to accept marriage as "the major factor in their life planning."[75]

What response should perceptive deans of women offer? Although both MacFarlane and Westervelt acknowledge the challenge deans of women face in addressing the complex expectations and desires of traditional women students, they suggest pragmatic, practical strategies and goals. MacFarlane concludes that deans of women must impart to women students an honest sense of the scope of life and what that means for most women. To do so effectively, they must also expand the purview of the office of dean of women to assist students not only in their residence and extracurricular life but also in articulating "life goals" and in selecting the curriculum necessary for their achievement.[76]

Westervelt concludes that if deans of women wish to change students, or at least to offer them reasonable options for their lives, they must reject neither cultural nor individual change. Discontent with "stereotyped femininity," she maintains that a growing number of women students "are more comfortable with their humanness than with their femaleness."[77] Deans of women should listen to, as well as advise the students, encouraging them to explore "richer and more varied conceptions of femininity."[78] However, to do so effectively, deans of women must be "courageous, aggressive, and autonomous"[79] in evaluating, protecting, and expanding their institutional role and in securing the widest possible opportunities for their students.

For what purpose do women need higher education? Within the context of U.S. history, this question has sparked spirited debate since the colonial era. Historians of the early national period maintain that education—at least through the secondary level—produced republican mothers, women well suited to raise patriotic and productive sons. In response to the rapid economic growth of the antebellum period, social critics argued that higher education for women provided an army of single women teachers for the burgeoning West.

By the 1870s, the number of women attending colleges began its dramatic increase. Furthermore, a small but growing number of women entered various graduate and professional programs, both in the United States and abroad. These pioneers and their advocates argued that women needed intellectual stimulation because they could do the work, because they needed to be independent, and because they relished the individual reward and satisfaction.

These women, whom Barbara Miller Solomon termed "pioneers," articulated the essential purpose of women's higher education that endures to this day. During the socially conservative 1920s, some saw women's higher education as yet another attack on the moral fiber of the nation. During the Great Depression, families were more likely to spend precious funds on a son's rather than a daughter's education. During World War II, the nation needed its women to perform industrial and other labor rather than to toil over academic minutiae.

For what purpose did women need education during the Cold War years? Undoubtedly, many women considered institutions of higher education to number among the best marriage markets in the country. However, among thoughtful college women and, significantly, among their most articulate advocates, deans of women, the purpose of the pioneers persisted. Throughout the *Journal of NAWDC*, 1956–73, deans of women articulated the goal of higher education for women, the obstacles that threatened its achievement, and the roles of the residence hall and the dean of women in helping women students attain this goal.

Writing at the height of the Cold War, Eunice Dowse and Mary Harrison, assistant deans of women at the University of Illinois, sounded a persistent, if often unwelcome note, when they concluded that the goal of higher education for women was to create "mature and self-directing individuals."[80] In an increasingly complex and challenging world, meaningful collegiate experience, they contended, produced mature women, capable of taking responsibility for their lives. To attain such maturity, however, Evelyn Gardner, dean of women at Grinell College, insisted that women students need academic and residential environments that engender both personal introspection and independence.[81]

Postwar institutional priorities, startlingly reflective of the larger culture, presented the most troubling obstacles both to deans of women and to many of their students, determined, respectively, to provide and to procure a meaningful college experience. Throughout the 1950s, students entered colleges and universities in unprecedented numbers. By the middle of the decade, institutional authorities, aware but not displeased by even greater projected enrollment increases in the 1960s, launched massive building programs. Construction abounded as colleges and universities expanded classrooms, dining halls, and most ominously for deans of women, residence halls.

One of the most persistent issues plaguing both advocates and opponents of higher education for women has been the issue of housing. Whether in single-sex or coeducational institutions, the questions remain the same. Should women live on the campus? In what size structures should they live? How closely should institutional authorities supervise them? Should residence life have a specific educational function?[82]

At the heart of the educational goals of deans of women in the Cold War era was the development of individuality, independence, and introspection. These goals, in their essential nature, conflicted with the political and social orthodoxy of the 1950s. Not only perceptive scholars such as David Riesman and C. Wright Mills, but also the authors of the Port Huron Statement and the founders of the Free Speech Movement, addressed the distressing loss of individualism in a mass corporate, media, and institutional culture. Deans of women, in their concern for the quality of residence life, raised the same questions, albeit in a less overtly provocative manner.

May Brunson, dean of women at a growing institution, the University of Miami, feared that increasingly "the business aspect of student housing may dominate educational goals."[83] Convinced that projected student numbers and construction costs drove administrative decision-making, Evelyn Gardner cautioned her colleagues of just how far the student personnel profession had indeed departed from upholding the conventional wisdom concerning quality of residence life. In the 1930s, student personnel experts concluded that "housing units of sixty to seventy five"[84] at most, represented the ideal environment to nurture individuality and independence.

Scarcely twenty years later, however, deans of women encountered administrative colleagues, who, replicating the cultural love affair with bigger and better and identical, dismissed a larger number of modest living facilities as financial liabilities. Troubled by the consequences of such a worldview, Evelyn Gardner warned her colleagues that in pursuit of financial expediency institutions would sacrifice the students' need for "privacy and independence."[85]

Reflective of the growing concern for the fate of the individual in an increasingly impersonal society, Gardner attacked not only the size of dormitories but also their proximity to campus life. By the mid-1970s, she concluded that the vast majority of women students would live in "larger and larger residence halls . . . on the edge of . . . campus."[86] Consigned to these collegiate Levittowns, college women would forfeit not only their individuality but also their sense of belonging to the larger university community.

Scholars agreed that residence halls for women occupied a central place in their collegiate experience and in fostering their attainment of individualism, independence, and introspection. Dowse and Harrison pragmatically reminded deans of women that students, in fact, spent the majority of their college life in their residence facility rather than in the classroom. Deans of women and other student personnel officers, thus, exerted potentially greater control or influence than did faculty over the development of young women.[87]

May Brunson encouraged her colleagues to bring to residence life "a fusion of living and learning."[88] Evelyn Gardner concurred, advocating the expansion of the scope of residence life beyond the basic "provision of mere shelter and social respectability."[89] From the earliest days of women's higher education—in either single-sex or coeducational institutions—living space incorporated the academic and social function of college life. By the 1950s, however, in large, impersonal, almost hotel-like structures housing hundreds of women, the closeness of students, of students to counselors, and of residence life to academic life, remained, if they remained at all, fragile commodities indeed.

Evelyn Gardner offered deans of women practical advice concerning their involvement in the future of residence life, advice directly relevant to their place in the administrative councils of higher education. Determined that they assume a far less restrictive role, she advised deans of women to assume a proactive stance, openly criticizing policies detrimental to women's higher education. To do so more effectively, they should claim a greater responsibility in both architectural and admission policymaking.[90] If in the end, however, deans of women could not alter the institutional propensity to build large residence hall complexes, they nevertheless must remain the vocal and active advocate of student welfare, striking a balance between the alienation and indifference endemic to a large, impersonal institution and the proper sort of space to develop as an introspective, independent person.

In the postwar era, deans of women experienced changes in both the population and purposes of higher education for women. A wide variety of women enrolled in colleges and universities. African American women and older women, who matriculated in growing numbers, demanded a different response from both deans of women and their institutions. For many women, of all ages and colors, higher education ceased to be only either a hobby or a form of job training, but rather crucial to the development of independence, individualism, and introspection vital to their inner well-being.

Yet a third, essentially intrinsic transformation also occurred, encompassing the entire paradigm of women's lives. By the mid-1960s, both the larger culture and deans of women confronted a portentous reconfiguration of women's potential longevity and activity. In so doing, they addressed three questions. What has changed in the paradigm of women's lives? How have both the larger culture and women themselves reacted to this? How must deans of women respond in the best interests of their students?

Discussion of this paradigm shift appeared repeatedly in the *Journal* throughout the 1950s and 1960s. According to Lois Stolz, a psychologist at Stanford University, nothing less than a " 'feminine revolution' " had occurred "in the timing of events in the life cycle of women."[91] Women married earlier, most likely by twenty-two,[92] and bore their last child earlier. Pursuant to advances in medicine and improvement in general health, women lived longer. Thus, by their mid-to-late thirties, women, with at least half of their lives remaining,[93] increasingly addressed the question, "what will I do with the rest of my life?"

Stolz and other scholars identified and suggested various responses to this query. Women between the ages of thirty and sixty, Stolz found, constituted the largest cohort of women entering the labor force during the 1950s. She concluded that they reflected a new and uniquely variegated pattern in the lives of women: "work-stop-work."[94] Such a pattern, Bernice Neugarten of the University of Chicago counseled her colleagues, demands that women live in a constant process of reexamination and revision of self-image and of goals. Such reexamination and revision are especially essential for middle-aged women.[95]

This new paradigm, Stolz and Linda Bruemmer, director of placement at Elmhurst College, concurred, intensified the presence and intensity of choice in women's lives, more so in the lives either of their ancestors or of men. No longer then could most women expect with any certainty that they would experience the predictable and culturally sanctioned path of marriage, motherhood, unpaid domestic labor, and economic security for the balance of their adult lives. While their grandmothers expected "a lifetime of domestic effort" and men accepted the inevitability of paid labor, women in the postwar era increasingly encountered "the far heavier burden of choice."[96]

Both the larger culture and many women either doubted the need for such choices or were ill-prepared to make them. Stolz cautioned deans of women that by the time their traditional charges, women between the ages of eighteen and twenty-two came to college, powerful forces of cultural conditioning profoundly influenced their perceptions of possible choices—of life stories and of work prospects. From their birth, this culture imposes upon women conflicting expectations. First, as children, parents treat girls differently from boys—in dress, toys, even color scheme. Subsequently, during the school years, girls often become even more confused when parents and culture expect them to achieve, yet to do so while retaining charm and a submissive temperament,[97] a combination that effectively precludes their ability either to perceive or to value informed choices.

Challenges to women's likelihood of selecting sensible options do not disappear when they complete their education. Although Stolz correctly cites the growth of mature women in the workplace, she explores neither the extent of their work nor the cultural barriers they encounter. Linda Bruemmer identifies a troubling "cultural set of myths"[98] concerning women's suitability for paid labor.

Quite simply, she contends that as late as 1969, most employers retained several crippling prejudices against women in the labor force. Women are not serious workers. Women intend to work only part time. Women defer to their husbands in scheduling their lives and their work. Bruemmer reminds deans of women that such a scenario sends an even more dismal message to college women. Paid labor for women is at best "a 'feminine' or secondary career."[99]

Unsettled by this troubling circumstance, deans of women repeatedly alert their colleagues to the threat that college women face in fashioning productive lives and, implicitly, to the unavoidable challenge which they face as advisors of these students. Most college women, Bruemmer observes, remain incapable of making sensible choices because seldom do they know that such choices exist. "Never have American women lived so long," concludes Ruth Useem, a sociologist at Michigan State University, "yet been so little concerned with preparing themselves for that . . . life. . . . Never has the younger generation been more in need of guidance."[100]

Patricia Tautfest, interim dean of women at the University of Wisconsin, offered imminently practical advice to assist deans of women in directing young women's response to this new paradigm. First, students must know that they will assume many roles in their lives, for which they must continue to learn. They must also accept the reality that they will, in all probability, join the paid labor force at some time in their lives.

Personal experience, common sense, and inspiration will serve deans of women well in advising their students. Either alumnae or returning mature women might share their experiences with young undergraduates. In making curricular choices, students should understand that women best serve their long-term interests by acquiring the central skills in the traditional liberal arts curriculum, particularly logical thinking and orderly writing, rather than a more narrow vocational skill that often becomes quickly outdated. Finally, deans of women render their greatest service by encouraging women to take risks, a genuine challenge to either gender in any culture.[101]

Of what possible value are these scholarly articles concerning women's higher education, written nearly thirty years ago, by and for members of a profession that no longer exists? Despite the demise of the office of dean of women, this perceptive scholarship retains both historiographic and practical significance. First, this collection of primary materials, in which these women identify a host of competing perspectives among women lends strong support to revisionists such as Meyerowitz and Hartmann. Articles in the *Journal of NAWDC*, 1956–73, which reflect the concerns of both activist deans of women and a wide spectrum of women students, reinforce the revisionist contention that women in the postwar era represented a multiplicity of realities, domestic life being but one.

Furthermore, these sources enhance the work of these scholars in the process of reclaiming the lives and reinterpreting the contributors of the deans of women, surely the most misunderstood office in the administrative ranks of higher education in the United States. Cognizant of its decreasing numbers in 1956, the NADW, deeming survival preferable to professional exclusivity and reflecting its essentially innovative and pragmatic nature, expanded its ranks. Despite such challenges to their profession, these tireless advocates of the rights of women published in their *Journal*, 1956–73, articles suffused with feminism and foresight concerning the vitality of women's education. Such primary sources lend effective support to a revisioning of the profession from one of timid conformity to one of outspoken advocacy.

Finally, these articles retain an imminently practical significance within contemporary higher education. In their recognition of and response to changes in population, purpose, and paradigm, like other women administrators examined in this volume, deans of women demonstrate a disturbing clairvoyance. Undoubtedly, *Journal* contributors identified and addressed issues of housing, curriculum, advisement, and gender equity with which colleges and universities still contend, two decades after the demise of the dean of women.

How did deans of women at mid-century evaluate themselves, particularly in light of the growing precariousness of their profession? Perhaps because of the challenges they had met, and even in response to those that they faced, leaders in the profession retained a rightly deserved self-respect and a realistic self-concept. Addressing NAWDC members at the fiftieth anniversary of the organization in 1966, JoAnn Fley, of the College of Education at the University of Illinois, attacked the disturbingly persistent, oversimplistic view of the dean of women "as a petty snoop and as a maintainer of the status quo."[102] Reflecting on half a century of dedication to the vitality of higher education for women, she concluded that "deans were more *out* of step than *in* step with conformity."[103]

Barbara Catton, Executive Secretary of NAWDC, speaking at that fateful annual meeting in 1956, supports Fley's observation. Faced with decreasing numbers and persistent challenge to women's place in higher education, the organization could have taken the low road of cultural accommodation and stereotypical behavior—house the women, protect them from the men, prepare them for marriage. Firmly claiming the higher ground, however, Catton credited the accomplishments of this profession to its tireless activism, its determination to look "a little farther ahead"[104] in its pursuit of educational opportunity for women.

Notes

1. Barbara Miller Solomon, *In the Company of Educated Women: A History of Women and Higher Education in America* (New Haven: Yale University Press, 1985), 207.

2. Dorothy Truex, "Education of Women, the Student Personnel Profession, and the New Feminism," *Journal of NAWDC* 35 (Fall 1971): 13.

3. Ibid., 16.

4. Ibid., 14.

5. Joanne Meyerowitz, "Women and Gender in Postwar America," in *Not June Cleaver: Women and Gender in Postwar America, 1945–1960*, ed. Joanne Meyerowitz (Philadelphia: Temple University Press, 1994), 3.

6. Ibid., 4.

7. Ibid., 2.

8. Ibid., 5.

9. Susan M. Hartmann, "Women's Employment and the Domestic Ideal in the Early Cold War Years," in *Not June Cleaver: Women and Gender in Postwar America, 1945–1960*, ed. Joanne Meyerowitz (Philadelphia: Temple University Press, 1994), 88–89.

10. Ibid., 90.

11. Ibid., 98.

12. Paula A. Treichler, "Alma Mater's Sorority: Women and the University of Illinois, 1890–1925," in *For Alma Mater: Theory and Practice in F3eminist Scholarship*, ed. Paul A. Treichler, Cjeris Kramarae, and Beth Stafford (Urbana: University of Illinois Press, 1985), 24.

13. Geraldine J. Clifford, ed., *Lone Voyagers: Academic Women in Coeducational Institutions, 1870–1937* (New York: The Feminist Press, 1989), 10.

14. Robert Arthur Schwartz, "The Feminization of a Profession: Student Affairs Work in Higher Education, 1890–1945," Ph.D. dissertation, Indiana University, 1990, 9–10, 358.

15. Jana Nidiffer, "More than a 'Wise and Pious Matron': Origins of the Position of Deans of Women, 1895–1916," Ed.D. dissertation, Harvard University, 1994.

16. Kathryn N. Tuttle, "What Became of the Dean of Women? Changing Roles for Women Administrators in American Higher Education, 1940–1980," Ph.D. dissertation, University of Kansas, 1996.

17. Hilda A. Davis and Patricia Bell-Scott, "The Association of Deans of Women and Advisers to Girls in Negro Schools, 1929–1954: A Brief Oral History," *Sage: A Scholarly Journal on Black Women* VI (Summer 1989): 40.

18. Carolyn Terry Bashaw, *Stalwart Women: An Historical Analysis of Deans of Women in the South* (New York: Teachers College Press, 1999).

19. Burton Bledstein, *The Culture of Professionalism: The Middle Class and the Development of Higher Education in America* (New York: W. W. Norton, 1976), 105.

20. Robert W. Wiebe, *The Search for Order 1877–1920* (New York: Hill & Wang, 1967), 14, 146.

21. In her study of women's higher education in the United States, Barbara Miller Solomon identifies three generations of college women: the

first generation (1860s–1880s) "pioneers," the second generation (1890s–1900s) "new woman," and the third generation (1910s–1920s) "more sophisticated 'new woman.' " See Solomon, *In the Company of Educated Women,* 95.

22. Walter Crosby Eells, "Earned Doctorates for Women in the Nineteenth Century," *Bulletin of the American Association of University Professors* 42 (Winter 1956): 648. For a more recent discussion of women and graduate degrees, see Margaret W. Rossiter, *Women Scientists in America: Struggles and Strategies to 1940* (Baltimore: The Johns Hopkins University Press, 1982), 29–50, and Margaret W. Rossiter, "Doctorates for American Women, 1868–1907," *History of Education Quarterly* 22 (Summer 1982): 159–83. See also Solomon, *In the Company of Educated Women*, 130–38, 154–56.

23. Joyce Antler, "The Educated Woman and Professionalization: The Struggle for a New Feminine Identity, 1890–1920" (Ph.D. dissertation, State University of New York at Stony Brook, 1977), 204.

24. Ibid., 415–16.

25. Nancy Cott, *The Grounding of Modern Feminism* (New Haven: Yale University Press, 1987), 238.

26. Penina M. Glazer and Miriam Slater, *Unequal Colleagues: The Entrance of Women into the Professions, 1890–1940* (New Brunswick: Rutgers University Press, 1987), 217. For a discussion of these four strategies see Glazer and Slater, *Unequal Colleagues*, 1–23, 209–27.

27. Mary Ross Potter, "History of the Conference of Deans of Women to the Organization of the National Association in 1917," in *Proceedings of the Fourteenth Regular Meeting of the National Association of Deans of Women*, Dallas, Texas, 1927, 213, 217. See also Eleanor Schetlin, "Fifty Years of Associations—Ninety Years of Dreams," *Journal of the National Association of Women Deans, Administrators, and Counselors* 29 (Spring 1966): 113.

28. Mrs. Ellis L. Phillips, Mina Kerr, and Agnes Wells, "History of the National Association of Deans of Women," in *Proceedings of the Fourteenth Regular Meeting of the National Association of Deans of Women*, Dallas, Texas, 1927, 228. See also Kathryn McLean Phillips, "Beginnings," *Journal of the National Association of Deans of Women* 16 (January 1953): 143–45 and Schetlin, "Fifty Years of Association," 114.

29. Kathryn Sission Phillips, *My Room in the World: A Memoir*, as told to Keith Jennison (New York: Abingdon Press, 1964), 67.

30. Phillips, "Beginnings," 143.

31. Phillips, *My Room in the World*, 67.

32. Phillips, "Beginnings," 143. See also Phillips, *My Room in the World*, 67–68.

33. Phillips, "Beginnings," 145.

34. For a discussion of the challenges that the NADW and its leadership faced in the 1930s, see Carolyn Terry Bashaw, "Agnes Ellen Harris and

Leadership in the NADW, 1929–1941," *The Alabama Review* 46 (October 1993): 243–65.

35. Barbara Catton, "Our Association in Review," *Journal of NAWDC* 20 (October 1956): 7. For additional comment concerning the founding of the *Journal*, see Past Presidents of the Association, "Twenty-Five Years in Review," *Journal of the National Association of Deans of Women* 4 (March 1941): 118–19.

36. Solomon, *In the Company of Educated Women*, 191.

37. Ibid., 190.

38. Ibid., 194–95.

39. Ibid., 198.

40. Ibid., 77.

41. Antler, "The Educated Woman and Professionalization," 111–12.

42. Mabel Newcomer, *A Century of Higher Education for Women* (New York: Harper & Brothers, 1959), 47, 49.

43. Lois Kimball Mathews, *The Dean of Women* (Boston: Houghton Mifflin, 1915), 305.

44. Solomon, *In the Company of Educated Women*, 95. For a more detailed discussion of the varieties of college women, see Helen Lefkowitz Horowitz, *Campus Life: Undergraduate Cultures from the End of the Eighteenth Century to the Present* (New York: Alfred A. Knopf, 1987), 193–219, and Lynn D. Gordon, *Gender and Higher Education in the Progressive Era* (New Haven: Yale University Press, 1990).

45. Horowitz, *Campus Life*, 201. David O. Levine maintains that although the number of men and women attending colleges and universities increased dramatically between 1915 and 1940, certain groups, especially women and minorities, functioned as second-class citizens on the campuses. See David O. Levine, *The American College and the Culture of Aspiration, 1915–1940* (Ithaca: Cornell University Press, 1986), 19–21.

46. Ibid. See also Solomon, *In the Company of Educated Women*, 78 and Antler, "The Educated Woman and Professionalization," 111–12.

47. Gloria I. Josephs, "Black Students on the Predominantly White Campus," *Journal of NAWDC* 32 (Winter 1969): 63.

48. Ibid.

49. Ibid., 64.

50. Ibid., 65.

51. Ibid., 66.

52. Ibid.

53. Annie M. Lee, "A Study of Married Women College Students," *Journal of NAWDC* 24 (April 1961): 132.

54. Ibid., 136.

55. Barbara A. Doty, "Why Do Mature Women Return to College," *Journal of NAWDC* 29 (Summer 1966): 173.

56. Ibid., 172.

57. Cora H. Myers, "Special Problems Encountered by Mature Women Undergraduates," *Journal of NAWDC* 27 (Spring 1964): 139.

58. Ibid., 137.

59. Lee, "Married Women College Students," 137.

60. Ibid. For a similar discussion of the specific campus concerns of older women students, see Myers, "Special Problems," 137–39.

61. Lee, "Married Women College Students," 136.

62. Irma T. Halfter, "The Comparative Academic Achievement of Young and Old," *Journal of NAWDC* 25 (January 1962): 60.

63. Ibid., 64.

64. Doty, "Why Do Mature Women," 171–72.

65. Patricia K. Cross, "College Women: A Research Description," *Journal of NAWDC* 32 (Fall 1968): 12.

66. Ibid., 20.

67. Ruth S. Tokey, "Intellectually-Oriented and Socially-Oriented Superior College Girls," *Journal of NAWDC* 27 (September 1964): 120–24.

68. Ibid., 127.

69. Jean W. MacFarlane, "Intellectual Functioning in High School Girls and College Women," *Journal of NAWDC* 21 (October 1957): 3.

70. Esther Manning Westervelt, "Femininity in American Women: The Influence of Education," *Journal of NAWDC* 35 (Fall 1971): 5.

71. MacFarlane, "Intellectual Functioning," 6.

72. Westervelt, "Femininity in American Women," 8.

73. Ibid., 2.

74. Ibid., 3.

75. Ibid., 8.

76. MacFarlane, "Intellectual Functioning," 7; 4.

77. Westervelt, "Femininity in American Women," 9.

78. Ibid., 10–11.

79. Ibid., 11.

80. Eunice M. Dowse and Mary E. Harrison, "The Educational Program of the Residence Hall," *Journal of NAWDC* 20 (January 1957): 59.

81. Evelyn Gardner, "The Sociology of Residence Halls," *Journal of NAWDC* 20 (January 1957): 56.

82. For a comprehensive discussion of the issues surrounding dormitories for women in single sex institutions, see Helen Horowitz, *Alma Mater: Design and Experience in the Women's Colleges from Their Nineteenth-Century Beginnings to the 1930s* (New York: Alfred A. Knopf, 1984).

83. May A. Brunson, "Residence Halls as Centers of Learning," *Journal of NAWDC* 27 (October 1963): 32.

84. Gardner, "Sociology of Residence Halls," 53.

85. Ibid., 52.

86. Ibid., 53. For a more detailed examination of the issue of collegiate women, dormitories, and campus space, see Bashaw, *Stalwart Women.*

87. Dowse and Harrison, "Educational Program," 58.

88. Brunson, "Residence Halls as Centers of Learning," 36.

89. Gardner, "Sociology of Residence Halls," 56–57.

90. Ibid., 52, 55–56.

91. Lois Meek Stolz, "Woman's Search for a New Self," *Journal of NAWDC* 22 (April 1959): 125.

92. Solomon, *In the Company of Educated Women*, 187.

93. Ruth Hill Useem, "Changing Cultural Concepts in Women's Lives," *Journal of NAWDC* 24 (October 1960): 29–30. Useem contends that at age thirty-five, most women begin a "second life."

94. Stolz, "Woman's Search," 127.

95. Bernice L. Neugarten, "Women's Changing Roles Through the Life Cycle," *Journal of NAWDC* 24 (June 1961): 163.

96. Linda Bruemmer, "The Condition of Women in Society Today: A Review-Part I," *Journal of NAWDC* 33 (Fall 1969): 18. See also Stolz, "Woman's Search," 127.

97. Ibid., 128–29.

98. Bruemmer, "Condition of Women," 19.

99. Ibid., 21.

100. Useem, "Changing Cultural Concepts," 29. See also Bruemmer, "Condition of Women," 18.

101. Patricia B. Tautfest, "Continuing Education Programs and Their Implications for Counselors," *Journal of NAWDC* 27 (Summer 1964): 196–97.

102. JoAnn Fley, "An Honorable Tradition," *Journal of NAWDC* 29 (September 1966): 106.

103. Ibid., 109.

104. Barbara Catton, "Our Association in Review," 8–9.

CHAPTER 8

Agents of Social Control

The Role of Physical Educators as Guardians of Women's Health, 1860–1960

JOAN PAUL

Catharine Beecher relinquished the idea of marriage after her fiancé drowned in a shipwreck while traveling to Europe to pursue advanced study. Beecher turned to education as the only acceptable career option in the 1820s. Given her emotional state following this tragedy, she found that active exercise both released her mind from its troubled condition and helped her improve her physical health. She was first in a long line of American women to see the relationship of exercise to health and to recognize the educational role it could play in schools. Beecher's efforts in creating a fairly sophisticated system of exercise and incorporating it into the various women's seminaries she founded set the stage for other women to choose physical education as a career by mid to late nineteenth century.

Some of the most powerful and dominant women in education were the physical educators who, like the women students, were new to institutions of higher education in the mid-nineteenth century. From the time they entered the halls of academia, they assumed responsibility for their young female charges by governing almost every aspect of their lives. Out of concern for their physical well being, they supervised their women students' diets, the amount of rest they received, regulated their exercise, monitored their weight, and worked to improve their posture. Furthermore, much like deans of women discussed in earlier chapters, they monitored their behavior in and out of class, prescribed proper dress, neatness, and cleanliness. Conservative and traditionalist physical educators, who believed their calling was to mold these women students in accordance with acceptable social mores of femininity, carefully scrutinized the lives of their students. Health, as the perceived outcome, was an encompassing notion that comprised physical, mental, and social behavior. From mid-nineteenth to mid-twentieth century, these women educators were strong agents of social control in their perceived role as the guardians of women's health.

Physical Education Arrives in the United States

German political refugees who fled their country after falling into disfavor with the Prussian government introduced physical education into the United States. Charles Beck, Charles Follen, and Francis Lieber, all members of Friedrich Jahn's political gymnastic Turnverein Society, came to America between 1825 and 1827 and introduced German gymnastics to boys at the Round Hill School in Northampton, Massachusetts, and to the students at Harvard College. This inauspicious beginning and its promise for improving students' health resulted in the creation of organized exercise programs that slowly spread to schools and colleges across the country. Joined at mid-century by Per Henrik Ling's Swedish system of gymnastics, these two exercise systems, along with a few hybrid programs, competed for dominance in education in the United States from mid-nineteenth into the early twentieth century. All were formal and militaristic systems of exercise, but women's programs favored Swedish gymnastics because of its more direct application to health.

As the country became more industrialized in the late nineteenth century, there were fears of a society growing physically weaker because mechanized work required less physical effort. The health problems created when people moved from the healthy, open-air of the countryside into the unsanitary living conditions of the city also caused concern. These troubling circumstances were instrumental to the inclusion of collegiate physical education as an antidote to the problem.

Women in Physical Education

At the time women's colleges opened in the mid-nineteenth century, cultural prescription held that women were both physically and mentally inferior to men. In fact, as Jana Nidiffer suggests in chapter 1, critics of higher education for women maintained that such education would ruin their physical and mental health. Some of the grave consequences cited were physical deformities and mental derangement.[1] But perhaps the greater fears were those predicted by educators such as Dr. Edward Clarke of Harvard, who, in the 1870s, attempted to present scientific evidence to show that college women who ventured beyond their sphere would be unfit wives or mothers. His most influential work, *Sex in Education* (1873), used biological terms to explain how higher education for women could draw blood from their reproductive organs to their brains, thus causing them to either have no children or to produce invalids.[2] Writings by such noted scholars caused young women and their families to consider higher education more of a stigma than a great social and intellectual advantage. The founders and administrators of women's colleges were inordinately preoccupied with the health of their students, and they took precautions because of the numerous problems attendant to the rigors of college life.[3] They considered physical exercises and games the preferred intervention for predicted problems college life presented to young women. It was in this context of fear that women's colleges accepted the necessity for physical education.[4]

This new field of physical education attracted many women in the early years even though males in the discipline appeared less than enthusiastic about having them as colleagues. Dioclesian Lewis, first to introduce teacher preparation in the neophyte field of physical education in the United States in 1861, attracted more women than men to his Normal Institute for Physical Education in Boston. As other private normal schools opened in the nineteenth century—Boston Normal School of Gymnastics (BNSG), Sargent's School of Physical Education, Anderson's School of Physical Education, Posse's School, and others—women continued to be the most eager students.[5] Edward Hartwell, American Physical Education Association (APEA) president, stated in his address at the famous 1889 Boston Conference that the future did not look as bright as it might because a "disproportionate number" of those who wished to come into the field as new recruits were women "with bees in their bonnets."[6] In spite of this open prejudice, women continued to flock to the new field in greater numbers than males.

Women chose the developing field of physical education for numerous reasons. First, other than teaching, there were few approved careers for the nineteenth-century woman beyond wife and mother. Physical education, which became an organized profession in 1885 with the creation of the Association for the Advancement of Physical Education,[7] offered new and unexplored opportunities for adventurous women. Because societal norms prohibited girls and women from the playing fields "red-blooded" American males frequented, the promise of a more active life through a career in physical education certainly was attractive to the more vigorously spirited young woman. Also, the new field was enticing to women because it appeared to offer personal freedom from convention and it held a missionary-like appeal for contributing to the health of the "weaker sex." Furthermore, as crusaders for women's higher education, these women believed they could be "enablers" for women by protecting them from the stress of academic study.

Early Teacher Preparation

From the 1860s until the 1890s, private normal schools, Chatauquas, and special summer schools offered the only pedagogical preparation for "physical training." In the 1890s, a few colleges and universities began the practice of offering one- and two-year certificates in physical education. However, most males seeking careers in the new field continued to pursue medical training. Because of the highly gendered nature of medicine, women had great difficulty gaining admittance to medical school, so they most often took advantage of the opportunity to attend private normal schools or to earn academic certification in collegiate institutions.[8] Perhaps it was because of this phenomenon that women's collegiate departments were first to offer specialized work toward academic certification in physical education. The two roads for teacher preparation were disparate, with women's education more applied than theoretical. The sciences of physiology, anatomy, and anthropometry were central to men's studies while women were prepared as classroom teachers who could lead healthful exercises for children during recess.[9]

The passing of legislation for compulsory public school physical education in states from Ohio to California to Louisiana in the 1890s, spurred progressive colleges to offer a bachelor's degree to prepare their graduates better for school and college teaching.[10] In 1900, only three colleges or universities offered majors in the field, but the acceptance of physical education as a collegiate offering was obvious since approximately 270 institutions offered classes in physical training. Harvard University in 1891, Stanford University in 1892, and the University of Nebraska in 1898 were the first institutions to establish a four-year major in physical education.[11]

As colleges and universities adopted teacher preparation programs in physical education, the old private normal schools either closed or affiliated with institutions of higher education.[12] The Boston Normal School of Gymnastics (BNSG) was the first of the private normal schools to affiliate with a college or university when in 1909 it became a department in Wellesley College with Amy Morris Homans as its director.[13] In 1929 Dudley Sargent's son transferred the ownership of the Sargent School to Boston University where it was placed in its School of Education. Today it is known as the Sargent College of Allied Health Professions.[14] The Posse School of Gymnastics in Boston closed its doors in 1942, after fifty-two years of service.[15] By the 1950s, virtually all of the old private normal schools of physical education had closed or achieved college/university affiliation.[16]

Early Programs of Physical Education

The first exercise programs for women in America began in female seminaries during the first half of the nineteenth century by such women as Catharine Beecher, Emma Willard, and Mary Lyon. Each recognized the important health benefits, but favored different forms of exercise. Beecher, with her strong Calvinistic background, preferred calisthenics performed to music because she said one could receive necessary exercise in a pleasant way while avoiding the evils of dance. Lyon, more conservative and traditional, had her students at Mount Holyoke obtain their exercise through required household or domestic duties. Willard, founder of the Emma Willard School in Troy, New York, believed that dancing was the best exercise for women because it was a proper feminine activity that taught graceful movement.[17]

Scholars of physical education recognize Catharine Beecher as the first American woman to make a meaningful contribution to the nascent field of physical education. She developed a system of exercise that she named "calisthenics." Because she believed her exercise system lacked the sophistication to be titled "gymnastics," Beecher devised the name "calisthenics" from two Greek words, "kalos" signifying "beautiful," and "sthenos" meaning "strength."[18]

Vassar College was first to accord exercise, games, and eventually organized physical education a regular place in a college curriculum for women. Mathew Vassar, who founded the college in 1861, believed that physical exercise should be a fundamental part of education for women. Consequently, he appointed a lady physician to monitor the health of the young women students.[19] In 1868, the college required daily health courses and outdoor exercises for students.[20] The inclusion of these exercise and sport classes introduced at Vassar created a domino effect since Wellesley patterned its program after Vassar, Goucher patterned after Wellesley, and other women's colleges developing around the country also followed Vassar's lead.

The women who introduced physical activity to the students in women's colleges in the 1870s and 1880s usually had teaching duties in addition to calisthenics classes. Pioneer deans of women, discussed in an earlier chapter, had a similar assignment — the supervising of women students alongside a teaching schedule. Colleges hired these first instructors of physical education as combination teachers, and catalogs seldom mentioned the institutions where they trained. Some of the common teaching combinations listed in early catalogs were: gymnastics or physical culture with history, elocution, English composition, and Latin. Sometimes the teacher of physical education also served as the registrar, librarian, or the president's assistant. Rarely did early catalogs list physical education as part of a course of study, but placed it under such categories as "the College Home" or "Domestic Arrangement."[21]

Although Vassar College was first in the United States to offer physical activity class work for women in 1868, Wellesley College hired the first full-time teacher in physical education in 1881. Other women's colleges and women's departments in private schools throughout the United States soon followed this pattern. For example, Vassar hired its first full-time physical educator in 1883, Bryn Mawr and Oberlin in 1885, Smith in 1887, Goucher in 1888, Sophie Newcomb in 1891, and the University of Chicago in 1892.

Between 1889 and 1900, many state universities including California Berkeley, Indiana, Washington, Kansas, Utah, Illinois, Michigan, Oregon, Wisconsin, Iowa, Minnesota, Ohio, and Missouri organized departments of physical education for women.[22]

When full-time teachers headed women's programs, they usually had the title, "Director." Early in the twentieth century a certain amount of elitism accompanied this position. Beginning in 1910, Amy Morris Homans invited women directors of physical education from the New England colleges to the Wellesley campus, with which the BNSG had affiliated in 1909, to discuss the status of the field.

From this grew a national body, the American Association of Directors of Physical Education for Women in Colleges and Universities, composed of several regional associations. Only directors had an opportunity to join the association, and even then the process for admittance resembled that of an exclusive club. To be eligible for membership, at least two sponsors had to suggest candidates who had to be a "director" in an accredited four-year college or university, hold membership in the American Physical Education Association (APEA), and receive a two-thirds vote by the membership.[23]

In time, some directors were radical enough to suggest that all staff members should be eligible for association membership because they might not only learn something from their meetings, but also might make a contribution. Several years passed before the association seriously considered this, because the response was always that small group discussions were more profitable, that administrative problems were not the staffs' concern, and if that the organization grew too large, members might as well be in an APEA meeting. The discussions among directors were sometimes polite and friendly and sometimes argumentative. The issues before them ranged from large curricular decisions to determining the proper length of swimming suits.[24] Members changed the name of the organization to the National Association for Physical Education of College Women (NAPECW) in 1932, when they invited physical educators other than directors to join. However, until 1942, only directors could vote, hold office, or attend business meetings, even though members paid the same dues.

Obstacles Early Women Physical Educators Faced

Nineteenth- and early-twentieth-century female physical educators confronted numerous obstacles. The most pervasive were the lack of academic respect, seriously inadequate facilities, controversy over gymnasium costumes, and the stigma of masculinity. Regardless of the obstacles, these early women physical educators were compelled to continue their struggle to enhance education for women by offering them an avenue to good health, while overseeing and directing their conduct into proper channels.

When physical education penetrated the walls of academia in the nineteenth century, its instructors often faced ridicule from other educators who believed physical training to be antithetical to mental training.[25] John M. Tyler, in his 1901 address offering congratulations to Edward Hitchcock for the forty years spent at Amherst College, described nineteenth century attitudes toward the young profession. He explained that one could not define physical education as "academic" because its applied approach to physical activity was not "intellectual," and to require it of college students dignified the subject "far beyond its desserts."[26]

Women physical educators early in the twentieth century were especially sensitive to their backgrounds. Most had private normal school certificates rather than college degrees.[27] Reinforcing the presumption that physical education lacked genuine academic credibility, institutions awarded students neither grades nor credit toward diplomas although leaders in the field such as Dudley Sargent had advocated course credit as early as 1900.[28] Some physical educators used the quest for academic respectability as a driving force to produce programs that were more educational and academic. However, sentiments on this issue varied as other leaders openly questioned academic awarding credit "for perspiration." J. B. Nash, president of the APEA, further accused some programs in physical education of not even guaranteeing that, and he believed giving academic credit was questionable until students had experiences that caused reflective thinking.[29]

The absence of academic faculty rank was another area of concern to the earliest collegiate physical educators. Although a handful of physical educators received professorial titles prior to the twentieth century, most did not. Physical educators accepted any semblance of equality with pride. They interpreted serving on committees with other faculty members as progress. When students taking their courses received grades, even though not counted toward graduation, they reveled. Thus, in spite of its lowly status, physical education secured an unquestioned and permanent position in academic institutions.[30] Physical educators reassured themselves that "no professor on the academic faculty [had] a larger opportunity to influence the health, happiness and character of the student."[31]

The second obstacle women physical educator encountered was the poor facilities in which they were expected to implement their programs. College and university officials considered almost any unused room, however uninviting and unsanitary, adequate to teach the subject.[32] Women's colleges were more likely to provide appropriately for their physical education programs, but the facilities in coeducational institutions for women were usually very meager. Many of the early physical educators, such as Delphine Hanna at Oberlin College, used their own modest salaries to buy equipment for their programs.

Women's classes in coeducational institutions frequently had access to the men's gymnasium floor and playing fields only when the men did not wish to use them. Otherwise, they attended classes in a basement room or even in condemned facilities.[33] Not until the 1920s did most collegiate women's programs have gymnasiums of their own. Many deans of women as well served as advocates for women students' access to the athletic spaces on campus.

A third obstacle was having students, parents, and administrators understand the need for special performance costumes in physical education. Standards for women's clothing during the Victorian era demanded modesty and conformed to accepted notions of woman's place and appearance. Gymnasium costumes were no exception. In the mid-nineteenth century, students came to campus wearing tightly fitted corsets, bustles, hoops, and petticoats beneath long-skirted dresses. Social mores, as well as dress styles, were antithetical to the idea of exercise, sports, and games. Women's clothing was for display more than utility, and when physical education instructors introduced the gymnasium suit into college classes, practical considerations were secondary to style and decorum. Dio Lewis was first to require the special gymnasium costume, based on the "Camelia Outfit" first worn in public in the 1850s by suffragist Amelia Bloomer, for American physical education in the 1860s.

Ever mindful of Victorian modesty, physical educators sought to design a "gym suit," that hid the fact that women were bipeds. Yards and yards of heavy material intentionally made the gymnasium suit resemble a full skirt. When women initially wore the costume, they were sometimes overcome with shame even though men were never allowed in the area. There are stories from many institutions describing women sinking to the floor of the gymnasium in a heap, tears coming down their cheeks, huddling together and refusing to take part in the activities because of the shame of the "gym suit."

Because beauty was an ever present ideal in all clothing designs, even the creation of the radical "bloomer" suit was not immune to criticism.[34] The suits, which weighed several pounds, were made of either a stiff, scratchy blue serge or a "heating and absorbing flannel," and neither was washable. Because the suits were so hot, most students wore one or two cloth belts around their waists to help absorb the perspiration. Bands sewn on the bottoms kept them from riding up and showing the legs, but these cut into the student's flesh as she moved. Although health and hygiene were the major purposes for physical education, the gym suits created a most unhygienic problem for teachers and students.[35]

Because the new field of physical education placed women in new roles with new demands, it created a fourth obstacle that became a pervasive problem. The more elite women attending college in the mid- to late-nineteenth century were raised in a society that conditioned them to remain indoors and engage in feminine pastimes such as sewing, painting, or playing the piano. Ill health was not only the common lot of upper-class women; many even considered it feminine. Because physical education promoted a more active life and required a trousered costume, people often considered it to be the antithesis of gentility.

Women physical educators were aware that other educators and the general public often regarded them as less feminine than others, but this only exacerbated their efforts to guard against masculinity in their students. Entering a field associated with male activities such as exercise and sport, usually being unmarried, and wearing tailored clothes more suitable to teaching activity, all fostered the appearance of masculinity. It was not unusual that women physical educators were single since most early women educators had to choose between marriage and a career. However, it appears that throughout the twentieth century, people categorized both women physical educators and deans of women as "old maids" more often than they did other women faculty members.[36]

It is clear that twentieth-century physical educators were aware of the masculine stereotype with which critics branded them. Mabel Lee, first woman president of the APEA in 1931, told of being fearful of appearing mannish, especially since she was working in physical education "which too many lay persons still looked upon as a calling for mannish women." She tells of carefully selecting her accessories for her suit so that she would look as feminine as possible and "give the public a different picture of what a woman director of physical education could look like."[37]

Although social values dominated competition in women's sport, a homophobic anxiety appeared in the early 1900s through the fear that sport could pervert normal gender relations and negatively affect the "prescribed" role of wife and mother.[38] Women physical educators often feared the social ostracism which could result from their "unfeminine" occupation.[39] Consciously or unconsciously, homophobia was perhaps a major factor in shaping the women's sporting tradition from earliest times into the 1960s.

Fear of criticism prevented women physical educators from taking more positive steps in the promotion of women's athletics.[40] As early as the 1920s, the professional associations urged organizations to stop giving recognition awards such as medals, bracelets, loving cups, and expensive college letter blankets and letter sweaters to individuals for intramural and class competition.[41] Even in 1974 when Title IX legislation was enacted to force society toward more equal sporting opportunities, a physical educator lamented: "It is . . . appalling to realize the number of people, men and women alike, who believe that a woman's place in an athletic contest should be relegated to cheering or waving a pom pom."[42]

Emerging Curriculum

Before the advent of sport as a regular part of the curriculum in the 1890s, the earliest programs in physical education for women were almost exclusively composed of calisthenics, marching, and synchronized drills performed with or without light apparatus such as wands, dumbbells, and Indian clubs. To gain physical strength and stamina, students worked on treadle machines, the forerunners of stationary bicycles, and exercised on various pieces of equipment to improve their posture. In daily physical education classes, students used Swedish apparatus, such as stall bars, the vaulting box, and window bars.

Very few women's programs included German gymnastics in their curriculum because of the great strength and vigorous movement required to perform on the parallel and horizontal bars, the vaulting and pommel horses, and the flying rings, trapeze, and other such equipment. Those few programs that did teach German gymnastics were usually in coeducational colleges influenced by the men's programs.[43] The French Delsarte gymnastics, more theatrical and dance oriented, joined the Swedish in popularity in women's programs in the 1890s. These systems dominated women's programs into the early twentieth century.

Between 1880 and 1920, the scientific focus of women's physical education was on anthropometry, patterned after the men's programs. Physical educators considered the practice of taking anthropometric measurements on students as unquestionably their most significant work. Edward Hitchcock of Amherst College, who developed the first significant college program for men in 1861, and Dudley Sargent of Harvard College, began the first anthropometric work in the United States.[44] The conduct of anthropometry in the United States was based on the studies of the British scientist, Archibald Maclaren, who was the first physical educator in the world known to apply anthropometric measurements to his work. Through anthropometry, physical educators created the forerunner of the exercise science laboratory, and it became the symbol of academic respectability for both men's and women's programs.

Through the use of anthropometric measurements common to all good programs, physical educators planned prescriptive exercise schedules for female students judged to be in poor health. They placed many students in corrective work, assigned breathing exercises, or even prescribed rest in place of exercise.[45] The role of physical education through the 1910s was to protect and preserve women's health, and these early physical directors took their jobs very seriously.

Both a Blessing and a Curse

The 1890s, the decade of the "New Woman," was also a time of innovation in women's physical education programs. Physical educators introduced dance and sport as a regular part of women's curricula in the 1890s. Dance caused some administrative headaches because conservative taxpayers had concerns with morality, but the issue of sport in women's programs became the most critical issue from this time onward.

At the 1889 Boston Conference, Thomas Wood and others called for the advancement of sport and games over the formal activities taught in physical education. The plea was for educational sport, not the commercialized and professionalized athletics which college men independently foisted on academe. Intercollegiate athletics for men began in 1852 as student organized, governed, and financed activities played with youthful exuberance, but without financial or official support of educational institutions. Many a college administrator frowned upon sport because of classes missed, bones broken, or behavior that seemed unfair and discourteous, such as throwing curve balls to visiting baseball teams. Even though recognized only as extracurricular activities, sport for boys and men was encouraged as "manly" activity that could help develop desirable traits such as bravery, collegiality, and fair play. Some of the very attitudes that supported and promoted men's sport became problematic to the promotion of women's sport.

Apparently the first effort to teach sport to women occurred at Vassar College in 1876, when a young teacher substituted games for exercise.[46] Between 1860 and 1880, women's college catalogues mentioned the recreational sports of riding, boating, baseball, archery, tennis, and swimming, but rarely were they part of the required curriculum until the 1890s.[47] From sport's first introduction to women's classes, physical educators emphasized its social rather than competitive value. A good example of this attitude was the selection of the crews at Wellesley based on singing ability rather than rowing skill. Before 1893, members of the crew had rowed and serenaded from their boats until Wellesley's President Helen Shafer enthusiastically announced that crew members would now be given lessons in the science of oarsmanship for the new objective of developing physical fitness.[48]

By 1910, sport replaced gymnastics, calisthenics, and synchronized drills as the mainstay of women's physical education but controversy ensued. Critics claimed that sport promoted manliness. How could women continue in sports without violating ideals of womanhood? To address this dilemma, female physical educators had to create a different sporting sphere for women. They promoted women's sport to instill traditional social expectations rather than feminist ideals. The only acceptable objectives in women's sport were the promotion of health, good character, and the provision of desirable social interaction. These sports programs emphasized proper conduct as ladylike behavior.

Society accepted sport in the nineteenth and early twentieth centuries as long as it was genteel enough for women to play in their dress clothes, for healthful exercise only, and displayed no competitive spirit. Many people considered sport to be inappropriate for girls and women when it required strenuous activity such as running, jumping, or coming in contact with other players or the ground. Consequently, basketball and track and field attracted sustained criticism.

When Senda Berenson Clara Baer introduced basketball to women, first in the spring of 1892 at Smith College and subsequently in the fall of 1893 at Sophie Newcomb College, both received severe criticism because they played the game using boys' rules. They quickly modified basketball to eliminate criticism of its masculine features. Baer's 1895 rules were so Victorian that running was limited, and players received fouls for making noise on the court, for not shooting the ball after taking aim, for falling down, and for guarding opponents who were shooting for a basket.[49] When Harriet Ballintine introduced track and field at Vassar in 1896, she received much ridicule by other physical educators for hosting a field day of running and jumping for her students.[50] She made clear to students and the public that the objective was not to teach sport, "but to teach girls to play."[51]

Emergence of Intercollegiate Sport

Between 1910 and 1920, sport became the focus of the physical education curriculum, and college women became more and more interested in competitive games. Although few physical educators favored competition between institutions, there were a number of colleges playing limited schedules in intercollegiate tennis and basketball. By the 1920s, because of the growth of women's sport beyond class competition, women physical educators organized to form a unified opposition to all highly competitive sport beyond the walls of their own institutions.

The Women's Division of the National Amateur Athletic Federation (WDNAAF), formed under the auspices of Lou Henry Hoover in 1923, served as the earliest governing body for girls' and women's sport. Its members argued that the biological differences in boys and girls dictated that they be treated differently in sporting situations. Although physical strain was beneficial for males, many authorities claimed that excessive activity would cause irrational nervousness in females. Critics argued that "external stimuli such as cheering audiences, bands, lights, etc., cause a great response in girls and are apt to upset the endocrine balance."[52]

The WDNAAF developed a twelve-plank platform that promoted playing sport for enjoyment, good sportsmanship, and character development rather than making and breaking records or winning championships. Physical educators promoted sport for the greatest good of all women and not just the skilled few. These women considered elitist sport and the promotion of star players as the greatest "evils" of "old athletics."[53] The WDNAAF extended its efforts to curtail competitive sport from colleges to high schools, churches and other recreation leagues, YMCAs, and even the Olympic Games. Its members promoted the philosophy that sport should be developed for the girl and not the girl for the sport.[54]

Influence as Agents of Social Control

Collegiate physical educators, perhaps more than any other faculty members, knew their students personally and listened willingly to their problems. Although deans of women were the logical choice for hearing student concerns, some students believed the deans were too much a part of the college disciplinary machinery to share certain problems.[55] Instead, physical educators assumed the protector role and acted as the parent or guardian away from home for their students.

This parental role empowered them to exert influence in ways that would be considered an infringement of rights today. As self-appointed guardians of women's health, they enforced strict regulations concerning diet and sleep. They usually prohibited sweets, afternoon teas, and eating between meals.[56] Physical educators closely monitored students' dress and behavior, and chided students for social or moral behavior they thought inappropriate.[57]

Amy Morris Homans is a classic example of a strong agent of social control. From the founding of the Boston Normal School of Gymnastics in 1889, through her years at Wellesley College, Homans and her predecessors generated legendary accounts of their attempt to control students and mold them into better citizens by adhering to feminine expectations. Miss Homans, who believed in the direct approach with her students, met with them both individually and in groups to discuss their shortcomings. Students told of the powerful influence Miss Homans exerted over them and described it as both fear-inspiring and painful.[58] Her view of life and work was broad and liberal, but she was openly "scornful of pettiness, of cheap and tawdry things, ostentation, unseemly or undignified behavior. . . . She stressed the importance of self-respect, self-control and dignity; of the good taste, grooming and manners of well bred people."[59]

Merely the swish of Miss Homans's skirts as she walked down the hall caused students to sit more erect and their hearts to pound. At the BNSG, she walked around observing students. Unpolished shoes, crooked hose seams, or hosiery insufficiently opaque would be cause for chastisement. She deemed unclean gym suits to be an even worse offense.[60] Homans demanded ladylike demeanor from students on the playfield, in social settings, and in the classroom. She expected her students to be "the epitome of womanliness in decorum and dress." She posted signs in her building to remind students that they should "speak with a well-modulated voice."[61] Even a student's disheveled hair after exercise was reason enough to have the student called to her office. Rolling up a sleeve or spilling milk also caused encounters with the strict Miss Homans. Her control was so total that when Mabel Lee first attended the Boston Normal School of Gymnastics, Homans gave her the choice of gaining ten pounds or being sent home.[62]

Homan's students loved her dearly despite all of her sternness. She also cared greatly for them in return, seeing that they were placed in the best teaching positions and continuing to follow their careers long after they left the BNSG. Homans was so influential that through the network she created with administrators throughout the country, her recommendation to school and college administrators was sufficient to place her students in jobs without an interview. College presidents eagerly hired her students, and they even allowed Miss Homans to suggest their salary.

Physical educators were obsessed with monitoring their female students' behavior. The gymnasium and playing fields became arenas for critical judgments by their teachers from the 1880s through the 1950s. Dudley and Kellor, who taught at the University of Chicago and advocated sport for girls, cautioned women athletes in 1909 against gum chewing, lying or sitting on the floor when there was idle time in a game, clapping their hands, and talking to each other while playing. They stated, "few girls have thus far learned the beauty, joy and science of the silent game. Grace and silence are among the anticipations rather than the realizations, and some still confuse noise with sport and having a good time."[63]

The 1920s was an exciting era for physical educators. Yet it was also a time when many felt some of their control wane. With the ratification of the Suffrage Amendment, women exhibited behavior indicative of the new political and social status they envisioned because of having the vote. Women bobbed their hair for the first time, wore short skirts, smoked publicly, wore hip flasks in defiance of prohibition, and behaved in ways traditionalists considered outrageous. Mabel Lee, who taught at the University of Nebraska during this decade, stated that she had never seen the word "sex" in print or heard anyone say the word aloud before the 1920s.[64]

The physical educators spoke out forcefully against any behavior they believed inappropriate for women. Because the world seemed to move toward more liberal ideas in the 1920s, they found many activities unacceptable. The physical educators took strong campuswide stands against drinking and smoking, against the athletic swagger exhibited by women in sport, and against what they saw as college practices that sexually exploited women. They campaigned against women playing basketball games as openers for the men's games, claiming that the male athletic hierarchy used women in their abbreviated costumes to draw crowds. They fought the idea of marching bands instituting the new practice of having drum majorettes, "strutteresses," twirlers, and golden girls perform on the athletic field as blatant exhibitionism.[65]

As guardians of women's health, physical educators believed they were most knowledgeable and best prepared to guide women in healthful practices. This became obvious in 1926 when women physical educators took exception to the National Association of Deans of Women for organizing a Committee on Student Health without consulting or including them on the committee. They were indignant with the deans. Physical educators believed they were the logical choice for this work because they were more knowledgeable about women's health problems. The NAPECW set its next meeting to coincide with the Deans' Association meeting both to show their cooperation with groups outside physical education and to convince the deans that they should be the decision makers in issues of women's health.[66]

Although women physical educators became less overt in their control of students' personal lives, they still felt duty bound to govern activities within their jurisdiction for the betterment of womanhood. By the 1930s, the Women's Division successfully eliminated women's intercollegiate sport in all but 12 percent of colleges. Women physical educators preferred some competition for all rather than intensive competition for a few.[67] Play Days, Sports Days, telegraphic meets, and intramural sports became the correct outlets for the athletic girl to display her skills.[68]

The National Association for Physical Education of College Women, still acting as guardians of their students, continued through the 1950s to recommend Sports Days in lieu of varsity competition. They supported the exclusion of women as members of men's athletic teams and adamantly opposed colleges sponsoring tournaments or meets for women to determine championships. In 1963 when the predecessor of the WDNAAF, the Division for Girls' and Women's Sports (DGWS), officially approved interscholastic and intercollegiate competition, a more liberal future for women in sport was evident. Even with the formation of the College Intercollegiate Athletic Association (CIAA) in 1966, many of the old guard physical educators clung to their traditional values. The president of NAPECW, Marian Broer, urged the members to alter their historically conservative views on women's sport in 1967. She almost pleaded with the women physical educators when she said: "We cannot set the clock back. We must go on from where we are."[69]

Conclusion

Beginning in the nineteenth century, women physical educators demonstrated strong scholarship and shaped the profession. They wrote books and articles, delivered principal convention speeches, and held high offices in professional organizations.[70] However, their approach to physical education and their attitudes toward their students differed from men. The availability of collegiate education for males preceded females by more than two hundred years because the mental and physical capabilities of men in higher education was never an issue. As earlier chapters in this volume suggest, for women, nineteenth- and early-twentieth-century collegiate education was fraught with dreadful consequences—mental derangement, physical deformity, and social ostracism. Women physical educators, with progressive social service motives, entered teaching careers with high ideals of contributing to the betterment of society. They chose a field that held promise for instilling social and moral values in young women whom they hoped would lead healthier and happier lives because of their efforts. These female physical educators, like the deans of women before them, exerted a powerful and far-reaching influence on their students from the nineteenth through mid-twentieth century.

Their approach to teaching was both nurturing and controlling. In hindsight, it appears that they often spent more time enforcing trivial rules than addressing larger academic matters. From the 1860s to the 1960s, dress codes were as dear to their hearts as national policy. They participated in endless faculty meetings in the 1930s and 1940s to determine penalties to be imposed over broken dress codes, such as wearing yellow instead of white socks. A semester of discussion and debate ensued at Wellesley before it was decided whether to purchase tank suits "Wellesley blue" when dry or when wet.[71] Through the 1950s women P.E. majors were still required to wear their all-white, starched shorts and shirts with identifiable labels and polished white tennis shoes. Inspection occurred at each activity class and grades suffered if students' violated uniform codes.

Women physical educators made curricular adjustments through the years. The notion that physical education's purpose was correcting deformities and providing other therapeutic health benefits shifted to the new aim of making students more self-directing individuals who would be better equipped for happy and efficient living.[72] With these changing objectives, programs in the 1930s dropped the old anthropometric measurements and adopted tests and measurements aimed at attacking weight problems, posture, and the improvement of motor skills, such as running, jumping, throwing, and catching. Through the new use of skill and written tests, physical educators also had a better argument for giving grades in their courses. They could now base grades on measurable objectives rather than on time served or docile obedience as in the past.[73]

Their tactics of control moved from overt preaching at students to more subtle means such as grading and awarding graduate assistantships to students conforming to expectations. Women continued to work through professional organizations to impose their values by limiting sporting opportunities, and they were largely successful through the 1960s. Only because they feared losing control of women's sport did they eventually bend, but they bitterly opposed the idea of women following in men's athletic footsteps.

The 1960s was another decade of change for women, and their traditional power base was almost exhausted. The field of collegiate physical education was on the brink of radical transformation because a new academic rigor created philosophical differences and caused great unrest between academicians and practitioners. These differences were causing a near impasse between public school physical education, which continued along traditional lines, and collegiate programs that were becoming specialized. Physical education was becoming discipline-oriented in its "efforts to establish itself as a scientific and scholarly profession."[74] In the guise of efficiency, upper administrators mandated the merging of women's departments with the men's. In almost all circumstances men occupied the administrative positions. The 1960s set the course for the last three decades of the twentieth century that resulted in new academic structures and altered titles for departments and schools of physical education within universities.[75] In the next chapter, Linda Carpenter and Vivian Acosta discuss the troubling nature of such change in the pivotal 1970s.

With collegiate physical education relinquishing much of its applied emphasis, academic goals transcended the preoccupation with physical activity. It was a new day, a day the more traditional physical educators regretted. Predictably, younger women physical educators and sports leaders retained less reverence for these pioneers who upheld the old guard philosophy and took pride in their social conservatism. Many of the younger feminist leaders believed the term "old guard" was an appropriate synonym for "obstructionists." The women coming into the field of physical education in the 1970s and later, whether influenced by the male model or because of rejecting the older women's model, were academicians with more traditionally male-oriented goals.

Although their goals and methods may be criticized by today's standards, these early women physical educators dedicated their lives to molding young lives. Still standing are older gymnasiums bearing their names. They remain as memorials to the power and influence such women wielded over collegiate life. According to the plethora of recordings left by former students, they loved or respected no faculty member more than the physical educator who loved and respected her students in return. Whether these women teachers and administrators were misguided or simply a product of their time, there was nobility in their struggle. They lived their lives, not for money or prestige, but for the high-principled purpose of acting as guardians of women's health.

Notes

1. It appears that the physical malady most probably caused from extended study was "distortions" of the spine. See Ainsworth, *The History of Physical Education in Colleges for Women* (New York: A. S. Barnes, 1930), 102.

2. See Lynn D. Gordon, *Gender and Higher Education in the Progressive Era* (New Haven: Yale University Press, 1990); Nancy Woloch, *Women and the American Experience* (New York: Alfred A. Knopf, 1984).

3. Ibid.; Joan S. Hult, "The Governance of Athletics for Girls and Women: Leadership by Women Physical Educators, 1899–1949," *Research Quarterly for Exercise and Sport* (Centennial Issue, 1985): 64–77.

4. Betty Spears, "The Emergence of Women in Sport," in *Women's Athletics: Coping with Controversy,* ed. Barbara J. Hoepner (Washington, D.C.: AAHPER, 1974): 26–42.

5. H. Harrison Clark, "Select Your Physical Educator with Care," *Education* 68 (April 1948): 463–69; Debbie Mauldin Cottrell, "The Sargent School for Physical Education," *Journal of Health, Physical Education, Recreation, and Dance (JOHPERD)* 65.3 (March 1994): 32–37; Paula Rogers Lupcho, "The Harvard Summer School of Physical Education," *JOHPERD* 65.3 (March 1994): 43–46.

6. Edward M. Hartwell, "President's Address—The Condition and Prospects of Physical Education in the United States," *Proceedings of the American Association for the Advancement of Physical Education* 6 (1893): 13–40 in Lockhart and Spears, *Chronicle of American Physical Education, 1855–1930*, 1972, 130–52.

7. The association went through a series of name changes from its founding. Today, the national organization for the multititled programs across the country is the American Alliance for Health, Physical Education, Recreation, and Dance. Modern collegiate membership divides its loyalty between the Alliance and various academic subdiscipline organizations, for example, North American Society for Sport History.

8. Mabel Lee, *A History of Physical Education and Sports in the U.S.A.* (New York: John Wiley & Sons, 1983); Joan Paul, "H. Sophie Newcomb Memorial College," *JOHPERD* 65.3 (March 1994): 53–56; Joanna Davenport, Feature ed., "The Normal Schools: Exploring Our Heritage," *JOHPERD* 65.3 (March 1994): 25–28; Luther Halsey Gulick, M.D., "Report of the Commission on the Status of PE in Public Normal Schools and Public High Schools in the U.S.," *American PE Review* 15.6 (June 1910): 453–54. The two schools that produced the greater number of college physical educators from the late 1890s through the first decade of the twentieth century were the BNSG and the Sargent School. Schwendener erroneously notes that the Anderson Normal School of Physical Education in New Haven, along with the BNSG, served for a time as almost the only source of preparation for women teachers of physical education. Not only were there a number of private normal schools, but more women graduates were produced by the Sargent School than Anderson's. See Norma Schwendener, *A History of Physical Education in the United States* (New York: A.S. Barnes and Company, 1942).

9. J. W. Seaver, "A Plea for More Theoretical Instruction in Our Normal Schools of Gymnastics," *American Physical Education Review* 6.1 (March, 1901): 217–21. Delphine Hanna and Anna Norris were among the first women in physical education with M.D. degrees, both earning them in the late nineteenth century. See Betty Spears, "Success, Women, and Physical Education,"

in M. Gladys Scott and Mary J. Hoferek, eds., *Women as Leaders in Physical Education and Sports* (Iowa City: The University of Iowa, 1979), 5–19.

10. Lee, *A History of Physical Education and Sports in the U.S.A.*, 1983; Norma Sue Griffin and Kathryn Weick, eds., *Seventy-Five Years of Professional Preparation in Physical Education for Women at the University of Nebraska-Lincoln: 1893–1973* (Lincoln: University of Nebraska-Lincoln, April 1973).

11. See Mabel Lee, *Memories beyond Bloomers* (Reston, Va.: AAHPER, 1978). Many colleges required students to take courses in physical education because of its health benefits, but rarely was academic credit awarded toward a degree. For example, out of the 270 colleges mentioned, only 8 percent reported giving any credit to their students toward a diploma. See Dudley A. Sargent, "Ideals in Physical Education," *American Physical Education Review* 62 (June, 1901): 110–21; Lee, *A History of Physical Education and Sports in the U.S.A.*, 1983.

12. Deobold B. Van Dalen and Bruce L. Bennett, *A World History of Physical Education*, 2nd ed. (Englewood Cliffs, N.J.: Prentice Hall, 1971).

13. See Mary L. Remley, "Amy Homans and the Boston Normal School of Gymnastics," *JOHPERD*, 65.3 (March 1994): 47–49, 52; Ruth Elliott, Mabel Lee, Helen McKinstry, and Ethel Perrin. "Resolution of Eastern District Society American Physical Education Association," *Mary Hemenway Alumnae Association Graduate Department of Hygiene and Physical Education, Wellesley College Bulletin, 1934–1935*, 4–5. When Wellesley decided to return to the status of a purely liberal arts college and divested itself of all teacher education in 1953, this department was terminated after a long and distinguished career. See Lee, *A History of Physical Education and Sports in the U.S.A.*, 1983.

14. Sargent's son took over the school when his father died in 1924. See Cottrell, "The Sargent School for Physical Education," March 1994, 32–37.

15. Lee, *A History of Physical Education,* 1983.

16. Ibid.; Clark, "Select Your Physical Educator with Care," April 1948. Schwendener erroneously notes that the Anderson Normal School of Physical Education in New Haven, along with the BNSG, served for a time as almost the only source of preparation for women teachers of physical education. Not only were there a number of private normal schools, but more women graduates were produced by the Sargent School than by Anderson's. See Schwendener, *A History of Physical Education in the United States*, 1942.

17. Ainsworth, *The History of Physical Education in Colleges for Women*, 1930.

18. See Ellen W. Gerber, *Innovations and Institutions in Physical Education* (Philadelphia: Lea & Febiger, 1971), 225.

19. Spears, "The Emergence of Women in Sport," 1974.

20. Ainsworth, *The History of Physical Education in Colleges for Women*, 1930.

21. Ibid.

22. Lee, *A History of Physical Education and Sports in the U.S.*A, 1983.

23. Membership was also restricted to white physical directors. It was 1965 before the American Association for Health, Physical Education and Recreation, the national organization of all physical educators, male and female, adopted a resolution urging all state associations to accept members regardless of race. Only one year earlier the NEA had passed a similar resolution. See Bruce L. Bennett, "This Is Our Heritage: 1960–1985," *Research Quarterly for Exercise and Sport,* Centennial Issue (1985): 102–20.

24. Elizabeth Halsey, "The Life and Lights of the NAPECW," NAPECW Booklet, 1962, eight pages; Phyllis Hill, "The Way We Were," *A History of the Purposes of NAPECW, 1924–1974* (NAPECW, December, 1975); Joan Paul, ed., *A Fifty-Year History of the Southern Association for Physical Education of College Women: 1935–1985* (Hammond, La.: Carr Office Environments, 1985).

25. Ainsworth, *The History of Physical Education in Colleges for Women*, 1930; "Editorial Note and Comment," *American Physical Education Review* 3.1 (March 1898): 69–70; Ira N. Hollis, "Intercollegiate Athletics," *The Atlantic Monthly* 90 (1902); 534–44.

26. "Address by John M. Tyler (congratulating Dr. Edward Hitchcock for his forty years at Amherst)," *American Physical Education Review* 6.1 (March 1901): 264–66.

27. By 1905 only 10 percent of physical educators had bachelor's degrees, but by 1911, 30 percent had received degrees. After 1915, there was a marked increase in academic degrees held by physical educators. Around the 1930s professorial titles were being awarded to physical educators and the academic degrees now held undoubtedly played a role. See George L. Meylan, "Presidential Address," *American Physical Education Review* 16.6 (June 1911): 353–59 in Lockhart and Spears, *Chronicle of American Physical Education, 1855–1930* (1972): 292–300; Ainsworth, *The History of Physical Education in Colleges for Women*, 1930.

28. D. A. Sargent, "The Place for Physical Training in the School and College Curriculum," *American Physical Education Review* 5.1 (March 1900): 1–17.

29. Rosalind Cassidy, "Changing Perspectives . . . A Personal Journey," *HPER Omnibus* (Washington, D.C.: AAHPER, 1976), 71–81.

30. In 1907 Thomas Storey, medical doctor and leader in the field, explained that for a subject to be educational it did not have to be intellectual. See Thomas A. Storey, "The Academic Status of the Gymnasium," *American Physical Education Review* 12.4 (December 1907): 303–6 in Lockhart and

Spears, *Chronicle of American Physical Education, 1855–1930* (1972): 239–42; Luther Gulick, "Physical Education: A New Profession," *Proceedings of the American Association of Physical Education*, 5th Annual Meeting, no. 4 (1890): 59–67 in Lockhart and Spears, *Chronicle of American Physical Education, 1855–1930* (1972): 91–97.

31. Quoted on page 240 in Storey, "The Academic Status of the Gymnasium" (December 1907).

32. Helen M. McKinstry, "Administration of Physical Education of Girls and Women," *American Physical Education Review* 16.6 (June, 1911): 364–79.

33. Lee, *A History of Physical Education and Sports in the U.S.A.*, 1983, 11.

34. McKinstry, "Administration of Physical Education of Girls and Women" (June 1911). Newspaper reporters, not knowing what to call the Indian pant outfit worn by Amelia Bloomer, referred to them as "bloomers" and the name stuck.

35. Felix Fuld Leonhard, "Gymnastic Costume for Women," *American PE Review* 15.8 (November 1910): 572–78.

36. Mabel Lee, "The State of the Profession from World War I to Women's Lib," in Bruce L. Bennett, ed., *The History of Physical Education and Sport* (Proceedings of the Big Ten Symposium), Chicago: The Athletic Institute, 1972, 101–20; Joan S. Hult, "The Story of Women's Athletics: Manipulating a Dream: 1890–1985" (unpublished paper), n.d.: 1–55.

37. Quoted on page 52 in Lee, *Memories beyond Bloomers*, 1978.

38. Remley, "Amy Homans and the Boston Normal School of Gymnastics" (March 1994); Joan Wallace Scott, "Women's History as Women's Education," *Women's History as Women's Education* (Sophia Smith Collection and College Archives, Northhampton, Mass., 1985): 23–40.

39. Jan Felshin, "The Full Court Press for Women in Athletics," in *Women's Athletics: Coping with Controversy,* ed. Barbara J. Hoepner (Washington, D.C.: AAHPER, 1974): 89–92.

40. Hult, "The Story of Women's Athletics: Manipulating a Dream: 1890–1985," n.d.

41. Lee, *Memories beyond Bloomers*, 1978.

42. Quoted on p. 94 in Charlotte West, "The Environmental Effect on the Woman in Athletics," in *Women's Athletics: Coping with Controversy,* ed. Barbara J. Hoepner, (Washington, D.C.: AAHPER, 1974): 93–97.

43. Lee, *A History of Physical Education and Sports in the U.S.A.*, 1983.

44. Both Hitchcock and Sargent were physicians. This was the career path most often taken by male physical educators seeking administrative positions in colleges and universities from 1861 through the first decade of the twentieth century. These first two "scientific" interests in the field, anthro-

pometry and physiology of exercise, preoccupied physical educators through the nineteenth and at least the first decade of the twentieth century. See Roberta J. Park, "Science, Service, and the Professionalization of Physical Education: 1885–1905," *Research Quarterly for Exercise and Sport* (Centennial Issue, 1985): 7–20.

45. McKinstry, "Administration of Physical Education of Girls and Women," June 1911.

46. Spears, "The Emergence of Women in Sport," 1974.

47. Ainsworth, *The History of Physical Education in Colleges for Women*, 1930.

48. Spears, "The Emergence of Women in Sport," 1974.

49. Baer published the first set of women's basketball rules in 1895. Berenson is credited with the first "official" rules because they were approved by the APEA when published in 1901. See Joan Paul, "Clara Gregory Baer: Harbinger of Southern Physical Education," *Research Quarterly for Exercise and Sport* (Centennial Issue, 1985): 46–55; Joan Paul, "Clara Gregory Baer: Catalyst for Women's Basketball," in *A Century of Women's Basketball,* ed. Joan S. Hult and Marianna Trekell (Reston, Va.: AAHPERD, 1991): 37–52.

50. *Mind and Body*, one of the leading periodicals in the field, was highly critical of Ballintine. See Harriet Ballintine, "The Value of Athletics to College Girls," June 1901.

51. Helene Saxe MacLaughlin, "Field Hockey—Girls," *American Physical Education Review* 26.1 (January 1911): 41–43 in Lockhart and Spears, *Chronicle of American Physical Education, 1855–1930* (1972): 277–79.

52. Quoted from Marjorie Sloan Loggia, "On the Playing Fields of History," *Ms* 2.1 (July 1973), on p. 63 in Richard A. Swanson, "From Glide to Stride: Significant Events in a Century of American Women's Sport," in *Women's Athletics: Coping with Controversy,* ed. Barbara J. Hoepner (Washington, D.C.: AAHPER, 1974): 43–53.

53. Ibid.

54. Alice Allene Sefton, ed., *The Women's Division: National Amateur Athletic Federation* (Stanford, Calif.: Stanford University Press, 1941).

55. Lee, "The State of the Profession From World War I to Women's Lib," 1972.

56. Ballintine, "The Value of Athletics to College Girls," June 1901.

57. Many claimed it was not from a moral standpoint that they opposed many behaviors, such as drinking and smoking, but for health reasons. See Lee, *Memories beyond Bloomers*, 1978.

58. Elizabeth Halsey, *Women in Physical Education* (New York: G. Putnam's Sons, 1961); Mabel Lee, "Looking Back over Seventy-Five Years of Work in Physical Education," *HPER Omnibus* (Washington, D.C.: AAHPER, 1976): 52–65.

59. Quoted on page 8 in William Skarstrom, "Amy Morris Homans—In Memoriam," *Mary Hemenway Alumnae Association Graduate Department of Hygiene and Physical Education, Wellesley College Bulletin, 1934–1935*, 6–9.

60. Helen McKinstry, "Vignettes," *Mary Hemenway Alumnae Association Graduate Department of Hygiene and Physical Education, Wellesley College Bulletin, 1934–1935*, 16–20.

61. Quoted on page 48 in Remley, "Amy Homans and the Boston Normal School of Gymnastics," March 1994.

62. Spears, "Success, Women, and Physical Education," 1979.

63. Quoted on page 41 in Gertrude Dudley and Frances A. Kellor, *Athletic Games in the Education of Women* (New York: Henry Holt and Company, 1909).

64. Lee, "The State of the Profession from World War I to Women's Lib," 1972.

65. Ibid.

66. Hill, "The Way We Were," 1975.

67. Swanson, "From Glide to Stride: Significant Events in a Century of American Women's Sport," 1974; Lucille E. Hill, "Introduction," *Athletics and Outdoor Sports for Women* (New York: Macmillan, 1903): 1–15 in Lockhart and Spears, *Chronicle of American Physical Education, 1855–1930* (1972): 227–33.

68. See Ruth Elliott, "Modern Trends in Physical Education," *The Research Quarterly* 1.2 (May 1930): 74–85. The Play Day (a day when sports were held for girls from several different institutions but organized as a social affair rather than a competition between schools) was introduced in colleges in 1928 by Helen Norman Smith and Helen Coops at the University of Cincinnati. See Schwendener, *A History of Physical Education in the United States*, 1942. It is interesting to note that Schwendener fails to even mention Mabel Lee, who was the chief proponent of the Play Day and who was one of the most well-known physical educators of the period. Lee, first woman president of the APEA in 1931, is not even mentioned in Schwendener's 1942 book. Perhaps this is a bias because Schwendener was an advocate of athletics for women while Lee's position was the antithesis, writing articles and speaking against women's athletics at every opportunity.

69. Hill, "The Way We Were," December 1975. Feelings became even more divisive with the creation of the Association for Intercollegiate Athletics for Women (AIAW) that took control from the Commission on Intercollegiate Athletics for Women (CIAA) in 1971. However, the bitterness and hostility was electric when the NCAA eventually became the major ruling body for all college sports in 1982.

70. Spears, "Success, Women, and Physical Education," 1979.

71. Stories told to me by the late Dr. Eleanor Metheny about her experiences teaching at Wellesley.

72. Elliott, "Modern Trends in Physical Education," May 1930; McKinstry, "Administration of Physical Education of Girls and Women," June 1911.

73. Elliott, "Modern Trends in Physical Education," May 1930.

74. Quoted on pp. 16–17, Park, "Science, Service, and the Professionalization of Physical Education: 1885–1905," 1985; Joan Paul, "Centuries of Change: Movement's Many Faces," *Quest* 48 (1996): 531–45.

75. By the early 1990s there were over 250 titles given to former collegiate departments of physical education that ranged from kinesiology to sport studies. The most widely used term across the country is "kinesiology." This was first used to describe physical education by Baron Nils Posse in 1886. See June A. Kennard, "The Posse Gymnasium," *JOHPERD* 65.3 (March 1994): 50–52. Rosalind Cassidy protested the name "physical education" in every book and article she wrote from 1923 until her death. Like Posse, she favored the name "kinesiology." This is a Greek word that connotes human movement. See Cassidy, "Changing Perspectives . . . A Personal Journey," 1976.

CHAPTER 9

"Let Her Swim, Climb Mountain Peaks"

Self-Sacrifice and Success in Expanding Athletic Programs for Women

LINDA JEAN CARPENTER AND R. VIVIAN ACOSTA

> Let her swim, climb mountain peaks, pilot airplanes, battle against the elements, take risks, go out for adventure, and she will not feel before the world . . . timidity.
>
> —Simone de Beauvoir

Epochal change was in the air in the late 1960s and early 1970s. Two parallel issues: the anti–sex discrimination legislation known as Title IX[1] and a new commitment on the part of female sports leaders to provide elite-level female athletes with appropriate competitive challenges, would, in the years to come, have great impact on hundreds of thousands of girls and women. Indeed, Title IX caused great change for both the female leaders and participants in athletics programs. Conversely, female leaders of sports programs, like their predecessors in chapter 8, caused great change in the implementation of Title IX and also altered the face of athletics for both men and women in the United States.

Title IX gave legal sanction to the wider opening of gymnasium doors for female athletes. The legislative activities of female sports leaders ensured that, but they did not open such doors without great cost. In the presence of the post–Title IX massive increase in programs and participation opportunities for female athletes, leadership opportunities for women in those same programs dwindled.

The cost was not a surprise to the female sports leaders nor was the increase in participation judged to be unworthy of the price paid. Indeed, the continuing, dynamic dialogue concerning the mission of athletics and the role of females as participants and leaders in athletics continues to invigorate and challenge virtually all who are involved. The first words exchanged in that dialogue, a dialogue the outcome of which has become vital to the future of both men's and women's athletics, would not have been uttered if not for the courageous and self-sacrificing engagement of females in the two parallel issues, equity and female involvement in athletic governance, which frame the state of athletics today.

Title IX

No single event nor solitary person decreed change, but there existed a strong cadre of individuals, organizations and a series of coincidences that acted together as functional agents of change. This critical mass of people and events intensified debate and sensitized society and its legislators to the point where, on June 23, 1972, federal legislation known as Title IX became the law of the land.

Title IX would not have been enacted a decade earlier. The nation's developing awareness of civil rights issues was still too new and unsettling in the early 1960s. Within the area of sports, the few female physical educators and coaches who advocated more competitive opportunities for the elite female athlete, national championships, full-length seasons, and athletic scholarships found little or no support among their peers. In fact, peers often ostracized such women for supporting a "male" model of athletics rather than keeping the best interests of the female participants foremost in mind.

By the late 1960s though, society, even if not yet comfortable with the notion of equity for all, had at least acquiesced to increasing equity with the passage of antiracial and rudimentary antigender discrimination legislation. For instance, Title VII prohibited sex discrimination but is only applicable in the workplace and thus is not useful to protect students. In the early 1960s few footfalls echoed in the halls of Congress from female members, and voices of female lobbyists seldom filled the air. In the late 1960s, however, the sounds were changing; females were finding their voices and beginning to be heard more distinctly in the halls of Congress. The 1972 enactment of Title IX told the nation that, "No person in the United States shall, on the basis of sex, be excluded from participation in, be denied the benefits of, or be subjected to discrimination under any education program or activity receiving Federal financial assistance."[2]

Women's Athletics—Prologue

Many of the same agents of change that produced Title IX also culminated in a significant change in the governance and direction of women's athletics just a few months before Title IX's enactment. No publicity accompanied events. In the 1950s and 1960s intercollegiate competition for women was informal and predominantly social. The only way anyone on campus would know a competition was to occur would be by seeing one of the notices taped to the back of the restroom doors in the women's dorm, noticing a flier tacked to a school bulletin board before someone removed it, or by being invited by one of the participants. This was true for both coeducational and single-sex institutions.

No championships were held, and colleges provided little, if any, support. Female physical educators volunteered as coaches, and a handful received small remuneration for their services. Athletes bought their own uniforms, packed brown bag lunches, and paid their own transportation and motel bills for games at other schools.

At the close of the decade, the 1970 collegiate athlete still had little or no competitive opportunities on campus. Only 16,000 collegiate women had any varsity opportunities at all. Over 160,000 women participate as varsity athletes in full length competition today.

Competition, when it did exist, was rudimentary. The 1970 woman was not believed to have the necessary stamina to survive a season length comparable to that of the male athlete. Competitive seasons were therefore truncated to less than a third of what they are today.

Athletes frustrated with the low level of support and competition on campus sought participation on off-campus teams such as Amateur Athletic Union teams, church, or privately sponsored teams and leagues. The off-campus teams gave the athletes an increased number of games, more intense competition, better coaching, local, regional and national recognition, and an increased opportunity for travel. Female physical educators found that more and more talented female athletes left school teams to engage in sporting events on outside teams. The athletes sought what did not exist for them on campus, even in the face of advice against such participation from their physical educators who feared for their exploitation.

At the time, many physical educators were just beginning to realize that they could not deny the assertive athlete highly competitive opportunities. Many of the physical educators sought competitive opportunities for themselves via these same outside teams because of the desire to compete but still wished to protect their students from the potential damage, as they saw it, from highly competitive environments. The students saw this as hypocritical; the physical educators saw it as a matter of maturity.

Many physical educators believed that high-level competition replicated the male model of athletics. The male model of athletics included the potential for gambling, exploitation, commercialism, loss of focus on academics, masculinization, and aggression. Often the physical educators thought it would take a great deal of maturity to avoid such pitfalls. In the absence of substantive physiological research on exercising female subjects, an absence that continued well into the late 1970s, health fears for the exercising female abounded. It would not be until 1984 that women would be allowed to demonstrate that they were physically able to tolerate the first running of an Olympic marathon for women. In that year, the first women's marathon trials for the USOC team were held in Olympia, Washington.

Perhaps a change in the historically protective and thus restrictive point of view of the female physical educators was overdue. However, even if the point of view changed, would the collegiate opportunities follow? Without funding, access to paid coaches, facilities other than the old and typically dilapidated "women's" gym, how could they implement a change in point of view?

Concurrently, forces outside the school-based environment affected women in general and women in sports specifically. The Olympic movement included more female athletes, and women discovered success as Olympians. Female athletes finally earned a small degree of media recognition. Society altered its views toward women as full participants in the workforce and in athletics. The number of women attending colleges and universities increased as did their participation in intercollegiate sports programs.

These underlying forces caused female physical educators to recognize the need for well administered, educationally based, on-campus varsity-level athletics programs that would provide opportunities for the athletically talented collegiate woman. Change did not come about easily, and philosophical differences often divided those involved in the creation of a new model for intercollegiate athletics for women. They had made many compromises, but without a new model it was apparent that many athletically talented young women would be lost to outside influences and indeed, would be lost to the physical education profession.

Women's Athletics—A New Governance Organization

In 1966, the Division of Girls and Women in Sport (DGWS), part of the then titled American Association of Health, Physical Education, and Recreation (AAHPER), established the Commission on Intercollegiate Athletics for Women (CIAW). DGWS had, until that time, governed whatever sport existed on the nation's campuses but did so with a focus on the majority, rather than on the highly skilled athlete. The purpose of the newly formed CIAW was to sanction intercollegiate athletic events and to establish, conduct, and promote national championships. The first national championship occurred in 1966, when the CIAW sanctioned the twenty-five-year-old golf event held at the Ohio University. Soon thereafter, seven other national championships emerged under the guidance of the CIAW in the sports of gymnastics, track and field, badminton, swimming and diving, volleyball, and basketball.

The CIAW was successful in providing a viable athletic forum for intercollegiate competition while maintaining the educationally based philosophy paramount to the leaders, coaches, and participants of the time. However, the CIAW lacked a membership-based constituency needed for financial and administrative control. The DGWS/AAHPER administrative umbrella for the CIAW was safe, but cumbersome and slow in the decision-making process. In reality, the CIAW was not an independent entity and relied on two separate boards of directors to approve decision and policies.

The CIAW membership structure consisted of individuals rather than institutions. Enforcement of rules and regulations was difficult, if not impossible, to impose on non-member institutions. The financial backing of DGWS/AAHPER was critical to the CIAW and thus critical to the development of an educationally based intercollegiate athletics program for women. But the financial entanglements with DGWS/AAHPER to which CIAW was married were problematic because CIAW could not be financially independent and could not expend monies without the permission of the other two organizations.

The CIAW existed until October 1971, when the Association for Intercollegiate Athletics for Women (AIAW) replaced it with the full blessing of DGWS/AAHPER. To best serve women's intercollegiate sport it was necessary to have a strong financial base, and that base could only come from institutional membership dues. Institutions would be more likely to comply with policies and regulations which they themselves had helped establish. The rationale appeared to be well founded because the membership of AIAW grew from its charter year membership of 278 in 1971–72 to 973 in 1979–80. With the formation of AIAW, women's intercollegiate programs took a giant leap forward.

The following statements from the AIAW Constitution illustrate the principles and philosophy that gave initial substance and form to the AIAW:

- Women should have the opportunity to strive for excellence in sport.
- Women should plan, administer, coach, and officiate sports programs for women and, in so doing, provide viable role models that will empower other women. Women should have power over their sports lives.
- Programs should be designed for women and should be inclusive rather than exclusive, encouraging the growth of sport and the inclusion of many different sports and different levels of skill.
- The system should provide many competitive opportunities on state, regional, and national levels in colleges, universities, junior colleges, community colleges and public and private colleges.
- Sport programs should be educational, not just athletic; they should be developmental, honoring the best but not negating the achievements of those who do not win.
- The rights of the athletes should be considered, especially as they relate to students who transfer, who return to school after dropping out, or who are making an Olympic bid.[3]

A Different Model for Governance: AIAW versus NCAA

The female physical educators/athletics personnel in the member institutions developed regulations for the AIAW. The philosophical goal of these women was to develop a different model for sports that would not mirror that of the men or of the NCAA. Four clear principles, among others, made the AIAW unique. First, the voting representatives were to be predominantly faculty members directly involved in the women's athletics program. In fact, over 70 percent of these representatives were females. Second, the organization designed an all-inclusive representational structure to include elected student athletes in the decision-making process. The NCAA, unlike the female-designed AIAW, had no elected student input and the few selected to serve on NCAA committees were appointed.

Third, minority representation was mandated at all level of AIAW governance through the organization's bylaws. From the outset, the AIAW's governance plan included a seven-member committee on the Status of Minority Women. The committee was charged to identify minority needs and concerns, encourage the involvement, and enhance the visibility of women of racial minorities within the AIAW. Now, twenty-seven years later, outside constituencies are urging the NCAA to identify minority needs and concerns, encourage the involvement and enhance the visibility of racial minorities within its membership. The NCAA has not been unaware of the need to include members of minority groups over the years, but the women of the AIAW were affirmatively acting on that awareness years before the NCAA. Inclusion of all constituencies was a clear founding principle of the AIAW, not merely a strategy of political expediency.

The fourth guiding principle which made the AIAW unique was its decision to make no distinctions between "major" and "minor" sports. To the participant, the sport in which the athlete participated was the most important. Therefore, the AIAW treated all sports equitably in terms of eligibility, recruitment, financial aid, and other areas, unlike the NCAA that gave preferential treatment to football and basketball. Under the structure of AIAW all student athletes had the same rights as students not involved in athletics and were not restricted in the acceptance of academic scholarships, work-study jobs, or governmental entitlements based upon financial need.

A significant difference between AIAW and NCAA concerned the transfer rule. AIAW permitted student athletes who transferred from one institution to another to continue their athletic involvement without interruption, whereas the NCAA required transfer student athletes to forego intercollegiate participation for one year.

The first statement in AIAW's position paper on Intercollegiate Athletics (1974) is a concise summary of AIAW's goal: "The enrichment of the life of the participant is the focus and reason for the existence of any athletic program. All decisions should be made with this fact in mind."[4]

So, in October 1971, the AIAW was born. Its birth was not easy but it had drawn its first breath. Some women in physical education and athletics were elated by dreams of a freer and more fulfilling future for the more highly skilled female athletes. Others were filled with dread for the inevitable abuses of female athletes which they feared lay ahead.

With AIAW's 1971 birth, members had resolved the debate of *if* women could compete intensely. The debate of *how* women should compete was just beginning. The women of the AIAW actively defined what the structure of a highly competitive opportunity for females would look like as they also walked the halls of Congress lobbying for Title IX's passage.

Congress enacted Title IX into law on June 23, 1972. Its subsequent application to athletics has been the focus of a quarter century of debate. Its wording is straightforward and has never changed. The three critical elements for Title IX jurisdiction are: *education* programs, *sex* discrimination, *federally funded* program. If any of the three elements is lacking, Title IX's jurisdiction does not apply. Title IX's jurisdiction does however, extend, not just to physical education and athletics but to all parts of almost all schools in the country.

The women of AIAW who worked for Title IX's passage surmised that legislatively mandated equality of opportunity would surely ease the way for female athletes. It did, but it also placed unanticipated challenges and opponents into the mixture of issues facing the infant AIAW. These same challenges and opponents would ultimately cause the death of AIAW and end the only female-dominated organizational structure that had the opportunity to design a female model of intercollegiate athletics programs. However, through the valiant efforts of its female leadership, the AIAW lived long enough to indelibly change the history of women's intercollegiate athletics in America.

Government officials accorded postsecondary schools six years until the 1978 mandatory compliance date to comply with Title IX. In that six-year period from enactment to the mandatory compliance date, the United States Department of Health, Education and Welfare, now the Department of Education, developed regulations so that those who must comply with Title IX would know the details of what full compliance entails.

Those six years were quite a roller coaster ride. Walter Byer, the charter executive director of the NCAA[5] told press that Title IX will be the "possible doom of intercollegiate sports."[6] It is understandable, yet not excusable, that years of privilege or a sense of sole ownership of the field of athletics could engender such sentiments. Understandable or not, such sentiments provided strong challenges for the female sport leaders to overcome as they developed the AIAW and sought to have input and impact on Title IX's yet-to-be-adopted Regulations.

Women's voices, particularly those of the female leaders in physical education and athletics, made a difference in the final content of the Regulations that, when Congress adopted them in 1975, had the force of law. The

NCAA worked unremittingly to remove athletics from Title IX jurisdiction. Fortunately reason and women's voices foiled the NCAA proposal.

When the NCAA lost its battle to exclude athletics from Title IX's jurisdiction, it supported the Tower Amendment, which proposed to exempt "revenue"[7] sports from Title IX's jurisdiction. Three hundred institutional members of the NCAA gave money to hire a public relations firm to encourage the adoption of the proposal. Against great odds, reason and women's voices again led to a rejection of the proposal.

Proposals for Title IX's regulations were sometimes neither logical nor realistic. For instance, the fielding of a single, coeducational team in each sport was proposed. If this proposal had been adopted, female students would have been given the choice to compete with their generally physiologically stronger and anatomically bigger male counterparts for positions on that single team or not compete at all. The reality of the dual sex team proposal would have resulted in very few females having any opportunity to compete. Courageous and insightful female leaders in physical education and athletics opposed the proposal. Their arguments were logical, based in reality and, in the end resulted in the defeat of the single-team proposal.

It is impossible to discuss the changing status of women as athletes and as leaders of athletics programs without understanding the interrelationships of the triad of AIAW, NCAA and Title IX. Each member of the triad affected the other members. These women developed the AIAW and its emerging design for women's athletics and worked for the passage of Title IX. They sought to defuse the efforts of the NCAA to alternately remove athletics from the reach of Title IX or to take over the governance of women's athletics. Sometimes the women acted proactively, sometimes reactively, in response to actions and decisions of the NCAA concerning Title IX. But the women always acted in support of expanded participation opportunities for female athletes.

Securing the expansion of participation opportunities for female athletes was not an easy task. The activities related to that task presented challenges of monumental proportions to the female sport leaders. In addition to struggling to have Title IX regulations that would be effective adopted, the female sport leaders frequently wore two and sometimes three professional hats—teacher, coach, administrator. Many of their male counterparts needed to focus only on one professional task while relying on the NCAA to develop strategies for fighting the regulations. In addition, 27 percent of these female sport leaders were mothers and thus carried much of the load of home and family duties as well.

In addition to their varied professional duties, home responsibilities, and regulation lobbying, the women were involved in organizing the infant AIAW, barely eight months old when Congress enacted Title IX, and within this context developed a female vision for intercollegiate athletics. Should athletic-based scholarships be offered to women? Should men's playing rules be adopted for specific women's sports? How could females maintain a place in the officiating of sports now that males were seeing a new field of endeavor within the women's programs? How should state and regional affiliates of AIAW be organized and function? Should AIAW membership be dues driven or financed by media contracts? Questions, questions, questions—all needed time and energy to address these in the best interests of the new organization. Commitment was the wellspring of time and energy, yet both were finite.

Although the AIAW was a fledgling organization, it had attracted the attention of the all-powerful NCAA and the smaller National Association for Intercollegiate Athletics (NAIA). The NCAA and the NAIA reacted differently to the developing AIAW.

The NAIA's executive director offered NAIA's assistance and maintained that women direct their own programs. The NAIA shared its materials with the AIAW and was constant in its recognition that the AIAW should represented women's interests in intercollegiate sports and conduct national championships for women. The NAIA assured the AIAW that it would not interfere with the business of the AIAW and that it would not offer programs or championships for women's intercollegiate programs. The NAIA kept its promises.

The NCAA took a different view. Early in the development of the AIAW, the NCAA sent a letter to Roswell D. Merrick, the executive director of AAHPER. In part it read:

> As you probably know, there is a growing interest in intercollegiate athletics for women in NCAA member institutions. . . . The prevailing attitude among our member institutions is to increase the scope of intercollegiate athletic programs by providing more sports for the male student-athlete and creating opportunities for female students through organized competition. It is inevitable that if this trend continues there will be a demand for national championship competition for women.[8]

Merrick's statement might appear benign, but it signaled a 180-degree change in NCAA philosophy concerning women's athletics. Prior to the establishment of the female-controlled AIAW, there had been absolutely no interest whatsoever by the NCAA in women's intercollegiate athletics. The NCAA's sole interest was with men's intercollegiate athletics.

Concomitant with the development, growth, and success of the AIAW, the NCAA politically maneuvered itself into a more powerful and influential position in the nation's sport arena. A power struggle with the Amateur Athletic Union (AAU), which had influence within the United States Olympic Committee, ensued. The AAU was the recognized leader in the United States as the "feeder" of Olympians of both genders into the U.S. National and

Olympic Teams. The NCAA wanted to usurp the AAU's position, but because the NCAA dealt with male athletes only, it had to find a way to bring women into its fold. Thus, for self-serving reasons, the NCAA developed a new interest in the AIAW's female constituency.

The NCAA sent duplicitous messages to the leadership of the AIAW. The Merrick letter indicated that the NCAA wanted to develop programs for women. However, a later communication from the male chairperson of the newly formed NCAA Committee on Women's Intercollegiate Competition sent to Lucille Magnusson, President of the AIAW, told the women clearly and emphatically that the NCAA had no interest in assuming the governance of women's athletics and indeed only wanted to serve as a resource of experience.[9]

The leadership of the AIAW and the NCAA held many meetings over a period of several years wherein dialogue concerning the role of both organizations in intercollegiate athletics for women occurred. It became increasingly clear to the AIAW leadership that, despite NCAA camouflage, the NCAA's goal was to overtake the AIAW and to silence the voices of the female sport leaders.

Soon incredible accusations by the NCAA surfaced. Among its unsubstantiated charges were the following: women were incompetent when it came to governing in the sport area; the NCAA has virtually a divine right to regulate women's intercollegiate competition; AIAW programs are deficient and the NCAA could not overcome such deficiencies; and furthermore, the NCAA, rather than the AIAW, could best solve the female athletes' lack of competitive opportunities.

Battle lines were drawn, and ugliness became the norm. A few of the AIAW women, either because they believed the NCAA accusations or because of self-serving ambition, left the AIAW and allied themselves with the NCAA. These were difficult organizational times for all of the female leaders.

Declining Representation of Female Administrators

Added to the NCAA battles, personal/professional time constraints, Title IX regulation design, and AIAW development struggles, the female sport leaders suddenly found themselves fighting to preserve their employment status on their individual campuses. Almost universally, their jobs were in jeopardy because the majority of college presidents either believed, or hoped Title IX required the merger of previously separate men's and women's athletics programs or departments of physical education.

Title IX never advocated merger as an appropriate action. The words from the journal of a college physical educator/coach describing the merger of her previously autonomous women's program provide a picture of what was happening across the country in the middle in 1970s. Women in a great number of the nation's colleges and universities shared the fear, frustration, and self-doubt found on the journal pages of a female sports leader of the 1970s:

> Journal entry: February 14, 1974. The president of the college came to our P.E. department faculty meeting today and said, "Title IX requires me to merge the men's and women's departments as well as athletics." Did it? We thought the Regulations were still being debated and we hadn't heard anything about such a requirement.
>
> Pat asked the president if he was sure. The president gave her one of his glowering looks and said, "Of course I'm sure and starting today, this is how the new structure will be: Joe will be the director of athletics and John will be the chair of the physical education department. If either Joe or John decides he wants help, he can appoint Amanda (up until that moment, the women's athletic director) or Pat (up until that moment, the chair of the women's physical education department) as their [*sic*] assistants.
>
> If you have any complaints, direct them to Joe or John. I don't want to hear them.
>
> We were stunned, too stunned to even protest, not that it would have done much good. Amanda and Pat had obviously had no forewarning and looked devastated. I feel so sorry for them.
>
> How can Amanda and Pat, both strong personalities, survive as the underlings for Joe and John? We thought Title IX was going to finally help us and our students find equity. Did what we had worked so hard for cause this to happen? What have we wrought? Maybe we should have left things as they were—but then our students would have been the one's [*sic*] hurt, not us. It's tempting to think that a crumb of the pie is better than none of the pie.[10]

All across the nation, autonomous, but greatly unequal, men's and women's programs were merged into greatly unequal programs with the former director of the men's program becoming the head of the newly merged program. Decades earlier, deans of women experienced the same phenomenon, as chapter 11 indicates. The female who, without significant resources, had skillfully administered positive and educationally sound athletics programs for females had no choice but to accept the secondary position, if she were to be retained at all. Mergers sent shock waves throughout the nation.

In the years prior to Title IX's enactment, females administered 90 to 95 percent of women's intercollegiate athletics programs. By 1977, one year before mandatory compliance, only 20 percent of women's programs had a female administrator in charge.[11] Title IX's Regulations never even contemplated requiring the merger of men's and women's departments, but many female leaders disappeared from their leadership positions because of these mergers. Some women stayed in the secondary position; some wearied of the fight and left the field.

Once done, reversing the change has been impossible. In 1998, two decades after the mass mergers, only 19.4 percent of women's athletics programs have female head administrators, and 20.8 percent had no female involved at any level in the athletic administration.[12] It has become painfully obvious that the doors have opened only one way; it still makes the newspapers when a female is the head administrator over a combined program of men's and women's athletics. Indeed, it is easier to be a female college president than it is to be a female head athletic director over a combined men's and women's Division I program.

After the mass mergers, a decade passed before the number of women in athletic administrations began to increase. However, in 1998, the number had only increased to 1.01 females within the administrative structures of women's athletics programs, an average of barely more than one female athletic administrator per campus. The average number of athletic administrators per campus has grown from 2.32 in 1988 to 2.57 in 1998, but the growth of female voices within those structures has not kept pace.[13]

In 1988, there were 1,827 administrative positions within women's NCAA-governed intercollegiate athletics programs; females held 528 (28.9%) of such posts. In 1996, there were 2,433 such jobs (an increase of 820) and women held 863 of them. Put another way, in the twelve-year period from 1988 to 1996, *men* gained 60 percent of the new jobs as administrators in *women*'s intercollegiate athletics.[14]

The original female administrators who remained after the mergers were often finding authority and decision-making tasks removed from their portfolios. One such women said, "After 10 years, I have a title but my authority is off the bottom of the chart."[15] So, with fewer than one female per campus, and with the females who were serving as administrators within women's athletics programs enjoying less and less authority, female leaders no longer shaped women's programs.

Women did not expect such a loss of authority, but it did mean women were no longer the designers of athletic programs for females. But, the loss of authority is not the end of the story. It is vital to realize that the female sports leaders would not have chosen to protect their own professional positions at the expense of the increased student participation. The female leaders have proven their commitment to their students through their courage in personal loss. The female leaders have also proven their courage and commitment to their students, and themselves, by not shrinking from the continuing challenge of increasing the presence of female role models in sport. Scholars have not written the end of the story of women as leaders in athletics.

Representation of Female Coaches

Female administrators paid quite a price for reaching toward equity early in the years of Title IX, but they continue to be engaged in the process to increase their representation among the ranks of athletic administrators. They have developed new tools and gained new skills in the endeavor. The same is true of female coaches.

Before Title IX's enactment, women coached over 90 percent of women's teams. It was a job most males did not seek because typically it was a job without pay or released time from teaching responsibilities. It was a job executed simply because of a dedication to the students and an awareness of the value of athletics in the full education of its student participants. Once Title IX began to have a positive impact on the pay scale for coaches of women's teams, the job market included an ever-increasing number of male applicants. Title IX prohibited the administrator from only considering female applicants, so more and more coaching positions for women's teams were being held by males.

By 1978, the percentage of coaching positions held by females had dropped to 58.2 and in 1998 it had further dropped to 47.4%.[16] In the same eighteen years, the number of head coaching positions among women's intercollegiate athletics had increased by almost 2,400 yet fewer than 700 of the new jobs went to women. The percentage of females coaching men's intercollegiate teams has not changed significantly during the entire life span of Title IX. It was and is less than 2 percent. Equity-induced expansion of employment opportunities has eluded the female professional in intercollegiate athletics.

Initially, the swift proliferation in the number of teams for women increasing the need for coaches may have eased the entrance of men into the ranks of coaches. However, after the first few years, one could no longer successfully argue that this influx was in any way correlated with the lack of qualified female coaches in numbers sufficient to cover the newly formed teams. In no case was it ever possible to apply the same argument to the declining representation of females as administrators over women's programs.

Why Did the Representation of Females Decrease?

Perception of truth is sometimes of greater significance than truth itself. The perception of truth in the mind of the hiring personnel is what generally carries the day. By 1996, 81.5 percent of the hiring personnel was male. Two national surveys, conducted four years apart, sought to determine the perceived causes of the declining representation of women in sport.[17] In 1988, the five most important reasons that male administrators identified were:

1. Lack of qualified female coaches
2. Failure of females to apply for job openings
3. Lack of qualified female administrators (tie)
4. Time constraints placed on females due to family duties (tie)
5. Female's "burnout" and leave coaching/administration sooner than males

The top three perceptions held by males for the declining representation of females could be categorized as job market dynamics. The female respondents perceived the causes differently. The top three could be categorized as communication and interpersonal interactions. The women's list includes:

1. Success of the "old boys' club" network
2. Failure of the "old girls' club" network
3. Lack of support systems for females (tie)
4. Unconscious discrimination in selection/hiring process (tie)
5. Females "burnout" and leave coaching/administration sooner than males

Does It Matter If Female Athletes See Females Fulfilling Leadership Positions?

Males and females almost universally mentioned the need for female athletes to have female role models as a vitally important reason to increase the representation of women. Among their responses were:

- We need role models for young women that say women can be #1, not just somebody's assistant.
- Women's perspective offers a different way of viewing things—not necessarily right or wrong compared to men's perspective—just different.
- Women bring a different set of values, priorities, ways of dealing with people and problems to their positions as coaches and administrators which should be a part of the mix in athletics, as well as providing good role models for young student athletes (both male and female).
- Female role models are important not just for females but, to change the future, it is important for *males* to see females as leaders and decision makers rather than solely as supporter and nurturers.[18]

Increased Student Participation

The efforts of the female leaders may have been counterproductive for their own benefit, but the opposite was true for the female athletes. Before Title IX's passage about 16,000 females engaged in intercollegiate athletics. Today, more than 150,000 do so. If athletics programs are designed correctly, they can be a significant and effective laboratory in which to learn decision making, teamwork, risk evaluation, self-esteem-enhancement techniques, and other skills that increase success for this generation's young women as they enter a broader array of employment and life choices.

The participation of female intercollegiate athletes has increased from about 2.1 teams per school in 1972 to 7.5 teams today, but the nature of those teams has changed. Team sports such as basketball and soccer have replaced individual sports, junior varsities, and sports often considered to be female sports. For instance, field hockey, traditionally a women's sport in the United States was offered at 36.3% of colleges in 1977 and in 1996 appears at only 27.1%. Other sports that are now found at less than a third of their previous strength include badminton (5.9% down to 0.3%), fencing (4.6% down from 9.8%), and gymnastics (11.2% down from 25.9%). The decrease in schools offering gymnastics may have been due, in part, to non-gender-based reasons such as the modernization of equipment requirements, greater risk, and the greater difficulty the rules of the sport now require.

One might argue that such sports as badminton, fencing and gymnastics, all Olympic sports, were always minor sports. However, the term minor has no meaningful significance beyond an indication that the male-dominated sponsoring institutions elected not to provide the sport with full funding. Such decisions have withdrawn viable options for excellence from the list of women's choices.

The demise of the previously strong junior varsity system for women has had an even greater impact. Without junior varsity teams, the number of entry level coaching positions for less experienced coaches has decreased. Without junior varsity teams, participation slots for athletes who need to bridge the gap from sufficiently-skilled-for-competition to ready-for-elite-level-competition ceased to exist, and those students needing growth in competitive skills have no field on which to grow.

If the female-dominated AIAW had survived would the female sports leaders' wish for gender equity among athletes have been closer to being fulfilled than it is today? If the AIAW had survived as the governance body for women's intercollegiate athletics, would there be a more diverse offering of participation opportunities for the nation's female athletes today? If the AIAW had survived would there be more employment opportunities for females within athletics? If the AIAW had survived would the implementation of Title IX's provisions still be a goal rather than a reality in the majority of schools? We think so. But the fact that equity is not yet a reality and the fact that the face of women's athletics is different than it might have been in no way should lessen the significance of the dedication and commitment female sports leaders have given. The massive increase in participation opportunities for their students is testimony of the effect of their quiet, and not-so-quiet, inspiration. This increase is due to the female sports leaders' defense of Title IX, their efforts through AIAW, and their self-sacrifice.

Motivation provided by Title IX's requirement to meet the interests and abilities of the historically underrepresented sex has prodded many institutions to increase the number of participation slots for their female athletes.

Institutions have done this most frequently by adding sports that require many participants, such as soccer or crew. Soccer has grown from a 1977 presence in 2.8 percent of women's intercollegiate programs to a 1996 68.9 percent presence. Crew has not grown as fast simply because of the geographic and facility based issues associated with it, but many schools are finding their new women's crew teams populated with forty to sixty participants.

The Death of the AIAW

Pride and a sense of empowerment gained from AIAW's defense of Title IX in the 1970s and the tenfold increase in the number of female students benefiting from athletics since Title IX's passage sustained many of the female sports leaders even though their own departments had been merged and their authority on campus lessened. Although participation continued to increase, by 1981 other factors brought depression and frustration to the women in AIAW. Leotus Morrison, president of the AIAW, said that the greatest moment of depression for her, and perhaps for all involved in the AIAW, came in 1981 when the NCAA, at its national convention, narrowly voted to offer championships for women despite a plea from the AIAW to postpone the vote for a year. After that critical vote, the other motions related to rules accommodations for women passed quickly. It was difficult for the women who were serving as representatives for their institutions to return to the next day's meeting amidst snide and sexist remarks, "The men in NCAA were not gracious winners."[19]

The impact of the NCAA vote upon the AIAW was swift. Within six months, membership dropped by 20 percent; championship participation dropped by 32 percent; NBC, under pressure of the NCAA, reneged on its contract to televise AIAW's championships and would not honor its $500,000 contract with the AIAW. It was clear that continuing to fight was senseless and would only hurt female student athletes by pulling them in two different directions. The AIAW filed an antitrust lawsuit against the NCAA, but when it lost the appeal in 1982, the life of the AIAW was over. In President Morrison's words, "In 1982, the AIAW Executive Board determined that it could not accomplish its stated goals . . . and voted to dissolve the Association. Women created the AIAW, and women disbanded it, in the interest of women's sports."[20]

President Morrison's choice of words is significant. In terminating the AIAW, the female sports leaders continued to act in the best interests of their students rather than to extend an organization structure and its unwinnable fight against the NCAA to the detriment of current generation of athletes. The decision of the women did not however signal their relinquishing the notion that equity was necessary in women's athletics. Instead, they healed themselves, regrouped, and refocused their efforts on behalf of their future students.

Physical Education and Title IX

The impetus of Title IX, the altered governance base from AIAW to the NCAA, and the society's changing views about female sports participants have all affected the face of sports for women in a number of less obvious ways too. For instance, Title IX requires physical education classes to be conducted on a coeducational basis, except in contact sport classes. On its face, this seems like a reasonable way of guaranteeing an automatically equitable scheduling of facilities, teachers, and equipment. However, in reality, the presence of hormones and disparate growth rates in high school physical education classes have made compliance with this requirement very difficult.

High school girls of average skill are frequently intimidated by the same aged boys who are trying to exert their masculinity and perception of dominance. The girls then either elect not to participate, thus cutting themselves off from the education otherwise available to them in the laboratory of sport, or they face demeaning situations, or they register for activities less frequented by the boys, such as aerobics and dance. The result is that the females who select aerobics and dance do not gain the skills which they could later use for athletics scholarship opportunities on the college level.

A concomitant result is that the boys never learn to deal appropriately with females in competitive situations. Physical educators either encourage the de facto segregation into dance and aerobics, or they acquiesce in the face of frustration in coeducational classes or they face time consuming challenges in creating effective coeducational sports opportunities in their classes. Unfortunately, few have the time, energy, support and facilities to select the third alternative. Teacher training programs lag far behind in preparing future teachers for the challenges of coeducational high school classes and so physical education programs have constructed comfortable learning zones for high school girls.

Remaining Challenges and Issues

Salaries

Salaries for coaches of women's teams have increased but have not reached parity with those of men, particularly within the premier sports such as basketball. Women do not move laterally or vertically in the job market as freely as men, and the lack of female applicants for coaching and administrative positions remains a concern. Senior women have indicated that increases in salary would entice them to move to new jobs, but those increases seldom occur. Data indicate that the increases seldom happen because the hiring institutions typically recruit with such enticements for males but not for females. Thus women do not apply.

Cuts of Men's Minor Sports

As is so often the case in discriminatory environments, people often blame the victim. Such occurs in women's athletics. Some college presidents and their male athletic directors have made the unconscionable decision to cut men's minor sports for the ostensible purpose of using the small amount of money saved to fund women's sports in the name of Title IX, which neither requires nor even recommends that men's participation opportunities be cut to provide opportunities for women. Poor administrative decisions, not the demands of gender equity, cause this to happen.

Principled View of Athletics Funding

Schools most likely to cut men's minor sports in the name of equity are those that have ignored the requirements of Title IX for decades. Such schools now face with the threat of compensatory and punitive damages for their Title IX violations as a consequence of the 1992 unanimous U.S. Supreme Court decision in *Franklin v Gwinnett.*[21] Such schools are also those that have consistently protected sports such as football from any budgetary review. Administrators claim that football makes money for the school and thus such excesses as hotel stays for upwards of 130 players, coaches, and support staff on nights preceding home games cannot be withheld, they say, without hurting the profit-making ability of the team. Logic, reality, and NCAA's own data, clearly demonstrate that 80 percent of Division I schools lose money on their football teams. The data also show that 32 percent of Division IA programs, the most competitive and commercialized football programs, lose more than one million dollars per year on their football teams.

The establishment of an alternative view to the commercial model of athletics currently found on many of the nation's campuses is vital. It is prerequisite to the continuation of a viable athletics program for men as well as women. Gender equity and participation opportunities for both men's minor sports and women's programs will be limited if colleges and universities continue the commercial model of athletics. Funding gender equity through a hoped-for profit generated by funding football richly enough to guarantee success is akin to funding gender equity by buying a lottery ticket. It is uncertain, unlikely, and unrelated to the facts.

Isolation and Networks

Discrimination and discriminatory mind sets of their peers isolate women on campus. Athletics and physical education programs, as a consequence of a typical physical location cross campus or a lack of collegial understanding about their roles in the educational endeavor, are often isolated from other programs on campus. In addition, almost two-thirds of the time female athletic administrators are the sole female within their programs so their cadre of female peers is small and they often feel misunderstood by their male administrators. For instance, one female assistant athletic director/coach wrote in her baby's book:

> Within a week of your birth I had to start going back to help my replacement coach a few hours a day. While at home, students called, I scheduled the games for the season, ordered uniforms and buses and basically worked full time from home. My joy was being with you but I will always regret having my mind at school. This was supposed to be a non-working, paid six week maternity leave! I think they think I should have paused during team practice to give birth to you, my wonderful daughter, scooped you up in my arms and continued to coach from the sidelines without missing a step. Why did they agree to the leave in the first place? My prayer is that your life will include bosses, male or female, who finally "get it." It's 1998 and my boss certainly doesn't get it.[22]

Two-thirds of female leaders in intercollegiate athletics programs find their support systems with professionals outside their schools walls, with professionals within the field of athletics at other institutions. The National Association for Girls and Women in Sport (NAGWS) is now almost one hundred years old. It has provided an effective and ongoing network base for female physical educators and secondary school coaches. NAGWS has also provided an organizational base for lobbying on behalf of Title IX's enforcement.

On the college level, the National Association of Collegiate Women Athletic Administrators (NACWAA), has provided a forum of support as well as a foundation for a growing degree of power within the male dominated NCAA. NACWAA was the moving force causing the NCAA, which had consistently denied even the existence of discrimination, to issue its Gender Equity Study in 1992, and again in 1997. Data had certainly been available prior to 1992 that unequivocally demonstrated grave problems in gender equity within athletics. But, without the NCAA imprimatur, some male directors of athletics still followed the ostrich strategy. NACWAA has also demonstrated strength in its efforts to increase female representation on NCAA committees of significance, to exert influence over NCAA legislation, and to have an impact on gender-equity legislation enacted by Congress relating to reporting requirements for the NCAA.

NACWAA and NAGWS, both of which have as their members female sports leaders, continue to encourage the Office for Civil Rights, the enforcement agency for administrative Title IX complaints, to develop both more appropriate investigation techniques and a stronger will to enforce the law. They also file amicus briefs for significant lawsuits relating to gender equity.

These organizations serve as the organizational framework within many female sports leaders network for gender equity. Women in athletics have learned to network.

Sensitization of Males to Equity Issues

More men understand the issues of gender equity in sports now than ever before. Some have obtained such understanding as a consequence of court decisions while others have learned from the outcome of lawsuits filed against their peers. One such decision was the outcome of *Franklin v Gwinnett*[23] where the United States Supreme Court made it clear that compensatory and punitive damages were available to victims of intentional discrimination covered by Title IX. Financial imperatives for equity flowing from the *Franklin* decision have caused many male administrators to find methods for increasing equity before lawsuits force them to do so.

For others, it is a matter of having been sensitized to the issues by female sports management/physical education/athletics administration professors through the inclusion of the topic in updated college curriculum. Increased media coverage and NCAA workshops on gender equity issues, although late in the day, have sensitized others. The media coverage has continued to inform administrators through the pattern of court cases such as Brown University[24] that the Regulations and Policy Interpretations for Title IX mean what they say.

Observation of high-profile, courageous female professionals in the field of athletics, the efforts of NACWAA and NAGWS to define and enforce gender equity, and the realization by the male administrators that their own daughters deserve better have also worked together to increase awareness and sensitivity about the issues of gender equity. Studies indicate that scholarship football players and other high-profile college athletes demonstrate sexist attitudes and have a statistical propensity to fit the profile of sexual assaulters more frequently than their nonathletic peers. However, the pool from which the current coaching and athletic administration cadre has been drawn now includes professionally trained individuals rather than jock-turned-coach individuals in any large numbers. This change in the makeup of the hiring pool has been prevalent for the last decade or so. It is likely to continue, supported by the many excellent sports management programs now found on college campuses.

Court Challenges

Using the law to produce gender equity has always been difficult. Most female coaches have only a one-year contract, and if they file or are suspected of having anything to do with the filing of a Title IX OCR complaint or a

Title IX lawsuit, their jobs are over, and they are unlikely to find another. Yet many women have filed. Most have filed because of inequities their students have faced rather than solely for inequities they have encountered. The courage of the women who have filed on behalf of their students is a quiet inspiration.

One coach, who lost her job due to her involvement with a Title IX complaint, filed a lawsuit on behalf of her loss. She remarked at the conclusion, six years later, of her Title IX and Equal Pay Act lawsuit, which she won:

> I cried tears of vindication when they read the verdict in our favor. It has been decades of the college cheating its female athletes, 8 years of its administrators harassing me and 5 years of legal maneuverings. It's over, the college lost and even after all this, I'm glad it's finally over and I'm glad I stood up for my students and myself.[25]

By the time of her vindication, this former coach had been out of college athletics for six years; no college or university would hire her because of her suspected involvement in the Title IX complaint. Instead, she has built a fine program for high school female athletes where she now serves as coach and director of athletics. She survived, she won, and makes a difference in the lives of others by giving them courage to stand for principle.

Student life spans on campus are short, yet even some brave female students have filed Title IX complaints and lawsuits; none has filed without irrevocably altering their collegiate experience by adding isolation and retribution to their lives. One of the first students to file was Rollin Haffer, who won a landmark lawsuit against Temple University.[26] She won, but the price was very high. Unenlightened faculty members and students on campus ostracized this quiet young woman who only wanted to be treated fairly and to gain the knowledge necessary to become a skilled elementary schoolteacher. The lawsuit occupied days, weeks, and months of her study time. Yet she survived; she won and she made a difference for others, even though not for herself since she had graduated by the time the case was settled.

Amy Cohen,[27] now an elementary schoolteacher, took on Brown University, as well as many outside interests who exerted great pressure on the courts. Her successful protest made a difference for others, if not for herself since she had graduated by the time the case was concluded. Amy's case has made it clear for all colleges across the country that a pivotal principle of Title IX's equal participation test, often referred to as proportionality, is valid.

Renee Smith, a student athlete, has sued the NCAA concerning its post-baccalaureate bylaw that limits the eligibility of transfer students. The significance of Smith's *pro se* lawsuit is that it has resulted in United States Third Circuit Court of Appeals ruling[28] that the NCAA is subject to the jurisdiction of Title IX. If the ruling stands, the quiet courage of a young female athlete, strong enough to file her own lawsuit, will have made a significant impact on the role NCAA plays in the governance of women in intercollegiate sports.

Quiet Inspiration: Courageous, Goal-Oriented Women

Gender equity is not a field for the faint of heart. The early female leaders had great dedication and quiet courage. The current female leaders, like their foremothers, also have great dedication, but their courage is more often put to the test in a public arena. Old and young, new and experienced, these women have woven a tapestry of self-sacrifice, dedication, and courage that is of great value. The tapestry includes massive increases in participation opportunities, well developed networking systems, a long line of successful court cases, an increased sensitivity to equity issues, and strong strategy for expanding the presence of female voices in the future of athletics programs for the nation's youth. The gauge and colors of the individual threads have not always been harmonious when placed next to each other but the fabric produced is sturdy.

This generation's young women did not often see the tapestry being woven. They seldom saw the cost of each thread. They only see the completed scene that includes more equity than their mothers and older sisters enjoyed. The tapestry is strong, and the current female leaders are working to strengthen it, but threads can weaken and unravel if not carefully tended. Those who view and use the tapestry need to value it. In order to do so, they need to hear of the courage, quiet inspiration and loving self-sacrifice involved in its creation.

Notes

1. 20 U.S.C. Section 1681 (a).

2. 20 U.S.C. Section 1681–87 (1988) as amended by the Civil Rights Restoration Act of 1987, Pub.L. No. 100-259, 102 Stat. 28 (1988) (codified USC section 1687).

3. L. Leotus Morrison, "The AIAW: Governance by Women for Women," in *Women in Sport: Issues and Controversies*, ed. Greta L. Cohen (Sage Publications, 1993), 61.

4. Ibid., 62.

5. The NCAA, National Collegiate Athletic Association, governed the majority of intercollegiate sport for men in the United States and had done so for decades.

6. B. Barnes and B. N. Scannell, "No Sporting Change: The Girls in the Locker Room," *The Washington Post* (May 12, 1974): A-14.

7. We place the term "revenue," in quotation marks because it is now well documented that only a handful of colleges receive any positive cash flow from their "revenue" sports.

8. Charles M. Neinas to Roswell D. Merrick, December 22, 1966, unpublished correspondence in possession of the authors.

9. NCAA, Minutes of January 21, 1968 meeting of the Committee on Women's Intercollegiate Competition, unpublished document, 2.

10. Journal entry, in possession of the authors.

11. R. V. Acosta and L. J. Carpenter, "Status of Women in Intercollegiate Sport—Nineteen Year Update, 1977–1998," unpublished manuscript, Brooklyn College, 1996.

12. Ibid.

13. Ibid.

14. Ibid.

15. R. V. Acosta and L. J. Carpenter, "Job Stasis: Reflections of Immobility and Resistance to Job Change among Senior Women in Athletic Personnel," unpublished manuscript, Brooklyn College, 1992, 5.

16. Acosta and Carpenter, "Status of Women in Intercollegiate Sport," 8.

17. Vivian Acosta and Linda Jean Carpenter, "Perceived Causes of the Declining Representation of Women Leaders in Intercollegiate Sports," unpublished manuscript, Brooklyn College, 1984 and 1988.

18. Ibid.

19. Morrison, "The AIAW," 64.

20. Ibid.

21. *Franklin v Gwinnett County Public Schools,* 112 S. Ct. 1028 (1992).

22. Journal entry, in possession of the authors.

23. *Franklin v Gwinnett County Public Schools.*

24. *Cohen v Brown University* (809 F. Supp. 978, D.R.I. 1992, aff'd 991 F 2d 888 1993, 1996 US. App. LEXIS 30192).

25. Anonymous source in possession of the authors.

26. *Haffer v Temple University,* Pa civil Action No. 80-1362, 1988.

27. *Cohen v Brown University* (809 F. Supp. 978, D.R.I. 1992, aff'd 991 F 2d 888 1993, 1996 US. App. LEXIS 30192).

28. *Smith v National Collegiate Athletic Association,* Third Circuit, Nos. 97-3346 and 97-3347, March 16, 1998.

CHAPTER 10

Contemporary Issues of Women as Senior Student Affairs Officers

SUSAN R. JONES AND SUSAN R. KOMIVES

In 1979 Margaret C. Berry, then editor of *The Journal of the National Association for Women Deans, Administrators, and Counselors,* wrote: "During the seventies, the women's movement, with its charges of sexism and bias, became an all-important issue. Title IX of the 1972 Educational Amendments, for instance, aroused a considerable amount of interest in the position of women on our campuses and served as a means of consciousness raising for women never before equaled in academe."[1] That "interest in the position of women on our campuses" resulted in, through the 1980s, ample research, scholarship, and dialogue about the impact of women in higher education. The 1990s however, by comparison, have been sluggish in continuing to build upon the work that brought attention to issues of women in higher education. In fact, the literature of student affairs administration appears to have backed off scholarly interest in documenting the issues and experiences of women in the profession. Perhaps reflecting larger societal forces and a general backlash against women,[2] our attention has turned from a gender-related perspective to a gender-neutral approach that has diverted a focus away from gender and its relation to the career pathways and contemporary issues of women student affairs officers.

Further, despite scholarship on new paradigms of leadership that incorporate the feminist values of inclusion, collaboration, and empowerment, as discussed in chapter 5,[3] women are not represented in leadership positions in student affairs in proportion to their numbers in the profession. However, women have consistently contributed to the development of the student affairs profession and continue to provide leadership in both theory generation and practice. The influence of women in student affairs administration is deeply rooted in the history of the profession and permeates current administrative practice and leadership in the field.

As the stories told in earlier chapters suggest (see chapters 6 and 7), contemporary issues of women as senior student affairs officers emerge out of a rich, albeit underreported, history and tradition of leadership. This chapter explores the impact of women senior student affairs officers on higher education through an examination of the demographics of student affairs administration, career patterns and employment trends, and the context of leadership in student affairs administration. The status of women in student affairs will be described demographically as well as conceptually, with specific attention given to what has been called the "feminization of the profession." Contemporary issues of women as senior student affairs officers cannot be fully understood without revisiting the historical roots of the profession.

Historical Perspective

As earlier chapters document, the foundations for the profession of student affairs administration were built out of the inspiration and hard work of the early deans of women. Beginning in the 1950s when new administrative structures resulted in the erosion and subsequent elimination of the dean of women position on many campuses, our collective memory of the strong legacy of leadership provided by these deans eroded. Instead, the image of the "snooping battle axes"[4] is the most vibrant recollection of these women deans, while the massive contributions made to the creation of the profession of student affairs administration are overlooked. As James Appleton, Channing Briggs, and James Rhatighan suggested, "We have largely forgotten their essential courage in the face of formidable circumstances; their dedication in attempting to open new fields of study for women; their persistence even in failure; the stereotype they fought to overcome; the ethical standards evidenced in their work; the example they set for all who have followed. We have diminished them when they should stand as role models."[5]

A closer analysis of the history of the student affairs profession reveals the personal qualities, expertise, and leadership provided by the deans of women that provided the foundation of the field. As Carolyn Bashaw's chapter chronicles, the functional role of the deans of women became increasingly marginalized as student demographics changed, the practice of *in loco parentis* relaxed, and housing options expanded. However, the leadership, both explicit and subversive, exercised by the deans of women provided the foundation for the profession of student affairs administration. Clearly, their understanding of the roles and responsibilities of the dean of women was anchored by a philosophy of educating the whole person and character development, the cornerstone of the student affairs profession. Ironically, it was, in part, their work toward developing the profession that ultimately led to the elimination of the dean of women position. In the name of administrative efficiency, and in combination with the contextual forces at work, the positions of the dean of women and the dean of men were combined to create the new position of dean of students. These changes resulted in removing gender distinctions in titles and in special programs for women students; and in an administrative structure that rendered women marginal in campus leadership and removed them from positions of power and influence.[6]

As men assumed leadership positions in student affairs, the historical legacy of leadership from the deans of women became invisible and all but forgotten. Women continued to enter the profession in greater numbers than men, but the pattern of men holding senior leadership positions was well set by historical precedent and carried forward into contemporary times. Although relegated to lesser positions when deans of students were hired, women continued to perform the essential work of student affairs and played significant roles in the lives of young women students. However, the expectations of this role were frequently reduced to the need for control and discipline.[7]

The 1970s was an era of unprecedented growth in higher education. Public institutions were built, community colleges expanded their roles, and student protest and involvement in United States domestic affairs signaled a new wave of societal attention to higher education. Along with other administrative roles, student affairs grew with the proliferation of specialized functional areas. This expansion combined with the large influx of the early baby-boomer group of professionals moving into student affairs roles. Women clearly came into the leadership pipeline and new women professionals, without hesitation, envisioned careers as deans of students and vice presidents for student affairs.

Contemporary Issues in a Demographic Context

The current demographic picture for women senior student affairs administrators can best be understood in the context of this historical and contextual perspective. While women are entering the profession in growing ranks and graduating from doctoral programs in growing numbers, men continue to hold a disproportionate number of the senior student affairs positions and women remain clustered in mid-level positions. Even for those women who are in senior-level positions, their salaries lag behind those of their male counterparts.

Typically, the career pathway for student affairs positions begins in graduate preparation programs. Recent research on the demographics in graduate programs suggests a preponderance of women entering the field through enrollment in and graduation from preparation programs. In 1986, 65 percent of master's students and 47 percent of doctoral students were women.[8] In 1993–94, among those reporting enrollment data to a directory of graduate preparation programs, 66 percent of master's students and 55 percent of doctoral students were women.[9] Current data suggest that the higher proportion of women in masters' programs remains fairly consistent while the number of women in doctoral programs continues to increase. The graduation rate for women completing a doctoral program, generally regarded as an important credential for senior level positions,[10] increased from 16 percent in 1970–71 to 59 percent in 1986–87.[11] However, participation in doctoral programs by underrepresented groups such as African Americans, Asian Americans, Latino/as, and Native Americans is very low.[12]

Given the increased participation of women in graduate preparation programs, the representation of women in the leadership pipeline would appear to be high. Although reporting results of research conducted in the early 1980s, David Holmes described a phenomenon still applicable today: "The present circumstance is one in which women may be dominant numerically in one setting and distinct minorities in another setting. Specifically, women are in the majority of many masters programs and frequently among all student affairs professionals at a particular institution. They are a minority at the top of the profession—dean of students and vice president for student affairs position—and at the top policy levels of most institutions."[13]

In a study of women senior student affairs officers conducted in 1980, Nancy Evans and George Kuh described a profile that is descriptive of current demographic realities for women in student affairs. Their findings indicated that women hold senior level positions at smaller and private institutions. Only 39 percent had graduate degrees from higher education or student affairs programs. In addition, women were younger than their male counterparts and more likely to hold the title of dean while men were appointed as vice presidents. Women were also more likely to have been promoted to their senior level positions from within the institution.[14]

The results of a longitudinal study examining membership in the National Association of Student Personnel Administrators (NASPA), a leading professional association in the field of student affairs administration, found that the percentage of women members increased from 38 percent of total membership in 1985–86 to 45 percent in 1991–92.[15] This is particularly significant. As Nidiffer's chapter on the history of deans reminds us, NASPA's origins are as the professional organization for deans of men, and NASPA is typically the association to which the majority of *senior* student affairs administrators belong. While the numbers of women in senior student affairs position increased over the same six-year period from 32 percent in 1985–86 to 37 percent in 1991–92, their representation in leadership positions was inversely proportionate to their overall increase in the profession. In addition, women were significantly underrepresented in the leadership positions of vice president, dean, and director.[16] Greater numbers of women were found in lower-level positions and in what are perceived as the more nurturing staff positions of student activities, student development, and hall director.[17]

Salary discrepancies mirror career patterns with women senior student affairs administrators generally earning less than their male counterparts. The 1995–96 NASPA Salary Survey results indicate that the mean salaries for male senior student affairs administrators are generally greater than the mean salaries for female senior student affairs administrators. In addition, when comparing salaries by gender and education, for all degree levels, male senior student affairs administrators earn more than their female counterparts. Including ethnic background in the analysis yields similar results with men earning more than the women of similar backgrounds, with the exception of Asian women, who earn more than their male counterparts.[18] Questions necessarily emerge about the existence of a glass-ceiling phenomenon in student affairs administration or the constriction of the leadership pipeline with fewer women advancing to senior-level positions than numbers in the pipeline warrant.

An indication of structural changes and hiring patterns is reflected in the survey data of the College and University Personnel Association (CUPA). In the 1975–76 salary survey, for example, CUPA researchers note that of the fifty-two titles tracked that year, they deleted the titles Dean of Men and Dean of Women and added titles such as Chief Executive Officer, Executive Vice President, Chief Planning Officer, Director of Information Systems, Affirmative Action/Equal Opportunity Employment Officer, and Chief Health Affairs Officer.[19] The title of Chief Student Life Officer continued from previous surveys.

In 1975–76, CUPA reported that white men held 79 percent of all fifty-two positions tracked at the 1,138 institutions surveyed. White women represented 14 percent of all positions, while minority men held 5 percent and minority women held under two percent of these roles. All women and persons of color in administrative roles were disproportionately represented on campuses compared with comparable student enrollments. The CUPA report summarized: "Women and minorities were generally best represented in positions relating to student affairs and external affairs."[20] Indeed, women and persons of color held from "10 to 20 percent of such jobs at white coeducational institutions and men's colleges, over 25 percent at public and over 80 percent at private women's colleges, and from 90–100 percent at minority institutions."[21] In this era, women and persons of color were likely most employable in student and alumni affairs in an attempt to appeal to the gender and racial diversity of the constituents served by those units. While talented and capable women and persons of color had assumed credibility in women's colleges and historically black institutions, access to senior level positions was not achieved in predominantly white, male-led institutions.

Among the nine new tables added in the 1980–81 CUPA report, one was a comparison of male and female salaries and one was a comparison

TABLE 10.1
Fifteen-Year Profile of Women Administrators in Select Student Affairs Roles*

Year	*1980–81*		*1985–86*		*1990–91*		*1995–96*		*15 years*
Responding institutions	*N=1,557*		*N=1,612*		*N=1,402*		*N=1,384*		
Position	*# women*	*%*	*# women*	*%*	*# women*	*%*	*# women*	*%*	*% change*
SSAO	224	17	297	22	258	25	306	33	+18%
Directors									
admissions	198	20	266	28	257	31	272	36	+16%
counseling	263	31	326	39	342	43	375	53	+22%
career placement	369	41	423	49	459	56	520	62	+21%
financial aid	439	35	500	40	536	47	526	52	+17%
registrar	475	38	494	43	481	49	502	56	+18%
residence life	206	33	246	40	214	37	229	42	+9%
student union	125	22	79	24	162	24	113	29	+7%

*Data from College and University Personnel Association (1981). *Administrative Compensation Survey, 1980–81* (Washington, D.C.: CUPA) and similar reports from 1986, 1991, 1996. Not all institutions provided data on each job code.

of non-minorities and minorities.[22] Table 10.1 compares women as a percent of the total reporting in each category over a fifteen-year span. Women held 17 percent of the senior student affairs officers roles in 1980–81 with a 27.2 percent lower salary. By 1985–86, women held 22 percent of the senior student affairs officer positions.[23] In 1990–91, the position of Dean of Students was added as a person reporting to the Senior Student Affairs Officer (SSAO).[24] Women were in 25 percent of the SSAO positions in 1991, which increased to 33 percent by 1995–96.[25]

Women have increased in each student affairs employment category with the smallest increases in positions reflecting a broad span of leadership, supervision, and budget authority (e.g., residence life, student union, admissions, SSAO). The largest gains for women have been in direct service positions emphasizing counseling and educational roles (e.g., career planning and placement, counseling, registrar). Table 10.2 reflects the patterns among various categories of institutions. In 1996–97, approximately one-third of all SSAOs are women. The numbers of women exceed the mean percentage in virtually every position studied in general baccalaureate institutions and are below the mean in every category in doctoral institutions.

TABLE 10.2
1996–97 Profile of Women Administrators in Select Student Affairs Positions by Type of Institution (N = 1,496)*

	Doctoral universities N=202	*%*	*Comprehensive univ. N=375*	*%*	*General baccalaureate N=353*	*%*	*Two-year colleges N=344*	*%*	*Total*	*%*
SSAO	48	27.3	106	33.4	120	40.5	78	35.6	352	34.9
Associate SSAO	31	39.2	48	44	48	54.5	9	40.9	136	45.6
Dean of Students	35	42.2	53	40.2	49	48.5	40	42.6	177	43.2
Directors										
admissions	41	30.4	99	38.1	90	34	53	45.7	283	36.5
counseling	59	40.1	132	50	118	60.5	71	54.6	380	51.2
career placement	87	52.4	190	63.5	195	69.1	82	61.2	554	62.9
financial aid	65	39.4	176	53	181	57.1	149	56.4	571	53
registrar	68	41.5	177	57.8	182	58.5	92	63.9	519	56.1
residence life	46	30.3	98	40	97	55.7	9	30	250	41
student union	34	22.7	52	31.1	42	50.6	7	31.8	135	32

*Data from College and University Personnel Association (1997). *Administrative Compensation Survey, 1996–97* (Washington, D.C.: CUPA). (222 institutions in this survey were classified as other and not included in this data.)

In another study that provides a demographic profile, Scott Rickard found significant differences between male and female senior student affairs administrators. Specifically, in a study of 162 newly appointed senior student affairs administrators, he found that women were appointed at a younger age, had less education, moved to their top positions from positions titled assistant director or coordinator and assumed titles such as dean or director rather than vice president, had less full-time experience, and were more likely to take senior positions at smaller institutions.[26]

Career mobility and access to senior-level positions remains an issue in the student affairs profession. The dynamics at work that limit access and disadvantage women in reaching leadership roles as senior student affairs administrators are complex, persistent, and interactive. While the route to the senior student affairs position is not always clear,[27] the path for women is particularly difficult.[28] In studies of mobility and position change in student affairs, findings suggest that women were more likely to be promoted from within an institution than hired from another, whereas men were selected from both within the institution and hired from outside.[29] In addition, women apply for new positions at the same rate as men, yet are hired at lower rates.[30] Interpreting these results, Mary Ann Sagaria noted that such findings are more reflective of organizational selection practices than individual aspirations and decisions regarding mobility. Those making decisions about hiring and promotion tend to select those individuals most similar to themselves, where trust is perceived, and a commonality in values is understood.[31] These dynamics have served to disadvantage women and separate women from the hiring and promotion processes in student affairs and higher education; and help to explain the underrepresentation of women in senior student affairs positions.

Feminization of the Profession

The cumulative effect of the demographics of women in student affairs administration is captured in the phrase used to describe student affairs: feminization of the profession. Borrowing from the sociological term, "feminization of poverty," the term "refers to the demographic representation of women within student affairs and changes in the profession that may be related to this demographic shift."[32] Further, feminization is discussed and understood in the context of the mission and purpose of the profession, whose core values center on the "feminine" beliefs in the development of the whole person, community, and compassion.[33] Similar to the critique of the term "feminization of poverty," such a concept incorrectly suggests the commonality of experience for all women and shifts an analysis to gender without attention to the dynamics of classism, racism, and sexism at work. In their qualitative study of feminization in student affairs, Marylu McEwen, Cathy Engstrom, and Terry Williams made the point that "the feminization of the profession and the representation of men and women is probably more of an issue for white professionals, members of the racial majority, than it is for professionals who are members of visible racial/ethnic groups."[34]

New theories of leadership also emphasize feminist values of inclusion, relationships, cooperation, and empowerment as was discussed in an earlier chapter.[35] The intersections of demographics, leadership theory and experiences, social constructions of gender, and the gendered nature of organizations have combined to produce the notion of feminization of the profession. However, while discussion about feminization of student affairs has focused attention on numbers of women in the profession, it has also served to further alienate and marginalize women by creating the artificial category of "women's work."[36] Jane Fried explains that the experience of women in student affairs administration cannot be fully understood without consideration of three central issues: the predominance of positivist assumptions in higher education, the marginalization of the profession because of the overlap between the relational values of the student affairs profession and female socialization, and the outsider perspective of women in student affairs administration.[37] While understanding these dynamics is critical to an analysis and understanding of women's experiences in the academy, they also emphasize the unique contribution to be made and position of strength women gain from their "outsider-within" status.[38] Marvalene Hughes issued a charge to the profession in stating: "The profession of student affairs must claim its alignment with transformative leadership values, such as feminist values, which offer nonhierarchical principles."[39] This stance is challenged by competing calls for accountability, credibility, and efficiency;[40] and an organizational hierarchy which historically has limited access to women in senior student affairs positions.

Contemporary Issues

Contemporary issues of women as senior student affairs officers and the influence of women in student affairs must be viewed in the context of historical legacy, the demographics of career mobility and access to senior level positions, and an analysis of the "feminization of the profession." The interaction of these perspectives has framed the discussion about the influence of women in student affairs and led to a shifting of the attention in the profession away from an analysis of gender to a more gender-neutral approach. Current issues emerge out of the intersection of these factors.

"Each One Reach One"

One of the central issues for the future of student affairs administration is access and representation of women and persons of color in upper-level student affairs leadership positions.[41] Women remain stacked in lower- and mid-level student affairs positions and in functional areas deemed more "feminine." For those women who achieve senior-level status in student affairs, support systems and the availability of mentors are in short supply. This situation is exacerbated for women of color.[42] With greater numbers of women in the leadership pipeline for senior level positions in student affairs, institutions, as well as professional associations, must create structures for mentoring women for leadership positions. Mentoring opportunities will not only introduce aspiring women senior student affairs administrators to the skills, knowledge, and competencies of this leadership position, but will also provide the support for the development of a professional identity consistent with the profession and with personal values and ethical standards. Women aspiring to senior-level positions are in need of mentors, sponsors, and positive role models. Young professionals are also in need of the same. Effective mentoring may take many forms and includes the sponsorship and supportive relationships provided by peers as well as those in leadership positions.[43] There is a great need for institutional structures to be put in place that acknowledge the importance of mentoring and developing supportive networks if women are to advance in their careers and gain access to senior-level positions in student affairs administration in increasing numbers.

The Opportunities in Professional Associations

Involvement in professional associations has provided women in student affairs with significant networking, mentoring, and leadership opportunities from the earliest conferences of deans of women through the nadir years of post-World War II to the modern day. Women have held significant leadership roles in professional associations that provide rich training ground for developing institutional leadership skills. In addition to the National Association for Women in Education (NAWE, originally the National Association of Deans of Women), whose history and mission have promoted women in leadership, both NASPA and ACPA have been well served by growing numbers of women in leadership positions. Since its founding in 1924, twenty-three of ACPA's fifty-six presidents have been women. In what some would say is a rather dramatic reversal from its roots as a group for deans of men, NASPA's 1996–97 elected leadership for example, included women in all seven regional vice presidencies, as past president and president-elect, and as journal editor. The executive directors for all three of these major student affairs professional associations are currently women. Clearly, leadership is being provided and influence generated by women in the profession.

In addition, several programs offered by professional associations specifically target the professional and leadership development of women in student affairs administration. For example, NASPA's symposium which targets women in senior level positions or those aspiring to that role, the HERS program for women aspiring to senior leadership positions, and NAWE's newly created Institute for Emerging Women Leaders all focus on the development of women leaders in the academy. These programs "groom" and prepare women for access to and success in senior level positions in student affairs administration. They also introduce women to one another so that supportive growth environments are created and professional sharing of struggles and expertise takes place—conversations that occur rarely among one's predominately male colleagues. In addition, NASPA's Minority Fellows Program targets new professionals in the field in an effort to recruit and support persons of color in student affairs. While the Minority Fellows Program does not focus specifically on women entering the profession, growing numbers of women of color have participated as both mentors and fellows.

Professional associations can play an instrumental role in reopening the dialogue about gender issues in general and the role and "place" of women in particular in student affairs administration. Leadership might also be provided by professional associations in stressing the importance of broadening the conversation about the "feminine" values of inclusion, collaboration, and caring to address the core values of the profession that all members embrace, but also the unique contributions and leadership roles women play in the field. In fact, as chapter 5 suggests, women leaders my prove to be a strategic advantage for the institution.

We have been diligent in the collection of data that describes the profession demographically, but less focused on the experiences of women in the field. Such attention would add depth to our professional understanding about the career pathways, mobility, and issues of women aspiring to or in senior-level student affairs positions. We also need research that focuses not exclusively on the experiences of individuals, but also on the institutions' policies, practices, and cultures that support or curtail the advancement of women. What are the institutional dynamics at work that result in fewer women in leadership positions at consistently lower salaries than their male counterparts?

Stresses and Strains of Leadership

Women in senior student affairs positions appear to be held to a different standard with differing expectations for style and success. For example, in their qualitative study of 210 exemplary practitioners in student affairs administration, Linda Clement and Scott Rickard found that women were expected to be more nurturing, more collaborative and less hierarchical, and more forgiving than their male counterparts.[44] In addition, "hidden work loads" were identified by women senior student affairs administrators as a variable in the gendered nature of their positions.[45] Differential expectations for women that placed them in advisory roles or on many committees moved them out of the perceived inner circle as well as added to work loads.

The demands of the senior student affairs position are great and seem to exact a greater toll for women who are balancing multiple commitments. In a study on stress and senior student affairs officers, Nancy Scott found that women were significantly more stressed than their male counterparts both in the work setting and outside it. In fact, for all eighteen items measured in this study, women reported higher levels of stress, six of which were related to work, nine to their personal lives, and three items describing the intersection of work and personal life.[46] For example, women were significantly more stressed over "change in relationships" than men and by "conflicts between own and other units." In another study that was a replication of Scott's but focused on mid-level student affairs officers, Jean Schober Morrell found that gender was a much greater predictor of stress than role or status among senior- and mid-level student affairs officers.[47] In other words, one might expect that the move from mid-level to senior-level student affairs positions would produce greater stress. However, as Schober Morrell found, high levels of stress were experienced by women regardless of position level.

While a "balanced life" continues to be an elusive goal for many women professionals, women in senior-level student affairs positions must reconcile the great demands of their work with other interests and responsibilities. The irony in this situation is that successful women leaders often suggest that part of their success is due to the well-rounded lives they lead, which includes time for relaxation and renewal, family, and interests outside the workplace. However, the realities of senior leadership positions do not always support the matching of espoused values with such activities.

A Critical Mass

The reality is that it will take more women in leadership positions in student affairs to reclaim the rich historical legacy of leadership and to increase the visibility of women in institutions of higher education. It is crucial that those who are currently making the hiring and promotion decisions recommit to gender equity and to developing women in—and all the way through—the student affairs leadership pipeline. This commitment includes institutional policies and procedures affecting the campus climate for women as well as hiring, promotion, and salary decisions. As Florence Hamrick and Wayne Carlisle suggest, "Our campuses should be more assertive in providing equitable access to upper-level positions through the selection process, and our associations should provide professional development opportunities for women aspiring to dean and vice president positions."[48]

However, there are unique opportunities in student affairs administration to lead the way in this effort because of the number of women entering and progressing in the field. Student affairs is the institutional division with large numbers of professional women, including women of color, with the administrative and leadership skills for advancement. The leadership pipeline for women in student affairs is full. However, the institutional gauge must be opened so that access to leadership positions is achieved.

Institutional Restructuring

The current climate of restructuring may not have the same effects as the restructuring that led to the elimination of the position of the dean of women, however, it holds the potential for diminished institutional prestige for student affairs and lessened opportunities for women and other underrepresented groups. As Kathryn Nemeth Tuttle summarized, those most affected, in any decade, by restructuring efforts aimed at improving efficiency and reducing redundancy, are those in less powerful positions.[49]

Current efforts at restructuring have, in some cases, led to changes in the reporting structure of senior student affairs administrators from the president to the provost. Whether motivated by increased interest in academic and student affairs collaborations and partnerships or other, less admirable, goals, the senior student affairs officer loses some access to the president and parity with other senior cabinet members. Restructuring has also led to the outsourcing of more traditional student affairs functions such as food services, housing, and psychological services that changes the nature, purposes, and make-up of the student affairs division. The impact on women leaders in student affairs of restructuring remains to be seen. However, early indications hold both promise and peril. Many presidents are fully aware that student affairs is the most viable division from which to hire a vice president who is a woman or professional of color. Search committees know they can find qualified and visionary leadership from the division of student affairs. Women will likely continue to increase at a faster rate of new hires in the SSAO category than in the past. Indeed, doctoral institutions that currently employ only slightly more than one-quarter women in these roles will likely receive applications from women SSAOs in baccalaureate and regional public institutions, bringing a well-qualified applicant pool. In some sectors such as community colleges, women can move into the presidency from the SSAO role and increases in women in these positions hold promise of further career progress.

Professional Issues

The most pressing professional issues currently have directed the attention of the higher education community to topics such as student learning, the creation of community, accountability, and outcomes assessment. While these issues are critical to the success and future of the profession, we must not abandon our commitment to and interest in the experiences of women and persons of color and our active pursuit of the creation of institutional climates and leadership opportunities so that all may flourish and succeed. As a profession, we must hold ourselves accountable for the realization of professional goals and values that include equity, justice, and care.

The erosion of affirmative action policies will no doubt have a significant impact on the leadership pipeline for women, particularly women of color. Earlier research has suggested that many institutions easily accomplished affirmative action goals primarily by promoting white women from within the institution.[50] While white women have been the primary beneficiaries of affirmative action, there will be a negative impact on the hiring, promotion, and career mobility of all women and persons of color by recent decisions about the future of affirmative action.

The Landscape of Higher Education

The contributions of women in student affairs administration hold great potential to increase as higher education recommits to issues and concerns congruent with women's leadership and to the values of the student affairs profession. Institutional commitments to interdisciplinary programs, collaborative efforts between units and divisions, and partnerships between the university and communities, businesses, and the schools, reflect values and interests congruent with women's leadership. Even the current emphasis on "seamless learning" reflects the integrated and connected way in which women approach leadership and professional practice. Women administrators often have strong relational networks across campus that are now being tapped in the move toward the cross-functional work-team environment prompted by such strategies as Continuous Quality Improvement. Indeed, skills such as relational empathy (i.e., seeing an issue from another's perspective) are now recognized as an integral competency for building bridges and opening dialogue among diverse constituent groups.

Likewise, student affairs will assume new centrality with institutional efforts to emphasize the student experience and the undergraduate curriculum. The ACPA/NASPA "Principles of Good Practice for Student Affairs" mirror and affirm the qualities reflected in women's ways of leading. Specifically, "good practice" in student affairs is defined by such principles as active learning, developing values and ethical standards, educational partnerships, and inclusive communities.[51] In addition, women in senior student affairs positions frequently identify interaction with students as of central importance to them, although the demands of these positions often remove them from close contact. The expertise of women in senior level positions, as well as their more relational orientations, will be needed as institutions create and sustain campus communities in which students and the student experience are central.

Summary

As a profession we have long struggled to achieve our "place" in the academy. So too have women worked for recognition, access, and visibility in the leadership ranks of student affairs. Such effort has provided women with a special angle of vision, the "outsider-within" status that describes those existing on the margins yet having to work at the center. Both worlds, that of insider and outsider, are known and understood, with a depth and clarity not perceived by those who take their insider status for granted. The success of women leaders in student affairs depends upon one's ability to walk in both worlds. As Kathryn Moore eloquently describes: "Such gifts are the heritage of those who have struggled outside the gates, and they offer significant consequences for women and minority leaders and for their institutions once such people are inside the gates and in substantive administrative positions."[52] The student affairs profession is rich with historical examples of effective leadership generated by early deans of women. The field continues to benefit from women serving in senior student affairs positions who have shaped the profession, provided leadership to the field, and served as superb role models and mentors to colleagues and those who aspire to leadership positions in student affairs administration.

Historically, women have been shaping and influencing the profession of student affairs administration both from the margins and increasingly from positions of authority, power, and in senior leadership positions. Women are now toiling inside the gates, and some in significant administrative positions. The contemporary issues of limited representation and isolation in senior leadership positions, inclusion, managing both professional and personal commitments, and changes in organizational and institutional restructuring and climates combine to suggest a complex picture of life as a woman in a senior student affairs leadership position. There are indicators of change with women in significant leadership positions in professional associations and with changing institutional commitments that accent women's ways of leading and the values of the student affairs profession. There is no reason to believe that women will not continue to provide the quiet inspiration and hard work that has anchored the historical and continuing influence they have on higher education.

Notes

* The authors would like to acknowledge the assistance of Kathleen Hill, doctoral student at The Ohio State University, in the preparations for the writing of this chapter.

1. Margaret C. Berry, *Women in Educational Administration: A Book of Readings* (Washington, D.C.: The National Association for Women Deans, Administrators and Counselors, 1979), v.

2. Susan Faludi, *Backlash: The Undeclared War against American Women* (New York: Crown Publishers, 1991).

3. Susan R. Komives, "New Approaches to Leadership," in *Different Voices: Gender and Perspective in Student Affairs Administration*, ed. Jane Fried (Washington, D.C.: National Association of Student Personnel Administrators, 1994).

4. Joanne Fley, *"Discipline in Student Personnel Work: The Changing Views of Deans and Personnel Workers,"* unpublished doctoral dissertation, University of Illinois, 1963.

5. James R. Appleton, Channing M. Briggs, and James. J. Rhatigan, *Pieces of Eight* (Portland, OR: National Association of Student Personnel Administrators, 1978), 16–17.

6. Kathryn N. Tuttle, "What Became of the Dean of Women? Changing Roles for Women Administrators in American Higher Education, 1940–1980," unpublished manuscript, University of Kansas, 1996.

7. Appleton, Briggs, and Rhatigan, *Pieces of Eight.*

8. Marybelle C. Keim, "Student Personnel Preparation Programs," *NASPA Journal* 28 (1991): 231–42.

9. Susan R. Komives, "An Update on Graduate Education," *NASPA Region II Newsletter* 15 (1996): 6.

10. Barbara K. Townsend and Michael Wiese, "The Value of the Doctorate in Higher Education for Student Affairs Administrators," *NASPA Journal* 30 (1992).

11. Keim, "Student Personnel Preparation Programs," 231–42.

12. Michael D. Coomes, Holley A. Belch, and Gerald L. Saddlemire, "Doctoral Programs for Student Affairs Professionals: A Status Report," *Journal of College Student Development* 32 (1991): 62–68.

13. David R. Holmes, "Exploring Career Patterns in Student Affairs: Problems of Conception and Methodology," *NASPA Journal* 20 (1982): 34.

14. Nancy J. Evans and George D. Kuh, "Getting to the Top: A Profile of Female Chief Student Affairs Officers," *Journal of NAWDAC* (1983): 18–22.

15. Darla J. Twale, "Gender Comparisons of NASPA Membership," *NASPA Journal* 32 (1995): 293–301.

16. Ibid.

17. Ibid.

18. National Association of Student Personnel Administrators, *NASPA Salary Survey Results: 1995–96 Senior Student Affairs Officers' Salary Data* (Washington, D.C.: NASPA, 1996).

19. College and University Personnel Association, *Administration Compensation Survey, 1975–76* (Washington, D.C.: CUPA, 1976).

20. College and University Personnel Association, *Administrative Compensation Survey, 1975–76: Special Supplement—Women and Minorities in Administration of Higher Education Institutions* (Washington, D.C.: CUPA, 1976).

21. Ibid.

22. College and University Personnel Association, *Administrative Compensation Survey, 1980–81* (Washington, D.C.: CUPA, 1981), 2.

23. College and University Personnel Association, *Administrative Compensation Survey, 1985–86* (Washington, D.C.: CUPA, 1986), 9.

24. College and University Personnel Association, *Administrative Compensation Survey, 1990–91* (Washington, D.C.: CUPA, 1991).

25. College and University Personnel Association, *Administrative Compensation Survey, 1995–96* (Washington, D.C.: CUPA, 1996).

26. Scott T. Rickard, "Career Pathways of Chief Student Affairs Officers: Making Room at the Top for Females and Minorities," *NASPA Journal* 22.4 (1985): 52–60.

27. D. David Ostroth, Frances D. Efird, and Lewis S. Lerman, "Career Patterns of Chief Student Affairs Officers," *Journal of College Student Development* 25.5 (1984): 443–48.

28. Nancy J. Evans, "Attrition of Student Affairs Professionals: A Review of the Literature," *Journal of College Student Development* 29.1 (1988): 19–24.

29. See Mary Ann D. Sagaria, "Administrative Mobility and Gender: Patterns and Processes in Higher Education," *Journal of Higher Education* 59 (May/June 1988): 305–26, and Mary Ann D. Sagaria and Linda K. Johnsrud, "Mobility within the Student Affairs Profession: Career Advancement through Position Change," *Journal of College Student Development* 29.1 (1988): 30–40.

30. Sagaria, "Administrative Mobility and Gender."

31. Ibid.

32. Florence A. Hamrick and L. Wayne Carlisle, "Gender Diversity in Student Affairs: Administrative Perceptions and Recommendations," *NASPA Journal* 27 (1989): 306.

33. Marvalene S. Hughes, "Feminization and Student Affairs," *NASPA Journal* 27 (1989): 18–27.

34. Marylu K. McEwen, Cathy McHugh Engstrom, and Terry E. Williams, "Gender Diversity Within the Student Affairs Profession," *Journal of College Student Development* 31 (1990): 47–53.

35. See Kathleen E. Allen and Cynthia Cherrey, "Shifting Paradigms and Practices in Student Affairs," in *Different Voices: Gender and Perspective in Student Affairs Administration*, ed. Jane Fried (Washington, D.C.: National Association of Student Personnel Administrators, 1994); James McGregor Burns, *Leadership* (New York: Harper & Row, 1978); Florence Guido-DiBrito, Patricia. A. Noteboom, Laura Nathan, and Joseph Fenty, "Traditional and New Paradigm Leadership: The Gender Link," *Initiatives* 58 (1996); and Komives, "New Approaches to Leadership."

36. Marvalene S. Hughes, "Feminization and Student Affairs," *NASPA Journal* 27 (1989): 18–27.

37. Jane Fried, "In Groups, Out Groups, Paradigms, and Perceptions," in *Different Voices: Gender and Perspective in Student Affairs Administration*, ed. Jane Fried (Washington, D.C.: National Association of Student Personnel Administrators, 1994).

38. Patricia Hill Collins, "Learning from the Outsider Within: The Sociological Significance of Black Feminist Thought," *Social Problems* 33 (1986): 14–32.

39. Hughes, "Feminization and Student Affairs."

40. Marylu K. McEwen, Terry E. Williams, and Cathy McHugh Engstrom, "Feminization in Student Affairs: A Qualitative Investigation," *Journal of College Student Development* 32 (1991): 440–46.

41. Margaret J. Barr and M. Lee Upcraft, "Identifying Challenges for the Future in Current Practice," in *New Futures for Student Affairs*, ed. Margaret. J. Barr and M. Lee Upcraft (San Francisco: Jossey-Bass, 1990).

42. Mary F. Howard-Hamilton and Vicki A. Williams, "Assessing the Environment for Women of Color in Student Affairs," in *Against the Tide: Career Paths of Women Leaders in American and British Higher Education*, ed. Karen Doyle Walton (Bloomington, IN: Phi Delta Kappa Educational Foundation, 1996).

43. Susan R. Komives, "The Middles: Observations on Professional Competence and Autonomy," *NASPA Journal* 29 (1992): 83–90.

44. Linda M. Clement and Scott T. Rickard, *Effective Leadership in Student Services: Voices from the Field* (San Francisco: Jossey-Bass, 1992).

45. Cynthia M. Anderson, "A Case Study of the Career Acquisition and Professional Experiences of Female Chief Student Affairs Officers," unpublished manuscript (Northern Arizona University, 1993).

46. Nancy A. Scott, "Chief Student Affairs Officers: Stressors and Strategies," *Journal of College Student Development* 33 (1992): 108–115.

47. Jean Schober Morrell, "Sources of Stress for the Student Affairs Mid-Manager," unpublished manuscript, University of Northern Colorado, 1994.

48. Hamrick and Carlisle, "Gender Diversity in Student Affairs."

49. Tuttle, "What Became of the Dean of Women?"

50. Sagaria, "Administrative Mobility and Gender."

51. See the American College Personnel Association and National Association of Student Personnel Administrators, "Principles of Good Practice for Student Affairs" (Washington, D.C., 1998).

52. Kathryn M. Moore, "Creating Strengths Out of Our Differences: Women and Minority Administrators," in *New Directions for Higher Education* 72 (1990): 94.

CHAPTER 11

"To Serve the Needs of Women"

The AAUW, NAWDC, and Persistence of Academic Women's Support Networks

CAROLYN TERRY BASHAW

Members of the National Association of Women Deans and Counselors (NAWDC) attending the 1957 annual meeting eagerly awaited Eunice M. Hilton's convention address concerning the continuing value of the organization both to the members and to the women whom they served. Director of the highly regarded graduate program in student personnel at Syracuse University, Hilton contended that undergraduate women, despite their apparently impressive enrollments, needed the advocacy and advice of the dean of women even more than did their less numerous predecessors. Furthermore, she observed that the increasing challenge to women's higher education only reinforced the necessity of single-sex professional organizations such as NAWDC. Thus, at mid-century, Hilton concluded, academic women—college students and the administrators who served them—confronted a society in which "the education of women is again on trial."[1]

Cultural proscription and demographic evidence confirm Hilton's conclusions. Postwar cultural conservatism affected women's options both off and on campus. Immediately following World War II, business and industry quickly reaffirmed traditional work patterns, simultaneously welcoming male veterans and releasing a significant contingent of women wartime workers. Responding to the subsequent communist military threat to and social critique of life in the United States, political and religious leaders, as well as the media, reemphasized the role of the nuclear family as the foundation of a democratic society. Central to the strength of that nuclear family was a distinctly gendered work pattern, in which men earned wages and women provided unpaid domestic labor.

The advent of the Cold War also reordered campus life for women. In fact, a numerical increase in the number of women pursuing undergraduate education throughout the 1950s masked the reality of their experience. The percentage of women attending college actually decreased, with not only fewer matriculating, but more significantly, with a larger percentage dropping out to marry.[2] Furthermore, the return of veterans to campus, the majority of whom sought professional employment, coupled with the cultural preoccupation with domesticity, combined to discourage many women either from graduating or from pursuing study in traditionally male fields.

Within the troubling context, Eunice Hilton reiterated the need for NAWDC, which provided its members with both "a sense of pride and security" and a framework for "revising and extending" the profession. She maintained that despite their participation in institutions of higher education for over a century, "women still have certain unique needs and problems." There remain troubling questions concerning their education, their professional prospects, and their role within institutions of higher education. Hilton claimed that only an all-women support network like the NAWDC, designed "to serve the needs of *women*"[3] could adequately understand and address the challenges that academic women face.

Women's professional societies remained active into the mid-twentieth century because, even when formerly all-male organizations admitted women, they seldom extended the full, affective benefits of membership. Thus, throughout the 1950s and 1960s, NAWDC numbered among a tenacious core of women's professional societies. The most long-lived, significant, and complex of these was the American Association of University Women (AAUW). Founded in 1881 by Marion and Emily Talbot as the Association of Collegiate Alumnae (ACA), the organization by the mid-fifties, functioned as a generic support network for the political, social, and educational activities of women college graduates.

By the mid-1950s, the two organizations forged close bonds. The AAUW offered office space to the fledgling National Association of Deans of Women (NADW) during the 1920s.[4] Many deans of women belonged to both AAUW and NAWDC. Journals of both societies published articles by the same authors. Founded in response to the specific educational and cultural challenges women faced, AAUW and NAWDC, by the mid-1950s, formed extensive, and in their view essential, support networks, especially for women administrators.

The historical reality for academic women in the United States and their support networks at mid-century and for contemporary scholars seeking to interpret this era remains complex indeed. Anxious to reduce historical nuance to scholarly sound bite, scholars often employ two terms to encompass women's activities in the 1950s and 1960s, respectively, domesticity and activism. Recent studies, however, suggest a far more variegated and often-threatening reality, especially for organizations such as AAUW and NAWDC.

Were domesticity and activism the totality of women's experience in the decades immediately following World War II, AAUW and NAWDC would have encountered familiar enemies and allies. Recent historical analysis, however, reveals a more complex pattern. In fact, women engaged in a variety of activities during both decades. Professional networks, including AAUW and NAWDC, persisted throughout the 1950s alongside suburban domesticity and increased workforce participation among women. In the 1960s, while civil rights workers, antiwar protesters, and radical feminists dominated the media, domesticity, nevertheless, remained a remarkably resilient norm for women.

Paradoxically, AAUW and NAWDC encountered their most formidable challenges—to the validity of a separate woman's culture and of an administrative office charged with the well-being of women—from activist women. Many professional women, who, by the early 1960s, found some modicum of acceptance within formerly all-male organizations, questioned the practicality of segregation within a woman's culture. Furthermore, undergraduate college women, imbued with the rhetoric of the civil rights movement, questioned the justice, let alone the necessity, of *in loco parentis* and, hence, the function of the dean of women. In response to such challenges, AAUW and NAWDC reaffirmed their commitment to the unique scholarly and administrative contributions of women to the academic community.

Historical Context

Members of both AAUW and NAWDC and their larger constituencies could only benefit from such reaffirmation of purpose. Nothing less was at stake, for these organizations and the women who supported and benefited from them, than the perennially divisive issue of essential gender difference. Throughout the '50s and '60s—in response to Cold War conservatism and provocative civic protest—traditionalists and activists addressed several familiar, unresolved questions. Do similarities outweigh differences between women and men? Do women benefit from a separate woman's culture? How should this issue play out in the larger culture?

Founded at least partly in response to discrimination against women in higher education, AAUW and NAWDC acknowledged differences between women and men, but considered such difference to be a source of strength and community. Women indeed differed from men on many levels. Women indeed benefited from the support of a woman's culture, particularly the support that single-sex professional organizations could provide.

Academic women drew strength from organizations such as AAUW and NAWDC because the reality of life for women in the 1950s and 1960s remained far more complex than the apparent dichotomy between private domesticity and public activism. In their analyses of the 1950s, Joanne Meyerowitz and Susan Hartmann successfully undermine the conventional wisdom of pervasive domesticity. Women participated in a variety of activities, Meyerowitz contends, including public activism, paid labor, and domestic management.[5] Exploding the myth of the ubiquity of the one-paycheck household in the fifties, Hartmann maintains that not only did women go out to work, but among those workers, married women's participation increased most dramatically.[6]

Such an expansive revisioning of women's lives in the 1950s cannot, however, obliterate certain disturbing realities, particularly in the lives of academic women, many of whom held membership in AAUW and NAWDC. Despite the increase in the number of women enrolled in undergraduate study, Rosalind Rosenberg discovered that nearly two-thirds of them did not graduate. Particularly troubling is her observation that numerous young women considered a college degree a distinct impediment to achievement of financial security through marriage.[7]

Historians of women in the 1950s cite the launching of Sputnik in 1957 and the subsequent publication of the National Manpower Council's (NMC) report *Womanpower* as turning points in women's educational and professional opportunities. Commissioned by NMC, *Womanpower* concluded that essential to success in the space race was the expanding education and employment of women in traditionally male fields such as science and mathematics. While such recommendations boded well for women, Rosenberg, through close reading of the report, disputes such optimism. While, on the one hand, welcoming women into the intensive study of science and mathematics, the report, on the other hand, consigned them to secondary school teaching, enabling more men to pursue academic and industrial research.[8]

If the culture of the 1950s sent women mixed messages, the 1960s, conclude Blanche Linden-Ward and Carol Hurd Green, further perpetuated such confusion, unfolding in "a pattern of fits and starts, pauses and surges." Evocative media images of the decade reflect women's front-line activism in the civil rights, antiwar, and women's movements. Such images, however, obscure the disturbing dissonance between superficial change and its actual effect on women both off and on college and university campuses. Perception of this threat led both AAUW and NAWDC to reaffirm the value of their financial and professional support of academic women.

Linden-Ward and Green contend that appearance and reality in the women's rights movement of the 1960s worked at cross purposes for all but a few activist women. In fact, for most white, suburban women in particular, the domestic ideal retained its vitality. Despite the increasing number of women "raising their voices, publishing manifestos, and demanding justice,"[9] by 1970, relatively few women experienced substantial change in their domestic lives or vocational opportunities.

Academic women on coeducational campuses, many of whom belonged either to AAUW or NAWDC, sustained the brunt of the antagonism between feminist opportunity for and traditional expectations of women. Between 1960 and 1970, both the percentage and number of women attending colleges and universities increased dramatically. In fact, by decade's end, nearly half of the eligible college-age women enrolled in undergraduate programs, reflecting an increase of 10 percent since 1960.[10]

Numbers alone, however, contend Linden-Ward and Green, cannot hide both the persistent traditionalism of many young women, and, even more significant for NAWDC, their growing hostility toward their unique institutional status on campus. Despite increasingly varied curricular options and political rhetoric, most undergraduate women pursued marriage as ardently as did their cohorts a decade earlier.[11] More troubling however, for deans of women was the growing antagonism among many women students toward both the policy of *in loco parentis* and the official charged with its implementation, the dean of women.

The issue of gender difference lay at the heart of this conflict. If the civil rights movement had, by the late 1960s, erased many of the legal differences between black and white Americans, did not women college students possess the same right to equality in the eyes of campus authorities? Why should institutions and their officers, most notably the dean of women, segregate women as a different class, subject to curfews and dress codes?[12] Discounting the long-term damage of such activism to the profession of dean of women and to women students, in the short term, it precipitated an immediate crisis within NAWDC.

Having confronted and surmounted challenge since its inception in 1916, NAWDC members did not shrink from yet another attack on their purpose and profession. Such a forthright response, on the part of both NAWDC and AAUW, highlights the persistence of ageism that Linden-Ward and Green discover in historical portrayal and common perception of the 1960s. Indeed some of the most provocative media images of the decade include young persons, under thirty, participating in civil rights, antiwar, and women's rights activism. Such a perspective, while accurate in part, obscures the activism and commitment of mature women, including members of AAUW and NAWDC.

For these women, virtually all of whom were substantially over thirty, the sixties not only complicated their still-tenuous place on the coeducational campus but also threatened the progress they had achieved. The influx of baby boomers to campus in the 1960s coincided with disheartening changes in the composition of the professoriate and increasing attacks on deans of women. Academic women, who achieved their greatest gain among the faculty ranks in the 1930s, saw their opportunities decrease dramatically as the postwar boom of male Ph.D. holders obtained most of the new faculty appointments.[13] Deans of women, as well, in the postwar years encountered increasing skepticism, if not hostility. Clearly Cold War campuses became chilly environments for virtually all academic women, as several of the historical accounts in this volume suggest.

Nevertheless, with verve and determination, equaling, if not surpassing that of the young, AAUW and NAWDC members confronted these challenges. To do so, they drew on the strength of a woman's culture to sustain them in their struggle. Their untold story immeasurably enriches historical understanding of the varied nature of activism in the 1960s. Most importantly, however, time has vindicated their recognition—over three decades ago—of the immutable problems which gender created for academic women and of the value of single-sex professional support networks in meeting such challenges.

The AAUW and "Practical Educational Work"

Indeed, the cultural challenges that the relatively few college-educated women faced in the late nineteenth century led to the founding of the Association of Collegiate Alumnae in 1881. The moving force behind the organization, Marion Talbot, daughter of the dean of the school of Medicine at Boston University, graduated—despite many obstacles—from that same institution in 1880, only to find virtually no productive employment opportunities beyond school teaching. Confronting a culture which placed little value on her academic skills and personal energy, Talbot, and other women alumnae, faced "as barren an outlook . . . as one can imagine."[14]

Determined that such attitudes be changed and that women graduates not face such circumstances alone, Talbot and seventeen college-educated friends met at the Massachusetts Institute of Technology in November of 1881, to establish the Association of Collegiate Alumnae. Not content with mere discussions and commiseration, the founders boldly stated their goal for ACA—"to unite alumnae of different institutions for practical educational work."[15]

Imbued with great energy and single-minded determination ACA founders, within thirty years, crafted the most well-known, long-lived, and financially secure professional women's organization in the United States. Within a decade of its founding, ACA established its most significant program—the awarding of fellowships for women to pursue postdoctoral study in both Europe and the United States. Eschewing the mantle of the voluntary nonscholarly organization, in 1897, the society hired a full-time secretary and commenced publication of the scholarly *Journal of the ACA*.[16] Coincidentally, some of the earliest deans of women published their work in this journal.

During the decade immediately following the First World War, the organization further consolidated its growing strength and prestige. In addition to sponsoring fellowships and publishing the *Journal*, the ACA also established study groups and committees on college accreditation and legislative action. In 1921, the ACA merged with the Southern Association of Collegiate Alumnae to become a truly national organization, the AAUW. The following year, it purchased a property in Washington, D.C., that became its national headquarters.[17] Thus by the mid-1920s, historian Susan Levine contends that AAUW had become "a mature professional organization,"[18] sponsoring an array of activities, devoted to fostering "practical educational work" for women.

What did it mean for AAUW to be "a mature professional organization" for women? What possible value could such an entity have in obviously male-dominated culture? In her analysis of AAUW, Levine concludes that the society pursued "feminism in its own way."[19] It did, indeed, provide valuable psychological and fiscal support, both of which allowed generations of educated women to pursue lives of autonomy and achievement, surely the benchmarks of feminism.

Like Eunice Hilton and NAWDC, leadership in AAUW perceived the fundamental difference between women and men and concluded that "a woman-centered culture and organization"[20] best met their needs as professionals. Of course, not everyone agreed, and by the post–World War II era, the organization sustained direct attack for this very reason. However, many women, denied membership in numerous professional societies and discriminated against in others, found essential social outlets and professional recognition in AAUW. Surely the greatest service of women-centered organizations such as AAUW, observes Margaret W. Rossiter, was their creation of "a little mental space and virtual support for isolated women doing atypical things."[21]

Undoubtedly, the AAUW Fellowship Program represented the most provocative and effective response of this woman-centered organization to the plight of women wishing to pursue academic careers at the highest levels. AAUW members, from the organization's founding, hoped to increase the number of women holding academic posts in institutions of higher education. Essential to securing such appointments was postgraduate study, usually in European universities. Women aspiring to such posts in the 1880s, soon discovered that "there was no room in the masculine procession . . . no funds available [for] their postgraduate training."[22]

Determined that talented women have the opportunity to do "work of the highest quality,"[23] ACA members began their greatest contribution to the fortunes of educated women by establishing, in 1889, the Committee on Fellowships. The next year, the society awarded its first European fellowship of $500 and, subsequently, an American fellowship of $300, each to support one year of postgraduate study. In addition, local branches across the country also collected funds and offered support to women in their region.[24] One cannot underestimate the significance of this growing philanthropic network, for talented women had virtually no institutions offering such a lifeline to professional achievement.

No shrinking violets these, AAUW women shrewdly perceived the connection between the power of money and the potential for professional careers. Throughout her work, Margaret Rossiter lauds such programs as provocative examples of "creative" or "coercive" philanthropy.[25] Women, many of whom were unlikely to pursue professional careers, nevertheless used funds at their disposal—whether large or small—to foster equal opportunity for promising women scholars. Although AAUW members not only recognized but valued the differences between women and men, they also knew that if talented women had an equal chance, they could succeed as women, and thus coerce the dominant culture to accept them.

The AAUW devoted its greatest efforts to the Fellowship Program, with gratifying results. In 1924, the society established the International Fellowship Program, enabling talented women around the world to pursue postgraduate study. Determined to expand its programs, in 1927, the AAUW inaugurated the Million Dollar Fellowship Fund, which became a reality in 1953. To recognize outstanding mature women scholars, whom most professional organizations often ignored, the AAUW instituted its annual Achievement Award.[26] Continuing this work during the daunting 1950s, the AAUW, anxious to systematize its fundraising activities, established the tax-exempt Educational Foundation. By 1957, a low point for educated women and for organizations such as AAUW and NAWDC, the Fellowship Committee made eighty-four awards to outstanding women, dramatic testimony indeed to the "practical educational work" of AAUW.[27]

AAUW Fellowships and the Search for Knowledge

From its inception, AAUW not only recognized the right of women to make original contributions to the advancement of knowledge but also drew on its own organizational and financial resources as a woman-centered organization to raise funds sufficient to make such contributions a reality. In assessing the significance of the Fellowship Program during the Cold War, one needs to address four questions. How do historians value the program? How did AAUW members justify the program in the 1950s? What did the program encompass? What does the AAUW Fellowship Program reflect concerning the supportive value of woman-centered organizations?

Historians Susan Levine and Margaret Rossiter acknowledge both the genuine threat to women's educational and scholarly opportunities and the undisputed values of the AAUW Fellowship Program in the 1950s and 1960s. Throughout these years, the educational and professional gains of women sustained verbal and financial attack. The full range of academic women—administrators, faculty, students—suffered as a consequence. However, Levine contends that the unexpected, provocative response of the AAUW compels scholars to reconsider the fortunes of feminism during the Cold War era.[28]

In addition to increasing cultural and institutional assault on the value of women's educational and scholarly advancement, Levine found that AAUW also faced disconcerting internal dissension. By the 1960s, as various professions and organizations made grudging concessions to an increasing number of women, these same women, in turn, began to doubt the value of woman-centered organizations, including AAUW.[29] Such a turn of events only reflects the perennial dilemma of women's organizations. If male acceptance and male standards are the benchmarks of a society, and if men concede that some women can meet those standards, then can any similar all-female organizations, in turn, retain any value?

In response to such external and internal attacks, AAUW could have merely maintained, if not curtailed, the Fellowship Program. This it did not do. Instead, reflecting gumption worthy of the founders, AAUW reaffirmed its commitment to the value of women's contributions to original research by reaching and surpassing the Million Dollar goal and by consistently increasing the number of annual awards.

Levine concludes that the AAUW's commitment to the Fellowship Program provides compelling evidence of the persistence of feminism during the Cold War. Convinced of the value of their woman-centered organization, AAUW members drew on that unique source of strength to "establish one of the nation's premier fellowship endowments."[30] While many members might well have rejected the feminist label, Levine concludes that their obvious dedication to "equity and respect for women's intellectual potential"[31] reflects the essence of the feminist spirit.

Concurring with Levine, Margaret Rossiter contends that the AAUW Fellowship Program played an essential role in the scholarly fortunes of many women scientists during the Cold War. Women wishing to pursue original scientific research in these years faced almost insurmountable obstacles. "Big Science," Rossiter contends, required big money. "Big Philanthropy," however, more often than not, awarded such funds to men.[32]

Secure in its own seven decades of sustained philanthropy, the AAUW reaffirmed its faith in women scientists through an increasing number of awards. Such a response, Rossiter maintains, reflects "the power of female philanthropy,"[33] in face of cultural indifference, if not hostility, toward women's research potential. Among women scientists these fellowships met an essential need as "a kind of female Guggenheim,"[34] which made scientific careers a reality for a core of talented women.

Alongside their active financial support of the Fellowship Program, members vigorously defended it in the *Journal*. Convinced that the success of the program grew directly from the unique contributions of a woman-centered organization, these women emphatically reminded members of its value to a wide spectrum of women. In their articles, contemporaries cast the value of the Fellowship Program in a much wider cultural context, moving from a very specific defense of the awards to a broad-ranging defense of the life of the mind—of whatever gender—in an increasingly suspicious society.

Ada Comstock, whom Nidiffer discusses in some detail in chapter 6, held a variety of administrative posts, including dean of women, provost, and, finally, president of Radcliffe College. As president of the organization, she maintained that the recipients, the larger culture, and the AAUW all benefited from the Fellowship Program. Financing of graduate study is difficult, at best; however, women usually confront a disproportionate share of obstacles. Through the Fellowship Program, which alleviates much of this pressure, talented women can experience the "spiritual release inherent in the search for knowledge."[35]

Cold War culture, suspicious of the motivation for the personal introspection and analytic propensity endemic to the life of the mind, cruelly stereotyped the professional scholar, but reserved its most virulent contempt for women academics. Comstock hoped that the Fellowship Program could decrease, if not alleviate, such hostility. As a wider range of women entered academic ranks and successfully produced original research, the larger culture might more readily accept their work as genuine contribution, and not threat, to the social order.[36]

Although only a small percentage of women could directly benefit from the awards, Comstock insisted that both the membership and the organization itself drew strength from the Fellowship Program. AAUW members, the majority of whom by the 1950s would not hold full-time employment, much less conduct original research, nevertheless derived "pride and a sense of vicarious achievement"[37] from their role in the productivity of fellowship recipients. Furthermore, the program, which fostered "the achievement of women in the highest reaches of scholarship," enhanced the status of AAUW, elevating it from a mere "ladies auxiliary"[38] to a legitimate woman-centered professional organization.

Helen C. White, a former AAUW president and the first woman to hold the rank of full professor at the University of Wisconsin, focuses more directly upon the value of the awards for recipients. Cognizant of the circumstances of most members, White identifies the criteria essential to initiating and completing "long-term original work."[39] Drawing on her own career, White evocatively describes both the challenges of the scholarly endeavor and the necessity of adequate financial support if one is to make any discernible progress.

"Creative work," White concludes, is both "lonely [and] uncertain." Such uncertainty assumes both emotional and financial dimensions. Conception and production of original research require time—time to think, to fail, to think again. Unfortunately, few talented women, or men for that matter, possess the financial security essential to thought, creation, and recreation. As a consequence of the Fellowship Program, deserving women can "take chances and risk being different . . . in order to do first class work."[40]

In her description of the minimal requirements for productive scholarship, White only hints at the more pervasive cultural malady. The simple truth is that during the Cold War years, most Americans remained suspicious of any person of either gender who appeared to think too deeply or for too long, for fear he or she might think of and act upon something subversive. Quite, clearly, this culture remained stubbornly unaware of and insensitive to the nature and requirements of scholarship. Mary E. Dichmann, fellowship recipient, explicitly warns *Journal* readers that hostility to the Fellowship Program is but one facet of the clear and present threat to intellectualism in the United States.

Anxious that her audience not confuse intellectualism with the mere "photographic memory" of successful quiz show participants, Dichmann maintains that intellectualism involves "the action of the mind upon a body of facts."[41] Such successful action requires "time to think without distractions,"[42] time that fellowship can provide. Maintaining such opportunity assures more than individual success, Dichmann concludes. Rather it enhances the ability of thoughtful persons to combat a growing anti-intellectual, passive culture, which "the forces of complacency and materialism"[43] nurture.

The AAUW Fellowship Program itself reflected judicious and dedicated use of material resources in the service of women's intellectual growth. Between 1958 and 1967, not only the annual budget, but also the sizes and number of awards consistently increased. During this period, the Endowment Fund virtually doubled, from $1.8 to $3.7 million dollars.[44] Both the largest and smallest awards increased, respectively from $4,000 to $5,000 and from $2,000 to $3,000.[45] The total number of awards across the decades grew as well, from 776 (1948–57) to 911 (1958–67), an increase of 17.4 percent.[46]

The fellowship also accomplished the AAUW's goal—affording talented women the chance to contribute to the fund of knowledge through the production of original research. Proposal descriptions reflect the astonishing range of their work. The 1957-58 recipients alone pursued topics as diverse as the origin of the Republican Party in New York to the theories of Boolean algebra to the behavior of liquid helium.[47] The Fellowship Program, in allowing recipients to claim all knowledge as their province, set generations of young scholars on the path to productive, satisfying careers.

The AAUW, like so many other organizations during the Cold War, experienced intense scrutiny. Politicians-turned-cultural-gatekeepers, who looked askance at most intellectual endeavors, regarded scholarly women and their advocates with particular suspicion. Women banding together outside the home for almost any purpose posed danger enough, but women supporting women's academic advancement with growing financial resources threatened the social order. Furthermore, as some male-dominated professions extended growing recognition to women by the early to mid 1960s, many of this number began to discount the value of organizations such as AAUW.

Fellowship recipients and a significant number of AAUW members, however, did not share this opinion. Those young women scholars, seeking to launch careers, never ceased to recognize the value of and to be grateful for the Fellowship Program, without which their contributions to original research would have been virtually impossible. Historians would do well, also, to recognize the courage of AAUW members—bound together in a woman-centered organization—in this period. The entire Fellowship Program required time, effort, and organization. In the face of growing skepticism, the society could have decreased or discontinued this endeavor. However, cognizant of the needs of women and the organization's dedication to "practical educational work," AAUW drew on the strength of a woman-centered culture not only to reaffirm, but also to realize its most significant mission.

The NADW and Support for a Woman-Centered Profession

Deans of Women, as well, during the Cold War era, drew on the strength of their woman-centered profession. Indeed, by the 1950s, the office of dean of women had survived since the mid-nineteenth century, in one form or another. Crucial to that survival was the shared belief that competent women leaders assume a special and required role in the higher education of women and in support of their colleagues.

Kathryn N. Tuttle, in a recent study of the dean of women, contends that for over a century, the office remained "central to the history of women's higher education."[48] Deans of women functioned as dedicated advocates for women's interests in large measure because of the support they drew from their own professional society, the National Association of Deans of Women (NADW). To appreciate the significance of this as a woman-centered organization in the Cold War era, one must consider the establishment of the NADW, which Nidiffer outlines in chapter 6, the growth of the organization, and the status of the profession in the post-World War II period.

The founding of the National Association of Deans of Women in the summer of 1916, also discussed in chapter 7, however, fell not to a member of the eastern educational elite but to a practitioner on the geographical and educational fringes. Kathryn S. McLean, dean of women at State Teachers College, Chadron, Nebraska, had, for several years, attended the summer session at Teachers College, Columbia University. Determined to enhance her status, McLean was one of a growing contingent of pragmatic, ambitious deans of women who recognized the value of graduate training and obtained it, usually at their own expense.

Isolated for most of the year at their widely scattered institutions, these women relished the community they discovered at Teachers College. From lengthy discussions of shared councilors and deans, McLean and her cohorts, cognizant of the virtual epidemic of professionalization in the United States since the 1880s, articulated two common goals. First, they requested that Teachers College initiate formal coursework for deans of women. More significantly, however, they established a formal, national professional society.

In the summer of 1916, the goals of these energetic and focused women reached fruition. Teachers College offered its first graduate courses for deans of women, which became the basis of the profession's premier training program.[49] Furthermore, on July 6, 1916, following a meeting of nearly two hundred persons at the Horace Mann auditorium, McLean and her colleagues founded the NADW.[50]

Like most woman-centered professional organizations, the NADW operated on a limited budget and relied extensively on volunteer labor. Nevertheless, within two decades, it became a full-fledged professional society, with regular publications, a permanent headquarters, and paid staff personnel. The NADW established the *Yearbook*, which contained in addition to officers, committee assignments, and membership list, papers presented at the annual convention.[51] Three years later the organization initiated the *Bulletin*, published quarterly, which informed members of news among deans and of the newest scholarly publications in the field.[52] In that same year, reinforcing the close ties between the two organizations, AAUW invited NADW to establish a headquarters office within its facility in Washington, D.C.

Despite the financial challenges that the Great Depression brought to many deans of women and to the NADW, the society, nevertheless, in these years achieved two of its most cherished goals. In 1931, the organization moved its headquarters to the larger facility of the National Education Association (NEA) and hired a full-time secretary. NADW also attained an unmistakable mark of professional status in 1938, when under the editorship of Ruth Strang at Teachers College, it established the *Journal*.[53] Thus, the organization and the profession survived the economic crises and entered the 1940s not only as a legitimate professional society, with a national membership but also as a ubiquitous office in virtually every coeducational institution in the country. Both the national headquarters office and the *Journal* strengthened the profession, offering not only a supportive network for deans of women but also a respectable outlet for their research.

In the post–World War II era, however, four additional forces inflicted serious damage on the profession, threatening, in fact, its very survival. Cultural conservatism, student hostility, and professional and institutional reorganization created for the NADW the greatest challenge in its history. In the politically and socially conservative 1950s, critics increasingly questioned the suitability of rigorous undergraduate and professional education for women. Within this context, both deans of women, particularly those outspoken advocates of educational and professional equity for women, and their woman-centered professional organization, the NAWDC, became targets of intense hostility that is detailed in chapter 7.

By the 1960s, many women students as well commenced spirited attacks on the policy of *in loco parentis* and the official most immediately responsible for its enforcement. Influenced by the free speech, civil rights, and antiwar movement, they identified the dean of women as an obstacle to their rights as citizens and their personal independence as adults. Determined to claim their equality with men, these students considered the woman-centered culture of the dean of women to be needlessly oppressive and hopelessly outdated.

Recent scholarship on the dean of women, however, focuses most closely on professional and institutional reorganization endemic to the Cold War era. What occurred in the profession as a consequence of such reorganization? What did this mean for the profession?

The question of perception, that is, how deans of women saw themselves and how the culture saw deans of women, plagued the profession from its inception. While most mid-nineteenth-century lady principals, the very first deans of women, lacked impressive academic credentials, a second cohort, between 1880 and 1930, marked a dramatic change in the profession. Most of these women, with earned doctorates in traditional academic disciplines, held joint faculty and administrative rank. Jana Nidiffer identifies these women and enumerates their contributions in chapter 6. Closely, if not primarily allied, with the academic mission of the institutions, they considered their scholarly status to be an essential component of their administrative work.

While the 1930s represented a milestone in the development of the NADW as a professional organization, that same decade saw the beginning of the end of the traditional scholar/dean, which, according to several historians, almost fatally weakened the profession. Susan Jones and Susan Komives in chapter 10, examine the contemporary results of such action. The growth of graduate programs in student personnel, an internal reorganization on behalf of a segment of the profession, emphasized administrative efficiency as an end in itself. Geraldine Clifford and Margaret Rossiter conclude that such a fundamental professional reorganization either effectively excluded traditionally trained women or made the job considerably less attractive to them.[54] Furthermore, in severing most deans of women from their purely academic responsibilities, such professional redefinition inadvertently diminished their influence on campus.

World War II, in both its conduct and aftermath, claims Kathryn Tuttle, precipitated a thoroughgoing institutional reorganization among colleges and universities that proved especially detrimental to the office of dean of women and to the NAWDC. Concern for administrative efficiency and for the well-being of the over two million male military personnel, many of whom either trained on campus during the war or returned to pursue degrees afterward, prompted high-level administrators to reconfigure the entire student personnel structure. Responding to the perennial needs of the male veterans, most institutions created a new administrative post, the dean of students, under whose authority served several assistants, one of whom was almost invariably the dean of women.[55]

Such institutional reorganization, Tuttle found, meant that numerous deans of women often lost both their title and, more importantly, their direct access to the highest levels of administration.[56] In the explicit name of administrative efficiency and in the implicit desire for a masculinized administrative structure perhaps more familiar and congenial to the male veterans, institutions across the country embarked on a pattern of "demotion and dismissal."[57] Regrettably, many mature, experienced deans of women faced a stark choice: either accept the lesser titles of "assistants, associates, or even counselors"[58] or resign. Facing such dismal alternatives, deans of women turned increasingly to the NADW for personal support and corporate response.

NAWDC and "Professional Survival"

Kathryn Tuttle suggests that such hope was misdirected indeed, for by the mid-1950s, protests subsided. Cognizant of the forces arrayed against the profession, NAWDC pursued two strategies. First, it suggested that members "adapt for personal and professional survival." Furthermore, convention addresses and articles in the *Journal* reinforced this strategy, focusing primarily on "professional development for . . . members."[59]

Close reading of articles in the *Journal*, especially in the 1960s, fifteen years into the maelstrom of "demotion and dismissal," challenge Tuttle on these very conclusions. To appreciate the persistent strength of NAWDC as a woman-centered organization dedicated to sustaining a woman-centered profession, one must examine these articles in light of two questions. Did protests against the attacks on the profession subside? How did NAWDC members, in fact, revision professional survival?

NADW members did not cease protesting against attacks on their professions. In fact, *Journal* articles throughout the 1960s reflect explicit protest in defense of professional survival that reemphasized the significance of the academic component of the dean of women's work. In fact, such arguments correlate directly with AAUW's defense and expansion of the Fellowship Program.

It is not at all surprising that the two organizations concurred in their unqualified support of women's right to intellectual development and to a voice in the academic life of institutions of higher education. Neither is it surprising that many deans of women, even those trained in student personnel programs, recognized the significance of those dean/scholars, who, for nearly half a century, 1880–1930, maintained close ties to and earned the respect of the academic community. Both NAWDC and AAUW perceived that attaining and retaining academic integrity, the particular institutional coin of the realm in the Cold War era, provided expanded access to opportunity within the university.

NAWDC members maintained that only through regaining academic influence and respect in the university could deans of women reaffirm their professional significance on college and university campuses. In pursuance of this goal, numerous *Journal* articles in the 1960s posed and responded to two questions. Why must deans of women regain the academic component of their work? What does an effective academic role entail?

For too long, observed Martha Peterson, dean of women at the University of Wisconsin, deans of women have settled for membership in a profession not "noted for its self-confidence and clarity of purpose."[60] Rather than confront the demise of the academic component of the profession, contends, Melvene Hardee of Florida State University, deans expended excessive energy on those issues "tangential to the major concerns of higher education." Unduly preoccupied with such issues, the women have unfortunately become "second-class educational citizens,"[61] whose very profession is in jeopardy.

Determined that the profession survive, May Brunson, dean of women at the University of Miami, offered both explicit advice and a detrimental alternative. To survive in an acceptable form, that is, to exert "significant educational leadership" on campus, she challenged her cohorts to regain both administrative and academic integrity. Should they fail in this, the risks were substantial. "Others will define our jobs for us," she contended, "or they may even write us out of the picture."[62] Linda Carpenter and Vivian Acosta, in chapter 9, conclude that women administrators in collegiate athletic programs faced similar problems in the 1970s.

Deans of women must regain and maintain an active academic role, contends Malvene Hardee, for the most self-evident of reasons—"the main business of the campus . . . is *learning*."[63] To function most effectively in the interests of women, May Brunson advised her cohorts to "maintain significant relationships with the total academic community."[64] Numerous *Journal* articles throughout the 1960s agree that to attain and retain academic respect within institutions of higher education, deans of women must redefine their relationships to students and faculty.

Unwilling to accede to student demands that the dean of women's office either be diminished in authority or be abolished altogether, Malvene Hardee nevertheless conceded that her colleagues must reconfigure their present relationship with students. Cognizant of the enduring value of the academic enterprise, she advocated a more direct integration of academic skills in residence life.[65] Jean Straub of the University of Pennsylvania concurred. However continually college students might advocate relevance in their relationships with authority figures, she maintained that deans of women can best retain long-term student respect by being who they are—educated women, who speak English and not jargon and are comfortable with both their maturity and authority.[66]

To regain and maintain respect within faculty ranks, Straub advises her colleagues once and for all to dispel the prevalent view of the dean of women as the behavioral "paragon" of the campus, who polices the actions of women students "with staunch and grim determination."[67] To realize this goal, they must, like many of their predecessors, draw more consistently on their academic skills. Patricia Thrash encourages deans to return, in some measure, to the classroom, the center of the academic enterprise.[68] Martha Peterson and May Brunson emphasize the value of conducting and disseminating research, both for their own satisfaction and for the respect of the academic community.[69] Deans of women, then, must do some of the things that faculty do, if they wish to retain academic credibility and to survive as an essential component of campus life. Professional survival, then, did not entail, as Tuttle suggests, resigned capitulation to cultural hostility, but rather, reaffirmation of the essential academic component of the office.

Women's Support Networks and "Historical Recovery"

Woman-centered organizations such as AAUW and NAWDC encountered suspicion, if not outright hostility, from their very inception. In response to the persistent external and internal challenges of the Cold War era, both societies reaffirmed their commitment to the unique scholarly and administrative contributions of women to the academic community. They provided invaluable support networks that not only perceived the connection between academic credibility and access to institutional centers of power, but also implemented policies to gain greater access for women. Despite intense cultural skepticism, AAUW retained and expanded its Fellowship Program, while NAWDC reaffirmed the academic component of the profession of dean of women.

What is the value of studying woman-centered support networks? How does such research enhance what Geraldine Clifford terms "historical recovery"?[70] First, research concerning societies such as AAUW and NAWDC often bring the historian in contact with somewhat obscure, but often provocative, sources. Reflecting the conscience of founders and members, many woman-centered organizations left a variety of institutional and personal records.

Second, study of woman-centered groups may also confirm Linden-Ward's and Green's findings concerning mature women and activism. Rather than dismiss such women as either indifferent, if not opposed to change, or highly invested in maintaining the status quo, historians might well consider the ways in which their age and experience actually encouraged them to embrace activism in various, unexpected forms. Furthermore, consideration of AAUW and NAWDC, particularly in the Cold War era, enriches recent historical reinterpretation of the breadth and depth of women's activism.

Finally, evaluation of the initiatives of AAUW and NAWDC in the Cold War years not only reaffirms their perception of the challenges administrative women face but also the validity of their response and the resiliency of these organizations. Nearly four decades after many of these articles appeared, the principal concerns of their authors remain unresolved. Women scholars still face challenges in obtaining financial support to free them to produce original research. An increasing number of women students and faculty also recognize the need for a woman's advocate in the administrative councils of colleges and universities. Nevertheless, despite such challenges, both woman-centered organizations persist in addressing their goals: the AAUW, in distributing its fellowships and the NAWDC through articulating the rights of women in higher education.

Most importantly, these organizations continue to offer support networks which sustain women administrators. However, they do so in a way that reflects both a keen sense of self-interest and a realistic perception of the academic environment and the place of women administrators in it. For instance, NAWDAC, founded initially for members of a single profession that disappeared by the 1970s, is now the National Association of Women in Education (NAWE), open to all women in higher education. Nevertheless, both NAWE and AAUW retain their essential goal—sustaining women in the academy whose quiet inspiration and hard work enhances the collegiate experience of contemporary women.

Notes

1. Eunice M. Hilton, "The Professional Organization's Role in a Democratic Society, "*Journal of NAWDC* 20 (June 1957): 146.

2. Barbara Miller Solomon, *In the Company of Educated Women: A History of Women and Higher Education in America* (New Haven: Yale University Press, 1985), 189–91.

3. Hilton, "Professional Organization," 141–42.

4. Founded in the summer of 1916, at Teachers College, Columbia University, the National Association of Deans of Women (NADW) changed its name several times, primarily to reflect expanded membership. For a discussion of these changes, see pages 158–59.

5. Joanne Meyerowitz, "Women and Gender in Postwar America, 1945–1960," *Not June Cleaver: Women and Gender in Postwar America, 1945–1960*, ed. Joanne Meyerowitz (Philadelphia: Temple University Press, 1994), 4–5.

6. Susan M. Hartmann, "Women's Employment and the Domestic Ideal in the Early Cold War Years," in *Not June Cleaver: Women and Gender*

in Postwar America, 1945–1960, ed. Joanne Meyerowitz (Philadelphia: Temple University Press, 1994), 86.

7. Rosalind Rosenberg, *Divided Lines: American Women in the Twentieth Century* (New York: Hill and Wang, 1992), 147.

8. Ibid., 167. See also Hartmann, "Women's Employment," 87–89.

9. Blanche Linden-Ward and Carol Hurd Green, *American Women in the 1960s: Changing the Future* (New York: Twayne Publishers, 1993), xvii, see also ix and xiv.

10. Ibid., 68.

11. Ibid., 88.

12. Ibid., 69, 90.

13. Ibid., xxi, 82–83.

14. Marion Talbot and Lois Kimball Mathews Rosenberg, *The History of the American Association of University Women 1881–1931* (Boston: Houghton Mifflin, 1931), 5.

15. Ibid., 12.

16. Ibid., 7, 147.

17. Ibid., 36, 118–19, 262.

18. Susan Levine, *Degrees of Equality: The American Association of University Women and the Challenge of Twentieth Century Feminism* (Philadelphia: Temple University Press, 1995), 14.

19. Ibid., 22.

20. Ibid., 156.

21. Margaret Rossiter, *Women Scientists in America: Before Affirmative Action 1940–1972* (Baltimore: The Johns Hopkins University Press, 1995), 359.

22. Talbot and Rosenberry, *History of AAUW*, 143.

23. Ibid., 147.

24. Ibid., 148, 157–61.

25. Margaret Rossiter, *Women Scientists in America: Struggles and Strategies to 1940* (Baltimore: The Johns Hopkins University Press, 1982), 39.

26. Talbot and Rosenberry, *History of AAUW*, 166, 170. See also Rossiter, *Women Scientists in America: Struggles and Strategies to 1940*, 309.

27. Levine, *Degrees of Equality*, 95. See also Rossiter, *Women Scientists in America: Before Affirmative Action*, 72.

28. Levine, *Degrees of Equality*, 67.

29. Ibid., 143.

30. Ibid., 93.

31. Ibid., 96.

32. Rossiter, *Women Scientists in America: Before Affirmative Action*, 359.

33. Ibid., 72.

34. Ibid., 355.

35. Ada Comstock Notestein, "Fellowships . . . Their Deeper Meaning," *Journal of the AAUW* 48 (January 1955), 80.

36. Ibid., 79.

37. Ibid.

38. Ibid., 80.

39. Helen C. White, "The Fellowship Program in 1957," *Journal of the AAUW* 51 (October 1957): 30.

40. Ibid., 32.

41. Mary E. Dichmann, "The Rising Tide of Anti-Intellectualism," *AAUW Journal* 51 (May 1958): 222.

42. Ibid., 223.

43. Ibid., 224.

44. "Financial Statements," *AAUW Journal* 52 (January 1959): 127. See also "Financial Statements," *AAUW Journal* 60 (March 1967): 150.

45. "AAUW Offers 1958–1959 Fellowships," *AAUW Journal* 50 (May 1957): 251. See also "American Association of University Women Educational Foundation," *AAUW Journal* 58 (March 1965): 140.

46. Doris C. Davies, *Idealism at Work: AAUW Educational Foundation Programs 1967–1981* (Billings, Mont., 1981), 10.

47. "Fellowship Awards for 1957–58," *AAUW Journal* 50 (May 1957): 240–49.

48. Kathryn N. Tuttle, "What Became of the Dean of Women? Changing Roles for Women Administrators in American Higher Education, 1940–1980," Ph.D. dissertation, University of Kansas, 1996, 2: 364.

49. Mrs. Ellis L. Phillips, Mina Kerr, and Agnes Wells, "History of the National Association of Deans of Women," in *Proceedings of the Fourteenth Regular Meeting of the National Association of Deans of Women*, Dallas, Texas, 1927, 228. See also Kathryn McLean Phillips, "Beginnings," *Journal of the National Association of Deans of Women* 16 (January 1953): 143–45, and Schetlin, "Fifty Years of Association," 114.

50. Kathryn Sission Phillips, *My Room in the World: A Memoir*, as told to Keith Jennison (New York: Abingdon Press, 1964), 67–68. See also Phillips, "Beginnings," 143.

51. Ibid., 145.

52. "Growth of the Deans' Association, 1914–1930," NADW *Bulletin*, March 18, 1930, 4.

53. Barbara Catton, "Our Association in Review," *Journal of the National Association of Women Deans and Counselors* 20 (October 1956): 5–6.

54. Geraldine J. Clifford, *Lone Voyagers: Academic Women in Coeducational Institutions, 1870–1937* (New York: The Feminist Press, 1989), 15. See also Rossiter, *Women Scientists in America: Struggles and Strategies to 1940*, 204.

55. Tuttle, "What Became of the Dean of Women?" 3–4, 8–9, 100, 189.

56. Ibid., 286, 358.

57. Ibid., 167.

58. Ibid., 270.

59. Ibid., 360.

60. Martha Peterson, "NAWDC in a Time of Change," *Journal of NAWDC* 30 (Summer 1967): 146.

61. Melvene D. Hardee, "Personnel Services for Improving the Campus Climate of Learning," *Journal of NAWDC* 24 (April 1961): 126.

62. May A. Brunson, "Professional Development in a Time of Change," *Journal of NAWDC* 30 (Summer 1967): 151.

63. Hardee, "Personnel Services," 125.

64. Brunson, "Professional Development," 152.

65. Hardee, "Personnel Services," 123.

66. Jean S. Straub, "To New Deans: 'Catch a Falling Star,' " *Journal of NAWDC* 30 (Winter 1967): 95–96.

67. Ibid., 95.

68. Patricia A. Thrash, "The Changing Role of the Student Personnel Dean," *Journal of NAWDC* 29 (Fall 1965): 11.

69. Peterson, "NAWDC in a Time of Change," 150. See also Brunson, "Professional Development," 153.

70. Clifford, *Lone Voyagers*, 37.

CONCLUSION

Women Administrators in Higher Education Today and in the Future

CAROLYN TERRY BASHAW AND JANA NIDIFFER

Nearly ten years ago, we met through a mutual professional colleague. Each of us was heartened to find another scholar conducting research on deans of women. The fortuitous circumstance that our work was related, but not overlapping, doubtless encouraged our friendship and facilitated our eventual collaboration.

Although the idea for this volume originated with Jana, we—individually at first and then together—found inspiration in Geraldine Clifford's volume, *Lone Voyagers: Academic Women in Coeducation Institutions, 1870–1930,* which appeared in 1989. At that time, each of us was pursuing enthusiastically, if gingerly, our own research on deans of women, a lonely path indeed. Within that context, *Lone Voyagers,* with its examination of an array of women faculty and administrators on the relatively unexplored terrain of the coeducational campus, offered hope, inspiration, and instruction. As virtually "lone voyagers" ourselves in our work on deans of women, we were encouraged to identify other scholars both in history and contemporary higher education who were also charting new scholarly territory.

What can we say, ten years later, in this volume, to enhance both Clifford's innovative work and the growing body of scholarly literature on women leaders in higher education? In our final reflections on this book, we must address two questions. First, what have we learned from our work and that of our contributors? Second, how does this work effect our understanding of the future of women administrators in higher education?

At first, one marvels at the wide variety of women in higher education in the last century and a half. Daughters of the wealthy, the middle class, and the poor—women religious and secular skeptics—they varied dramatically in their educational attainment, commitment to scholarship, and leadership skills. However, in the end, we find deep, unmistakable connections among these women who pursued wholeheartedly a common goal—to attain for women students "genuine access" to a full college life. Across generations, across institutions, across the administrative spectrum, these women shared tenacious activism and pragmatism.

Unwilling to rely solely either on chance or on the good offices of male mentors and advocates, the women chronicled in this volume sought opportunities and pursued them with gumption and courage. We have learned that women presidents, deans of women, physical educators, CAOs, and SSAOs pursued activist strategies dedicated to deepening and broadening opportunities for women administrators, faculty, and students. Determined to include women in the administrative ranks of higher education, many women worked tirelessly both to found professional organizations and to encourage respect for and growth within these nascent professions.

Deans of women were in the forefront of this initiative. In chapter 6, Jana chronicles Marion Talbot's efforts to establish the Conference of Deans of Women of the Middle West, beginning in 1903. As both the numbers of and educational opportunities for deans of women expanded, there grew a desire for a national professional society for this new occupation, which Carolyn examines in chapter 7. During the summer of 1916, another enterprising dean of women, this time from the Plains State of Nebraska, Kathryn Sisson McLean, while pursuing summer graduate study at Teachers College, initiated the meeting which resulted in the founding of the National Association of Deans of Women.

Women physical educators as well perceived the need for professional organizations not only to reflect administrative concerns but also to chart the parameters of women students' athletic opportunities. Linda Carpenter and Vivian Acosta, in chapter 9, discuss the founding in 1971 of the Association for Intercollegiate Athletics for Women (AIAW). Despite its grudging capitulation to the National Collegiate Athletic Association in the wake of the passage of Title IX, the organization, nevertheless, was significant, Carpenter and Acosta contend, because it represented a female-dominated vision of women's intercollegiate athletics.

Individually and through professional organizations, women administrators sought both increasing respect for themselves and for their colleagues and an expansion of employment opportunities for women in the administrative ranks of higher education. Nidiffer, also in chapter 6, examines Lois Kimball Mathews's efforts at the University of Wisconsin to attain not only administrative but also faculty status. Among the earliest women to hold the office of dean of women, Mathews shrewdly recognized an issue which plagued the profession for its entire history—the establishment of academic credibility among the faculty. Although she and many colleagues of her generation succeeded in retaining scholarly ties to the faculty, in the end the profession rejected this combination, which may well have facilitated its demise.

Susan Jones and Susan Komives, in chapter 10, in their discussion of the contemporary descendent of the dean of women—Senior Student Affairs Officers (SSAOs)—examine current efforts to increase both the numbers and the prestige of women holding this post. While they chart an increase in women SSAOs in the last two decades, they find that few of them hold top positions. Determined to counter this trend, women SSAOs are increasingly pursuing activist strategies such as mentoring, encouraging involvement in professional organizations, and recognizing and promoting leadership skills among women.

In their study of women Chief Academic Officers (CAOs) in chapter 4, Karen Doyle Walton and Sharon McDade follow an activist strategy on two levels. First, this chapter represents some of the initial research on the small, but growing, number of women in this pivotal administrative post. Walton and McDade render an invaluable addition to the literature by their collective portrait of Women CAOs—well-educated, energetic, savvy women, who relish their vocation despite inevitable conflict and stress. Second, in their results, these authors find that their research subjects, women CAOs, embrace their work because of the challenge it offers and heartily encourage other women to pursue these jobs.

Not surprisingly, women presidents often took the initiative in enhancing the opportunities for and role of women faculty at their institutions. Candace Introcaso, in chapter 3, recounts the dilemma of Roman Catholic women's colleges in their attempts to secure religiously acceptable but professionally valid training for the women religious who would fill faculty positions. Deterred neither by the mission nor by the skepticism of the local bishop, Mother Mary Kenneth Kearns fulfilled the requirements necessary to establish La Roche College, designed to meet this crucial need.

The most elite women's colleges as well struggled with enhancing the quality of their women faculty. In chapter 2, Cynthia Farr Brown chronicles the efforts of two of the premier woman's college presidents, M. Carey Thomas at Bryn Mawr and Alice Freeman Palmer at Wellesley, to raise the level of academic expertise among the faculty and demonstrate that women presidents could wield power and exercise leadership. Confident of the ability of these faculty women to contribute to decision making within the institution Palmer also championed their increased involvement in institutional governance.

Presidents, deans of women, and physical educators evidenced their greatest activism on behalf of their women students, attempting to secure for them access to the full range of college life. The chapters that examine this work suggest at least five aspects of administrative activism in the service of women students. First, Candace Introcaso, in chapter 3, reminds us that the moving force behind the founding of the earliest Roman Catholic colleges for women were the women religious who subsequently served as the first presidents of these institutions. Determined that Roman Catholic women have access to higher education that integrated religious principle with rigorous collegiate curriculum, women such as Sr. Mary Euphrasia and Mother Irene Gill, citing the support of their respective orders and discerning God's blessing on their mission, succeeded in founding, respectively, Trinity College, in Washington, D.C., and the College of New Rochelle, in New York State.

Second, despite the obviously essential task of founding colleges for women, Nidiffer maintains that deans of women worked tirelessly answering the critics of rigorous higher education for women. Marion Talbot considered academic equity to be at the center of constant struggle to enhance opportunities for women students at the University of Chicago. To prevent the sex-segregation of students in the classroom, Talbot let the women speak for themselves in her annual reports to President William R. Harper, thus reminding the university of their thoroughly excellent academic performance.

Third, Jana Nidiffer and Joan Paul both attest to the activism of both deans of women and physical educators in claiming campus space for women. For decades after the first women students came to campus, institutional authorities, usually with the enthusiastic support of male students, sought to limit women's access to the social, ceremonial, and athletic spaces of the campus. In response to this policy, Ada Comstock, dean of women at the University of Minnesota, as Nidiffer reminds us, tirelessly and successfully campaigned for the establishment of Alice Shevlin Hall, a building dedicated solely to the interests of the women students on the campus. Joan Paul, in her consideration of the earliest women physical educators, found them to be continually lobbying institutional authorities for appropriate facilities for women's athletic activities.

Fourth, women physical educators and deans of women, usually single, self-supporting women, recognized the importance of identifying career opportunities for women students, thus increasing their chances of economic self-sufficiency. Joan Paul, in chapter 8, tells the story of Amy Morris Homans, founder of the Boston Normal School of Gymnastics, a tireless advocate of the professional fortunes of her women students. In fact, she was so well known around the country that not only could she place most of her students but also could dictate the financial terms of their employment. Nidiffer discovered that Ada Comstock was concerned with the inequities in the employment of women students at the University of Minnesota, many of whom were paying for their own education. She even went so far as to encourage local merchants to hire Minnesota women as dependable workers.

Finally, Joan Paul identified intriguing and thought-provoking evidence of the determination of women physical educators in the 1920s to reaffirm the dignity of the women students. As college and university athletics for men expanded, the whole question of pep bands, baton twirlers, and other ancillary personnel, more often than not scantily clad women, deeply troubled women physical educators. Many of them did not hesitate to oppose this exploitation of young women for purposes of entertainment. While such opposition might seem to be mere over-concern on the part of "old-maid" physical education professors, the questions they raised now appear to be more than legitimate in the culture that celebrates the Dallas Cowboy cheerleaders. While women physical educators never tired of celebrating the benefit of appropriate athletic activities for women's physical and mental well-being, they quickly perceived the dangers, particularly to the women, of their exploitation at the hand of promoters of a male-dominated athletic system.

We have also learned that in addition to such wide-ranging activism, women administrators were also capable of shrewd pragmatism in pursuance of their goals. Rather than abandon an initiative, presidents, deans of women, and women physical educators were often willing to change course, to pursue diverse strategies to achieve their goal, or at least a part of their goal. Examination of their careers reveals at least three examples of such pragmatism.

First, a number of these women were sufficiently perceptive and flexible to forge alliances with supportive men to realize their goals. Cynthia Farr Brown, in chapter 2, includes two such women. M. Carey Thomas, both as dean and as president of Bryn Mawr, made productive use of her powerful male relatives and friends in gaining and retaining power and in implementing high academic standards. Brown finds that women religious were equally as perceptive in pursuance of their larger goals. Determined to establish a college for Roman Catholic women, Mother Irene knew she could not realize this dream without cultivating male allies, which she did quite effectively.

Second, presidents and deans of women, like so many of their male colleagues, did not hesitate to solicit financial contributions, in their case invoking the financial clout of women, to improve women's higher education. Cynthia Farr Brown reminds us that the generous and well-placed contribution of Mary Garrett played a defining role in the selection of her friend M. Carey Thomas as the president of Bryn Mawr. Candace Introcaso identified the same sense of financial savvy among certain women religious. As a consequence of the generous contribution of Edith and Genevieve Neylan, sister presidents formed the Neylan Commission, an agency central to efforts to enhance the leadership of women religious in higher education.

In chapter 11, an examination of the persistence of academic women's support networks during the Cold War, Carolyn found yet a further instance of the pragmatic collection of funds for the support of women and higher education. Cognizant of the difficulty of women to secure adequate funds for graduate study and research, the American Association of University Women (AAUW), to whom numerous women administrators belonged, instituted its Fellowship Program. Undeterred by the indifference, if not hostility, of the culture, this organization, drawing on the capabilities of various contributors, made possible the graduate study of generations of women who otherwise might have deserted their work.

Finally, both women physical educators and deans of women accepted a refocusing of their mission to realize their larger goal of achieving access for women to the full range of college life. In her study of the earliest women physical educators, Joan Paul, in chapter 8, examined the strategy these women employed to change the fundamental focus of their programs from gymnastics to sport. Convinced that competitive sport, at least on the campus level, was preferable to gymnastics, they then had to convince a skeptical administration and larger culture that such activity would not challenge cultural standards of femininity. Crucial to this strategy was the assurance that sport, which emphasized health and good character, would, in fact, reinforce ladylike behavior. Whether this strategy was honest, or even advisable, remains irrelevant to the larger goal of securing athletic opportunities for women.

Linda Carpenter and Vivian Acosta, in chapter 9, recount a particularly poignant instance of pragmatism. Despite the obvious value of the passage of Title IX for women students, the legislation had both the immediate and long-term effect of decreasing the number and influence of women physical educators in women's intercollegiate athletics. Carpenter and Acosta remind us however, that many of these women knowingly made this sacrifice because it would result in higher quality sport programs for women students.

Since the inception of the profession, deans of women found themselves almost continually under attack, whether from skeptical administrators anxious to cut the budget, professional colleagues who dismissed the value of women's professional organizations, and of course, women students. In chapter 7, an examination of the major issues confronting deans of women in the Cold War era, Carolyn found student skepticism of, if not indifference to, deans of women to be disturbingly intense. Responding to this problem, deans of women recognized the need to refocus their efforts to serve more fully the changing student population. Numerous articles in the *Journal of NAWDC* during this period reflect their understanding of the nature of this changing population, including most specifically both racial and age variation. Cognizant of the influx of both black and nontraditional students, deans of women devised strategies to address their specific concerns.

In reflecting on the answer to our first question—what have we learned from our work and from that of our contributors—we find generations of women administrators who got things done. Through their shared activism and pragmatism, they enhanced the fortunes of women professional colleagues, faculty members, and students. Neither whining victims nor thoroughgoing victors, women presidents, deans of women, physical educators, CAOs, and SSAOs worked consistently and cleverly in pursuance of an unwavering goal—attaining for women "genuine access" to the full range of college life and opportunity.

How does this volume effect our understanding of the future of women administrators in higher education? Recognizing that history is neither predictive nor prescriptive, a failure to understand the past dramatically limits one's ability to think clearly about the future. Within this context a knowledge of history can facilitate both assessment of the present and speculation concerning future scholarship and practice.

This volume brings together groundbreaking research, both historical and contemporary, concerning women administrators in higher education. Cynthia Farr Brown and Candace Introcaso are among a growing number of scholars expanding knowledge of women presidents through their work on women religious presidents of Roman Catholic women's colleges. Joan Paul, Linda Carpenter, and Vivian Acosta raise significant questions concerning both the earliest and contemporary women physical educators.

Carolyn and Jana, whether working individually or cooperatively, have substantially enhanced the small body of contemporary, revisionist scholarship on deans of women. Our individually authored books on deans of women in the South and Midwest are the very first full-length historical studies of this office. We maintain that deans of women, so central to the fortunes of women on the coeducational campus, pursued activist strategies both in their establishment of the components of a legitimate profession and in their largely successful advocacy on behalf of women students.

In addition to the contribution this volume makes to historical scholarship concerning women administrators in higher education, it furthermore raises some significant issues concerning women leaders as they interact on campus. Karen Doyle Walton and Sharon McDade, in their pathbreaking study of women CAOs, offer valuable insights for both the scholar and the practitioner. Not only have they created the primary resources for future scholars of this office, they also, through their research, let their subjects speak for themselves, advising future leaders of the pitfalls, workable strategies, and hard-won rewards of the job. Susan Jones and Susan Komives offer similar information to contemporary and future SSAOs. While they chronicle the challenges women SSAOs have faced in the last twenty-five years, they also remind practitioners of the strategies contemporary SSAOs are implementing to increase their numbers, influence, and rank.

In chapter 5, Nidiffer offers provocative advice to both future presidential search committees and candidates. This authoritative review of the literature on leadership in the last fifteen years posits that old-style, top-down leadership has little relevance in a contemporary university community. On a daily basis, presidents must deal with a variety of constituencies—across class, age, gender, and race.

Instead she concludes that effective presidencies actually require not only expert and referent power, which both genders possess, but also the skills frequently associated with women's socialization, which enhance their connective leadership. Thus, she contends that while putting women in such powerful positions as presidencies is on one level an equity issue; it is also a strategic one. Future leaders in higher education need a collection of skills. Because women have these skills, it simply makes good sense to utilize them in the highest leadership positions.

Women students now compose over half of the undergraduate population. Their numbers are growing in graduate programs, some of which they actually dominate. Women are increasingly occupying senior faculty and administrative positions. Within this context, discussion of the role women play in the administration of institutions of higher education remains essential to the future welfare of women.

It is our hope that the research in this volume will inspire response from future scholars and practitioners. The nature of that response—whether it be support, reinterpretation, or outright opposition—is less important than the fact that our research and that of our contributors enhance contemporary and future research and practice. From such informed interaction, we all benefit.

Contributors

R. Vivian Acosta, Ph.D., is Professor Emerita of Physical Education and Exercise Science at Brooklyn College of the City University of New York. During many of her thirty-one years at Brooklyn College she has also served as Graduate Deputy Chairperson, Director of Women's Athletics, and the Senior Associate Director of Athletics for both men and women. She has written several books and has an extensive record of publication, speaking and grant preparation. Jointly with Linda Carpenter, she has investigated many aspects of the experience of females in sport including the national longitudinal study on the status of women in sport. In addition to a term as president of the National Association for Girls and Women in Sport, she was active on the national level in the Association for Intercollegiate Athletics for Women during its existence and has served as a Board of Governors member for the American Alliance for Health, Physical Education, Recreation and Dance. She holds the A.A. degree from Los Angeles City College, the B.S. and M.S. from Brigham Young University, the Ph.D. from the University of Southern California and has been the recipient of the coveted Billie Jean King Award from the Women's Sports Foundation and the Honor Award and two Presidential Awards from the National Association for Girls and Women in Sport.

Carolyn Terry Bashaw received her B.A. from Vanderbilt University, MA from the University of Illinois, and earned an Ed.D. and a Ph.D. from the University of Georgia. She has published articles and book chapters concerning women and leadership in higher education in the South and has won awards for her writing from the Alabama Historical Association and from the Filson Club Historical Society in Louisville, Kentucky. Bashaw has presented her research to various professional organizations, including AERA, the History of Education Society, and the Southern Historical Association. She is also the author of *Stalwart Women: A Historical Analysis of Deans of Women in the South* (Teachers College Press, 1999). Bashaw is Professor of History at Le Moyne College, Syracuse, New York.

Cynthia Farr Brown is Assistant Professor and in 1998–99 served as Director of the Curriculum and Instruction Program in the Lesley College School of Education. In addition to the history of women's higher education, her research interests include technology in education, adult learners, and formal education and professional development for experienced classroom teachers. She has taught history, education, research and writing courses at Lesley and Simmons College.

Linda Jean Carpenter, Ph.D., J.D., Professor Emerita of Physical Education and Exercise Science at Brooklyn College of the City University of New York, is also a member of the New York State and United States Supreme Court Bars. She has written six books, some of which are co-authored with Vivian Acosta, and is currently under contract to prepare the second edition of *Legal Concepts in Sport.* She has also prepared hundreds of articles, presentations, and successful grants. Her research, including the national longitudinal study on the status of women in sport, co-authored with Vivian Acosta, now in its twenty-first year, has been the focus of much of her extensive publishing and presentation record. The longitudinal research is frequently cited in scholarly writing as well as the lay press and has been used frequently in Senate and Congressional hearings on Title IX and equity in sport. She holds the B.S. and M.S. from Brigham Young University, the Ph.D. from the University of Southern California, and the J.D. from Fordham Law School

Candace Introcaso is Vice President for Administrative Affairs and Associate Professor of Education at Barry University in Miami Shores, Florida. She works as a consultant with the board of directors of the Neylan Commission, an organization of colleges and universities founded by women religious. She is a member of the Congregation of the Sisters of Divine Providence in Pittsburgh, Pennsylvania, founders of La Roche College. She holds a B.A. in Psychology from Shippensburg University and an M.A. in Sociology from Fordham University. She has conducted research on organizational culture and institutional identity and received her Ph.D. in higher education from the Claremont Graduate University.

Susan R. Jones is Assistant Professor and Director of the Student Personnel Assistantship Program in the School of Educational Policy and Leadership at the Ohio State University. She served as Dean of Students at Trinity College of Vermont as well as Assistant Director of Campus Programs and the Stamp Student Union at the University of Maryland. She is currently a member of the editorial board for the *Journal of College Student Development* and past board member of the National Association for Women in Education as Vice President for Leadership Development and Secretary. She is also a member of the Board of Trustees for an AIDS service organization in Columbus. Her primary research interests are identity development and service-learning in higher education.

Susan R. Komives is program director for the College Student Personnel graduate program and Associate Professor at the University of Maryland. She served as Vice President for Student Development at the University of Tampa and Vice President and Dean of Student Life at Stephens College and held other student affairs positions at Denison University and the University of Tennessee. She is past-president of the American College Personnel Association (ACPA) and serves as co-chair of the Senior Scholars of ACPA. She is co-editor of *Student Services: A Handbook for the Profession* (Jossey-Bass, 1996) and co-author of *Exploring Leadership: For College Students Who Want to Make a Difference* (Jossey-Bass, 1998).

Sharon A. McDade is Assistant Professor of Higher Education in the Department of Educational Leadership at the George Washington University. Previously, she was a member of the faculty at Teachers College, Columbia University. Her research, teaching, and consulting center on the leadership development of higher education administrators as well as the management of colleges and universities. Publications include: *Developing Administrative Excellence: Creating a Culture of Leadership* as a volume in the New Directions for Higher Education series (Fall 1994, with Phyllis Lewis), *Investing in Higher Education: A Handbook of Leadership Development* (with Madeleine Green, reprinted in 1994 by American Council on Education/ORYX), and *Higher Education Leadership: Enhancing Skills through Professional Development Programs* (1990, ERIC/ASHE). She has developed leadership programs for and worked with senior administrators of higher education and business, in the United States and abroad. Previously, she was director for Harvard University's Institute for Educational Management, Management Development Program and the Harvard Seminar for New Presidents. She served on the board of directors of the American Association for Higher Education from 1988 to 1992. Her degrees include an Ed.D. from Harvard University's Graduate School of Education, an M.F.A. from Ohio State University, and a B.S. from Miami University.

Jana Nidiffer is an assistant professor in the Center for the Study of Higher and Postsecondary Education at the University of Michigan, Ann Arbor. Her areas of specialization include both history and gender issues in higher education. She has also been the Assistant Dean of the College and Coordinator of Women's Studies at Brandeis University. She holds an undergraduate and master's degree from Indiana University and a doctorate from Harvard University. Her first book, *Beating the Odds: How the Poor Get to College,* is co-authored with Arthur Levine. She is also the author of *The First Professional Deans of Women: More than Wise and Pious Matrons* (Teachers College Press, 2000). She has presented papers on her work at conferences of the History of Education Society, the American Educational

Research Association, and the Association for the Study of Higher Education. In 1992, she was awarded the Alice E. Smith Fellowship for women in history.

Joan Paul, a sport and physical education historian, received her B.S. degree from Samford University, Birmingham, Alabama, and her M.S. and Ed.D. degrees from the University of Alabama, Tuscaloosa. After teaching six years in the Birmingham public schools, she taught at Southeastern Louisiana University until 1987. She has been at the University of Tennessee, Knoxville since 1987 where she is presently in the Department of Cultural Studies in Education and Sport. She served as a department head at both Southeastern and the University of Tennessee, and has received the Tunstall Award at University of Tennessee, Knoxville as the most outstanding professor in teaching, research, and service within the College of Education. She is also past president of the North American Society for Sport History. She is a member of the North American Society for Sport History, National Association for Physical Education in Higher Education, Southern History of Education Society, Southern Academy for Women in Physical Activity, Sport and Health, and American Alliance of Health, Physical Education, Recreation and Dance.

Karen Doyle Walton is Vice President for Academic Affairs and Professor of Mathematics at Allentown College of St. Francis de Sales. She earned degrees in mathematics from Vassar College, Harvard University, and the University of Pittsburgh, and a doctorate in higher education administration from Lehigh University. She previously chaired the mathematics departments of two colleges before assuming her current position. She has served as a Visiting Scholar at Wolfson College, Cambridge University, and as a Fulbright Administrative Fellow at La Sainte Union College of Higher Education in Southampton, England. Her inservice courses for teachers of mathematics, science, and computer science have received approximately $1.5 million in funding from the U.S. Department of Education, the Pennsylvania Department of Education, and other sources. She has published more than forty articles in a variety of journals. The focus of her writing has been on computer applications to the teaching of mathematics; higher education administration; and encouraging women and minority students in mathematics, science, and technology. Dr. Walton's book *Against the Tide: Career Paths of Women Leaders in American and British Higher Education* was published in 1996 by Phi Delta Kappa.

Index

SUNY series, Frontiers in Education
Philip G. Altbach, Editor

List of Titles

Excellence and Equality: A Qualitatively Different Perspective on Gifted and Talented Education—David M. Fetterman

Class, Race, and Gender in American Education—Lois Weis (ed.)

Change and Effectiveness in Schools: A Cultural Perspective—Gretchen B. Rossman, H. Dickson Corbett, and William A. Firestone (eds.)

The Curriculum: Problems, Politics, and Possibilities—Landon E. Beyer and Michael W. Apple (eds.)

Crisis in Teaching: Perspectives on Current Reforms—Lois Weis, Philip G. Altbach, Gail P. Kelly, Hugh G. Petrie, and Sheila Slaughter (eds.)

The Character of American Higher Education and Intercollegiate Sport—Donald Chu

Dropouts from Schools: Issues, Dilemmas, and Solutions—Lois Weis, Eleanor Farrar, and Hugh G. Petrie (eds.)

The Higher Learning and High Technology: Dynamics of Higher Education Policy Formation—Sheila Slaughter

Religious Fundamentalism and American Education: The Battle for the Public Schools—Eugene F. Provenzo, Jr.

The High Status Track: Studies of Elite Schools and Stratification—Paul W. Kingston and Lionel S. Lewis (eds.)

The Economics of American Universities: Management, Operations, and Fiscal Environment—Stephen A. Hoenack and Eileen L. Collins (eds.)

Going to School: The African-American Experience—Kofi Lomotey (ed.)

Curriculum Differentiation: Interpretive Studies in U.S. Secondary Schools—Reba Page and Linda Valli (eds.)

The Racial Crisis in American Higher Education—Philip G. Altbach and Kofi Lomotey (eds.)

The Great Transformation in Higher Education, 1960–1980—Clark Kerr

College in Black and White: African American Students in Predominantly White and in Historically Black Public Universities—Walter R. Allen, Edgar G. Epps, and Nesha Z. Haniff (eds.)

Critical Perspectives on Early Childhood Education—Lois Weis, Philip G. Altbach, Gail P. Kelly, and Hugh G. Petrie (eds.)

Textbooks in American Society: Politics, Policy, and Pedagogy—Philip G. Altbach, Gail P. Kelly, Hugh G. Petrie, and Lois Weis (eds.)

Black Resistance in High School: Forging a Separatist Culture—R. Patrick Solomon

Emergent Issues in Education: Comparative Perspectives—Robert F. Arnove, Philip G. Altbach, and Gail P. Kelly (eds.)

Creating Community on College Campuses—Irving J. Spitzberg, Jr. and Virginia V. Thorndike

Teacher Education Policy: Narratives, Stories, and Cases—Hendrik D. Gideonse (ed.)

Beyond Silenced Voices: Class, Race, and Gender in United States Schools—Lois Weis and Michelle Fine (eds.)

The Cold War and Academic Governance: The Lattimore Case at Johns Hopkins—Lionel S. Lewis

Troubled Times for American Higher Education: The 1990s and Beyond—Clark Kerr

Higher Education Cannot Escape History: Issues for the Twenty-first Century—Clark Kerr

Multiculturalism and Education: Diversity and Its Impact on Schools and Society—Thomas J. LaBelle and Christopher R. Ward

The Contradictory College: The Conflicting Origins, Impacts, and Futures of the Community College—Kevin J. Dougherty

Race and Educational Reform in the American Metropolis: A Study of School Decentralization—Dan A. Lewis and Kathryn Nakagawa

Professionalization, Partnership, and Power: Building Professional Development Schools—Hugh G. Petrie (ed.)

Ethnic Studies and Multiculturalism—Thomas J. LaBelle and Christopher R. Ward

Promotion and Tenure: Community and Socialization in Academe—William G. Tierney and Estela Mara Bensimon

Sailing Against the Wind: African Americans and Women in U.S. Education—Kofi Lomotey (ed.)

The Challenge of Eastern Asian Education: Implications for America—William K. Cummings and Philip G. Altbach (eds.)

Conversations with Educational Leaders: Contemporary Viewpoints on Education in America—Anne Turnbaugh Lockwood

Managed Professionals: Unionized Faculty and Restructuring Academic Labor—Gary Rhoades

The Curriculum (Second Edition): Problems, Politics, and Possibilities—Landon E. Beyer and Michael W. Apple (eds.)

Education / Technology / Power: Educational Computing as a Social Practice—Hank Bromley and Michael W. Apple (eds.)

Capitalizing Knowledge: New Intersections of Industry and Academia—Henry Etzkowitz, Andrew Webster, and Peter Healey (eds.)

The Academic Kitchen: A Social History of Gender Stratification at the University of California, Berkeley—Maresi Nerad

Grass Roots and Glass Ceilings: African American Administrators in Predominantly White Colleges and Universities—William B. Harvey (ed.)

Community Colleges as Cultural Texts: Qualitative Explorations of Organizational and Student Culture—Kathleen M. Shaw, James R. Valadez, and Robert A. Rhoads (eds.)

Educational Knowledge: Changing Relationships between the State, Civil Society, and the Educational Community—Thomas S. Popkewitz (ed.)

Transnational Competence: Rethinking the U.S.-Japan Educational Relationship—John N. Hawkins and William K. Cummings (eds.)

Women Administrators in Higher Education: Historical and Contemporary Perspectives—Jana Nidiffer and Carolyn Terry Bashaw (eds.)

Faculty Work in Schools of Education: Rethinking Roles and Rewards for the Twenty-first Century—William G. Tierney (ed.)

College in Black and White: African American Students in Predominantly White and in Historically Black Public Universities—Walter R. Allen, Edgar G. Epps, and Nesha Z. Haniff (eds.)

Critical Perspectives on Early Childhood Education—Lois Weis, Philip G. Altbach, Gail P. Kelly, and Hugh G. Petrie (eds.)

Textbooks in American Society: Politics, Policy, and Pedagogy—Philip G. Altbach, Gail P. Kelly, Hugh G. Petrie, and Lois Weis (eds.)

Black Resistance in High School: Forging a Separatist Culture—R. Patrick Solomon

Emergent Issues in Education: Comparative Perspectives—Robert F. Arnove, Philip G. Altbach, and Gail P. Kelly (eds.)

Creating Community on College Campuses—Irving J. Spitzberg, Jr. and Virginia V. Thorndike

Teacher Education Policy: Narratives, Stories, and Cases—Hendrik D. Gideonse (ed.)

Beyond Silenced Voices: Class, Race, and Gender in United States Schools—Lois Weis and Michelle Fine (eds.)

The Cold War and Academic Governance: The Lattimore Case at Johns Hopkins—Lionel S. Lewis

Troubled Times for American Higher Education: The 1990s and Beyond—Clark Kerr

Higher Education Cannot Escape History: Issues for the Twenty-first Century—Clark Kerr

Multiculturalism and Education: Diversity and Its Impact on Schools and Society—Thomas J. LaBelle and Christopher R. Ward

The Contradictory College: The Conflicting Origins, Impacts, and Futures of the Community College—Kevin J. Dougherty

Race and Educational Reform in the American Metropolis: A Study of School Decentralization—Dan A. Lewis and Kathryn Nakagawa

Professionalization, Partnership, and Power: Building Professional Development Schools—Hugh G. Petrie (ed.)

Ethnic Studies and Multiculturalism—Thomas J. LaBelle and Christopher R. Ward

Promotion and Tenure: Community and Socialization in Academe—William G. Tierney and Estela Mara Bensimon

Sailing Against the Wind: African Americans and Women in U.S. Education—Kofi Lomotey (ed.)

The Challenge of Eastern Asian Education: Implications for America—William K. Cummings and Philip G. Altbach (eds.)

Conversations with Educational Leaders: Contemporary Viewpoints on Education in America—Anne Turnbaugh Lockwood

Managed Professionals: Unionized Faculty and Restructuring Academic Labor—Gary Rhoades

The Curriculum (Second Edition): Problems, Politics, and Possibilities—Landon E. Beyer and Michael W. Apple (eds.)

Education / Technology / Power: Educational Computing as a Social Practice—Hank Bromley and Michael W. Apple (eds.)

Capitalizing Knowledge: New Intersections of Industry and Academia—Henry Etzkowitz, Andrew Webster, and Peter Healey (eds.)

The Academic Kitchen: A Social History of Gender Stratification at the University of California, Berkeley—Maresi Nerad

Grass Roots and Glass Ceilings: African American Administrators in Predominantly White Colleges and Universities—William B. Harvey (ed.)

Community Colleges as Cultural Texts: Qualitative Explorations of Organizational and Student Culture—Kathleen M. Shaw, James R. Valadez, and Robert A. Rhoads (eds.)

Educational Knowledge: Changing Relationships between the State, Civil Society, and the Educational Community—Thomas S. Popkewitz (ed.)

Transnational Competence: Rethinking the U.S.-Japan Educational Relationship—John N. Hawkins and William K. Cummings (eds.)

Women Administrators in Higher Education: Historical and Contemporary Perspectives—Jana Nidiffer and Carolyn Terry Bashaw (eds.)

Faculty Work in Schools of Education: Rethinking Roles and Rewards for the Twenty-first Century—William G. Tierney (ed.)